POWER · &
·CIVILITY

Also by Norbert Elias

THE HISTORY OF MANNERS

THE COURT SOCIETY

POWER · & ·CIVILITY

THE CIVILIZING PROCESS:
VOLUME II

BY
NORBERT ELIAS

Translated by Edmund Jephcott
with some notes and revisions
by the author

PANTHEON BOOKS, NEW YORK

Library of Congress Cataloging in Publication Data

Elias, Norbert.
Power and civility.

(The Civilizing process; v.2)
Includes bibliographical references and index.
1. Europe—Politics and government.   2. Europe—Social conditions.
I. Title.   II. Series: Elias, Norbert. Über den Prozess der
Zivilisation.   English; v.2
CB83.E413   1982 vol. 2   306'.2'094   82-8157   [D105]
ISBN 0-394-71134-3 (pbk.)

Contents

Dedicated to the memory of my parents
Hermann Elias, d. Breslau 1940
Sophie Elias, d. Auschwitz 1941 (?)

Acknowledgements

This translation could not have been produced without the aid of my friends. In particular, Professor Johan Goudsblom has spent a great deal of time and effort in comparing the English and German texts to ensure that the exact meaning has been interpreted. Eric Dunning has also throughout made a number of very useful suggestions. The exercise of checking the translation was in itself a most useful one for me as it enabled me to revise the text in minor, but important ways and to add notes which set the work in the context of my later thinking. None of this should be taken as any reflection on the translator, Edmund Jephcott, to whom I owe the greatest debt. My thanks are also due to Johan and Maria Goudsblom for reading the proofs and compiling the index.

Publisher's Note

Volume 1 of The Civilizing Process is entitled *The History of Manners* and consists of two Chapters. Volume 2, now published in English for the first time, originally consisted of Chapter Three (in two Parts) and the Synopsis. These divisions are here called Part One (divided into two Chapters) and Part Two: Synopsis.

The italic in the quotations in both volumes indicates the author's emphasis.

PART ONE

Feudalization and State Formation

Introduction

I

Survey of Courtly Society

1. The struggles between the nobility, the Church and the princes for their shares in the control and the produce of the land run through the entire Middle Ages. In the course of the twelfth and thirteenth centuries a further group emerges as a partner in this play of forces: the privileged town-dwellers, the "bourgeoisie".

The actual course of this constant struggle, and the power relations among the contestants, vary widely between countries. But the outcome of the conflicts is, in its structure, nearly always the same: in all the larger Continental countries, and at times in England˙ too, the princes or their representatives finally accumulate a concentration of power to which the estates are not equal. The autarky of the majority, and the estates' share of power, are curtailed step by step, while the dictatorial or "absolute" power of a single supreme figure is slowly established, for a greater or lesser period. In France, England and the Habsburg countries this figure is the king, in the German and Italian regions it is the territorial ruler.

2. Numerous studies describe, for example, how the French kings from Philip Augustus to Francis I and Henry IV increase

their power, or how the Elector Frederick William pushes aside the regional estates in Brandenburg, and the Medici the patricians and senate in Florence, or how the Tudors do the same to the nobility and parliament in England. Everywhere it is the individual agents and their various actions that we see, their personal weaknesses and gifts that are described. And it is no doubt fruitful and even indispensable to see history in this way, as a mosaic of individual actions of individual people.

Nevertheless, something else is obviously at work here besides the fortuitous emergence of a series of great princes and the fortuitous victories of numerous individual territorial rulers or kings over numerous individual estates at approximately the same time. It is not without reason that we speak of an *age* of absolutism. What finds expression in this change in the form of political rule is a structural change in Western society as a whole. Not only did individual kings increase their power but, clearly, the social institution of the monarchy or princedom took on new weight in the course of a gradual transformation of the whole of society, a new weight which at the same time gave new power chances to the central rulers.

On the one hand we might enquire how this or that man gained power and how he or his heirs increased or lost this power in the context of "absolutism".

On the other, we may ask on the basis of what social changes the medieval institution of the king or prince took on, in certain centuries, the character and power referred to by concepts such as "absolutism" or "despotism", and which social structure, which development in human relations, made it possible for the institution to sustain itself in this form for a greater or lesser period of time.

Both approaches work with more or less the same material. But only the second attains to the plane of historical reality on which the civilizing process takes place.

It is by more than a coincidence that in the same centuries in which the king or prince acquires absolutist status, the restraint and moderation of the affects discussed in the previous volume, the "civilizing" of behaviour, is noticeably increased. In the quotations assembled earlier to demonstrate this change in behaviour, it emerged quite clearly how closely this change is linked to the formation of the hierarchical social order with the absolute ruler and, more broadly, his court at its head.

3. For the court, too, the residence of the ruler, took on a new aspect and a new significance in Western society, in a movement that flowed slowly across Europe, to ebb away again, earlier here and later there, at about the time we call the "Renaissance".

In the movements of this period the courts gradually become the actual model and style-setting centres. In the preceding phase they had had to share or even wholly relinquish this function to other centres, according to the prevailing balance of power, now to the Church, now to the towns, now to the courts of the great vassals and knights scattered across the country. From this time on, in German and particularly in Protestant regions, the courts of the central authorities still share their function with the universities turning out the princely bureaucracy, whereas in Romanic and perhaps in all Catholic countries—this latter point remains to be established—the importance of the courts as a social authority, a source of models of behaviour, far exceeds that of the university and all the other social formations of the epoch. The early Renaissance in Florence, characterized by men like Masaccio, Ghiberti, Brunelleschi and Donatello, is not yet an unequivocally courtly style; but the Italian High Renaissance, and more clearly still the Baroque and Rococo, the style of Louis XV and XVI, are courtly, as finally is the "Empire", though in a more transitional way, being already permeated with industrial–bourgeois features.

At the courts a form of society is evolving for which no very specific and unequivocal term exists in German, for the obvious reason that in Germany this type of human bonding never attained central and decisive importance, except at most only in the final, transitional form it had at Weimar. The German concept of "good society", or more simply, of "society" in the sense of *monde*, like the social formation corresponding to it, lacks the sharp definition of the French and English terms. The French speak of *la société polie*. And the French terms *bonne compagnie* or *gens de la Cour* and the English "Society" have similar connotations.

4. The most influential courtly society was formed, as we know, in France. From Paris the same codes of conduct, manners, taste and language spread, for varying periods, to all the other European courts. This happened not only because France was the most powerful country at the time. It was only now

5

made possible because, in a pervasive transformation of European society, similar social formations, characterized by analogous forms of human relations came into being everywhere. The absolutist-courtly aristocracy of other lands adopted from the richest, most powerful and most centralized country of the time the things which fitted their own social needs: refined manners and a language which distinguished them from those of inferior rank. In France they saw, most fruitfully developed, something born of a similar social situation and which matched their own ideals: people who could parade their status, while also observing the subtleties of social intercourse, marking their exact relation to everyone above and below them by their manner of greeting and their choice of words—people of "distinction" and "civility". In taking over French etiquette and Parisian ceremony, the various rulers obtained the desired instruments to express their dignity, to make visible the hierarchy of society, and to make all others, first and foremost the courtly nobility themselves, aware of their dependence.

5. Here, too, it is not enough to see and describe the particular events in different countries in isolation. A new picture emerges, and a new understanding is made possible, if the many individual courts of the West, with their relatively uniform manners, are seen together as communicating organs in European society at large. What slowly begins to form at the end of the Middle Ages is not just one courtly society here and another there. It is a courtly aristocracy embracing Western Europe with its centre in Paris, its dependencies in all the other courts, and offshoots in all the other circles which claimed to belong to "Society", notably the upper stratum of the bourgeoisie and to some extent even broader layers of the middle class.

The members of this multiform society speak the same language throughout the whole of Europe, first Italian, then French; they read the same books, they have the same taste, the same manners and—with differences of degree—the same style of living. Notwithstanding their many political differences and even the many wars they wage against each other, they orientate themselves fairly unanimously, over greater or lesser periods, towards the centre at Paris. And social communication between court and court, i.e. within courtly-aristocratic society, remains for a long time closer than between courtly society and other strata in the same country; one expression of this is their common language. Then, from about the middle of the eighteenth century, earlier in one country and somewhat later in another, but always in conjunction with the rise of the middle classes and the gradual displacement of the social and political centre of gravity from the court to the various national bourgeois societies, the ties between the courtly-aristocratic societies of different nations are slowly loosened even if they are never entirely broken. The French language gives way, not without violent struggles, to the bourgeois, national languages even in the upper class. And courtly society itself becomes increasingly differentiated in the same way as bourgeois societies, particularly when the old aristocratic society loses its centre once and for all in the French Revolution. The national form of integration displaces that based on social estate.

6. In seeking the social traditions which provide the common basis and deeper unity of the various national traditions in the West, we should think not only of the Christian Church, the common Roman–Latin heritage, but also of this last great pre-national social formation which, already partly in the shadow of the national divergences within Western society, rose above the lower and middle strata in different linguistic areas. Here were created the models of more pacified social intercourse which more or less all classes needed, following the transformation of European society at the end of the Middle Ages; here the coarser habits, the wilder, more uninhibited customs of medieval society with its warrior upper class, the corollaries of an uncertain, constantly threatened life, were "softened", "polished" and "civilized". The pressure of court life, the vying for the favour of the prince or the "great"; then, more generally, the necessity to distinguish oneself from others and to fight for opportunities with relatively peaceful means, through intrigue and diplomacy, enforced a constraint on the affects, a self-discipline and self-control, a peculiarly courtly rationality, which at first made the courtier appear to the opposing bourgeoisie of the eighteenth century, above all in Germany but also in England, as the epitome of the man of reason.

And here, in this pre-national, courtly-aristocratic society, a part of those commands and prohibitions were fashioned or at least prepared that are perceptible even today, national differences notwithstanding, as something common to the West. Partly from them the Western peoples, despite all their differences, have taken the common stamp of a specific civilization.

That the gradual formation of this absolutist-courtly society was accompanied by a transformation of the drive-economy and conduct of the upper class in the direction of "civilization", has been shown by a series of examples. It has also been indicated how closely this increased restraint and regulation of elementary urges is bound up with increased social constraint, the growing dependence of the nobility on the central lord, the king or prince.

How did this increased constraint and dependence come about? How was an upper class of relatively independent warriors or knights supplanted by a more or less pacified upper class of courtiers? Why was the influence of the estates progressively reduced in the course of the Middle Ages and the early modern period, and why, sooner or later, was the dictatorial "absolute" rule of a single figure, and with it the compulsion of courtly etiquette, the pacification of larger or smaller territories from a single centre, established for a greater or lesser period of time in all the countries of Europe? The sociogenesis of absolutism indeed occupies a key position in the overall process of civilization. The civilizing of conduct and the corresponding transformation of human consciousness and libidinal make-up cannot be understood without tracing the process of state-formation, and within it the advancing centralization of society which first finds particularly visible expression in the absolutist form of rule.

II

A Prospective Glance at the Sociogenesis of Absolutism

1. A few of the most important mechanisms which, towards the end of the Middle Ages, gradually gave increasing power chances to the central authority of a territory, can be quite briefly described at this preliminary stage. They are broadly similar in all the larger countries of the West and are particularly clearly seen in the development of the French monarchy.

The gradual increase of the money sector of the economy at the expense of the barter sector in a given region in the Middle

Ages had very different consequences for the majority of the warrior nobility on the one hand, and for the king or prince on the other. The more money that came into circulation in a region, the greater the increase in prices. All classes whose revenue did not increase at the same rate, all those on a fixed income, were thus placed at a disadvantage, above all the feudal lords who received fixed rents from their estates.

The social functions whose income increased with these new opportunities were placed at an advantage. They included certain sections of the bourgeoisie, but above all the king, the central ruler. For the taxation apparatus gave him a share of the increasing wealth; a part of all the earnings in his area of rule came to him, and his income consequently increased to an extraordinary degree with the growing circulation of money.

As is always the case, this functional mechanism was only very gradually and, so to speak, retrospectively exploited consciously by the interested parties, being adopted at a relatively late stage by rulers as a principle of domestic politics. Its first result was a more or less automatic and constant increase in the income of the central lord. This is one of the preconditions on the basis of which the institution of kingship gradually gained its absolute or uncircumscribed character.

2. As the financial opportunities open to the central function grew, so too did its military potential. The man who had at his disposal the taxes of an entire country was in a position to hire more warriors than any other; by the same token he grew less dependent on the war services which the feudal vassal was obliged to render in exchange for the land with which he was invested.

This too is a process which, like all the others, begins very early but only gradually leads to the formation of definite institutions. Even William the Conqueror went to England with an army consisting only partly of vassals, the rest being paid knights. Between that time and the establishment of standing armies by the central lords, centuries intervened. A prerequisite for such armies, apart from the growing revenue from taxes, was surplus manpower—the discrepancy between the number of people and the number and profitability of jobs available in a particular society which we know today as "unemployment". Areas suffering from surpluses of this kind, e.g. Switzerland and parts of Germany, supplied mercenaries to anyone who could afford them. Much later, Frederick the Great's recruiting tactics show the solutions open to a prince when the manpower available in his territory is not sufficient for his military purposes. The military supremacy that went hand in hand with financial superiority was, therefore, the second decisive prerequisite enabling the central power of a region to take on "absolute" character.

A transformation of military techniques followed and reinforced this development. Through the slow development of firearms the mass of common foot-soldiers became militarily superior to the numerically limited nobles fighting on horseback. This too was to the advantage of the central authority.

The king, who in the France of the early Capetian period, for example, was not much more than a baron, one territorial lord among others of equal power, and sometimes even less powerful than others, gained from his increasing revenues the possibility of military supremacy over all the forces in his country. Which noble family managed in particular cases to win the crown and thus gain access to these power chances depended on a wide range of factors including the personal talents of individuals and often chance. The growth of the financial and military power chances that gradually attached themselves to the monarchy was independent of the will or talents of individuals; it followed a strict regularity that is encountered wherever social processes are observed.

And this increase in the power chances of the central function was therefore the precondition for the pacification of a given territory, greater or smaller as the case may be, from a single centre.

3. The two series of developments which acted to the advantage of a strong central authority were in all ways detrimental to the old medieval warrior estate. They had no direct connection with the growing money sector of the economy. They could scarcely derive any direct profit from the new opportunities of income that offered themselves. They felt only the devaluation, the rise in prices.

It has been calculated that a fortune of 22,000 francs in the year 1200 was worth 16,000 francs in 1300, 7,500 francs in 1400, and 6,500 in 1500. In the sixteenth century this movement accelerated; the value of the sum fell to 2,500 francs, and the case was similar in the whole of Europe.[1]

A movement originating far back in the Middle Ages underwent an extraordinary acceleration in the sixteenth century. From the reign of Francis I up to the year 1610 alone, the French pound was devalued in approximately the ratio 5 to 1. The importance of this developmental curve for the transformation of society was greater than can be stated in a few words. While money circulation grew and commercial activity developed, while bourgeois classes and the revenue of the central authority rose, the income of the entire remaining nobility fell. Some of the knights were reduced to a wretched existence, others took by robbery and violence what was no longer available by peaceful means, others again kept themselves above water for as long as possible by slowly selling off their estates; and finally a good part of the nobility, forced by these circumstances and attracted by the new opportunities, entered the service of the kings or princes who could pay. These were the economic options open to a warrior class that was not connected to the growth in money circulation and the trade network.

4. How the development of war technology operated to the nobility's disadvantage has already been mentioned: the infantry, the despised foot-soldiers, became more important in battle than the cavalry. Not only the military superiority of the medieval warrior estate was thereby broken, but also its monopoly over weapons. A situation where the nobles alone were warriors or, conversely, all warriors were nobles, began to turn into one where the noble was at best an officer of plebeian troops who had to be paid. The monopoly control of weapons and military power passed from the whole noble estate into the hands of a single member, the prince or king who, supported by the tax income of the whole region, could afford the largest army. Thereby the majority of the nobility were changed from relatively free warriors or knights into paid warriors or officers in the service of the central lord.

These are a few of the most important lines of this structural transformation.

5. There was another as well. The nobility lost social power with the increase in the money sector of the economy, while bourgeois classes gained it. But in general neither of the two estates proved strong enough to gain the upper hand over the other for a prolonged period. Constant tensions everywhere erupted in periodic struggles. The battle fronts were complicated

and varied widely from case to case. There were occasional alliances between groups within the nobility and groups within the bourgeoisie; there were transitional forms and even fusions between sub-groups from the two estates. But however that may be, both the rise and the absolute power of the central institution always depended on the continued existence of this tension between the nobility and the bourgeoisie. One of the structural preconditions for the absolute monarchy or princedom was that neither of the estates nor any group within them should gain the upper hand. The representatives of the absolute central authority therefore had to be constantly on the alert to ensure that this unstable equilibrium was maintained within their territory. Where the balance was lost, where one group or class became too strong, or where aristocratic and upper bourgeois groups even temporarily allied, the supremacy of the central power was seriously threatened or—as in England—doomed. Thus we often observe among rulers that while one protects and promotes the bourgeoisie because the nobility seems too powerful and therefore dangerous, the next inclines towards the nobility, this having grown too weak or the bourgeoisie too refractory, without the other side being ever quite neglected. The absolute rulers were obliged, whether they were entirely conscious of it or not, to manipulate this social mechanism that they had not created. Their social existence depended on its survival and functioning. They too were bound to the social regularity with which they had to live. This regularity and the social structure corresponding to it emerged sooner or later with numerous modifications in almost every country of the West. But it takes on clear delineation only if observed in the process of emergence through a concrete example. The development in France, the country in which this process, from a particular moment on, takes place in the most direct form, will serve here as an example.

Chapter One

Dynamics
of Feudalization

I

Introduction

1. If we compare France, England and the German Empire at the middle of the seventeenth century in terms of the power of their central authorities, the king of France appears particularly strong beside the English king and even more so beside the German emperor. This constellation is the outcome of a very long development.

At the end of the Carolingian and the beginning of the Capetian period the situation is almost the reverse. At that time the central power of the German emperors was strong as compared to the French kings. And England had yet to undergo its decisive unification and reorganization by the Normans.

In the German empire the power of the central authority crumbles persistently—though with occasional interruptions— from this time on.

In England, from Norman times on, periods of strong royal power alternate with the preponderance of the estates or parliament.

In France, from about the beginning of the twelfth century,

the king's power grows—again with interruptions—fairly steadily. A continuous line leads from the Capetians through the Valois to the Bourbons.

Nothing entitles us to presuppose that these differences follow any kind of compulsion. Very slowly the different regions of the three countries merge into national units. At first, as long as the integration of those areas which are later to become "France", "Germany", "Italy" and "England" is relatively slight, they do not weigh very heavily as social organisms in the balance of historical forces. And the main developmental curves in the history of these nations are in this phase incomparably more strongly influenced by the fortunes and misfortunes of individuals, by personal qualities, by sympathies and antipathies or "accidents", than later when "England", "Germany" or "France" have become social formations with a quite specific structure and a momentum and regularity of their own. At first the historical lines of development are co-determined very strongly by factors which, from the viewpoint of the later unit, have no inherent necessity.[2] Then, gradually, with the increasing interdependence of larger areas and populations, a pattern slowly emerges which, according to circumstance, either limits or opens opportunities to the whims and interests of powerful individuals or even of particular groups. Then, but only then, do the inherent developmental dynamics of these social units override chance or at least mark it with their stamp.

2. Nothing entitles us to presuppose any compelling necessity determining that it was the duchy of Francia, the "Isle de France", about which a nation would crystallize. Culturally, and also politically, the southern regions of France had much stronger ties with those of northern Spain and the bordering Italian regions than with the area around Paris. There was always a very considerable difference between the old, more Celto–Romanic regions of Provence, the *langue d'oc*, and the *langue d'oïl* parts, that is, regions with a stronger Frankish influence, above all those to the north of the Loire, together with Poitou, Berry, Bourgogne, Saintonge and Franche-Comté.[3]

Moreover, the eastern frontiers established by the Treaty of Verdun (843) and then by the Treaty of Meerssen (870) for the western Frankish empire, were very different from the borders between what gradually emerged as "France" and "Germany" or "Italy".

The Treaty of Verdun fixed as the eastern frontier of the western Frankish empire a line leading from the present Gulf of Lions in the south, and approaching the western side of the Rhône, in an approximately northerly direction as far as Flanders. Lorraine and Burgundy—except for the duchy west of the Saône—, and therefore also Arles, Lyons, Trier and Metz thus lay outside the borders of the western Frankish empire, while to the south the county of Barcelona was still within its frontiers.[4]

The Treaty of Meerssen made the Rhône the direct frontier in the south between the western and the eastern Frankish empires; then the frontier followed the Isère and, further north, the Moselle. Trier and Metz thus became frontier towns, as, to the north, did Meerssen, the place from which the treaty took its name. And the frontier finally ended north of the Rhine estuary in the region of southern Friesland.

But what such frontiers separated were neither states, nor peoples or nations, if by that we mean social formations that are in any sense unified and stable. At most they were states, peoples, nations in the making. The most striking feature of all the larger territories in this phase is their low level of cohesion, the strength of the centrifugal forces tending to disintegrate them.

What is the nature of these centrifugal forces? What peculiarity of the structure of these territories gives such forces their particular strength? And what change in the structure of society, from the fifteenth, sixteenth or seventeenth century onwards, finally gives the central authorities preponderance over all the centrifugal forces, and thus confers on the territories a greater stability?

II

Centralizing and Decentralizing Forces in the Medieval Power Figuration

3. The immense empire of Charlemagne had been brought together by conquest. Certainly the basic, though not the only function of his immediate predecessors, and more so of Charlemagne himself, was that of army leader, victorious in conquest and defence. This was the foundation of his royal power, his renown, his social strength.

As army leader Charlemagne had control of the land he conquered and defended. As victorious prince he rewarded the warriors who followed him with land. And by virtue of this authority he held them together even though their estates were scattered across the country.

The emperor and king could not supervise the whole empire alone. He sent trusted friends and servants into the country to uphold the law in his stead, to ensure the payment of tributes and the performance of services, and to punish resistance. He did not pay for their services in money; this was certainly not entirely lacking in this phase, but existed to only a very limited extent. Needs were supplied for the most part directly from the land, the fields, the forests and the stables, produce being worked up within the household. The earls or dukes, or whatever the representatives of the central authority were called, also fed themselves and their retinue from the land with which the central authority had invested them. In keeping with the economic structure, the apparatus for ruling in this phase of society was unlike that of "states" in a later stage. Most of the "officials", it has been said of this phase, "were farmers who had 'official' duties only for certain set periods or in the case of unforeseen events, and so were most directly comparable to landowners having police and judicial powers".[5] With this legal and law-enforcing role they combined military functions; they were warriors, commanders of a warlike following and of all the other landowners in the area the king had given them, should it be threatened by an external enemy. In a word, all ruling functions were drawn together in their hands.

But this peculiar power figuration—a measure of the division of labour and differentiation in this phase—again and again led to characteristic tensions arising from the nature of its structure. It generated certain typical sequences of events which—with certain modifications—were repeated over and again.

4. Whoever was once entrusted by the central lord with the functions of ruling in a particular area and was thus in effect the lord of this area, no longer depended on the central lord to sustain and protect himself and his dependants, at least as long as he was threatened by no stronger external foe. At the first opportunity, therefore, as soon as the central power showed the slightest sign of weakness, the local ruler or his descendants sought to demonstrate their right and ability to rule the district

entrusted to them, and their independence of the central authority.

Over many centuries the same patterns and trends show themselves over and again in this apparatus for ruling. The rulers over parts of the central lord's territory, the local dukes or chieftains, are at all times a danger to the central power. Conquering princes and kings, being strong as army leaders and protectors against external foes, strive, successfully at first, to confront this danger within the area they control. Where possible they replace the existing local rulers with their own friends, relations or servants. Within a short time, often within a generation, the same thing happens again. The erstwhile representatives of the central ruler do their best to take over the area entrusted to them, as if it were the hereditary property of their family.

Now it is the *comes palatii*, once the overseers of the royal palace, who want to become the independent rulers of a region; now it is the margraves, dukes, counts, barons or officials of the king. In repeated waves the kings, strengthened by conquests, send their trusted friends, relations and servants into the country as their envoys, while the previous envoys or their descendants fight just as regularly to establish the hereditary nature and the factual independence of their region, which was originally a kind of fief.

On the one hand the kings were forced to delegate power over part of their territory to other individuals. The state of military, economic and transport arrangements at that time left them no choice. Society offered them no sources of money taxes sufficient for them to keep a paid army or paid official delegates in remote regions. To pay or reward them they could only allocate them land—in amounts large enough to ensure that they were actually stronger than all the other warriors or landowners in the area.

On the other hand the vassals representing the central power were restrained by no oath of allegiance or loyalty from asserting the independence of their area as soon as the relative power positions of the central ruler and his delegates shifted in favour of the latter. These territorial lords or local princes in effect own the land once controlled by the king. Except when threatened from outside, they no longer need the king. They withdraw themselves from his power. When they need the king as military leader, the movement is reversed and the game starts all over again, assuming the central lord is victorious in the war. Then, through the power and threat emanating from his sword, he regains actual control over the whole territory and can distribute it anew. This is one of the recurring processes in the development of Western society in the early Middle Ages and sometimes, in somewhat modified form, in later periods too.

5. Examples of such processes are to be found even today outside Europe, in regions with a similar social structure. The development of Abyssinia shows such configurations in abundance, though they have latterly been somewhat modified by the inflow of money and other institutions from Europe. But the rise of Ras Tafari to the position of central ruler or emperor of the whole country was made possible only by the military subjugation of the most powerful territorial lords; and the unexpectedly quick collapse of opposition to Italy is explained not least by the fact that in this feudal and predominantly agrarian region, the centrifugal tendencies of the individual territories were multiplied as soon as the central ruler failed to fulfil his most important task, that of resisting the external enemy, thus showing himself "weak".

In European history traces of this mechanism are to be found as early as the Merovingian epoch. Here, already, are present "the beginnings of a development which changed the higher imperial offices into hereditary forms of rule".[6] Even to this period the principle applies that: "The greater the actual economic and social power of these officials became, the less could the monarchy contemplate transferring the office outside the family on the death of its incumbent."[7] In other words, large parts of the territory passed from the control of the central lord to that of the local rulers.

Sequences of this kind emerge more clearly in the Carolingian period. Charlemagne, much like the emperor of Abyssinia, replaces the old local dukes wherever he can by his own "officials", the counts. When, within Charlemagne's lifetime, these counts show their self-will and their effective control over the territory entrusted to them, he despatches a new wave of people from his entourage as royal envoys, *missi dominici*, to supervise them. Under Louis the Pious the function of count already begins to become hereditary. Charlemagne's successors are no longer able "to escape factual recognition of the claim to hereditariness".[8] And the royal envoys themselves lose their function. Louis the Pious is forced to withdraw the *missi domin-ici*. Under this king who lacked the military renown of Charlemagne, the centrifugal tendencies within the imperial and social organization emerge very clearly. They reach a first peak under Charles III, who in 887 can no longer protect Paris from his external enemies, the Danish Normans, by the power of the sword, and scarcely by the power of money. It is characteristic of this tendency that with the end of the direct line of the Carolingians, the crown goes first to Arnulf of Carinthia, the bastard son of Karlmann, nephew of Charles the Fat. Arnulf had proved his worth as a military leader in the border conflicts with the invading foreign tribes. When he leads the Bavarians against the weak central ruler, he quickly gains the recognition of other tribes, the eastern Franks, the Thuringians, the Saxons and the Swabians. As army leader in the original sense, he is raised to the kingship by the warrior nobility of the German tribes.[9] Once again it is shown very clearly from where the function of kingship in this society derives its power and legitimation. In 891 he succeeds in repelling the Normans at Louvain on the Dyle. But when, confronted by a new threat, he hesitates only slightly to lead his army into battle, the reaction is immediate. At once centrifugal forces gain the upper hand in his weakly unified domain: "Illo diu morante, multi reguli in Europa vel regno Karoli sui patruelis excrevere," says a writer of the time.[10] Everywhere in Europe little kings grew up when he hesitated for a time to fight. This illustrates in one sentence the social regularities which set their stamp on the development of European society in this phase.

The movement is once again reversed under the first Saxon emperors. The fact that rule over the entire empire fell to the Saxon dukes again shows what was the most important function of the central ruler in this society. The Saxons were particularly exposed to pressure from the non-German tribes pushing across from the east. The first task of their dukes was to protect their own tribal territory. But in so doing they also defended the land of the other German tribes. In 924 Henry I manages to conclude at least a truce with the Hungarians; in 928 he himself advances as far as Brandenburg; in 929 he founds the frontier fortress at Meissen; in 933 he defeats the Hungarians at Riade, but without destroying them or really averting the danger; and in 934 in Schleswig he succeeds in restoring the northern frontiers against the Danes.[11] All this he does primarily as a Saxon duke. These are victories of the Saxons over peoples threatening their frontiers and territory. But in fighting and conquering on their own frontiers, the Saxon dukes gain the military power and reputation that are needed to oppose the centrifugal tendencies within the empire. Through external victory they lay the foundation of a strengthened internal central power.

Henry I had by and large maintained and consolidated the frontiers, at least to the north. As soon as he dies the Wends revoke their peace with the Saxons. Henry's son Otto drives them back. In the following years 937 and 938 the Hungarians advance again and are likewise repelled. Then begins a new and more powerful expansion. In 940 the German territory is extended to the Oder region. And, as always, as in the present day, the conquest of new lands is followed by the ecclesiastical organization which—then much more strongly than now—serves to secure military domination.

The same thing happens in the south-east. In 955—still on German territory—the Hungarians are defeated at Augsburg and so driven out more or less finally. As a barrier against them the Eastern Marches, embryo of the later Austria, are established with their frontier roughly in the region of Pressburg. To the east, in the central Danube area, the Hungarians slowly begin to settle permanently.

Otto's military successes are matched by his power inside the empire. Wherever he can he tries to replace the descendants of lords installed by earlier emperors, who now oppose him as hereditary local leaders, with his own relations and friends. Swabia goes to his son Ludolph, Bavaria to his brother Henry, Lorraine to his son-in-law Conrad, whose son Otto is given Swabia when Ludolph rebels.

At the same time he seeks—more consciously, it seems, than his predecessors—to counteract the mechanisms which constantly weaken centralism. He does this on the one hand by limiting the powers of the local rulers he installs. On the other hand he and, more resolutely still, his successors, oppose these mechanisms by installing clerics as rulers over regions. Bishops are given the secular office of count. This appointment of high ecclesiastics without heirs was intended to put a stop to the tendency of functionaries of the central authority to turn into a "hereditary, landowning aristocracy" with strong desires for independence.

In the long run, however, these measures intended to counter decentralizing forces only reinforced them. They led finally to the conversion of clerical rulers into princes, worldly powers. The preponderance of centrifugal tendencies over centripetal ones that was rooted in the structure of this society emerged yet again. In the course of time the spiritual authorities showed themselves no less concerned for the preservation of their independent hegemony over the territory entrusted to them than the secular. It was now in their interests too that the central authority should not grow too strong. And this convergence of the interests of high ecclesiastical and secular dignitaries was a main contributory factor in keeping the actual power of the central authority of the German Empire low for many centuries, while the power and independence of the territorial rulers increased—the inverse of what happened in France. There the leading ecclesiastics hardly ever became great worldly rulers. The bishops, part of whose possessions were scattered among the lands of the various territorial lords, remained interested in preserving a strong central authority for their own security. These parallel interests of church and monarchy, extending over a considerable period, were not the least of the factors which, in France, gave the central power preponderance over centrifugal tendencies at a relatively early stage. Early on, however, by the same process, the western Frankish empire disintegrated even more rapidly and radically than the eastern one.

6. The last, western Frankish, Carolingians were by all accounts[12] courageous and clear-thinking men, some of them gifted with outstanding qualities. But they were contending with a situation that gave the central ruler little chance, and one which shows particularly clearly how easily, in this social structure, the centre of gravity could shift to the disadvantage of the central ruler.

Leaving aside his role as army leader, conqueror and distributor of new lands, the basis of the social power of the central lord consisted of his family possessions, the land he controlled directly and from which he had to support his servants, his court and his armed retainers. In this respect the central lord was no better off than any other territorial ruler. But the personal territory of the western Frankish Carolingians had in the course of long struggles been largely given away in exchange for services rendered. To obtain and reward support, their forefathers had had to distribute land. Each time this happened—without new conquests—their own possessions were reduced. This left the sons in a still more precarious position. All new help meant new losses of land. In the end the heirs had very little left to distribute. The retainers they were able to feed and pay became fewer and fewer. We find the last of the western Frankish Carolingians in a sometimes desperate position. To be sure, their vassals were obliged to follow them to war; but if they had no personal interest in doing so, only the open or concealed pressure of a militarily powerful liege lord could induce them to meet this obligation. The fewer vassals followed the king, the less threatening his power became and so the fewer vassals followed him. With military power as with land, therefore, these social mechanisms, once set in motion, progressively weakened the position of the Carolingian kings.

Louis IV, a brave man fighting desperately for survival, is sometimes called "le roi de Monloon", the king of Laon. Of all the family possessions of the Carolingians, little is left to him except the fortress at Laon. At times the last sons of the house have hardly any troops to fight their wars, just as they have hardly any land to support and pay their followers: "The time arrived when the descendant of Charlemagne, surrounded by landowners who were the masters of their domains, found no other means of keeping men in his service than by handing out territory to them with concessions of immunity, that is, attaching them to him by making them more and more independent, and continuing to reign by abdicating more and more."[13] Thus the function of the monarchy goes irremediably downhill, and whatever its occupants do to improve their position in the end turns against them.

7. The former territory of the western Frankish Carolingians, the embryo of what was to become France, had at that time disintegrated into a number of separately ruled areas. After a prolonged struggle between various territorial rulers of roughly equal strength, a kind of equilibrium had been established. When the direct line of the Carolingians becomes extinct, the chieftains and territorial lords elect the one of their number whose house has outdone the others in the fight against the hostile Normans, and has thus long been the strongest rival of the weakening monarchy. In a similar way in the eastern Frankish regions, with the end of the Carolingians, the local princes who had successfully defended the country against the invading

peoples from the east and north, Slavs, Hungarians and Danes, that is, the dukes of Saxony, are made kings.

This had been preceded by a protracted struggle between the house of Francia and the last, western Frankish Carolingians.

When the crown went to the former in the person of Hugh Capet, they were themselves already somewhat weakened by a process similar to the one that had brought down the Carolingians. The dukes of Francia too had had to form alliances, and obtain services in exchange for land and rights. The territory of the Norman dukes who had settled and become Christianized in the meantime, the duchies of Aquitaine and Burgundy, the counties of Anjou and Flanders, Vermandois and Champagne, was scarcely smaller, and in some respects more important, than the family territory of the new royal house of Francia. And it was family power and territory that counted. The power available to the king through his family possessions was the real basis of his royal power. If his family possessions were no greater than those of other territorial rulers, then his power was no greater either. It was only from the family possessions and territory that he drew regular income. From other territories he drew, at the most, ecclesiastical dues. What he received beyond that in his capacity as "king" was minimal. Moreover, the factor which in the German territories constantly restored the preponderance of the centralizing royal function over the centrifugal tendencies of the territorial rulers, their function as military leaders in the struggle against external enemies and in the conquest of new land, ceased at a relatively early stage to be of importance in the western Frankish area. And this is one of the decisive reasons why the disintegration of the royal domain into independent territories occurred earlier here and, at first, in a more radical form. The eastern Frankish region was exposed for far longer to attack and threat by foreign tribes. Hence the kings not only constantly re-emerged as leaders in wars fought in common by a number of tribes to protect their lands, but they also had the opportunity of invading and conquering new lands, which they then distributed. So they were at first able to keep a relatively large number of retainers and vassals dependent on them.

In contrast, the western Frankish area, since the Normans had settled, had scarcely been threatened by outside tribes. In addition, there was no possibility of conquering new lands directly outside its borders, unlike the situation in the eastern Frankish region. This accelerated its disintegration. The prime factors giving the king preponderance over the centrifugal forces, defence and conquest, were lacking. Since there was virtually nothing else in the social structure that made the various regions dependent on a central ruler, the latter's domain was in fact reduced to little more than his own territory.

This so-called sovereign is a mere baron who owns a number of counties on the banks of the Seine and the Loire that amount to scarcely four or five present-day *départements*. The royal domain just manages to sustain his theoretical majesty. It is neither the largest nor the richest of the territories making up the France of today. The king is less powerful than some of his major vassals. And like them he lives on the income from his estates, duties from his peasants, the work of his bondsmen and the "voluntary gifts" from the abbeys and bishoprics in his territory.[14]

Soon after the crowning of Hugh Capet the weakening not of the individual kings but of the royal function itself, and with it the disintegration of the royal territories, begins slowly and steadily to increase. The first Capetians still travel throughout the whole country with their courts. The places where the royal decrees are signed give us an idea of the way in which they journeyed back and forth. They still sit in judgement at the seats of major vassals. Even in southern France they have a certain traditional influence.

At the beginning of the twelfth century the wholly hereditary and independent nature of the various territories previously subject to the king is an accomplished fact. The fifth of the Capetians, Louis the Fat (1108–37), a brave and belligerent lord and no weakling, has little say outside his own territory. The royal decrees show that he hardly ever travels outside the borders of his own duchy.[15] He lives within his own domain. He no longer holds court in the lands of his great vassals. They hardly ever appear at the royal court. The exchange of friendly visits grows more infrequent, correspondence with other parts of the kingdom, particularly in the south, more sparse. France at the beginning of the twelfth century is at best a union of independent territories, a loose federation of greater and lesser domains between which a kind of balance has provisionally been established.

8. Within the German Empire, after a century filled with wars between the wearers of the royal and imperial crown and the families of powerful dukes, one of the latter, the house of Swabia, succeeds in the twelfth century in again subjugating the others and, for a time, bringing together the necessary means of power in the central authority.

But from the end of the twelfth century onwards the social centre of gravity moves ever more clearly and inevitably towards the territorial rulers in Germany too. However, while in the immense area of the German "Imperium Romanum" or "Sacrum Imperium", as it was later called, the territorial estates are consolidating themselves to the point that they can now for centuries prevent the formation of a strong central power and so the integration of the whole area, in the smaller area of France the extreme disintegration of the end of the twelfth century now begins gradually and—some setbacks notwithstanding—fairly steadily to give way to a restoration of the central authority and the slow reintegration of larger and larger regions around one centre.

The scene of this radical disintegration must be envisaged as in a way the starting point if we are to understand how the smaller areas join together to form a stronger unit, and by which social processes were formed the central organs of the larger units of rule that we designate by the concept of "absolutism"—the ruling apparatus which forms the skeleton of modern states. The relative stability of the central authority and the central institutions in the phase we call the "Age of Absolutism" contrasts sharply with the instability of the central authority in the preceding "feudal" phase.

What was it in the structure of society that favoured centralization in the later phase but strengthened the forces opposing centralization in the earlier one?

This question takes us to the centre of the dynamics of social processes, of the changes in human interweaving and interdependence in conjunction with which conduct and drive structure were altered in the direction of "civilization".

9. What constantly gave the decentralizing forces in medieval, particularly early medieval, society their preponderance over the centralizing tendencies is not difficult to see, and has been

emphasized by historians of that epoch in a variety of ways. Hampe, for example, in his account of the European High Middle Ages, writes:

> The feudalization of states 'everywhere forced rulers to provide their army leaders and officials with land. If they were to avoid being impoverished in the process, and to make use of the military services of their vassals, they were virtually driven to attempts at military expansion, generally at the expense of the power vacuums around them. At that time it was not economically possible to avoid this necessity by constructing a bureaucracy on the modern pattern.[16]

This quotation implicitly shows the essential nature of both the centrifugal forces and the mechanisms in which the monarchy was embroiled in that society, provided that "feudalization" is not understood as an external "cause" of all these changes. The various elements in this dilemma: the necessity of providing warriors and officials with land, the unavoidable diminution of the royal possessions unless new campaigns of conquest took place, the tendency of the central authority to weaken in times of peace—all these are parts of the great process of "feudalization". The quotation also indicates how indissolubly this specific form of rule and its apparatus of government were bound to a particular economic structure.

To make this explicit: as long as barter relationships predominated in society, the formation of a tightly centralized bureaucracy and a stable apparatus of government working primarily with peaceful means and directed constantly from the centre, was scarcely possible. The imminent tendencies we have described—conqueror-king, envoys sent by the central authority to administer the country, independence of these envoys or their descendents as territorial rulers and their struggle against the central power—correspond to certain forms of economic relationship. If in a society the production from a small or large piece of land was sufficient to satisfy all the essential everyday needs of its inhabitants from clothing to food and household implements, if the division of labour and the exchange of products over longer distances were undeveloped, and if accordingly—all these are different aspects of the same form of integration—roads were bad and the means of transportation undeveloped, then the interdependence of different regions was also slight. Only when this interdependence grows considerably can relatively stable central institutions for a number of larger areas be formed. Before this the social structure simply offers no basis for them.

A historian of the period writes: "We can scarcely imagine how difficult it was, given medieval transportation conditions, to rule and administer an extensive empire."[17]

Charlemagne, too, supported himself and his court essentially from the produce of his old family estate scattered between the Rhine, the Maas and the Moselle. Each "Palatium" or manor—in Dopsch's convincing account[18]—was associated with a number of households and villages in the vicinity. The emperor and king moved from manor to manor in this relatively small area, supporting himself and his followers on the revenue from the surrounding households and villages. Trade over long distances was never entirely lacking even at this time; but it was essentially a trade in luxury goods, at any rate not in articles of daily use. Even wine was not, in general, transported over long distances. Anyone who wanted to drink wine had to produce it in his own district, and only his nearest neighbours could obtain any surplus through exchange. This is why there were in the Middle Ages vineyards in regions where wine is no longer cultivated today, the grapes being too sour or their plantations "uneconomic", for example in Flanders or Normandy. Conversely, regions like Burgundy which are for us synonymous with viniculture, were not nearly as specialized in winemaking as they later became. There, too, every farmer and estate had to be, up to a certain point, "autarkic". As late as the seventeenth century there were only eleven parishes in Burgundy where everyone was a wine-grower.[19] Thus slowly do the various districts become interconnected, are communications developed, are the division of labour and the integration of larger areas and populations increased; and increased correspondingly is the need for a means of exchange and units of calculation having the same value over large areas: money.

To understand the civilizing process it is particularly important to have a clear and vivid conception of these social processes, of what is meant by "barter or domestic economy", "money economy", "interdependence of large populations", "change in the social dependence of the individual", "increasing division of functions", and so on. Such concepts too easily become verbal fetishes which have lost all pictorial quality and thus, really, all clarity. The purpose of this necessarily brief account is to give a concrete perception of the social relationships referred to here by the concept of the "barter economy". What it indicates is a quite specific way in which people are bound together and dependent on each other. It refers to a society in which the transfer of goods from the man who gets them from the soil or nature to the man who uses them takes place directly, that is without or almost without intermediaries, and where they are worked up at the house of one or the other, which may well be the same. This transfer very gradually becomes more differentiated. More and more people slowly interpose themselves as functionaries of processing and distribution in the passage of the goods from the primary producer to the final consumer. How and, above all, why this happens, what is the motive power behind this prolongation of the chains, is a question in itself. At any rate money is nothing other than an instrument which is needed and with which society provides itself when these chains grow longer, when work and distribution are differentiated, and which under certain circumstances tends to reinforce this differentiation. If the terms "barter economy" and "money economy" are used, it can easily appear as if an absolute antithesis exists between these two economic forms, and such an imagined antithesis has unleashed many a dispute. In the actual social process the chains between production and consumption change and differentiate very gradually, not to mention the fact that in some sectors of Western society economic communication over long distances and thus the use of money never entirely ceased. Thus, very gradually, the money sector of the economy increases again, as do the differentiation of social functions, the interdependence of different regions, and the dependence of large populations on one another; all these are different aspects of the same social process. And so too the change in the form and apparatus for ruling that has been discussed is nothing other than a further aspect of this process. The structure of the central organs corresponds to the structure of the division and interweaving of functions. The strength of the centrifugal tendencies towards local *political autarky* within societies based predominantly on a barter economy corresponds to the degree of local *economic autarky*.

10. Two phases can generally be distinguished in the

development of such predominantly agrarian warrior societies, phases which may occur once only or alternate frequently: the phase of the belligerent expansionist central lords and that of the conserving rulers who win no new land. In the first phase the central authority is strong. The primary social function of the central lord in this society manifests itself directly, that of the army leader. When over a long period the royal house does not manifest itself in this belligerent role, when the king is either not needed as army leader or has no success as such, the secondary functions lapse as well, for example that of the highest arbitrator or judge of the whole region, and the ruler has at bottom no more than his title to distinguish him from other territorial lords.

In the second phase, when the frontiers are not threatened and the conquest of new land is impossible for one reason or another, centrifugal forces necessarily gain the upper hand. Though the conquering king has actually controlled the entire country, in times of relative peace it increasingly slips away from his authority. Anyone with a piece of land regards himself as its first ruler. This reflects his actual dependence on the central lord which in more peaceful times is minimal.

At this stage, when the economic interdependence and integration of large areas is lacking or only beginning, a noneconomic form of integration appears all the more strongly: military integration, alliance to repel a common foe. Beside a traditional sense of community with its strongest support in the common faith and its most important promoters in the clergy—but which never prevents disintegration, nor of itself brings about an alliance, merely strengthening and guiding it in certain directions—the urge to conquer and the necessity of resisting conquest is the most fundamental factor binding together people in regions lying relatively far apart. For this very reason every such alliance in this society is, compared with later periods, highly unstable, and the preponderance of decentralizing forces very great.

The two phases of this agrarian society, the phases of conquering and of conserving rulers, or merely spurts in one direction or the other, may alternate, as has been noted. And this is what actually happened in the history of Western countries. But the examples of German and French development also show that despite all the countervailing movements in the periods of conquering rulers, the tendency for the larger dominions to disintegrate and for land to pass from the control of the central lord to that of his erstwhile vassals proceeds, up to a certain time, continuously.

Why? Had the external threat to the former Carolingian Empire, which really constituted the West at that time, abated? Were there yet other causes for this progressive decentralization of the Carolingian Empire?

The question of the motive forces of this process may take on new significance if seen in relation to a familiar concept. This gradual decentralization of government and territory, this transition of the land from the control of the conquering central ruler to that of the warrior caste as a whole is nothing other than the process known as "feudalization".

III

The Increase in Population after the Migration of Peoples

11. For some time, understanding of the problem of feudalization has been undergoing a pronounced change which perhaps merits more explicit emphasis than it has received hitherto. As with social processes in general, the older mode of historial research has failed to come properly to grips with the process of feudalization in the West. The tendency to think in terms of isolated causes, to look for individual creators of social transformations, or at most to see only the legal aspect of social institutions and to seek the examples on which they were modelled by this or that agent—all this has made these processes and institutions as inaccessible to our thought as natural processes were earlier to scholastic thinkers.

More recently historians have begun to break through to a new way of posing the question. Increasingly, historians concerned with the origins of feudalism are emphasizing that this is neither a deliberate creation of individuals, nor does it consist of institutions that can be simply explained by earlier ones. Dopsch, for example, says of feudalization: "We are concerned here with institutions that were not called into being deliberately and intentionally by states or the bearers of state power in order to realize certain political ends."[20]

And Calmette formulates still more clearly this approach to the social processes of history:

However different the feudal system is from the preceding one, it results directly from it. No revolution, no individual will has produced it. It is part of a long evolution. Feudality belongs to the category of what might be called the "natural occurrences" or "natural facts" of history. Its formation was determined by quasi-mechanical forces and proceeded step by step.[21]

Elsewhere in his study *La société féodale* he says:

To be sure, knowledge of antecedents, that is, of similar phenomena preceding a given phenomenon, is interesting and instructive to historians, and we shall not ignore it. But these "antecedents" are not the only factors involved and perhaps not the most important. The main thing is not to know where the "feudal element" comes from, whether its origins are to be sought in Rome or among the Germans, but why this element has taken on its "feudal" character. If these foundations became what they were, they owe this to an evolution whose secret neither Rome nor the Germans can tell us . . . its formation is the result of forces that can only be compared with geological ones.[22]

The use of images from the realm of nature or technology is unavoidable as long as our language has not developed a clear, special vocabulary for socio-historical processes. Why images are provisionally sought in these realms is readily explained: for the time being they express adequately the compulsive nature of social processes in history. And however much one may thereby expose oneself to misunderstanding, as if social processes and their compulsions, originating in the interrelationships of men, were really of the same nature as, for example, the course of the earth about the sun or the action of a lever in a machine, the endeavour to find a new, structural manner of posing historical questions reveals itself very clearly in such formulations. The relation of later institutions to similar institutions in an earlier phase is always of significance. But here the decisive historical question is why institutions, and also people's conduct and affective make-up *change*, and why they change in this particular way. We are concerned with the strict order of socio-historical *transformations*. And perhaps it is not easy even today to understand that these transformations are not to be explained by something that itself remains unchanged, and still less easy to realize that in history no isolated fact ever brings about any transformation by itself, but only in combination with others.

Finally, these transformations remain inexplicable as long as explanation is limited to the ideas of individuals written down in books. When enquiring into social processes one must look at the web of human relationships, at society itself, to find the compulsions that keep them in motion, and give them their particular form and their particular direction. This applies to the process of feudalization as to the process of increasing division of labour; it applies to countless other processes represented in our conceptual apparatus by words without process-character, which stress particular institutions formed by the process in question, for example, the concepts of "absolutism", "capitalism", "barter economy", "money economy" and so on. All these point beyond themselves to changes in the structure of human relationships which clearly are not planned by individuals and to which individuals were subjected whether willingly or not. And this applies finally to changes in the make-up of people themselves, to the civilizing process.

12. One of the most important motors of change in the structure of human relationships, and of the institutions corresponding to them, is the increase or decrease of population. It too cannot be isolated from the whole dynamic web of human relationships. It is not, as prevalent habits of thought incline us to assume, in itself the "first cause" of socio-historical movement. But amidst the intertwining factors of change this is an important element that should never be neglected. It also shows particularly clearly the compelling nature of these social forces. It remains to be established what role factors of this kind played in the phase under discussion. It may help understanding of them to recall briefly the last movements in the migration of peoples.

Up to the eighth and ninth centuries tribes migrating from the east, north and south push in recurrent spurts into the already populated areas of Europe. This is the last and biggest wave in a movement that has gone on over a long period. What we see of it are small episodes: the irruption of Hellenic "barbarians" into the populated areas of Asia Minor and the Balkan peninsula, the penetration by the Italian "barbarians" of the neighbouring western peninsula, the advance of the Celtic "barbarians" into the territory of the former who have now in their turn become to some extent "civilized" and whose land has become a centre of "ancient culture", and the definitive settling of these Celtic tribes to the west and partly to the north of them.

Finally the German tribes overrun a large part of the Celts' territory, which in the meantime has likewise given rise to an "older culture". The Germans in their turn defend this "cultured" land they have conquered against new waves of peoples advancing from all sides.

Shortly after the death of Mohammed in 632 the Arabs are set in motion.[23] By 713 they have conquered the whole of Spain with the exception of the Asturian mountains. Towards the middle of the eighth century this wave comes to a standstill at the southern frontier of the Frankish empire, as Celtic waves had earlier done before the gates of Rome.

From the east Slavonic tribes advance against the Frankish empire. By the end of the eighth century they have reached the Elbe.

If in the year 800 a political prophet had possessed a map of Europe as we can now reconstruct it, he might well have been misled into predicting that the whole eastern half of the Continent from the Danish peninsula to the Peloponnese was destined to become a Slavonic Empire or at least a powerful group of Slavonic countries. From the Elbe estuary to the Ionian sea ran an unbroken line of Slavonic peoples ... this seems to mark the frontier of Germanic territory.[24]

Their movement comes to a standstill somewhat later than that of the Arabs. Then the struggle remains long undecided. The frontier between Germanic and Slavonic tribes now moves somewhat forward, now back again. By and large the Slavonic wave is held at the Elbe from about 800 onwards.

What may be called the "originally settled territory" of the west had thus, under the rule and leadership of Germanic tribes, preserved its frontier against the migrating tribes. Representatives of earlier waves defend it against those following, the last waves of migration that pass across Europe. These, prevented from advancing further, slowly settle outside the borders of the Frankish empire. And so a fringe of populated regions forms about the latter in large areas in the interior of Europe. Previously nomadic tribes take possession of the land. The great migrations slowly come to rest, and the renewed intrusions of migrating peoples that occur from time to time, by the Hungarians and finally the Turks, founder sooner or later on the superior defensive techniques and the strength of those already in possession.

13. A new situation had been created. There were no longer any empty spaces in Europe. There was virtually no usable land—usable in terms of the agricultural techniques then available—that had not been pre-empted. By and large Europe, and above all its large interior regions, was now more completely populated than ever before, even if incomparably less densely than in the centuries that followed. And there is every indication that population increased to the same extent as the upheavals accompanying the great migrations abated. This changed the whole system of tensions between and within the various peoples.

In late antiquity the population of the "old cultural regions" diminishes more or less rapidly. In consequence the social institutions corresponding to relatively large and dense populations disappear also. The use of money within a society, for example, is bound up with a certain level of population density. It is an essential prerequisite for the differentiation of work and the formation of markets. If the population falls below a certain level—for whatever reasons—the markets automatically empty. The chains between the man producing a commodity from nature and its consumer grow shorter. Money loses its instrumental function. This was the direction of development at the end of antiquity. The urban sector of society grows smaller. The agrarian character of society increases. This development took place the more easily as the division of labour in antiquity was never remotely as great as, for example, in our own society. A proportion of urban households were always to a degree directly supplied, independently of commercial or manufacturing intermediaries, by the great slave estates. And as the overland transportation of goods over long distances was always extremely difficult, given the state of technology in antiquity, long-distance trade was essentially confined to waterborne transport. Large markets and towns and vigorous monetary activity developed in proximity to water. Inland areas always preserved a predominantly domestic type of economy. Even for the urban population, the autarkic household and economic self-sufficiency never declined to the extent that they have in modern Western society. With the fall in population this aspect of the social structure of antiquity regained prominence.

With the end of the migration of peoples, this movement was once again reversed. The influx and subsequent settling of so many new tribes provided the basis for a new and more comprehensive population of the whole European area. In the Carolingian period this population still had an almost completely domestic economy, perhaps even more so than in the Merovingian period.[25] One indication of this may be that the political centre moved still further inland, where hitherto—owing to the difficulties of overland transport—the political centres preceding those of the medieval West had never been situated, with few exceptions such as the Hittite Empire. We may assume that the population was beginning to increase very slowly in this period. We already hear of forest clearance, and that is always a sign that land is growing scarce, the density of population rising. But these are certainly only the initial stages. The migrations of peoples have not yet entirely abated. Only from the ninth century onwards do the signs of a more rapidly increasing population multiply. And not very long afterwards there are already indications of overpopulation here and there in the former Carolingian regions.

Fall in population at the end of antiquity, slow rise once more under different circumstances in the aftermath of the migrations of peoples: a brief retrospective summary must be enough to recall to mind the curve of this movement.

14. Phases of perceptible overpopulation alternate in European history with those of lower internal pressure. But the term "overpopulation" needs explaining. It is not a product of the absolute number of people inhabiting a certain area. In a heavily industrialized society with intensive utilization of the land, highly developed long-distance trade and a government favouring the industrial against the agrarian sector through import and export duties, a number of people can live more or less tolerably which, in a barter economy with extensive agricultural methods and little long-distance trade, would constitute overpopulation with all its typical symptoms. "Overpopulation" is therefore first of all a term for growth of population in a particular area to a point where, in the given social structure, the

35

satisfaction of basic needs is possible for fewer and fewer people. We thus encounter "overpopulation" only relative to certain social forms and a certain set of needs, a social over-population.

Its symptoms in societies which have attained a certain degree of differentiation are, broadly speaking, always the same: increased tension within society; greater self-encapsulation by those who "have", i.e., in a predominantly barter economy, those who "have land", over against those those who "have not", or at any rate not enough to support themselves in a manner conforming with their standards; and often, increased self-encapsulation, among the "haves", of those who have more than the rest; a more pronounced cohesion of people in the same social situation to resist pressure from those outside it or, inversely, to seize opportunities monopolized by others. In addition, increased pressure on neighbouring areas with lower population or weaker defences, and finally, an increase in emigration and in the tendency to conquer or at least settle in new lands.

It is difficult to say whether available sources can give an exact picture of population growth in Europe in the centuries following the migrations, and particularly of differences in population density between different regions. But one thing is certain: as the migrations slowly come to a standstill, once the major struggles among the different tribes have come to an end, one after another all the symptoms of such "social overpopulation" show themselves—a rapid growth of population accompanied by the transformation of social institutions.

15. The symptoms of increasing population pressure first appear clearly in the western Frankish empire. Here, about the ninth century, the threat from foreign tribes slowly recedes, unlike the situation in the eastern Frankish empire. In the part of the empire named after them the Normans have grown peaceable. With the help of the western Frankish Church, they rapidly absorb the language and the whole tradition about them, in which Gallo–Romanic and Frankish elements are mingled. They add new elements of their own. In particular, they bring about important advances in the administrative structure within the territorial framework. From now on they play a decisive part as one of the leading tribes in the federation of western Frankish territories.

The Arabs and Saracens cause occasional unrest on the

Mediterranean coast, but by and large they too, from the ninth century on, scarcely represent a threat to the survival of this empire.

To the east of France lies the German "Imperium" which under the Saxon emperors has again grown powerful. With minor exceptions the frontier between it and the western Frankish empire scarcely moves from the tenth to the first quarter of the thirteenth century.[26] In 925 Lotharingia is won back from the empire, and in 1034 Burgundy. Apart from this, tension along this line is not high until 1226. The empire's expansionist tendencies are directed essentially to the east.

The external threat to the western Frankish empire is therefore relatively slight. Equally slight, however, are the possibilities of expanding beyond the existing frontiers. The east in particular is blocked both by the population density and the military strength of the empire.

But within this area, now that the external threat has diminished, population begins to increase markedly. It grows so strongly after the ninth century that by the beginning of the fourteenth century it is probably almost as large as at the beginning of the eighteenth.[27]

This movement certainly did not proceed in a straight line, but there is an abundance of evidence to show that, by and large, population increased steadily; this evidence has to be seen as a whole if the strength of the overall movement, and the meaning of each individual piece of evidence within it, are to be understood.

From the end of the tenth century onwards, and more so in the eleventh, the pressure on land, the desire for new land and greater productivity from the old, are more and more visible in the western Frankish region.

As mentioned, forests were already cleared in the Carolingian period and no doubt earlier too. But in the eleventh century the tempo and extent of the clearance accelerate. Woods are felled and marshlands made arable as far as the technology of the time permitted. The period from about 1050 to about 1300 is the great age of deforestation, of the internal conquest of new land, in France.[28] About 1300 this movement slows down again.

Some Observations on the Sociogenesis of the Crusades

16. The great onslaught from outside has subsided. The earth is fruitful. Population grows. Land, the most important means of production, the epitome of property and wealth in this society, becomes scarce. Deforestation, the opening up of new land within, is not nearly sufficient to offset this scarcity. New land must be sought outside the frontiers. Hand in hand with internal colonization goes the external conquest of new territory elsewhere. By the beginning of the eleventh century Norman knights are going to southern Italy to hire themselves out as warriors to individual princes.[29] In 1029 one of them is enfeoffed for his services with a small piece of land on the northern boundary of the duchy of Naples. Others follow, among them other sons of a minor Norman lord, Tancrède de Hauteville. He has twelve sons in all; how are they to be sustained to a fitting standard on their father's land? Eight of them therefore go to southern Italy, and there obtain in time what is denied to them at home: control of a piece of land. One of them, Robert Guiscard, gradually becomes the acknowledged leader of the Norman warriors. He unites the scattered estates or territories that individuals have won for themselves. From 1060 onwards they begin under his leadership to advance into Sicily. By Robert Guiscard's death in 1085 the Saracens have been pushed back into the south-west corner of the island. All the rest is in Norman hands and forms a new Norman feudal empire.

None of this had actually been planned. At the outset we have the population pressure and the blocked opportunities at home, the emigration of individuals whose success attracts others; at the end we have an empire.

Something similar happens in Spain. In the tenth century French knights go to the aid of the Spanish princes in their struggles against the Arabs. As mentioned, the western Frankish area, unlike the eastern, does not border on an extensive area open to colonization and peopled by largely disunited tribes. To the east the empire prevents further expansion. The Iberian peninsula is the only direct way out. Up to the middle of the eleventh century only individuals or small bands cross the mountains; then, they gradually become armies. The Arabs, split internally, offer slight, sporadic resistance. In 1085 Toledo is taken, and in 1094 Valencia under the leadership of El Cid, only to be lost shortly afterwards. The struggle is waged back and forth. In 1095 a French count is invested with the reconquered territory of Portugal. But it is only in 1147, with the aid of members of the Second Crusade, that his son finally succeeds in gaining control of Lisbon and there to some degree stabilizing his rule as a feudal king.

Apart from Spain, the only possibility of gaining new land near France lay across the Channel. Even in the first half of the eleventh century individual Norman knights had struck out in this direction. Then in 1066 the Norman Duke with an army of Norman and French knights crosses to the island, seizes power and redistributes the land. The possibilities of expansion, the prospects of new land in the vicinity of France, grow more and more restricted. Eyes are cast further afield.

In 1095, before the great feudal lords begin to move, a band led by the knight Walter Habenichts, or Gautier Senzavoir, sets out for Jerusalem; it perishes in Asia Minor. In 1097 a mighty army under the leadership of Norman and French territorial lords advances into the Holy Land. The Crusaders first have themselves invested by the Eastern Roman Emperor with the lands to be conquered, then advance further, conquer Jerusalem and found new feudal dominions.

There is no reason to assume that without the guidance of the Church and the religious link with the Holy Land, this expansion would have been directed to precisely that place. But nor is it probable that without the social pressure first within the western Frankish region and then in all the other regions of Latin Christendom, the Crusades would have taken place.

The tensions within this society were not only manifested in desire for land and bread. They exerted mental pressure upon the whole person. The social pressure supplied the motive force as a generator supplies current. It set people in motion. The Church steered this pre-existing force. It embraced the general distress and gave it a hope and a goal outside France. It gave the struggle for new land an overarching meaning and justification. It turned this into a struggle for the Christian faith.

17. The Crusades are a specific form of the first great movement of expansion and colonization by the Christian West. During the migrations of peoples, in which for centuries tribes from

the east and north-east had been driven in a western and south-western direction, the utilizable areas of Europe had been filled up with people to the furthest frontiers, the British Isles. Now the migrations had stopped. The mild climate, fertile soil and unfettered drives favoured rapid multiplication. The land grew too small. The human wave had trapped itself in a cul-de-sac, and from this confinement it strained back towards the east, both in the Crusades and within Europe itself, where the German-populated area slowly spread, through heavy conflicts, further and further east beyond the Elbe to the Oder, then to the Vistula estuary, and finally to Prussia and the Baltic lands, even if it was only German knights, not German farmers, who succeeded in migrating so far.

But precisely this last fact shows very clearly one of the peculiarities distinguishing this first phase of social overpopulation and expansion from later ones. In general, with the advance of the civilizing process, and the concomitant constraint and regulation of human drives—and they always advance further, for reasons to be discussed later, in the upper than in the lower classes—the birthrate slowly declines, usually less rapidly in the lower than in the upper strata. This difference between the average birthrate of the upper and lower classes is often highly significant for the maintenance of the standard of the former.

This first phase of rapid population growth in the Christian West is distinguished from the later ones, however, by the fact that in it the ruling stratum, the warrior class or nobility, increases hardly less rapidly than the stratum of bondsmen, tenants and peasants, in short, of those who directly work the land. The struggle for the available opportunities which, with the growth of population, necessarily shrink for each individual; the incessant feuds that these tensions unleashed; the high rate of infant mortality, illness and plague: all that may have eliminated a part of the human surplus. And it is possible that the relatively unprotected peasantry were harder hit than the warriors. Moreover, the freedom of movement of the former group was so limited and, above all, communications between different regions were so difficult, that the surplus labour power could not be quickly and evenly distributed. Thus in one area shortage of labour might result from feuds and pillage, plagues, the opening up of new land or the flight of serfs, while a surplus was accumulating in others. And in fact we have, for the same period, clear evidence of an excess of bondsmen in one area, and of efforts in others to attract free tenants, *hospites*[30]—that is, rulers offering labourers improved conditions.

Be that as it may, what is above all characteristic of the processes operating here is that not only was a "reserve army" of bondsmen or serfs forming in this society, but also a "reserve army" of the *upper class*, of knights without property, or without enough to maintain their standards. Only in this way can the nature of this first Western expansionist phase be understood. Peasants, the sons of bondsmen, were certainly involved in one way or another in the struggles for colonization, but the main impulse came from the knights' shortage of land. New land could only be conquered by the sword. The knights opened a way by force of arms; they took the lead and formed the bulk of the armies. The surplus population in the upper class gave this first period of expansion and colonization its special stamp.

The rift between those who had land and those who had none or too little, runs right through this society. On the one hand are the land-monopolists—warrior families, noble houses and land-owners in the first place, but also peasants, bondsmen, serfs, *hospites*, who occupy a piece of land that supports them, however meagrely. On the other hand are those from both classes who have been deprived of land. Those from the lower classes —displaced by the shortage of opportunities or the oppression of their masters—play a part in the emigration or colonization, but above all they provide the population of the growing towns. Those from the warrior class, in short the "younger sons", whose inheritance is too small either for their demands or for their mere sustenance, the "have-nots" among the knights, appear down the centuries wearing the most disparate social masks: as Crusaders, as robber-leaders, as mercenaries in the service of great lords; finally they form the basis of the first standing armies.

18. The often-quoted dictum: "No land without a lord", is not only a basic legal principle. It is also a social watchword of the warrior class. It expresses the knights' need to take possession of every scrap of usable land. Sooner or later this has come about in all the regions of Latin Christendom. Every available piece of land is in firm ownership. But the demand for land continues and even increases. The chances of satisfying it diminish. The pressure for expansion rises, as does the tension within so-

ciety. But the specific dynamic which is thus imparted to society as a whole does not emanate solely from the malcontents; it is necessarily communicated also to those rich in land. In the poor, debt-ridden, declining knights the social pressure manifests itself as a simple desire for a piece of land and labourers to support them in keeping with their standards. In the richer warriors, the greater landowners and territorial lords, it is expressed likewise as an urge for new land. But what lower down was a simple desire for a means of subsistence appropriate to one's class, is higher up a drive for enlarged dominion, for "more" land and so more social power as well. This craving for enlarged property among the richer landowners, above all those of the first rank, the counts, dukes and kings, sprang not only from the personal ambition of individuals. We have already seen by the example of the western Frankish Carolingians, and also the first Capetians, how unremittingly, unless there was a possibility of conquering new land, even royal houses were forced into decline by a compelling social process centred on the ownership and distribution of land. And if, throughout this whole phase of outward and inward expansion, we see not only poor knights but also many rich ones striving after new land to increase their family power, this is no more than a sign of how strongly the structure and situation of this society imposed the same striving on all strata, whether simply to own land in the case of the dispossessed, or to own "more" land in the case of the rich.

It has been thought that this craving for "more" property, the acquisitive urge, is a specific characteristic of "capitalism" and thus of modern times. In this view medieval society was distinguished by contentment with the income appropriate to one's social standing.

Within certain limits this is no doubt correct, if the striving for "more" is understood as applying to money alone. But for a long period of the Middle Ages it was not ownership of money but of land which constituted the essential form of ownership. The acquisitive urge thus necessarily has a different form and a different direction. It demands different modes of conduct to those of a society with a money and market economy. It may be true it is only in modern times that there develops a class specializing in trade, with a desire to earn ever-increasing amounts of *money* through uninterrupted toil. The social structures which, in the predominantly barter economy of the Middle

Ages, lead to a desire for ever-increasing means of production—and it is structural features that are important in both cases—are less easy to perceive, because land not money is desired. In addition, political and military functions have not yet been differentiated from economic ones as they have gradually become in modern society. Military action, and political and economic striving, are largely identical, and the urge to increase wealth in the form of land comes to the same thing as extending territorial sovereignty and increasing military power. The richest man in a particular area, i.e. the one with most land, is as a direct result the most powerful militarily, with the largest retinue; he is at once army leader and ruler.

Precisely because the relationship between one estate owner and another in that society was analogous to that between states today, the acquisition of new land by one neighbour represented a direct or indirect threat to the others. It meant, as today, a shift of equilibrium in what was usually a very labile system of power balances in which rulers were always potential allies and potential enemies of one another. This, therefore, is the simple mechanism which, in this phase of internal and external expansion, kept the richer and more powerful knights in motion no less than the poorer ones, each being constantly on guard against expansion by others, and constantly seeking to enlarge his own possessions. When a society has once been put in such a state of flux by the blockage of territorial expansion and population pressure, anyone who declines to compete, merely conserving his property while others strive for increase, necessarily ends up "smaller" and weaker than the others, and is in ever-increasing danger of succumbing to them at the first opportunity. The rich knights and territorial lords of that time did not view the matter quite so theoretically and generally as we have put it here; but they did see quite concretely how powerless they were when their neighbours were richer in land than they, or when others around them won new land and sovereignty. This could be shown in more detail in relation to the Crusade leaders, for example Godefroi de Bouillon, who sells and mortgages his domestic possessions to seek larger ones far away, and in fact finds a kingdom. In a later period this could be shown by the example of the Habsburgs, who even as emperors were possessed by the idea of extending their "family power", and were in fact, even as emperors, completely impotent without the support of their own family power. Indeed, it was precisely because of his poverty and powerlessness that the first emperor from the family was selected for this position by mighty lords jealous of their power. It could be illustrated particularly clearly by the importance which the conquest of England by the Norman Duke had for the development of the western Frankish empire. In fact, this growth in the power of one territorial ruler meant a total displacement of equilibrium within the alliance of territorial rulers comprising this empire. The Norman Duke who, in his own territory, Normandy, was himself no less affected by centrifugal forces than any other territorial ruler, did not conquer England for the Normans as a whole but solely to increase his own family power. And the redistribution of English soil to the warriors who came with him was expressly designed to counter centrifugal forces in his new domain by preventing the formation of large territorial dominions on English soil. That he had to allot land to his knights was dictated by the necessity of ruling and administering it; but he avoided allocating a large self-contained area to any individual. Even to the great lords who could demand the produce of large areas for their maintenance, he assigned lands dispersed throughout the country.[31]

At the same time he had automatically risen, with this conquest, to be the most powerful territorial ruler in the western Frankish empire. Sooner or later there must be a confrontation between his house and that of the dukes of Francia, who held the kingship—a confrontation in which the crown itself was at stake. And it is known how greatly developments in subsequent centuries were determined by this struggle between the dukes of Francia and Normandy, how the rulers of the Isle de France slowly restored the balance of power by the acquisition of new territories, and how these struggles on both sides of the Channel finally gave rise to two different dominions and two different nations. But this is certainly only one of many examples of the compelling processes in this dynamic phase of the Middle Ages, which impelled both rich and poor knights to seek new land.

V

The Internal Expansion of Society:
The Formation of New Social Organs and Instruments

19. The driving force of this social expansion, the disproportion between rising population and land in fixed ownership, drove a large part of the ruling class to conquer new territory. This outlet was largely blocked to people of the lower classes, the workers. The pressures arising from the land shortage here led mainly in a different direction, to the differentiation of work. The bondsmen driven from the land comprised, as we have mentioned, material for the growing settlements of artisans which slowly crystallized around favourably situated feudal seats, the evolving towns.

Somewhat larger agglomerations of people—the word "town" perhaps gives the wrong impression—are already to be found in the society of the ninth century which operated a barter economy. But these were not the communities which "lived by crafts and trade instead of labour on the land, or had any special rights and institutions".[32] They were fortresses and at the same time centres of the agricultural administration of great lords. The towns of earlier periods had themselves lost their unity. They were juxtaposed pieces, groups often belonging to different knights and different dominions, some secular, others ecclesiastical, each leading its own independent economic life. The sole framework for economic activity was the estate, the domain of the territorial lord. Production and consumption took place at essentially the same place.[33]

But in the eleventh century these formations began to grow. Here too, as usually happened with knightly expansion but was now happening among bondsmen, it was at first unorganized individuals, surplus labourers, who were driven to such centres. And the attitude of rulers to the newcomers, who in each case had just left a different estate, was not always the same.[34] Sometimes they gave them a modicum of freedom; but mostly they expected and demanded the same services and tributes as from their own bondsmen and tenants. But the accumulation of such people changed the power relationship between the lord and the lower class. The newcomers gained strength through numbers and gradually obtained new rights in bloody and often protracted struggles. These struggles broke out earliest in Italy, somewhat later in Flanders: in 1030 in Cremona, in 1057 in Milan, in 1069 at Le Mans, in 1077 at Cambrai, in 1080 at Saint-Quentin, in 1099 in Beauvais, in 1108–9 in Noyon, in 1112 in Laon, in 1127 in Saint-Omer. These dates, together with those of the knights' expansion, give a general impression of the internal tensions which kept society in motion in this phase. These are the first struggles for liberation by working town-dwellers. That they were able, after some defeats, in their struggles with the warrior class in the most different areas of Europe, to secure rights of their own, first a limited and then a substantial degree of freedom, shows how great was the opportunity that social development placed in their hands. And this peculiar fact, the slow rise of lower, working, urban strata to political autonomy and finally—first in the form of the professional middle classes—to political leadership, provides the key to almost all the structural peculiarities distinguishing Western societies from those of the Orient, and giving them their specific stamp.

At the beginning of the eleventh century there are, essentially, only two classes of free people, the warriors or nobles and the clergy; below them exist only bondsmen and serfs. There are "those who pray, those who fight, those who work".[35]

By about 1200, that is to say, in the course of two centuries or even only one and a half—for like forest clearance and colonial expansion this movement too accelerates after 1050—a large number of artisan settlements or communes have secured rights and jurisdiction, privileges and autonomy. A third class of free men joins the other two. Society expands, under the pressure of land shortage and population increase, not only extensively but intensively as well; it becomes differentiated, generates new cells, forms new organs, the towns.

20. But with the increasing differentiation of work, with the new, larger markets that now form, with the slow process of exchange over longer distances, grows the need for mobile and unified means of exchange.

When the bondsman or small tenant brings his tribute direct to his lord, when the chain between producer and consumer is short and without intermediaries, society needs no unit of calculation, no means of exchange to which all other exchanged objects can be related as to a common measure. But now, with the gradual severance of craftsmen from the economic unit of the household, with the formation of an economically independent artisanry and the exchange of products through several hands and down longer chains, the network of exchange-acts becomes complicated. A unified object of exchange is needed. When the differentiation of labour and exchange grows more complex and more active, more money is needed. Money is indeed an incarnation of the social fabric, a symbol of the network of exchange-acts and human chains through which a commodity passes on its way from its natural state to consumption. It is only needed when extended chains of exchange form within society, that is to say, at a certain level of population density and a high level of social interdependence and differentiation.

It would take us too far afield to explore here the question of the gradual recession of the money economy in many areas in late antiquity and its resurgence from about the eleventh century onwards; but one observation on the question is necessary in connection with the foregoing.

It must be pointed out that money never went completely out of use in the older inhabited area of Europe. Over this whole period there were enclaves of money economy within the barter economy, and in addition, outside the Carolingian area there were large regions of the old Roman Empire where money traffic never receded to the same extent as it did here. One can, therefore, always and very rightly ask about the "antecedents" of the money economy in the Christian West, the enclaves in which it never disappears. One can ask: where did the money economy originate? From whom was the use of money relearned? This kind of enquiry is not without value; for it is difficult to imagine that this instrument should have returned to use so relatively quickly had it not been so far developed in other, preceding or neighbouring civilizations, or if it had never been known.

But the essential aspect of the question concerning the revival of money traffic in the West is not answered in this way. The question remains why Western society needed relatively little money over a long stretch of its development, and why the need and use of money, with all the consequent transformations of society, gradually increased once more. Here again the enquiry must be directed toward the *moving*, the *changing* factors. And this question is not answered by examining the origins of money and the antecedents of the money economy. It is answered only by examining the actual social processes which, after the slow ebb of money traffic in declining antiquity, once again brought forth the new human relationships, the new forms of integration and interdependence, which caused the need for money to increase again: the cellular structure of society is differentiated. *One* expression of this was the revival in the use of money. That it was not only internal expansion but also migration and colonization which—through the mobilization of property, the awakening of new needs, the establishment of trade relations over longer distances—played an important part in this revival is immediately evident. Each individual movement in the whole interplay of processes reacts on the others, either obstructing or reinforcing them, and the web of movements and tensions is from now on considerably complicated by the social differentiation. Single factors cannot be absolutely isolated. But without the differentiation within society itself, without the passing of the land into fixed ownership, without the sharp increase in population, without the formation of independent communities of artisans and tradesmen, the need for money within society would never have risen so sharply, nor the money sector of the economy have grown so rapidly. Money, the decrease or increase of its use, cannot be understood by itself, but only from the standpoint of the structure of human relationships. It is here, in the changed form of human integration, that the prime movers of this transformation are to be sought; of course, when the use of money had once begun to grow, it helped in its turn to propel this whole movement—population increase, differentiation, growth of towns—still further, up to a certain point of saturation.

"The beginning of the eleventh century is still characterized by the absence of large-scale money transactions. Wealth is to a large extent immobilized in the hands of the Church and the secular territorial lords."[36]

Then the need for mobile means of exchange gradually increases. The existing coinage is no longer sufficient. First of all people make do with plate and ornaments in precious metal that are weighed to provide a unit of calculation; horses too can serve as measures of value; new money is minted to meet the growing demand, that is to say: pieces of precious metal of a certain weight gauged by authorities. And probably, with the growing need for mobile means of exchange, the process was repeated on various levels; perhaps exchange by barter, when the supply of coinage no longer met the increased demand, repeatedly gained new ground. Slowly the increasing differentiation and interweaving of human actions, the growing volume of trade and exchange, pushes up the volume of coinage and then the reverse takes place. In between, disproportions continually arise.

By the second half of the thirteenth century, at least in Flanders, and somewhat earlier or later in other regions, mobile wealth is very considerable. It circulates fairly rapidly "thanks to a series of instruments that have been created in the meantime":[37] gold coinage minted within the country—hitherto even in France, as in Abyssinia to the present day, no gold coinage had been minted; what was in use, and stored in the treasuries, was Byzantine gold coin—together with small money, the letter of exchange and measurement—all these are symbols of how the invisible network of chains of exchange was growing more and more dense.

21. But how could exchange relations between different areas, and differentiation of work extending beyond the local region be established, if transport was inadequate, if society was incapable of moving heavy loads over long distances?

Examples from the Carolingian period have already shown how the king had to travel with his court from one imperial palace to another in order to consume the products of his estates on the spot. No matter how small this court may have been in comparison to those of the early absolutist phase, it was so difficult to move the quantities of goods that were needed for its sustenance that the people had to move to the goods instead.

But in the same period when population, the towns, interdependence and its instruments, were growing more and more perceptibly, transport too was developing.

In antiquity the harness of horses, as of all other beasts of burden, was little suited to the transportation of heavy loads over long distances. It is open to question what distances and loads it could cope with, but clearly this mode of conveyance was sufficient for the structure and needs of the inland economy of antiquity. Throughout the whole of that period land transport remained extraordinarily expensive,[38] slow and difficult, in comparison to waterborne transport. Virtually all major centres of trade were situated on the coast or on navigable rivers. And this centralization of transport about the waterways is very characteristic of the structure of the society of antiquity. Here, on the waterways and above all on the seacoasts, arose rich and sometimes very densely populated urban centres whose need for food and luxury articles was often met from very remote parts, and which formed central links in the highly differentiated chains of an extensive exchange traffic. In the enormous hinterlands, which by and large were open only to overland transport, that is, in by far the largest part of the Roman Empire, the population met their primary needs directly from the produce of their immediate environment. Here, short exchange chains predominated, in other words, what can be roughly called a "barter economy"; very little money circulated, and the purchasing power of this barter sector of the ancient economy was too low for the acquisition of luxury articles. The contrast between the small urban sector and the vast inland areas was thus very great. Like thin nerve strands the larger urban settlements along the waterways were embedded in the rural districts, drawing off their strength and the products of their labour until, with the decline of the centralized government, and partly through the active struggle of rural elements against the urban rulers, the agrarian sector freed itself from the domination of the towns. Then this narrow, more differentiated urban sector, with its extensive interdependencies, fell into decay, to be obliterated by a somewhat altered form of short, regionally limited exchange chains and barter-economy institutions. In this dominant urban sector of ancient society, however, there was clearly no need to develop overland transport further. Everything that its own country could not supply or only at a high transportation cost, could be more easily obtained from overseas.

But now, in the Carolingian period, the chief waterway of the ancient world, the Mediterranean, was closed, primarily through Arab expansion, to a large number of peoples. Overland transport and internal connections took on an entirely new significance. This generated a pressure for land transport to be developed to promote interdependence and exchange. And if subsequently, as in antiquity, sea connections such as those between Venice and Byzantium, the Flemish cities and England, again played a decisive part in the rise of the West, the specific character of Western development is no less determined by the fact that to the network of sea routes was attached an increasingly dense network of overland connections, and that major inland centres of trade were also gradually developed. The development of land transport beyond the level it had attained in the ancient world is a particularly clear illustration of this growing differentiation and interdependence of societies throughout the inland areas of Europe.

The use of the horse for haulage was, as has been mentioned, not very highly developed in the Roman world. The harness ran across the throat.[39] This was perhaps useful to the rider in guiding his horse. The thrown-back head, the "proud" posture of the horse frequently seen in ancient reliefs is connected with this mode of harnessing. But it makes the horse or mule fairly unusable for haulage, particularly of heavy loads, which necessarily constrict its throat.

The case is similar with the shoeing of animals. The ancients lacked the nailed iron horseshoe without which the full power of the horse cannot be exploited.

Both states of affairs slowly change from the tenth century onwards. In the same phase when the tempo of forest clearance is gradually increased, when society is differentiated and urban markets are formed, when money comes increasingly into use as a symbol of this interdependence, land transport too, in the form of devices for the exploitation of animal labour power, makes decisive progress. And this improvement, insignificant as it may appear to us today, had at that time scarcely less importance than the development of machine technology in a later age.

"In a mighty constructive effort", it has been said,[40] the scope of use of animal labour is slowly extended in the course of the eleventh and twelfth centuries. The main load in haulage is transferred from the throat to the shoulders. The horseshoe appears. And in the thirteenth century the modern haulage technique for both horses and oxen is created in principle. The foundation for the overland transport of heavy loads over long distances has been laid. In the same period the wheeled cart appears and the beginnings of metalled roads. With the development of transport technology, the water-mill takes on an importance it had lacked in antiquity. It was now profitable to transport grain to it over quite long distances.[41] That too was a step on the way to differentiation and interdependence, to the severance of functions from the closed sphere of the estate.

VI

Some New Elements in the Structure of Medieval Society as Compared with Antiquity

22. The change in drive-control and conduct that we call "civilization" is very closely related to the growing interweaving and interdependence of people. In the few examples that it has been possible to give here, this interweaving can be seen as it were in the process of becoming. And even here, at this relatively early phase, the nature of the social fabric in the West is in certain respects different from that of antiquity. As the cellular structure of society began once again to become differentiated, whatever institutions the preceding stage of high differentiation had left behind were used in many ways. But the conditions under which this renewed differentiation took place, and thus the nature and direction of the differentiation itself, diverged in certain respects from those of the earlier period.

People have spoken of a "renaissance of trade" in the eleventh or twelfth centuries. If this means that institutions of antiquity were now to a certain extent revived, it is certainly correct. Without the heritage of antiquity, the problems confronting society in the course of this development could certainly not have been successfully overcome in this way. In this respect it was a construction on earlier foundations. But the driving force of the movement did not reside in "learning from antiquity". It lay within the society itself, in its own inherent dynamics, in the conditions under which people had to accommodate themselves to one another. These conditions were no longer the same as in antiquity. There is a very widespread conception that the West only really regained and then surpassed the level attained by antiquity in the Renaissance. But whether or not we are here concerned with a "surpassing", with "progress", structural features and developmental tendencies departing from those of antiquity are visible not only in the Renaissance but already—at least to a certain extent—in the early phase of expansion and growth that has been discussed here.

Two such structural differences will be mentioned. Western society lacked the cheap labour of prisoners-of-war, slaves. Or when they were available—and they were not in fact entirely lacking—they no longer played any very significant part in the overall structure of society. This gave social development a new direction from the outset.

No less important was another circumstance that has already been mentioned. Resettlement did not take place as previously about a sea, or as exclusively along waterways, but very largely in inland areas by land transport routes. Both these circumstances, often in close interaction, confronted Western society from the start with problems that ancient society had not needed to solve and which guided social development into new paths. The fact that slaves played only a minor role in the working of estates may be explained by the absence of large slave reservoirs or by the sufficiency of the indigenous population of bondsmen for the needs of the warrior class. However that may be, the insignificance of slave labour is matched by the absence of the typical social patterns of a slave economy. And it is only against the background of these different patterns that the special nature of the Western structure can be fully appreciated. Not only do the division of labour, the interweaving of people, the mutual dependence of upper and lower classes, and concomitantly, the drive economy of both classes, develop differently in a slave society than in one with more or less free labour, but also the social tensions and even the functions of money are not the same, to say nothing of the importance of free labour for the development of work-techniques.

It must be enough here to contrast to the specific processes of Western civilization a brief summary of the different processes operating in a society with highly developed slave markets. These are no less compelling in the latter than in the former. In a *résumé* of present-day research, the mechanisms of a society based on slave labour have been summarized as follows:

... slave-labour interferes with the work of production by free-labour. It interferes in three ways: it causes the withdrawal of a number of men from production to supervision and national defence; it diffuses a general sentiment against manual labour and any form of concentrated activity; and more especially it drives free labourers out of the occupations in which the slaves are engaged. Just as, by Gresham's law, bad coins drive out good, so it has been found by experience that, in any given occupation or range of occupations, slave-labour drives out free; so that it is even difficult to find recruits for the higher branches of an occupation if it is necessary for them to acquire skill by serving an apprenticeship side-by-side with slaves in the lower.

This leads to grave consequences; for the men driven out of these occupations are not themselves rich enough to live on the labour of slaves. They therefore tend to form an intermediate class of idlers who pick up a living as best they can—the class known to modern economists as "poor whites" or "white trash" and to students of Roman history as "clientes" or "faex Romuli". Such a class tends to emphasize both the social unrest and the military and aggressive character of a slave-state. . . .

A slave society is therefore a society divided sharply into three classes: masters, poor whites and slaves; and the middle class is an idle class, living on the community or on warfare, or on the upper.

But there is still another result. The general sentiment against productive work leads to a state of affairs in which the slaves tend to be the only producers and the occupations in which they engage the only industries of the country. In other words, the community will rely for its wealth upon occupations which themselves admit of no change or adaptation to circumstances, and which, unless they supply deficiencies of labour by breeding, are in perpetual need of capital. But this capital cannot be found elsewhere in the community. It must therefore be sought abroad: and a slave community will tend, either to engage in aggressive warfare, or to become indebted for capital to neighbours with a free-labour system. . . .[42]

The use of slaves tends to disincline free men from work as an unworthy occupation. Alongside the non-working upper class of slave-owners a *non-working middle class* forms. By the use of slaves society is bound to a relatively simple work structure, embodying techniques that can be operated by slaves and which for this reason is relatively inaccessible to change, improvement or adaptation to new situations. The reproduction of capital is tied to the reproduction of slaves, and thus directly or indirectly to the success of military campaigns, to the output of the slave reservoirs, and is never calculable to the same degree as in a society in which it is not whole people who are bought for their lifetime but particular work services of people who are socially more or less free.

It is only against this background that we can understand the importance for the whole development of Western society of the fact that, during the slow growth of population in the Middle

Ages, slaves were absent or played only a minor part. From the start society was therefore set on a different course than in Roman antiquity.[43] It was subjected to different regularities. The urban revolutions of the eleventh and twelfth centuries, the gradual liberation of the workers displaced from the land—the burghers—from the power of the feudal lord, is a first expression of this. From this a line of descent leads to the gradual transformation of the West into a society where more and more people earn a living through occupational work. The very small part played by slave imports and slave labour gives the workers, even as the lower class, considerable social weight. The further the interdependence of people proceeds and the more, therefore, land and its produce are drawn within the circulation of trade and money, the more dependent the non-working upper classes, warriors or nobility, become on the working lower and middle classes and the more the latter gain in social power. The rise of bourgeois classes to the upper class is an expression of this pattern. In exactly the opposite way to that in which, in the ancient slave society, urban freemen were driven away from labour, in Western society, as a result of the work of freemen, the growing interdependence of all finally drew even members of the previously non-working upper classes more and more within the division of labour. And even the technical development of the West, the evolution of money to that specific form of "capital" which is characteristic of the West, presupposes the absence of slave labour and the development of free work.

23. The above is a brief sketch of one example of the specifically Western developments that run through the Middle Ages to modern times.

Hardly less significant was the fact that settlement in the Middle Ages did not take place around a sea. The earlier waves of migrating peoples had, as already mentioned, given rise to concentrated trade networks and to the integration of large areas in Europe, only along riverbanks and above all in coastal regions of the Mediterranean. This applies to Greece and above all to Rome. The Roman dominion slowly spread out around the Mediterranean basin and finally enclosed it on all sides. "Its outermost frontiers on the Rhine, the Danube, the Euphrates, and the Sahara formed an enormous defensive circle securing the coastal perimeter. Undoubtedly the sea was for the Roman Empire the basis both of its political and its economic unity."[44]

The German tribes too first drove from all sides towards the Mediterranean, and founded their first empires throughout the areas of the Roman Empire surrounding the sea, which the Romans had called "mare nostrum".[45] The Franks did not get so far; they found all the coastal regions already occupied. They tried to break through by force. All these changes and struggles may well have begun to upset and loosen the communications encircling the Mediterranean. But of course the old importance of the Mediterranean as a means of transport and communication, as the basis and centre of all higher cultural development on European soil, was more thoroughly destroyed by the invasion of the Arabs. It was only this that finally ruptured the weakened connecting threads. The Roman sea becomes in good part an Arab one. "The bond uniting eastern and western Europe, the Byzantine Empire and the German Empires in the West, is sundered. The consequence of the Islamic invasion . . . was to place these Empires in circumstances which had never previously existed since the beginning of history."[46] To put it somewhat differently: at least in the inland parts of Europe, away from the major river valleys and the few military roads, no highly differentiated society and therefore no differentiated production system had so far developed.

It is still difficult to decide whether the Arab invasion alone created the conditions for a development concentrated inland. The filling up of the European lands by tribes during the migration of peoples may also have played its part. But at any rate this temporary constriction of the hitherto main transport arteries had a decisive effect on the direction taken by the development of western and central European society.

In the Carolingian period a powerful territory was grouped for the first time around a centre situated far inland. Society was confronted by the task of developing inland communications more fully. When, in the course of centuries, it succeeded in doing so, the heritage of antiquity was placed under new conditions in this second way. The foundation was laid for formations unknown in antiquity. It is from this aspect that certain differences between the units of integration in antiquity and those which slowly form in the West are to be understood. States, nations, or whatever we call these entities, are now to a large extent collections of people grouped around inland centres or capitals and connected by inland arteries.

If, subsequently, these Western centres not only colonized the coast or riverbanks, but also large inland regions, if indeed large stretches of the earth were occupied and settled by Western nations, the preconditions for this lay in the evolution of inland forms of communication, which were not tied to slave labour, within the mother countries themselves. The beginnings of this course of development, too, are to be found in the Middle Ages.

And if, finally, even the inland agrarian sector of society is today integrated into the complex division of labour and the extensive exchange networks as never before, the origins of this development are likewise to be sought there. No one can say today that Western society, once set on this course, necessarily had to continue on it. A whole constellation of levers that can not yet be clearly disentangled, contributed to maintaining and stabilizing it on this course. But it is important to recognize that this society entered at this very early stage on a path on which it has remained up to modern times. One can readily imagine that, viewing the development of this whole period of human society, the medieval and modern periods together, later ages will see them as a single unified epoch, a great "Middle Age". And it is scarcely less important to observe that the Middle Ages in the narrower sense of the word were not the static period, the "petrified forest", which they are often taken to be, but that they contained highly dynamic phases and sectors moving in precisely the direction in which the modern age continued, stages of expansion, of advancing division of labour, of social transformation and revolution, of the improvement of the instruments of labour. Alongside these, admittedly, were sectors and phases in which institutions and ideas became more rigid and to a degree "petrified". But even this alternation of expanding phases and sectors with others where conservation is more important than growth and development, is by no means alien to modern times, even if the pace of social development and of this alternation has increased sharply since the Middle Ages.

VII

On the Sociogenesis of Feudalism

24. Processes of social expansion have their limits. Sooner or

later they come to a halt. So, too, the movement of expansion that began about the eleventh century gradually reached a standstill. It became increasingly difficult for the western Frankish knights to open up new land by forest clearance. Land outside their frontiers was obtainable, if at all, only by heavy fighting. The colonization of the eastern Mediterranean coastal regions petered out after these first successes. But the warrior population continued to increase. The drives and affects of this ruling class were less restrained by social dependencies and civilizing processes than in subsequent upper classes. The dominance of women by men was still unimpaired. "On every page in the chronicles of this time knights, barons and great lords are mentioned who have eight, ten, twelve or even more male children."[47] The so-called "feudal system" that emerged more clearly in the twelfth century and was more or less established in the thirteenth, is nothing other than the concluding form of this movement of expansion in the agrarian sector of society. In the urban sector this movement persists somewhat longer in a different form, until it finally finds its definitive form in the closed guild system. It becomes increasingly difficult for all those warriors within society who do not already have a piece of land and possessions to obtain them, and for families with small possessions to enlarge them. Property relations are ossified. It grows more and more difficult to rise in society. And accordingly class differences between warriors are hardened. A hierarchy within the nobility corresponding to the differing magnitude of land ownership emerges more and more clearly. And the various titles that earlier had designated positions within service to the ruler, much as civil service grades do today, take on a new and increasingly fixed meaning: they are linked to the name of a particular house as an expression of the size of its estates and thus of its military power. The dukedoms are descended from the royal servants once sent to represent the king in a territory; they gradually become more or less independent liege lords over this whole territory and possessors of a more or less expensive unenfeoffed family property within it. The case is similar with counts. The viscounts are descendants of a man whom a count has placed as his delegate over a particular smaller region and who now controls this land as his hereditary possession. The "seigneurs" or "sires" are descendants of a man whom a count has earlier installed as guardian of one of his castles or man-sions, or who may have built himself a castle in the small area he had been appointed to superintend.[48] Now the castle and land around it have become the hereditary possession of his family in turn. Everyone holds on to what they have. They relinquish nothing to those above them. And there is no room for anyone from below. The land is allocated. A society expanding internally and externally, in which social betterment, the acquisition of land or more land is not too difficult for a warrior, that is, a society with relatively open positions or opportunities, has become within a few generations a society in which most positions are more or less closed.

25. Transitions from phases with large possibilities of social improvement and expansion to those offering diminished satisfaction to these needs, in which the relatively deprived are sealed off and thus more strongly united with those in the same predicament—processes of this sort recur frequently in history. We are ourselves now in the midst of such a transformation, modified by the peculiar elasticity of industrial society which is able to open up new sectors when old ones are closed, and by the different levels of development of interdependent regions. But, taken as a whole, the situation is not only that each crisis marks a shift in one direction and each boom a shift in another: the overall trend of society points increasingly clearly towards a system with closed opportunities.

Such periods can be recognized from afar by a certain despondency of mind, at least among the deprived, by a hardening of social forms, by attempts to break them from below and, as already mentioned, by the stronger cohesion of those occupying the same position in the hierarchy.

The particular pattern of this process, however, is different in a barter economy than in a money society, though no less strict. What above all seems incomprehensible to the later observer in the process of feudalization, is the fact that neither kings nor dukes nor all the ranks below them were able to prevent their servants becoming independent owners of the fief. But precisely the universality of this fact shows the strength of the social regularity at work. We have already sketched the pressures which brought about the slow decline of the royal house in a warrior society with a barter economy, once the crown no longer succeeded in expanding, that is, in conquering new lands. Analogous processes were at work, once the possibility of expansion and the external threat had diminished, throughout the warrior society. This is the typical pattern of a society built up on land ownership, in which trade does not play a major part, in which each estate is more or less autarkic, and in which military alliance for defence or attack is the primary form of integration of large regions.

In the tribal unit the warriors live relatively close together. Then they slowly spread throughout the whole country. Their number grows. But with increase and dispersal across a large region the individual loses the protection once offered by the tribe. Single families ensconced in their estates and castles and often separated by long distances, the individual warriors ruling these families and a retinue of bondsmen and serfs, are now more isolated than before. Gradually new relationships are established between the warriors, as a function of the increased numbers and distance, the greater isolation of the individual and the intrinsic tendencies of land ownership.

With the gradual dissolution of the tribal units and the merging of Germanic warriors with members of the Gallo–Romanic upper class, with the dispersion of warriors over large areas, the individual has no other way of defending himself against those socially more powerful, than by placing himself in the protection of one of them. They in their turn have no other way of protecting themselves against others with similarly large estates and military power, than with the aid of warriors to whom they give land or whose land they protect in exchange for military services.

Individual dependencies are established. One warrior enters an alliance with another under oath. The higher-ranking partner with the greater area of land—the two go hand in hand—is the "liege lord", the weaker partner the "vassal". The latter in turn can, if circumstances so require, take still weaker warriors under his protection in exchange for services. The contracting of such individual alliances is at first the only form in which people can protect themselves from one another.

The "feudal system" stands in strange contrast to the tribal constitution. With the latter's dissolution new groupings and new forms of integration are necessarily set up. There is a strong tendency towards individualization, reinforced by the mobility and expansion of society. This is an *individualization relative to the tribal unit*, and in part relative to the family unit too, just as there will later be movements of individualization relative to the feudal unit, the guild unit, the class unit, and, again and again, to the family unit. And the feudal oath is nothing other than the sealing of a protective alliance between individual warriors, the sacral confirmation of the individual relationship between the warrior giving land and protection and the other giving services. In the first stage of the movement the king stands on one side. As the conqueror he controls the whole area and performs no services; he merely allocates land. The bondsman is at the other extreme of the pyramid; he controls no land and merely performs services or—what comes to the same thing—pays dues. All the degrees between them have at first a double face. They have land and protection to distribute below them and services to perform above them. But this network of dependencies, the need of those higher up for services, particularly military, and of those lower down for land or protection, harboured tensions that led to quite specific shifts. The process of feudalization is none other than one such compulsive shift in this network of dependencies. At a particular phase everywhere in the West the dependence of those above on services is greater than that of their vassals on protection. This reinforces the centrifugal forces in this society in which each piece of land supports its owner. This is the simple structure of those processes in the course of which, throughout the whole hierarchy of warrior society, the former servants over and again become the independent owners of the land entrusted to them, and titles deriving from service become simple designations of rank according to size of property and military power.

26. These shifts and their mechanisms would not in themselves be difficult to understand if the later observer did not constantly project his own idea of "law" and "justice" upon the relations between the warriors of feudal society. So compulsive are the habits of thinking of our own society that the observer involuntarily asks why the kings, dukes and counts tolerated this usurpation of sovereignty over the land which they had originally controlled. Why did they not assert their "legal rights"?

But we are not concerned here with what are called "legal questions" in a more complex society. It is a prerequisite for understanding feudal society not to regard one's own "legal forms" as law in an absolute sense. Legal forms correspond at all times to the structure of society. The crystallization of general legal norms set down in writing, an integral part of property relations in industrial society, presupposes a very high degree of social integration and the formation of central institutions able to give one and the same law universal validity throughout the area they control and strong enough to enforce respect for written agreements. The power which backs up legal titles and property claims in modern times is no longer directly visible. In proportion to the individual it is so great, its existence and the threat emanating from it are so self-evident, that it is very seldom put to the test. This is why there is such a strong tendency to regard this law as something self-explanatory, as if it had come down from heaven, an absolute "right" that would exist even without the support of this power structure, or if the power structure were different.

The chains mediating between the legal system and the power structure have today grown longer, in keeping with the greater complexity of society. And as the legal system often *operates* independently of the power structure, though never completely so, it is easy to overlook the fact that the law is here, as in any society, a function and symbol of the social structure or—what comes to the same thing—the balance of social power.[49]

In feudal society this was less concealed. The interdependence of people and regions was less. There was no stable power structure stretching across the whole region. Property relations were regulated directly according to the degree of mutual dependence and actual social power.*

*Note on the concept of social power. The "social power" of a person or group is a complex phenomenon. As regards the individual it is never exactly identical with his individual physical strength and, as regards groups, with their sum of individual strength. But physical strength and skill can under some conditions be an important element in social power. It depends on the total structure of society and the place of the individuals in it, to what extent physical strength contributes to social power. The latter varies in its structure as much as does society itself. In industrial society, for example, extreme social power in an individual can go together with low physical strength, although there can be phases in its development when bodily strength again takes on increased importance for everyone as an ingredient of social power.

In the feudal warrior society considerable physical strength is an indispensable element in social power, but by no means its sole determinant. Simplifying somewhat, one can say that the social power potential of a man in feudal society is exactly equal to the size and productivity of the land and the labour force he controls. His physical strength is undoubtedly an important element in his ability to control it. Anyone who is unable to fight like a warrior and commit his own body to attack and defence has in the long run little chance of owning anything in this society. But anyone who once controls a large piece of land in this society

There is in industrial society a kind of relationship which can in a certain sense be compared to the relationship between the warriors or liege lords in feudal society, and through which the pattern of this relationship can be clarified. It is the relation between states. Here, too, the decisive factor is quite nakedly social power, in which military power plays a relatively major part alongside the interdependencies arising from the economic structure. This military power is in its turn, however, much as in feudal society, largely determined by the size and productivity of a territory and the number and work potential of the people it can support.

There is no law governing the relations between states of the kind that is valid within them. There is no all-embracing power apparatus that could back up such an international law. The existence of an international law without a corresponding power structure cannot conceal the fact that in the long run the relationships between nations are governed solely by their relative social power, and that any shift in the latter, any increase in the power of a country within the various figurations of states in different parts of the world and now—with growing interdependence—within world society as a whole, means an automatic reduction of the social power of other countries.

And here too the tension between the "haves" and "have-

---

possesses, as monopolist of the most important means of production, a degree of social power, that is to say a quantity of opportunities, transcending his individual personal strength. To others dependent on it he can give land, taking their services in exchange. That his social power equals the size and productivity of the land he actually controls also means that his social power is as great as his following, his army, his military power.

But equally, it is obvious from this that he is dependent on services to maintain and defend his land. This dependence on followers of varying grades is an important element in the latters' social power. When this, his dependence on services, grew, his social power was reduced; when the need and demand for land grew among the propertyless, the social power of those controlling land was increased. The social power of an individual or group can be completely expressed only in proportions. The above is a simple example.

To investigate what constitutes "social power" in more detail is a task in itself. Its importance for understanding social processes in the past and present scarcely needs stating. "Political power", too, is nothing but a certain form of social power. One can therefore understand neither the behaviour nor the destinies of people, groups, social classes or states unless one finds out their actual social power regardless of what they themselves say or believe. Political life itself would lose some of its hazardousness and mystery if the structure of social power relationships between all countries were publicly analysed. To evolve more exact methods of doing so remains one of the many sociological tasks of the future.

nots", between those who do and those who do not have enough land or means of production to meet their needs and their standards, automatically increases the more world-wide bourgeois society approaches the state of a "system with closed opportunities".

The analogy that exists between the relationships among individual lords in feudal society and among states in the industrial world, is more than fortuitous. It has its basis in the developmental curve of Western society itself. In the course of this development, with its growing interdependence, relationships of an analogous kind are established, among them legal forms, at first between relatively small territorial units and then at higher and higher levels of magnitude and integration, even if the transition to groups of a different order of size does represent a certain qualitative change.

It will be shown later what importance the process which we have begun to delineate here, i.e. the establishment of increasingly large, internally pacified but externally belligerent units of integration, had for the change of the pattern of drive control and the social standard of conduct—for the civilizing process.

The relations of these individual feudal lords to one another did indeed resemble those of present-day states. Economic interdependence, exchange, the division of labour between individual estates was, to be sure, incomparably less developed in the tenth and eleventh centuries than between modern states, and so the economic dependence between warriors was correspondingly less. All the more decisive in their relationships, therefore, was their military potential, the size of their following and the land they controlled. It can be observed over and over again that in this society no oath of allegiance or contract—as is the case between states today—could in the long run withstand changes in social power. The fealty of vassals was in the end regulated very exactly by the actual degree of dependence between the parties, by the interplay of supply and demand between those giving land and protection in exchange for services on the one hand and those needing them on the other. When expansion, when the conquest or opening up of new land grew more difficult, the greater opportunities were first of all on the side of those who rendered services and received land. This is the background of the first of the shifts which now take place in this society, the self-enfranchisement of the servants.

Land, in this society, is always the "property" of the man actually controlling it, really exercising rights of possession and strong enough to defend what he possesses. For this reason the man with land to invest in exchange for services always starts off at a disadvantage to the man who receives it. The "liege lord" has the "right" to the invested land, to be sure, but the vassal actually controls it. The only thing making the vassal dependent on the liege lord, once he has the land, is the latter's protection in the widest sense of the word. But protection is not always needed. Just as the kings of feudal society are always strong when their vassals need their protection and leadership when threatened by external foes, and above all when they have freshly conquered lands to distribute, but are weak when their vassals are not threatened and no new territory is expected, so too the liege lords of lesser magnitude are weak when those to whom they have entrusted land do not happen to need their protection.

The liege lord at any given level can compel one or other of his vassals to fulfil his obligations, and drive him by force from his land. But he cannot do this to all, or even to many. For, as there can be no thought of arming bondsmen, he needs the services of one warrior to expel another, or he needs new land to reward new services. But for his conquests he needs new services. In this way the western Frankish territory disintegrated in the tenth and eleventh centuries into a multitude of smaller and smaller dominions. Every baron, every viscount, every seigneur controlled his estate or estates from his castle or castles, like a ruler over his state. The power of the nominal liege lords, the more central authorities, is slight. The compelling mechanisms of supply and demand, which make the vassal actually controlling the land generally less dependent on the protection of his liege lord than the latter on his services, have done their work. The disintegration of property, the passing of land from the control of the king to the various gradations of the warrior society as a whole—and this and nothing else is "feudalization"—has reached its utmost limit. But the system of social tensions that is established with this mighty disintegration, contains at the same time the driving forces of a counterthrust, a new centralization.

VIII

On the Sociogenesis of *Minnesang* and Courtly Forms of Conduct

27. Two phases can be distinguished in the process of feudalization: the one of extreme disintegration just discussed, and then a phase in which this movement begins to be reversed and the first, still loose, forms of reintegration on a somewhat large scale emerge. Thus begins, if we take this state of extreme disintegration as the starting point, a long historical process in the course of which ever larger areas and numbers of people become interdependent and finally tightly organized in integrated units.

In the tenth and eleventh centuries this fragmentation continues. It seems that no one will hold on to a portion of rule big enough to enable him to exert any effective action. Fiefs, the chances of ruling, and rights are split up more and more . . . from top to bottom, throughout the whole hierarchy, all authority is heading towards disintegration.

Then, in the eleventh and especially the twelfth century, a reaction sets in. A phenomenon occurs that has been repeated in history several times in different forms. The liege lords who are better placed and have the greatest chances, sequestrate the feudal movement. They give feudal law, that has begun to become fixed, a new turn. They fix it to the disadvantage of their vassals. Their efforts are favoured by certain large historical connections . . . and this reaction serves in the first place to consolidate the situation just reached.[50]

After the gradual transition of the warrior society from a more mobile phase with relatively large opportunities for expansion and social betterment for the individual, to a phase with increasingly closed positions, in which everyone tries to retain and consolidate what he has, power once again shifts among the warriors scattered across the land and ensconced like *reguli* (like little kings) in their castles. The few richer and larger lords gain in social power relative to the many smaller ones.

The monopoly mechanism which thus slowly begins to operate will be discussed in more detail later. Here we shall refer to only one of the factors that from now on act more and more decisively in favour of the few greater warriors at the expense of the many lesser ones: the importance of slowly proceeding commercialization. The network of dependencies, the interplay of supply of and demand for land, protection and services in the less differentiated society of the tenth and even the eleventh century, is simple in its structure. Slowly in the eleventh, and more quickly in the twelfth century, the network grows complex. At the present stage of research it is difficult to determine accurately the growth of trade and money circulating at this time. This alone would provide a possibility of really measuring the changes in social power relations. Suffice it to say that the differentiation of work, and the market and money sector of society, are growing, even though the barter form of economy continues to predominate as it will for a long time; and this growth in trade and money circulation benefits the few rich lords very much more than the many small ones. These continue by and large to live on their estates as they have done up to now. They consume directly what their estates produce, and their involvement in the network of trade and exchange-relationships is minimal. The former, by contrast, not only enter the network of trade relations through the surplus produce of their estates; the growing settlements of artisans and traders, the towns, generally attach themselves to the fortresses and administrative centres of the great dominions, and however uncertain relations between the great lords and the communes within their territory may still be, however much they waver between mistrust, hostility, open struggle and peaceful agreement, in the end they too, and the duties flowing from them, strengthen the great lords as compared to the small ones. They offer them opportunities of escaping the perpetual cycle of land investiture in exchange for services, and subsequent appropriation of the land by the vassal—opportunities that counteract the centrifugal forces. At the courts of the great lords, by virtue of their direct or indirect involvement in the trade network, whether through raw materials or in coined or uncoined precious metal, a wealth accumulates that the majority of lesser lords lack. And these opportunities are supplemented by a growing demand for opportunities from below, a growing supply of services by the less favoured warriors and others driven from the land. The smaller society's possibilities of expansion become, the larger grows the reserve army from all classes, including the upper class. Very many from this class are well content if they can simply find lodging, clothing and food at the courts of the great lords through performing some function. And if ever, by the grace of a great lord, they receive a piece of land, a fief, this is a special stroke of fortune. The story of Walther von der Vogelweide, well known in Germany, is typical in this respect of the lives of many men in France as well. And, realizing the underlying social necessities, we can guess what humiliations, vain supplications and disappointments may have lain behind Walther's exclamation: "I have my fief!"

28. The courts of the greater feudal lords, the kings, dukes, counts and higher barons or, to use a more general term, the territorial lords, thus attract, by virtue of the growing opportunities in their chambers, a growing number of people. Quite analogous processes will take place again some centuries later at a higher level of integration, at the courts of the absolute princes and kings. But by that time the interweaving of social functions, the development of trade and money circulation are so great, that a regular income through taxation from the whole dominion and a standing army of peasants' and burghers' sons with noble officers financed by the absolute ruler from these taxes, can totally paralyse the centrifugal forces, the landed aristocracy's desire for independence, through the whole country. Here, in the twelfth century, integration, the network of trade and communications, is not remotely so far developed. In areas the size of a kingdom it is still quite impossible to oppose the centrifugal forces continuously. Even in territories the size of a duchy or a county it is still very difficult, usually only after hard fighting, to restrain vassals who wish to withdraw their land from the control of a liege lord. The increase in social power falls firstly to the richer feudal lords on account of the size of their family property, their unenfieffed land. In this respect the bearers of the crown are no different from the other major feudal lords. The opportunities that they all derive, through their large holding of land, from trade and finance, give them a superiority, including military superiority, over the smaller self-sufficient knights, first of all within the limits of one territory. Here, even with the poor travelling conditions of the time, access by the central authority is no longer very difficult. All this converges at this stage of development to give the rulers of medium-sized territories, smaller than kingdoms or "states" in the later sense of this word, and larger than the bulk of the knightly estates, a special social significance.

But this is by no means to say that at that stage a really stable governmental and administrative apparatus could be established even within a territory of this size. The interdependence of regions and the permeation of the country by money had not yet advanced remotely far enough to permit the highest and richest feudal lord of a region to establish a bureaucracy paid exclusively or even primarily in money, and thus a more strict centralization. A whole series of struggles was needed, struggles that were constantly rekindled, before the dukes, kings and counts could assert their social power even within their own territory. And whatever the outcome of these battles, the vassals, the smaller and medium knights, still retained the rights and functions of rule within their estates; here they continued to hold sway like little kings. But while the courts of the great feudal lords became more populated, while their chambers filled and goods began to pass in and out, the bulk of the small knights continued to lead their self-sufficient and often very restricted lives. They took from the peasants whatever was to be got out of them; they fed as best they could a few servants and their numerous sons and daughters; they feuded incessantly with each other; and the only way in which these small knights could get hold of more than the produce of their own fields was by plundering the fields of others, above all the domains of abbeys and monasteries, and then gradually, as money circulation and so the need for money grew, by pillaging towns and convoys of goods, and ransoming prisoners of war. War, rapine, armed attack and plunder constituted a regular form of income for the warriors in the barter economy, and moreover, the only one open to them. And the more wretchedly they lived, the more dependent they were on this form of income.

The slowly increasing commercialization and monetarization therefore favoured the few large landowners and feudal lords rather than the mass of the small. But the superiority of the kings, dukes or counts was not remotely as great as later, in the age of absolutism.

29. Analogous shifts, as already mentioned, have often taken place in the course of history. The increasing differentiation between the upper middle class and the petty-bourgeois classes is probably most familiar to the twentieth-century observer. Here too, after a period of free competition with relatively good possibilities of social improvement and enrichment even for

small and medium property owners, the preponderance within the bourgeoisie is gradually shifting to the disadvantage of the economically weaker and in favour of the economically stronger group. Anyone with small or medium-sized property, leaving aside a few growth areas, finds it increasingly difficult to attain major wealth. The direct or indirect dependence of the small and middle-sized on the great is growing, and while the opportunities of the former diminish, those of the latter almost automatically increase.

Something similar took place in the western Frankish knightly society of the late eleventh and twelfth centuries. The possibilities for expansion of the agrarian sector of society, predominantly a barter economy, were as good as exhausted. The division of labour, the commercial sector of society, was—despite many reverses—still spreading, in the grip of growth. The bulk of the knightly landowners profited but little from this expansion. The few great landlords had a part in it and profited. In this way a differentiation took place within feudal knightly society itself that was not without consequences for attitudes and styles of life.

Feudal society as a whole [says Luchaire in his incomparable study of society in the age of Philip Augustus][51] has, with the exception of an élite . . . scarcely altered its habits and manners since the ninth century. Almost everywhere the lord of the manor remains a brutal and rapacious cutthroat; he goes to war, fights at tournaments, spends his peacetime hunting, ruins himself with extravagance, oppresses the peasants, practises extortion on his neighbours and plunders the property of the church.

The classes influenced by the slowly increasing division of labour and monetarization are in flux; the others remain stationary and are drawn only resistingly and, as it were, passively into the current of forces of change. It is no doubt never quite correct to say that this or that class is "without history". But what can be said is this: the living conditions of the lesser landlords or knights change only very slowly. They play no direct or active part in the exchange network, the money flow, the quicker movement that passes with it through society. And when they feel the shocks and convulsions of these social movements, it is practically always in a form detrimental to

70

them. All these things are disruptions which the landlords like the peasants usually fail to understand and often detest, until they are actually driven by them more or less violently from their autarkic base into the classes with a faster current. They eat what their land, their stables and the work of their bondsmen yield. In this nothing is changed. If supplies are short or more is wanted, it is taken by force, through pillage and plunder. This is a simple, clearly visible and independent existence; here the knights, and very much later the peasants too, are and remain in a certain sense always the lords of their land. Taxes, trade, money, the rise and fall of market prices, all these are alien and often hostile phenomena from a different world.

The barter sector of society which, in the Middle Ages and for long after, comprises the great majority of people, is certainly not entirely untouched even at this early stage by the social and historical movement. But despite all the upheavals, the pace of real changes in it is, compared to that in other strata, very small. It is not "without history"; but in it, for a very large number of people in the Middle Ages and for a smaller number even in recent times, the same living conditions are constantly reproduced. Here, uninterruptedly, production and consumption are carried on predominantly in the same place within the framework of the same economic unit; the supra-local integration in other regions of society is traceable only late and indirectly. The division of labour and work techniques which, in the commercialized sector, advance more quickly, here are only slowly changed.

It is only much later, therefore, that the personalities of men are here subjected to the peculiar compulsions, the stricter controls and restraints which arise from the money network and the greater division of functions, with its increasing number of visible and invisible dependencies. Feeling and conduct undergo far more hesitantly a civilizing process.

As already stated, in the Middle Ages and long after, this agrarian barter sector of the economy with its low division of labour, its low integration beyond the local level and its high capacity to resist change, contains by far the largest portion of the population. If we are really to understand the civilizing process we must remain aware of this polyphony of history, the pace of change slow in one class, more rapid in another, and the proportion between them. The rulers of this large, ponderous, agrarian sector of the medieval world, the knights, are for the most part scarcely bound in their conduct and passions by money chains. Most of them know only one means of livelihood—thus only one direct dependence—the sword. It is at most the danger of being physically overpowered, a military threat from a visibly superior enemy, that is to say direct, physical, external compulsion, that can induce them to restraint. Otherwise their affects have rather free and unfettered play in all the terrors and joys of life. Their time—and time, like money, is a function of social interdependence—is only very slightly subject to the continuous division and regulation imposed by dependence on others. The same applies to their drives. People are wild, cruel, prone to violent outbreaks and abandoned to the joy of the moment. They can afford to be. There is little in their situation to compel them to impose restraint upon themselves. Little in their conditioning forces them to develop what might be called a strict and stable super-ego, as a function of dependence and compulsions stemming from others transformed into self-restraints.

Towards the end of the Middle Ages, to be sure, a rather larger number of knights has been drawn within the sphere of influence of the great feudal courts. The examples from the life of a knight given earlier in connection with a series of pictures (cf. vol. 1, page 205ff.) come from this circle. But the bulk of the knights still live at this stage in much the same way as they had in the ninth or tenth century. Indeed, a gradually dwindling number of lords of the manor continued to lead a similar life long after the Middle Ages. And if we can believe a poetess, George Sand—and she expressly confirms the historical authenticity of what she says—there were still a few people leading these untamed feudal lives in provincial corners of France right up to the French Revolution, by now doubly savage, fearful and cruel as a result of their outsider situation. She describes life in one of these last castles, that have by now taken on the character of robbers' caves less because they had changed than because society around them had done so, in her short story "Mauprat".

My grandfather [says the hero of the story] was from then on, with his eight sons, the last débris our province had conserved of that race of petty feudal tyrants by which France had been covered and infested for so many centuries. Civilization, which was striding rapidly towards the great revolutionary upheavals, was increasingly stamping out these exactions and this organized brigandage.\ The light of education, a kind of good taste which was the distant reflection of a gallant court, and perhaps a presentiment of a close and terrible awakening of the people, penetrated the castles and even the semi-rustic manors of the down-at-heel gentry.

We would need to quote whole sections of this description to show how modes of conduct that in the tenth, eleventh and twelfth centuries were characteristic of the major part of the upper class, are still to be found among isolated outsiders thanks to their similar conditions of life. Still present among them is the low degree of regular drive-control. Still lacking is the transformation of elementary urges into the many kinds of refined pleasure known to society around them. There is mistrust towards women, who are essentially objects of sensual satisfaction, delight in plundering and rape, desire to acknowledge no master, servility among the peasants on whom they live, and behind all this the impalpable pressures that cannot be met with weapons or physical violence: debt, the cramped, impoverished mode of life contrasting sharply with their large aspirations, and mistrust of money whether in the hands of the masters or the peasants:

> Mauprat did not ask for money. Monetary values are what the peasant of these lands obtains with greatest difficulty and parts with most reluctantly. *"Money is dear"*, is one of his proverbs, because money represents for him something other than physical work. *It is a commerce with things and people from outside, an effort of foresight or circumspection, a market, a sort of intellectual struggle*, which jolts him out of his apathetic habits, in a word of mental effort; and to him this is the most painful and disturbing thing of all.

Here we still find enclaves of a predominantly barter economy within a large fabric woven of trade relations and the division of labour. Even here, no one can quite resist being drawn into the current of circulating money. Primarily taxes, but also the need to buy certain things one cannot produce oneself, force people in this direction. But the peculiarly opaque nature of the control and foresight, the restraint of inclination beyond what is required by necessary physical work, that any involvement in money chains imposes on people, remains in these enclaves a detested and uncomprehended kind of compulsion.

This quotation refers to masters and peasants at the end of the eighteenth century. It serves to illustrate once more the slow pace of change in this sector of society, and something of the attitudes of people within it.

30. From the broad landscape of the barter economy with its innumerable castles and its many greater and smaller dominions, therefore, there slowly emerged in France during the eleventh, and more clearly during the twelfth century, two new kinds of social organ, two new forms of settlement or integration, that marked an increase in the division of labour and in the interdependence of people: the courts of the greater feudal lords, and the towns. These two institutions are very closely connected in their sociogenesis, however mistrustful and hostile their members may often have been towards one another.

This should not be misunderstood. It is not as if the undifferentiated sector of the barter economy is confronted at one stroke with more differentiated forms of settlement in which rather larger numbers of people can be supported directly or indirectly on the basis of exchange and the division of labour. Infinitely slowly new, economically autonomous stations are built into the path of goods from the natural state to consumption. And so, step by step, towns and larger feudal courts grow out of the form of economic activity that survives on the small estates. In the twelfth century and long after it neither the urban settlements nor the great feudal courts are remotely as divided from the barter economy as the cities of the nineteenth century were from the so-called open country. On the contrary, urban and rural production are still intimately connected. The few great feudal courts are, to be sure, attached to the trade network and the market through their surplus produce, through the duties flowing into them, and also through an increased demand for luxury goods; but the major part of their everyday needs is still met directly by the produce of their own domains. In this sense they too still operate a predominantly barter economy. Admittedly, the very size of their domains brings about a differentiation of operations within them. Much as in antiquity the great slave estates work in part for the market and in part for the direct needs of the ruling household and in this sense still represent a more differentiated kind of non-market economy, so

74

too do these great feudal estates. This may apply to some extent to the more simple work carried out within them, but it applies above all to the organization of the estate. The domain of the great feudal lord hardly ever forms a single, powerful complex on a self-contained piece of land. The estates have often been acquired very gradually by very different means, conquests, inheritance, gift or marriage. They are usually scattered in different regions of a territory and are therefore not as easy to supervise as a small property. A central apparatus is needed, people to superintend incoming and outgoing goods, to keep accounts, however primitive they may at first be, people who both check the income from duties and administrate the territories. "The small feudal estate was from an intellectual point of view a rudimentary organ, particularly when the master could neither write nor read."[52] The courts of the great and rich feudal lords first attract a staff of educated clerics for administrative purposes. But through the opportunities opening to them at this time the great feudal lords are, as we have mentioned, the richest and most powerful men in their region, and with the possibility grows the desire to express this position by the splendour of their courts. They are not only richer than the other knights but also, to begin with, richer than any burgher. For this reason the great feudal courts have far more cultural significance than the towns at this time. In the competition between the territorial rulers, they become the places to show off the power and wealth of their lords. The latter therefore gather scribes around them not only for administrative purposes but also to chronicle their deeds and destinies. They are bountiful towards minstrels who sing the praises of themselves and their ladies. The great courts become "potential centres of literary patronage" and "potential centres of historiography".[53] As yet there is no book market. And within the framework of secular society, for anyone who has specialized in writing and composing and has to live by it, whether or not he is a cleric, court patronage is the only means of livelihood.[54]

Here, as always in history, higher and more refined forms of poetry develop from simpler ones in conjunction with a differentiation of society, with the formation of richer and more refined social circles. The poet does not work as a wholly self-sufficient individual writing for an anonymous public of which he knows at the most a few representatives. He creates and writes for people he knows through daily contact. And the conviviality, the forms of relationship and behaviour, the atmosphere of his social circle as well as his place within it, find expression in his words.

Players travel from castle to castle. Some are singers, many are merely clowns and fools in the simplest sense of the word. And as such they are to be found too in the castles of the simpler and smaller knights. But they visit them only in passing; there is no room here, no interest and often no means to feed and pay a player for any length of time. These are only available at the few larger courts. And by "players" we must understand a whole range of functions from the simple jester and fool to the *minnesänger* and troubadour. The function is differentiated with the public. The greatest, richest—which is to say the highest-ranking—lords were able to attract the best performers to their courts. More people were gathered there; there was a possibility of more refined conviviality and entertainment, so that the tone of poetry was also refined. The idea that "the higher the lord and lady, the higher and better the bard" was frequently uttered at the time.[55] It was taken for granted. Frequently, not one but several singers lived at the great feudal courts. "The higher the personal qualities and rank of a princess, the more brilliant her court, the more poets she gathered in her service."[56] Matching the power struggle between the great feudal lords was a constant struggle for prestige. The poet, like the historian, was one of its instruments. Thus a *minnesänger*'s change of service from one lord to another could often mean a complete change in the political convictions he expressed.[57] It has been rightly said of the *minnesang*: "In meaning and purpose it was a political panegyric in the form of a personal homage."[58]

31. Retrospectively, *minnesang* can easily appear an expression of knightly society in general. This interpretation has been reinforced by the fact that, with the decline of knightly functions and the growing subservience of the noble upper class with the rise of absolutism, the image of free, unfettered knightly society took on a nostalgic aura. But it is difficult to conceive that *minnesang*, especially in its more delicate tones—and it is not always delicate—springs from the same life as the coarse and unbridled behaviour that was proper to the bulk of knights. It has already been stressed that *minnesang* was actually "very

contradictory to the knightly mentality".[59] The whole landscape, with its incipient differentiation, must be kept in view if this contradiction is to be resolved and the human attitude expressed in troubadour poetry understood.

There are three forms of knightly existence which, with many intermediate stages, begin to be distinguishable in the eleventh and twelfth centuries. There are the smaller knights, rulers over one or more not very large estates; there are the great, rich knights, the territorial rulers, few in number compared to the former, and finally the knights without land or with very little, who place themselves in the service of greater ones. It is mainly, though not exclusively, from this last group that the knightly, noble *minnesänger* come. Singing and composing in the service of a great lord and a noble lady is one of the ways open to those driven from the land, whether from the upper class or from the urban–rural lower class. Former members of both groups are to be found as troubadours at the great feudal courts. And even though a great feudal lord may occasionally involve himself in singing and composing, nevertheless troubadour poetry and service are stamped by the dependent status of their practitioners within a rich social life that was slowly taking on more definite forms. The human relationships and compulsions established here are not as strict and continuous, or as inescapable, as they later become at the larger absolutist courts which are far more thoroughly formed by money relationships. But they already act in the direction of stricter drive-control. Within the restricted court circle, and encouraged above all by the presence of the lady, more peaceful forms of conduct become obligatory. Certainly, this should not be exaggerated; pacification is not nearly so far advanced as later when the absolute monarch could even prohibit duelling. The sword still hangs loosely, and war and feud are close at hand. But the moderation of passions, sublimation, is unmistakable and inevitable in feudal court society. Both the knightly and the bourgeois singers are socially dependent; and their subordinate status forms the basis of their song, their attitudes and their affective and emotional mould.

If the court singer wished to secure respect and regard for his art and his person, he could only raise himself permanently above the travelling player by being taken into the service of a prince or princess. Minnesongs addressed to a distant mistress whom he has not yet visited, had no other purpose than to express readiness and desire to serve at the court of the addressee. That was and remains by the nature of things the real goal of all who had to gain their livelihood from their art, for men of low origin as for younger, non-inheriting sons of noble houses. . . .

In Walther von der Vogelweide's conditions of service we can, as has been clearly demonstrated by Konrad Burdach, observe a typical example of the life of a Minnesänger. King Philip had taken Walther "to himself": this was the usual expression for entry to ministerial service. It was a service without payment or security of tenure lasting from four months to a year. When this time elapsed he could seek a new master with the permission of the old. Walther received no fief from Philip, nor from Dietrich of Meissen, nor from Otto IV or Hermann of Thuringia, to whose household he once belonged. Likewise his service to Bishop Wolfgar of Ellenbrechtskirchen was brief. Then, finally, Friedrich II, a connoisseur of art and a poet himself, granted him a salary that secured him a living. A fief of land or office (only later of money) was, in the barter economy of the feudal age, the highest honour for services rendered, and the ultimate goal. Seldom was it granted to court singers either in France or Germany. They usually had to be content to serve as court poets entertaining society and receiving board and lodging in exchange, and as a special honour . . . the dress needed for court service.[60]

32. The particular structuring of affects expressed in the *minnesang* is inseparable from the social position of the *minnesänger*. The knights of the ninth and tenth centuries, and the majority of knights even later, did not behave particularly delicately towards their own wives, or with women of lower rank in general. The women in the castles were always directly exposed to the rough advances of the stronger man. They could defend themselves by ruse, but here the man ruled. And relations between the sexes were regulated, as in every warrior society with more or less pronounced male rule, by power, and often by open or veiled struggles, that each waged with his own means.

We hear from time to time of women who by temperament and inclination differed little from men. The lady of the castle is in this case a "virago" with a violent temper, lively passions, subjected from her youth to all manner of physical exercise, and taking part in all the pleasures and dangers of the knights around her.[61] But often enough we hear of the other side, of a warrior, whether a king or a simple seigneur, beating his wife. It seems almost an established habit for the knight, flying into a rage, to punch his wife on the nose till blood flows:

"The king hears this and anger rises into his face: raising his fist he strikes her on the nose so hard that he drew four drops of blood. And the lady says: 'Most humble thanks. When it shall please you, you may do it again.'"

"One could quote other scenes of the same kind", says Luchaire.[62] "Always the blow on the nose with the fist." Moreover a knight is often censured for taking advice from his wife.

"Lady, go into the shade," the knight says for example, "and eat and drink with your retinue in your painted and guilded chambers, busy yourself hanging silk: that is your job. Mine is to strike with the sword of steel."

> The conclusion might be drawn [to quote Luchaire again] that even in the epoch of Philip Augustus the courtly, courteous attitude towards women was only exceptionally found in feudal circles. In the great majority of domains the old, less respectful, brutal tendency still prevailed, transmitted and, perhaps, exaggerated in the majority of the "chansons de geste". One should not be misled by the love theories of the Provençal Troubadours and a few "Trouvères" from Flanders and the Champagne: the feelings they expressed were, we believe, those of an élite, a very small minority. . . .[63]

The differentiation between the bulk of smaller and medium knightly courts and the few large ones more closely attached to the slowly developing network of trade and money, brings with it, as can be seen, a differentiation of behaviour too. No doubt this behaviour was not in such stark contrast as it may first appear from these reconstructions. Here, too, there may have been transitional forms and mutual influences. But by and large it can be said that a more peaceable social life formed about the lady of the court only in these few large courts. Only here did the singers have a chance of finding service of any length, and only here was established that peculiar attitude of the serving man towards the lady of the court that finds its expression in *minnesang*.

The difference between the attitude and feelings expressed in *minnesang* and the more brutal ones prevalent in the *chansons de geste*, for which history provides ample documentation, derives, in other words, from two different kinds of relation between man and woman, corresponding to two different classes in feudal society. These two modes of conduct therefore arise with the shift in the centre of gravity of society already discussed. In a society of landed nobility dispersed fairly loosely across the country in their castles and estates, the likelihood of a preponderance of the man over the woman and thus of a more or less unconcealed male dominance, is very great. And wherever a warrior class or a class of landed gentry has strongly influenced the overall behaviour of society, traces of male dominance, forms of purely male social life with its specific eroticism and a certain eclipse of women, are to be found more or less clearly in its tradition.

Relationships of this kind predominated in medieval warrior society. Characteristic of them is a particular kind of mistrust between the sexes, reflecting the great difference in the form and scope of the lives they each lead, and the spiritual estrangement which arises as a result. As in later times—as long as women are excluded from professional life—the men of the Middle Ages, when women were generally excluded from the central sphere of male life, military action, spend most of their time among themselves. And their superiority is matched by a more or less explicit contempt of man for woman: "Go to your ornamented chambers, lady, our business is war." That is entirely typical. The woman belongs in her own special room. And this attitude, like the social basis which produced it, persists for a very long time. Its traces are to be found in French literature as late as the sixteenth century, for precisely as long as the upper class is primarily a military and landed aristocracy.[64] Then this attitude disappears from literature, which by now in France is almost exclusively controlled and modelled by courtly people, but certainly not from the life of the landed nobility itself.

The great absolutist courts are the places in European history in which the most complete equality between the spheres of life of men and women, and also of their behaviour, has so far been achieved. It would take us too far afield here to show why even the great feudal courts of the twelfth century, and incomparably more so the absolutist courts, offered women special opportunities to overcome male dominance and attain equal status with men. It has been pointed out, for example, that in southern France women could at an early stage become liege ladies, own property and play a political role; and it has been surmised that this fact favoured the development of *minnesang*.[65] But to qualify this it has also been emphasized that "the succession to the throne by daughters was only possible if the male relations, the liege lord and the neighbours did not prevent the lady from taking up her inheritance".[66] In fact even in the narrow stratum of great feudal lords, the superiority of man over woman resulting from his warrior function is always perceptible. Within the great feudal courts, however, the military function of the men receded to some extent. Here, for the first time in secular society, a large number of people, including men, lived together in constant close contact in a hierarchical structure, under the eyes of the central person, the territorial lord. This fact alone enforced a certain restraint on all dependents. An abundance of unwarlike administrative and clerical work had to be done. All this created a somewhat more peaceful atmosphere. As happens wherever men are forced to renounce physical violence, the social importance of women increased. Within the great feudal courts a common sphere of life and a common social life for men and women were established.

To be sure, male dominance was by no means broken as it sometimes was later in the absolutist courts. For the master of the court, his function as knight and military leader was still the primary one; his education too was that of a warrior centred upon the wielding of arms. For just this reason the women surpassed him in the sphere of peaceful society. As so often in the history of the West it was not men but women of high class who were first liberated for intellectual development, for reading. The wealth of the great courts gave the woman the possibility of filling her leisure time and pursuing such luxury interests. She could attract poets, singers and learned clerics. And so it was about women that the first circles of peaceful intellectual activity were established. "In aristocratic circles in the twelfth century the education of women was on average more refined than that of men."[67] This certainly refers only to the man of the same status, the husband. The wife's relationship to him was not yet very different from that customary in warrior society. It was more moderate and somewhat more refined than in the case of the small knights; but the compulsion the man placed on himself, as compared with that he placed on his own wife, was in general not great. Here too the man was quite unmistakably the ruler.

33. It is not this relationship of husband to wife that underlies troubadour poetry and *minnesang*, but the relationship of a socially inferior man to a high-ranking woman. And it is only in these courts rich and powerful enough to generate such relationships that *minnesang* is to be found. But compared to the knighthood as a whole they represent a narrow stratum, an "élite".

The connection between the structure of relationships in society at large and the personality structure of people emerges very clearly here. In the greater part of feudal society, where the man ruled and the dependence of women was unconcealed and almost unrestricted, nothing compels the man to constrain his drives and to impose control on them. There is little talk of "love" in this warrior society. And one has the impression that a man in love would have appeared ridiculous among these warriors. Women are generally regarded by these men as inferior beings. There are enough of them available. They serve to gratify drives in their simplest form. Women are given to man "for his necessity and delectation". So it was once expressed at a later time; but this is exactly in keeping with the behaviours of warriors earlier. What they sought of women is physical pleasure; apart from this, "there is scarcely a man with the patience to endure his wife".[68]

The pressures on the libidinal life of women are throughout Western history, with the exception of the great absolutist courts, considerably heavier than on men of equal birth. The fact that women in high positions in this warrior society, and thus with a certain degree of freedom, always found it easier to control, refine and fruitfully transform their affects than did the men of equal status, may reflect habituation and early conditioning in this direction. Even in relation to the man of outwardly equal social status, she is a dependent, socially inferior being.

Accordingly it is only the relation of a socially inferior and dependent man to a woman of higher rank that leads to the restraint, renunciation and the consequent transformation of drives. It is no accident that in this human situation what we call "lyric poetry" evolves as a social and not merely as an individual event;* and—likewise as a social event—that transformation of pleasure, that shade of feeling, that sublimation and refinement of the affects that we call "love" comes into being. Not as exceptions but in a socially institutionalized form, contacts between man and woman arise which make it impossible even for the strong man simply to take the woman when he pleases; which make the woman unattainable or attainable only with difficulty; and perhaps, because she is higher placed and difficult to attain, particularly desirable. This is the situation, this the emotional setting of *minnesang*, in which henceforth down the centuries lovers recognize something of their own feelings.

No doubt a large number of songs by troubadours and *minnesänger* are essentially expressions of feudal courtly conventions, ornaments of social life and a mere part of the social game. There may have been many troubadours whose inner relationship to their lady was not quite so consuming, and who indemnify themselves with other, more attainable women. But neither this convention nor its expression could have arisen had genuine experiences and feelings of this kind been absent. They have a core of authentic feeling and real experience. Such tones cannot be simply thought out or invented. Some loved, and some had the strength and greatness to express their love in words; it is not even difficult to say in which poems feeling and

*In the German text I am speaking here of social and individual *phenomena*. At the time of writing this book my awareness of the ambiguities inherent in the term "phenomenon", especially of its near solipsistic undertones, was not yet sufficiently sharpened to avoid its use. In the English translation, however, it seemed preferable to replace it by expressions such as "events", "data", etc. It is, of course, highly significant for the influence which phenomenalistic types of philosophy have had not only on academic but also on non-academic linguistic usages that the term "phenomenon" has become the most common unspecific expression for data or events of all sorts. One may not be aware of it that it is tainted by the solipsistic doubt as to whether such data really exist, such events really occur. One can easily overlook that the term "phenomenon" carries with it the notion that the data to which it refers may be only appearances, conjured up by the constitution of the human subject. But whether or not one is conscious of the philosophical heritage represented by this concept, its continued use reinforces again and again the apparitionist tendencies of our age. It is better to look for expressions less woolly and less affected by this philosophical tradition. I felt that I owe my readers an explanation for the innocent use of this term in the German and its omission in the English edition. [*Author's note to the translation*] experience are genuine and in which they are more or less conventional. Some must first have found words and tones for their feelings, in order that others might play with them and give rise to a convention. "The good poets, undoubtedly, mix their own truth into even these poems of infatuation. From the fullness of their lives flowed the substance of their songs."[69]

34. The literary sources and precursors of *minnesang* have often been investigated. Its relationship with religious poetry addressed to the Virgin and with the Latin lyric of the Wandering Scholars has, probably correctly, been pointed out.[70]

But the emergence and essence of *minnesang* cannot be understood only in terms of literary antecedents. These earlier forms contained many different possibilities of development. Why did the manner in which people sought to express themselves change? To put the question quite simply: why did not these two forms of religious and secular lyric remain society's predominant forms of expression? Why were formal and emotional elements taken from them and fashioned into something new? Why did this new genre take on just that form which we know as *minnesang*? History has its continuity: wittingly or not, those coming later start with what already exists and develop it further. But what are the dynamics of this movement, the shaping forces of historical change? That is the question here. The investigation of sources and antecedents is doubtless of importance for understanding *minnesang*, but without sociogenetic and psychogenetic study its origins, its feudal connections, remain obscure. *Minnesang* as a supra-individual event, as a social function in relation to feudal society as a whole, cannot be understood, any more than its specific form and typical content, unless one is aware of the actual situation and relationship of the people who express themselves in it, and the genesis of this situation. This special question demands more space than is available here, where the main interest concerns movements and connections on a larger scale. If a more precise line of enquiry for analysing a specific institution such as *minnesang* within this context has now been indicated, and some of the main outlines of its socio- and psychogenetic conditions sketched, that is all that is necessary for the purposes of this study.

35. Great historical changes have a strict regularity of their own. It often appears from present-day studies as if particular social formations whose history constitutes history as such, fol-

low each other at random like the cloud-shapes in the mind of Peer Gynt; now they look like a horse, now like a bear, now society looks Romanic or Gothic, and now Baroque.

What has been shown here are a few basic interdependent trends that led to the shaping of society in the form of the "feudal system", and finally to the kind of relationship expressed in *minnesang*. One of these trends is the more rapid growth of population after the migration of peoples, closely connected with the consolidation of property relationships, the formation of a human surplus, among the nobility as in the class of bondsmen or serfs, and the pressure on these displaced persons from both groups to find new services.

Connected with this too is the slow insertion of discrete stations in the passage of goods from production to consumption, the growth of demand for unified, mobile means of exchange, the shift of the centre of gravity within feudal society in favour of the few great lords at the expense of the many small, the formation of large feudal courts at the centre of regions the size of a territory, where knightly-feudal traits combine with courtly ones in a peculiar unity, as barter and money relations do in this society as a whole.

Again, there is the great feudal lords' need of prestige and display in the more or less violent struggles between them; to their desire to distinguish themselves from lesser knights. And as an expression of all this, poets and singers who praise the lords and ladies, putting into words the interests and political opinions of the lord and the taste and beauty of the lady, become a more or less firmly established social institution.

Likewise one can observe, only in this small upper stratum of knightly society, a first form of emancipation, of greater freedom of movement, for women—very slight, to be sure, when compared to the freedom of women at the great absolutist courts—more continuous contacts between the lady of the court, the woman of high rank, and the troubadour, the man of lower rank and dependent, whether or not he be a knight; the impossibility or difficulty of attaining the desired woman, the selfrestraint imposed on the dependent man, the need for circumspection and a certain, still very muted, regulation and transformation of his elementary drives and needs; and finally the expression of such scarcely realizable wishes in the language of dreams, in poetry.

The beauty of one poem and the empty conventionality of another, the greatness of this *minnesänger* and the triviality of that, are facts in their own right. *Minnesang* as a social institution, however, the framework in which the individual develops—and this alone concerns us here—evolves directly from this interplay of social processes.

36. In this very situation, that is, at the great feudal courts, there emerge at the same time a more rigid convention in behaviour, a certain moderation of the affects, and a regulation of manners. It is that standard of manners, that convention of behaviour, that polishing of conduct to which this society itself gave the name of *courtoisie*, and we get a fully rounded picture of it only if we incorporate what was said in Volume One about *courtois* conduct into the account of feudal courts given in the present one.

Precepts of *courtois* society were given earlier, at the beginnings of various series of examples illustrating the civilization of conduct and sentiment. The sociogenesis of the great feudal courts is at the same time the sociogenesis of *courtois* conduct. *Courtoisie*, too, is a form of conduct that doubtless first developed among the more socially dependent members of this knightly-courtly upper class.[71] However that may be, one thing re-emerges here very clearly: this *courtois* standard of conduct is in no sense a beginning. It is not an example of how people behave when their affects have free, "natural" play unfettered by society, that is to say, by the relations between people. Such a condition of totally uncontrolled drives, of an absolute "beginning" simply does not exist. The relatively great licence for acting out instinctual and affective impulses characteristic of men in the *courtois* upper classes—great in comparison with the later secular upper classes in the West—corresponds exactly to the form of integration, the degree and kind of mutual dependence in which people live together here. The division of labour is less developed than in the phases when the stricter absolutist system of rule was developed; the trade network is smaller and so the number of people who can be sustained in one place is less. And whatever the form of individual dependencies may be, the social web of dependencies that intersect within the individual is here much coarser and less extensive than in societies with greater division of labour, where more people live continuously in close proximity in a more exactly ordered system. And, consequently, the control and restraint on the individual's drives and affects is here less strict, continuous and uniform. Nevertheless, it is already considerably greater at the larger feudal courts than at the small or in the warrior society at large, where the interdependence of people is much less extensive and complex, the network of individuals much more loosely woven, and where the strongest functional dependence between people is still that of war and violence. Compared to the behaviour and affective life to be found here, *courtoisie* already represents a refinement, a mark of distinction. And the polemics contained in fairly unchanging form in the many medieval precepts on manners—avoid this and refrain from that—refer more or less directly to the behaviour practised by the bulk of the knights, which changed as slowly and slightly between the ninth or tenth centuries and the sixteenth as did their conditions of life.

37. At the present stage of development we still lack linguistic instruments which do justice to the nature and direction of all these intertwining processes. It is an imprecise and provisional aid to understanding to say that the restraints imposed upon men and their drives became "greater", integration "closer", or interdependence "stronger", just as it does not quite do justice to socio-historical reality to say that one thing belongs to a "barter economy" and another to a "money economy", or, to repeat the form of expression chosen here, that "the money-sector of the economy grew". By how much did it "grow", degree by degree? In what way did the restraints become "greater", integration "closer", interdependence "more pronounced"? Our concepts are too coarse; they adhere too much to the image of material substances. In all this we are not concerned merely with gradations, with "more" or "less". Each "increase" in restraints and interdependencies is an expression of the fact that the ties between people, the way they depend on one another, are changing, and changing qualitatively. This is what is meant by differences in social structure. And with the dynamic network of dependencies into which a human life is woven, the drives and behaviour of people take on a *different* form. This is what is meant by differences in personality structure and in social standards of conduct. The fact that such qualitative changes are sometimes, despite all the fluctuations within the movement, changes in one and the same direction over long periods, that is, continuous, directed processes rather than a random sequence, permits and indeed causes us to speak in comparative terms when discussing different phases. That is not

to say that the direction in which these processes move is towards improvement, "progress", or towards the opposite, "retrogression". But nor is it to say that they involve merely quantitative changes. Here, as so often in history, we are concerned with structural changes that are most easily, visibly, but perhaps most superficially grasped in their quantitative aspect.

We see the following movement: first one castle stands against another, then territory against territory, then state against state, and appearing on the historical horizon today are the first signs of struggles for an integration of regions and masses of people on a still larger scale. We may surmise that with continuing integration even larger units will gradually be assembled under a stable government and internally pacified, and that they in their turn will turn their weapons outwards against human aggregates of the same size until, with a further integration, a still greater reduction of distances, they too gradually grow together and world society is pacified. This may take centuries or millennia; however that may be, the growth of units of integration and rule is always at the same time an expression of structural changes in society, that is to say, in human relationships. Whenever the centre of gravity of society moves towards units of integration of a new order of magnitude—and in the shift that first favoured large feudal lords at the expense of small and middle-sized ones, then kings against the great feudal or territorial lords, a displacement in this direction is expressed—whenever such changes occur they do so in conjunction with social functions that have grown more differentiated, and with chains of organized social action, whether military or economic, that have lengthened. Each time, the network of dependencies intersecting in the individual has grown larger and changed in structure; and each time, in exact correspondence to this structure, the moulding of behaviour and of the whole emotional life, the personality structure, is also changed. The "civilizing" process, seen from the aspects of standards of conduct and drive control, is the same trend which, when seen from the point of view of human relationships, appears as the process of advancing integration, increased differentiation of social functions and interdependence, and the formation of ever-larger units of integration on whose fortunes and movements the individual depends, whether he knows it or not.

It was attempted here to complement the general account of

the earliest and least complicated phase of this movement with some illustrative factual evidence; next the further progress of this movement and the mechanisms driving it will be examined. It has been shown how and why, in the early phase of Western history which had a predominantly barter economy, integration and the establishment of stable governments over large empires had little chance. Conquering kings can, it is true, subjugate huge areas through battle and hold them together for a time by respect for their sword. But the structure of society does not yet permit the creation of an apparatus for ruling sufficiently stable to administrate and hold together the empire by relatively peaceful means over long periods of peacetime. It remains to be shown what social processes make possible the formation of such a more stable government and with it a quite different bonding of individuals.

In the ninth and tenth centuries when, at least in the western Frankish regions, the external threat was small—and when economic integration was slight—the disintegration of the ruler-function reaches extraordinary heights. Each small estate is under its own rule, a "state" in itself, every small knight its independent lord and master. The social landscape comprises a chaotic multitude of governmental and economic units. Each of them is essentially autarkic with little dependence on others, with the exception of a few enclaves—foreign traders, for example, or monasteries and abbeys—which sometimes have links beyond the local level. In the secular ruling stratum integration through aggressive or defensive conflict is the fundamental form. There is not much to constrain members of this ruling stratum to control their affects in any continuous way. This is a "society" in the broader sense of the word which refers to every possible form of human integration. It is not yet a "society" in the narrower sense of a more continuous, relatively close and uniform integration of people with a greater constraint on violence, at least within its confines. The early form of such a "society" in the narrower sense slowly emerges at the great feudal courts. Here, where there is a larger confluence of goods, owing to the amounts produced and the attachment of these courts to the trade network, and where more people congregate in search of service, a sizeable number of people is obliged to maintain a constantly peaceful intercourse. This demands, particularly towards women of higher rank, a certain control and restraint of behaviour, a more precise moulding of affects and manners.

38. This restraint may not always have been as great as it was in the relation of singer to lady in the *minnesang* convention. The *courtois* precepts on manners give a more accurate picture of the standard of behaviour demanded in everyday life. They also occasionally throw light on the conduct of knights towards women that is not confined to the relation of the minstrel to the lady of the court.

We read in a "motto for men",[72] for example: "Above all, take care to behave well towards women. . . . If a lady asks you to sit beside her, do not sit on her dress, or too near her, and if you wish to speak softly to her, never clutch her with your arms, whatever you have to say."

Judging by the habitual standards of the lesser knights, this amount of consideration for women may have demanded considerable effort. But the restraint is slight, like that in other *courtois* precepts, in comparison to what became customary among courtiers at the court of Louis XIV, for example. This gives an idea of the different levels of interdependence and integration that shape the individual's habits in the two phases. But it also shows that *courtoisie* was indeed a step on the path that leads finally to our own affective and emotional mould, a step in the direction of "civilization".

On the one hand, a loosely integrated secular upper class of warriors, with its symbol, the castle on the autarkic estate; on the other, the more tightly integrated secular upper class of courtiers assembled at the absolutist court, the central organ of the kingdom: these are in a sense the two poles of the field of observation which has been isolated from the far longer and broader movement in order to gain initial access to the sociogenesis of civilizing change. The slow emergence from the castle landscape of the greater feudal courts, the centres of courtoisie, has been shown from a number of aspects. It remains to demonstrate the basic dynamics of the processes by which *one* of the great feudal or territorial lords, the king, gained preponderance over the others, and the opportunity to control a more stable government over a region embracing many territories, a "state". This is also the path that leads from the standard of conduct of *courtoisie* to that of *civilité*.

Chapter Two

On the Sociogenesis
of the State

I

The First Stage of the Rising Monarchy: Competition and Monopolization within a Territorial Framework

1. The crown signifies very different things in different phases of social development, even though all its wearers have in common certain actual or nominal central functions, above all that of military leader against external enemies.

At the beginning of the twelfth century the former western Frankish empire, hardly threatened any more by strong external foes, has finally decayed into a collection of discrete dominions:

The bond that formerly united the "provinces" and the feudal dynasties with the monarchy, is as good as completely ruptured. The last traces of real dominance that permitted Hugh Capet and his son, if not to act in the large regions controlled by his vassals, then at least to appear in them, have disappeared. The feudal groups of the first rank . . . conduct themselves like independent states impervious to the king's influence and more so to his actions. The relations between the great feudal lords and the monarchs are reduced to a minimum. This change is reflected even in the official titles.

The feudal princes of the twelfth century cease calling themselves "comtes du Roi" or "comtes du royaume".[73]

In this situation the "king" does what other great feudal lords do: he concentrates on consolidating his own possessions, increasing his power in the only region still open to him, the duchy of Francia.

Louis VI, king from 1108 to 1137, was preoccupied throughout his life with two tasks: to increase his own direct land ownership within the duchy of Francia—the estates and castles not yet, or only partly, enfeoffed, i.e., his own family property—and, within the same area, to subdue all possible rivals, every warrior who might equal him in power. One task assists the other: from the feudal lords he has subdued or conquered he takes all or part of their property without enfeoffing it to anyone else; thus by small steps he increases his family possessions, the economic and military basis of his power.

2. In this the monarch is, to begin with, no different from a great feudal lord. The means of power at his disposal are so small that medium and even lesser feudal lords—in alliance—can successfully oppose him. Not only has the preponderance of the royal house in the whole kingdom vanished with the decline of his function as the common army leader, and with advancing feudalization; even his monopoly power within his own hereditary territory has become extremely precarious. It is disputed by rival lords or warrior families. In the person of Louis VI, the Capetian house struggles against the houses of Montmorency, Beaumont, Rochefort, Montlhéry, Ferté-Alais, Puiset and many others,[74] just as centuries later the Hohenzollerns in the person of the Great Elector have to contend with the Quitzows and the Rochows. Only the Capetians had much less chance of success. The difference between the military and financial means of the Capetians and their opponents was smaller, given the less developed state of money, taxation and military technique. The Great Elector had already a kind of monopoly control of power within his territory. Louis VI was, leaving aside his support from the ecclesiastical institutions, essentially a great landowner who had to contend with lords with somewhat smaller possessions and military power; and only the victor of these battles could attain a kind of monopoly position within the territory, beyond the competition of other houses.

Only from reading contemporary reports can we judge by how little the military and economic means of the Capetians in this period surpassed those of other feudal houses in the duchy of Francia; and how difficult, given the low degree of economic integration, undeveloped transportation and communications, and the limitations of feudal military organization, was the "sovereign's" struggle for monopoly power even within this small area.

For example, there is the fortress of the Montlhéry family commanding the route between the two most important parts of the Capetian domain, the areas around Paris and Orléans. In 1015 the Capetian king Robert had given this land to one of his servants or officials, the "grand forestier", with permission to build a castle on it. From this castle the "grand forestier's" grandson already controlled the surrounding area as an independent lord. This is a typical example of the centrifugal movements that are taking place everywhere in this period.[75] After laborious struggles Louis VI's father finally manages to reach a kind of understanding with the Montlhérys; he marries a bastard son about ten years old to the Montlhéry heiress and thus brings the castle under the control of his house. Shortly before his death he says to his eldest son, Louis VI:

> Guard well that tower of Montlhéry, which by causing me so many torments has aged me before my time, and on account of which I have never enjoyed lasting peace or true repose ... it was a centre for perfidious people from far and near and disorder came only through it or with its help ... for ... Montlhéry being situated between Corbeil on one hand and Châteaufort on the other, each time a conflict arose Paris was cut off, and communication between Paris and Orléans was impossible except by armed force.[76]

Problems of communications of the kind which play no small role between states today, were at that earlier stage of social development no less troublesome on a different scale: in the relations between one feudal lord—whether he wore a crown or not—and others, and in regard to the comparatively microscopic distance between Paris and Orléans: Montlhéry is twenty-four kilometres from Paris.

A good part of Louis VI's reign was taken up by fighting for this fortress, until he finally succeeded in adding Montlhéry to

93

the Capetian possessions. As in all such cases, this meant a military strengthening and economic enrichment of the victorious house. The Montlhéry estate brought in an income of two hundred pounds—a handsome sum for those times—and belonging to it were thirteen direct fiefs and twenty indirect ones depending on these,[77] whose tenants now swelled the military power of the Capetians.

No less protracted and difficult were the other battles Louis VI had to fight. He needed three expeditions in 1111, 1112 and 1118, to break the power of a single knightly family in the Orléans district;[78] and it cost him twenty years to deal with the houses of Rochefort, Ferté-Alais and Puiset, and add their possessions to those of his family. By this time, however, the Capetian domain was so large and well-consolidated that, thanks to the economic and military advantages conferred by such large property, its owners had outstripped all other rivals in Francia, where they now took up a kind of monopoly position.

Four or five centuries later, the monarch has emerged as the monopoly controller of enormous military and financial means flowing from the whole area of the kingdom. Campaigns such as that of Louis VI against other feudal lords within the framework of one territory represent the first step on the way to this later monopoly position of the monarchy. At first the house of the nominal kings is scarcely superior to the feudal houses around it in terms of land ownership and military and economic power. The difference in property among warriors is relatively slight, as therefore is the social difference, no matter with what titles they adorn themselves. Then, through marriage, purchase or conquests, one of these houses accumulates more and more land and thus gains preponderance over its neighbours. The fact that it is the old royal house that succeeds in doing so in Francia may be bound up—apart from the never inconsiderable possessions that made its new start possible—with the personal qualities of its representatives, the support of the church, and a certain traditional prestige. But the same differentiation of property among warriors is taking place at the same time, as has been mentioned, in other territories too. It is the same shift in the centre of gravity of warrior society, favouring the few large knightly families at the expense of the many small and medium ones, that was discussed earlier. In each territory sooner or later one family succeeds, by accumulating land, in attaining a kind of hegemony. That the crown, that Louis the Fat should undertake the same thing looks like an abrogation of the royal function. But given this distribution of social power he has no choice. In this social structure, family property and control of the narrower hereditary area constitutes the most important military and financial basis of even the king's power. By concentrating his forces on the small area of Francia, by creating a hegemony in the restricted space of a territory, Louis VI lays the foundation for the subsequent expansion of his house. He creates a potential centre for the crystallization of the greater area of France, even though we may certainly not assume that he had any prophetic vision of this future. He acts under the direct compulsions of his actual situation. He *must* win Montlhéry if he is not to forfeit communication between parts of his own territory. He *must* subdue the most powerful family in the Orléans region if his power there is not to dwindle. Had the Capetians not succeeded in gaining preponderance in Francia, it would sooner or later—like the other provinces of France—have fallen to another house.

The mechanism leading to hegemony is always the same. In a similar way—through the accumulation of property—a small number of economic enterprises in more recent times slowly outstrip their rivals and compete with each other, until finally one or two of them control and dominate a particular branch of the economy as a monopoly. In a similar way—by accumulating land and thus enlarging their military and financial potential—states in recent times struggle for preponderance in a particular part of the world. But whereas in modern society, with its higher division of functions, this process takes place in a relatively complex way, with a differentiation of the economic and the military and political aspects of hegemony, in the society of Louis VI, with its predominantly barter economy, these aspects remained undivided. The house that rules a territory politically is at the same time by far the richest house in this territory, with the largest area of land; and its political power diminishes if its military power, stemming from the size of its domanial revenues and the number of its bondsmen and retainers, does not exceed that of all the other warrior families within its territory.

Once the preponderance of one house is fairly secure in this small region, the struggle for hegemony in a larger area moves into the foreground—the struggle between the few larger territorial lords for predominance within the kingdom. This is the task confronting the descendants of Louis VI, the next generations of Capetians.

II

Excursus on some Differences in the Paths of Development of England, France and Germany

1. The task implied in the struggle for dominance, i.e. for both centralization and rule, was for a very simple reason different in England and France from that in the German–Roman Empire. The latter formation was very different in size to the other two; geographical and social divergences within it were also much greater. This gave the local, centrifugal forces much greater energy, and made the task of attaining hegemony and thus centralization incomparably more difficult. The ruling house would have needed a far greater territorial area and power than in France or England to master the centrifugal forces of the German–Roman Empire and forge it into a durable whole. There is good reason to suppose that, given the level of division of labour and integration, and the military, transportational and administrative techniques of the time, the task of holding centrifugal tendencies in so vast an area permanently in check was probably insoluble.

2. The scale on which social processes take place is a not unimportant element of their structure. In enquiring why the centralization and integration of France and England was achieved so much earlier and more completely than in the German regions, we should not neglect this point. In this respect the trends of development in the three regions vary very widely.

When the crown of the western Frankish region falls to the Capetians, the area in which the house has real power extends from Paris to Senlis in the north and to Orléans in the south. Twenty-five years previously Otto I had been crowned Roman emperor in Rome. Resistance by other German chieftains he had ruthlessly put down, primarily supported, at first, by the experienced warriors of his own tribal area. At that time Otto's empire stretched roughly from Antwerp and Cambrai in the west, at least (i.e. without the margraviates east of the Elbe) as far as the Elbe, and beyond Brünn and Olmütz to the south-east; it stretched to Schleswig in the north and to Verona and Istria in the south; in addition it included a good part of Italy and for a time Burgundy. What we have here, therefore, is a formation on an entirely different scale, and consequently one fraught by far greater tensions and conflicts of interest, than the western Frankish area, even if we include in the latter the Norman–English colony acquired later. The task confronting the dukes of Francia and Normandy or of the Angevin territory as kings in the struggle for hegemony in this region, was entirely different to that with which every ruler of the German–Roman Empire had to contend. In the former area centralization or integration, despite numerous swerves to one side or the other, proceeded on the whole fairly continuously. In the latter incomparably larger area, one family of territorial rulers after another tried in vain to attain, with the imperial crown, a really stable hegemony over the whole empire. One house after another used up in this fruitless struggle what despite all else continued to be the central source of its income and power—their hereditary or domanial possessions. And after each unsuccessful bid by a new house, decentralization and the consolidation of centrifugal tendencies went a step further.

Shortly before the French monarchy gradually began to regain its strength in the person of Louis VI, the German–Roman Emperor Henry IV collapsed under the combined assaults of the great German territorial lords, the Church, the upper Italian cities and his elder son, that is to say, in face of the most diverse centrifugal forces. This provides a point of comparison with the early period of the French monarchy. Later, when the French King Francis I has his whole kingdom so completely in hand that he no longer needs to call assemblies of the estates and can raise taxes without asking the taxpayers, the Emperor Charles V and his administration have to negotiate even within his own hereditary lands with a whole multitude of local assemblies, before he can muster the duties needed to pay for the court, the army and the administration of the empire. And all this, including income from the overseas colonies, is not nearly enough to meet the cost of running the empire. When Charles V abdicates, the imperial administration is on the verge of bankruptcy. He too has exhausted and ruined himself in trying to rule such an enormous empire torn by such massive centrifugal forces. And it is an indication of the transformation of society in general, and of the royal function in particular, that the Habsburgs are nevertheless able to maintain themselves in power.

3. The mechanism of state-formation—in the modern sense of the word state—has been shown to be, in the European area at the time when society was moving from a barter economy to a money economy, in its main outlines always the same. It will be illustrated in more detail in relation to France. We always find, at least in the history of the great European states, an early phase in which units of the size of a territory play the decisive role within the area later to become a state. These are small, loosely structured dominions such as have arisen in many parts of the world where division of labour and integration are slight, their size corresponding to the limits placed on the organization of rule by the prevalence of barter relationships in the economy. One example is the feudal territorial dominions within the German–Roman Empire which, with the advance of the money economy, are consolidated to form small kingdoms, duchies or counties; another are areas like the principality of Wales or the kingdom of Scotland, now merged with England in the United Kingdom of Great Britain and Northern Ireland; and a further example is the duchy of Francia, whose development into a more tightly knit feudal dominion has just been discussed.

In its schematic outline, the process taking place *between* the different neighbouring territorial dominions takes a very similar course to the one previously followed *within* a firmly established territory between the individual lords or knights, until one of them attained predominance and a rather more solid territorial dominion was formed. Just as, in one phase, a number of estates placed in competition experience the need to expand if they are not to be subjugated by expanding neighbours, so in the next a group of units one degree larger, duchies or counties, find themselves in the same predicament.

It has already been shown in some detail how, in this society, the internal competition for land is intensified with the growth of population, the consolidation of land-ownership and difficulties of external expansion. It was shown how this drive for land was exerted in the poor knights as a simple desire for a mode of living appropriate to their status, and in the highest and richest as a spur to demand "more" land. For in a society with such competitive pressures, he who does not gain "more" automatically becomes "less". Here again we see the effect of the pressure running through this society from top to bottom: it sets the territorial rulers against one another; and thereby sets the monopoly mechanism in motion. At first the divergences of power are contained, even in this phase, within a framework that allows a considerable number of feudal territorial dominions to remain in contention. Then, after many victories and defeats, some grow stronger through accumulating the means of power, while others are forced out of the struggle. The victorious few fight on and the process of elimination is repeated until finally the decision lies between only two territorial dominions swollen through the defeat and assimilation of others. All the rest—whether they were involved in the struggle or remained neutral—have been reduced by the growth of these two to figures of second or third rank, though they still retain a certain social importance. The other two, however, are approaching a monopoly position; they have outstripped the others; between them lies the issue.

In these "elimination contests", this process of social selection, the personal qualities of individuals and other "accidental" factors such as the late death of one man or a ruling house's lack of male heirs, undoubtedly play a crucial part from time to time in deciding *which* territory triumphs, rises and grows.

The social process itself, however, the fact *that* a society with numerous power and property units of relatively equal size, tends under strong competitive pressures towards an enlargement of a few units and finally towards monopoly, is largely independent of such accidents. They can have an accelerating or retarding effect on the process. But no matter who the monopolist is, that a monopoly will sooner or later be formed has a high degree of probability, at least in the social structures that have existed so far. In the language of exact science this observation would perhaps be called a "law". Strictly speaking, what we have is a relatively precise formulation of a quite simple social mechanism which, once set in motion, proceeds like clockwork. A human figuration in which a relatively large number of units, by virtue of the power at their disposal, are in competition, tends to deviate from this state of equilibrium (many balanced by many; relatively free competition) and to approach a different state in which fewer and fewer units are able to compete; in other words it approaches a situation in which *one* social unit attains through accumulation a monopoly of the contended power chances.

4. The general character of the monopoly mechanism will be discussed in more detail later. It seems necessary to point out at this stage, however, that a mechanism of this kind is at work in the formation of states too, just as it was earlier involved in the formation of the smaller units, the territories, or will be later in the formation of yet larger ones. Only if we have this mechanism in mind can we understand which factors in the history of different countries modify or even impede it. Only in this way can we see with some clarity why the task facing a potential central ruler of the Germano–Roman Empire was incomparably more difficult than that which faced a potential ruler of the western Frankish region. In this empire too, through elimination struggles and the constant accumulation of territory in the hands of the victors, a territorial dominion would have had to emerge strong enough to absorb or eliminate all others. Only in this way could this disparate empire have been centralized. And there was no lack of struggles tending in this direction, not only those between the Welfs and the Hohenstaufens but also between Emperor and Pope, with their special complications. But they all missed their mark. In an area as large and varied as this, the probability of a clearly dominant power emerging was very much less than in smaller areas, especially as at this stage economic integration was lower and effective distances were many times greater than later. In any case, elimination struggles within so large an area would need far longer than in the smaller neighbouring ones.

How, nevertheless, states finally managed to be formed in the Germano–Roman Empire is well known. Among the German territorial dominions—to disregard the analogous process in Italy—a house emerged which, above all through expansion into the German or semi-German colonial region, slowly came into competition with the older Habsburgs: the Hohenzollerns. A struggle for supremacy ensued, leading to victory for the Hohenzollerns, to the formation of an unambiguous supremacy among German territorial rulers and eventually, step by step, to the unification of the German territories under a single apparatus for ruling. But this struggle for supremacy between the two most powerful components of the empire, while leading to greater integration, to the formation of states within them, meant a further step towards the disintegration of the old empire. With their defeat the Habsburg lands left the union. This was in fact one of the last stages of the slow and continuous decay of the empire. In the course of centuries more and more parts have crumbled away to become independent dominions. As a whole, the empire was too large and diverse to be other than a hindrance to state-formation.

To reflect on why state-formation in the Germano–Roman Empire was so much more laborious and belated than in its western neighbours certainly helps understanding of the twentieth century. Modern experience of the difference between the longer-established, better balanced and more fully expanded western states, and the recently established states descended from the old empire, states which expanded comparatively late, gives this question topical importance. From a structural point of view it does not seem difficult to answer, at any rate not more so than the complementary question which is scarcely less important for an understanding of historical structures—the question why this colossus, despite its unfavourable structure and unavoidable strength of centrifugal forces within it, held together so long, why the Empire did not founder earlier.

5. As a totality, it did indeed collapse late; but for centuries border areas of the empire—particularly to the west and south—had been crumbling away and going their own way, while incessant colonization and expansion of German settlements in the east to some extent compensated the losses in the west, though only to some extent. Up to the late Middle Ages, and to an extent even later, the empire spread to the west as far as the Maas and the Rhône. If we disregard the irregularities and consider only the general trend of this movement, we have the impression of the empire's constant attrition and diminution, accompanied by a slow shift in the direction of expansion, and a drift of the centre of gravity from west to east. The task remains to demonstrate this trend more exactly than is possible here. But purely in terms of area, the trend is still visible in the most recent changes in German territory proper:

The German Confederation before 1866   630,098 sq. km.
Germany after 1870   540,484 sq. km.
Germany after 1918   471,000 sq. km.

In England, and in France too, the trend is almost the reverse. The traditional institutions first develop in relatively small and restricted areas and then extend their scope. The fate of the central institution, the structure and development of the whole government apparatus in these countries, cannot be understood or the difference between them and the corresponding formations in the states descended from the old empire explained, unless this simple factor, this slow growth from small to larger, is taken into account.

Compared to the Germano–Roman Empire, the island territory that the Norman Duke William conquered in 1066 was quite small. It reminds us roughly of Prussia under the first kings. It comprises, apart from small areas on the northern border with Scotland, present-day England, an area of about 131,764 square kilometres. Wales is only completely united with England at the end of the thirteenth century (England with Wales 151,130 sq. km.). Union with Scotland has existed only since 1603. Such figures are visible but very crude indications of structural differences. They remind us that the formation of the English nation, and then the British, took place within a framework which, compared to that of the great Continental nations, scarcely extended, in its decisive phase, beyond that of a territorial dominion. What William the Conqueror and his immediate successors built up was in fact nothing other than a large territory of the western Frankish empire, and not very different from those which existed at the same time in Francia, Aquitaine or Anjou. The task with which the struggle for supremacy confronted the territorial rulers of this area—through the sheer necessity of expanding to avoid domination by others—this task could not in any way be compared with that facing a potential central ruler of the Continental empire. This is true even of the first phase in which the island territory formed a kind of western Frankish colony, when its Norman or Angevin rulers also controlled considerable territories on the Continent and when they were therefore still struggling for supremacy in the western Frankish area. But it is true above all of the phase when they were thrown back on the island from the Continent, and had to unite it under one government on the basis of England alone. And if the royal function, like the relation of king to estates, took a different form here than in the Continental empire, one of the factors at work, though certainly not the only one, was the relative smallness and also, of course, the isolated position of the area to be united. The likelihood of major regional differentiation was very much less, and the struggle for supremacy between two rivals simpler than between the many factions in the empire. The English parliament, as far as its manner of formation and therefore its structure is concerned, is in no way comparable to the German Imperial Diet, but rather with the regional estates. Much the same is true of all the other institutions. They grow, like England itself, from smaller to larger; the institutions of a feudal territory evolve continuously into those of a state and an empire.

In the British Empire too, however, centrifugal forces immediately begin to act again as soon as territory has been united beyond a certain point. Even with present-day integration and communications this empire is proving dangerously large. Only very experienced and flexible government holds it together with great difficulty. Despite very different preconditions from those of the old German Empire, it still illustrates how a very large empire, brought together by conquest and colonization, finally tends to disintegrate into a number of more or less independent units, or at least to be transformed into a kind of "federal state". Seen thus at close quarters, the mechanism seems almost self-evident.

6. The native region of the Capetians, the duchy of Francia, was smaller than the English territory controlled by the Norman dukes. It was roughly the same size as the Electorate of Brandenburg at the time of the Hohenstaufens. But there, within the framework of the empire, it took five or six centuries for the small colonial area to become a power capable of confronting the old-established territories of the empire. Within the more limited framework of the western Frankish area, the power of such a territory, together with the material and spiritual help given by the Church to the Capetians, was enough to enable the house to begin the struggle for supremacy over larger areas of France at a very early stage.

The area left behind by the western Frankish empire, the basis of the later France, occupied a roughly midway position, as far as its size was concerned, between what was to become England and the Germano–Roman Empire. Regional divergences, and thus centrifugal forces, were less here than in the neighbouring empire and the task of the potential central ruler

103

accordingly less difficult. But the divergences and attendant centrifugal forces were greater than on the British island.[79] In England, however, the very restrictedness of the territory facilitated, under certain circumstances, an alliance of the different estates and, above all, of warriors from the whole territory *against* the central ruler. Furthermore, William the Conqueror's distribution of land favoured contact and common interests among the landowning class throughout the whole of England, at least as far as relationships to the central ruler were concerned. It remains to be shown how a certain degree of fragmentation and disparateness in a dominion, not enough to permit disintegration but enough to make a direct alliance of the estates throughout the country difficult, strengthens the position of the central ruler.

Thus the chances offered by the former western Frankish region in terms of its size, were not unfavourable to the emergence of a central ruler and the formation of monopoly power.

It remains to be seen in detail how the Capetians took advantage of these opportunities and, in general, by what mechanisms monopoly rule was established in this territory.

III

On the Monopoly Mechanism

1. The society of what we call the modern age is characterized, above all in the West, by a certain level of monopolization. Free use of military weapons is denied the individual and reserved to a central authority of whatever kind,[80] and likewise the taxation of the property or income of individuals is concentrated in the hands of a central social authority. The financial means thus flowing into this central authority maintain its monopoly of military force, while this in turn maintains the monopoly of taxation. Neither has in any sense precedence over the other; they are two sides of the same monopoly. If one disappears the other automatically follows, though the monopoly rule may sometimes be shaken more strongly on one side than on the other.

Forerunners of such monopoly control of taxes and the army over relatively large territories have previously existed in societies with a less advanced division of functions, mainly as a result of military conquest. It takes a far advanced social division of functions before an enduring, specialized apparatus for administrating the monopoly can emerge. And only when this complex apparatus has evolved does the control over army and taxation take on its full monopoly character. Only then is the military and fiscal monopoly firmly established. From now on social conflicts are not concerned with removing monopoly rule but only with the question of who are to control it, from whom they are to be recruited and how the burdens and benefits of the monopoly are to be distributed. It is only with the emergence of this continuing monopoly of the central authority and this specialized apparatus for ruling that dominions take on the character of "states".

Within them a number of other monopolies crystallize around those already mentioned. But these two are and remain the key monopolies. If they decay, so do all the rest, and with them the "state".

2. The question at issue is how and why this monopoly structure arises.

In the society of the ninth, tenth and eleventh centuries it definitely does not yet exist. From the eleventh century—in the territory of the former western Frankish empire—we see it slowly crystallizing. At first each warrior who controls a piece of land exerts all the functions of rule; these are then gradually monopolized by a central ruler whose power is administrated by specialists. Whenever he pleases, he wages wars to gain new land or defend his own. Land-acquisition and the governmental functions going with its possession are, like its military defence, left to "private initiative", to use the language of a later age. And since, with the increasing population of the area, hunger for land is extremely keen, competition for it throughout the country is rife. In this competition both military and economic means are used, in contrast to that of the nineteenth century, for example, which, given the state monopoly of physical violence, is waged solely by economic means.

A reminder of the competitive struggles and the monopolization taking place directly under our own eyes is not without value for an understanding of monopoly mechanisms in earlier stages of society. In addition, consideration of the old in conjunction with the new helps us to see this social development as a whole. The later part of the movement presupposes the earlier, and the centre of both is the accumulation of the most important means of production of the time, or at least control over it, in fewer and fewer hands—earlier the accumulation of land, later that of money.

The mechanism of monopoly formation has already been briefly discussed:[81] if, *in a major social unit,*—so the mechanism may be roughly summarized—*a large number of the smaller social units which, through their interdependence, constitute the larger one, are of roughly equal social power and are thus able to compete freely—unhampered by pre-existing monopolies—for the means to social power, i.e. primarily the means of subsistence and production, the probability is high that some will be victorious and others vanquished, and that gradually, as a result, fewer and fewer will control more and more opportunities, and more and more units will be eliminated from the competition, becoming directly or indirectly dependent on an ever-decreasing number.* The human figuration caught up in this movement will therefore, unless countervailing measures are taken, approach a state in which all opportunities are controlled by a single authority: a system with open opportunities has become a system with closed opportunities.[82]

The general pattern followed by this sequence is very simple: in a social area there are a certain number of people and a certain number of opportunities which are scarce or insufficient in relation to the needs of the people. If we assume that to begin with each of the people in this area fights one other for the available opportunities, the probability that they will maintain this state of equilibrium indefinitely and that no partner will triumph in any of these pairs is extremely small, if this is indeed a free competition uninfluenced by any monopoly power; and the probability that sooner or later individual contestants will overcome their opponents is extremely high. But if some of the contenders are victorious, their opportunities multiply; those of the vanquished decrease. Greater opportunities accumulate in the hands of one group of the original rivals, the others being eliminated from direct competition with them. Assuming that each of the victors now struggles with the others, the process is repeated: once again one group is victorious and gains control of the power chances of the vanquished; a still smaller number of people controls a still greater number of power chances; a still greater number of people are eliminated from the free competition; and the process is repeated until finally, in the extreme case, one individual controls all power chances and all the others are dependent on him.

In historical reality it is certainly not always individual people who become embroiled in this mechanism; frequently it is large associations of people, for example territories or states. The course of events in reality is usually far more complicated than in this schematic pattern, and full of variations. It often happens, for example, that a number of weaker parties combine to bring down an individual who has accumulated too many possibilities and grown too strong. Should they succeed and take over the possibilities of this party, or some of them, they then fight among themselves for predominance. The effect, the shift in power balances, is always the same. In this way, too, an ever-increasing number of power chances tend to accumulate in the hands of an ever-diminishing number of people through a series of elimination contests.

The course and pace of this shift in favour of the few at the expense of the many depend to a large extent on the relation between the supply and demand of opportunities. If we assume that the level of demand and the number of opportunities remain unchanged overall in the course of the movement, the demand for opportunities will increase with the shift in the power relations; the number of the dependents and the degree of their dependence will increase and change in kind. If relatively independent social functions are increasingly replaced by dependent ones in society—for example, free knights by courtly knights and finally courtiers, or relatively independent merchants by dependent merchants and employees—the moulding of affects, the structure of drives and consciousness, in short the whole social personality structure and the social attitudes of people are necessarily changed at the same time. And this applies no less to those who are approaching a monopoly position than to those who have lost the possibility to compete and fallen into direct or indirect dependence.

3. For this process should in no way be understood merely as one whereby fewer and fewer people become "free" and more and more "unfree", although in some phases it appears to answer this description. If the movement is viewed as a whole, we can recognize without difficulty that—at least in highly differentiated societies—dependence undergoes a peculiar qualitative

change at a certain stage of the process. The more people are made dependent by the monopoly mechanism, the greater becomes the power of the dependent, not only individually but also collectively, in relation to the one or more monopolists. This happens not only because of the small number of those approaching the monopoly position, but because of their own dependence on ever more dependents in preserving and exploiting the power potential they have monopolized. Whether it is a question of land, soldiers or money in any form, the more that is accumulated by an individual, the less easily can it be supervised by this individual, and the more surely he becomes by his very monopoly dependent on increasing numbers of others, the more he becomes dependent on his dependents. Such changes in power and dependence relationships often take centuries to become perceptible, and centuries more to find expression in lasting institutions. Particular structural properties of society may place endless obstacles in the way of the process, yet its mechanism and trend are unmistakable. The more comprehensive the monopolized power potential, the larger the web of functionaries administering it and the greater the division of labour among them; in short, the more people on whose work or function the monopoly is in any way dependent, the more strongly does this whole field controlled by the monopolist assert its own weight and its own inner regularities. The monopoly ruler can acknowledge this and impose on himself the restraints that his function as the central ruler of so mighty a formation demands; or he can indulge himself and give his own inclinations precedence over all others. In the latter case the complex social apparatus which has developed along with this private accumulation of power chances will sooner or later lapse into disorder and make its resistance, its autonomous structure, all the more strongly felt. In other words, the more comprehensive a monopoly position becomes and the more highly developed its division of labour, the more clearly and certainly does it move towards a point at which its one or more monopoly rulers become the central functionaries of an apparatus composed of differentiated functions, more powerful than others, perhaps, but scarcely less dependent and fettered. This change may come about almost imperceptibly by small steps and struggles, or through whole groups of dependents asserting their social power over the monopoly rulers by force; in one way or another the power first won through the accumulation of chances in private struggles, tends, from a point marked by an optimal size of possessions, to slip away from the monopoly rulers into the hands of the dependents as a whole, or, to begin with, to groups of dependents, such as the monopoly administration. The privately owned monopoly in the hands of a single individual or family comes under the control of broader social strata, and transforms itself as the central organ of a state into a public monopoly.

The development of what we today call a "national economy" is an illustrative example of this process. The national economy develops from the "private economy" of feudal ruling houses. More precisely, there is at first no distinction between what are later opposed as "public" and "private" income and expenditure. The income of the central rulers derives primarily from their personal family or domanial possessions; expenses for the ruler's court, hunts, clothes or presents are met from this income in exactly the same way as the cost of the relatively small administration, paid soldiers if any, or the building of castles. Then, as more and more land comes together in the hands of one ruling house the management of income and expenditure, the administration and defence of his property become increasingly difficult for the individual to supervise. But even when the direct possessions of the ruling house, its domanial estate, are no longer by any means the most important source of the ruler's income, even when, with the increasing commercialization of society, duties from the whole country flow into the "chambers" of the central ruler and when, with the monopoly of force, the monopoly of land has become at the same time one of duties or taxes, even then the central ruler at first continues to control this revenue as if it were the personal income of his household. He can still decide how much of it should be spent on castles, presents, his kitchen and the court, and how much on keeping the troops and paying the administration. The distribution of the income from the monopolized resources is his prerogative. On closer examination, however, we find that the monopolist's freedom of decision is restricted more and more by the immense human web that his property has gradually become. His dependence on his administrative staff increases and, with it, the influence of the latter; the fixed costs of the monopoly apparatus constantly rise; and at the end of this development the absolute ruler with his apparently unrestricted power is, to an extraordinary degree, governed by and functionally dependent on, the society he rules. His absolute sovereignty is not simply a consequence of his monopoly control of opportunities, but the function of a particular structural peculiarity of society in this phase, of which more will be said later. But however that may be, even the budget of French absolutism still contains no distinction between the "private" and "public" expenditure of the king.

How the transformation into a public monopoly finally finds expression in the budget is well enough known. The wielder of central power, whatever title he may bear, is allocated a sum in the budget like any other functionary; from it the central ruler, king or president, meets the expenses of his household or court; expenditure necessary for the governmental organization of the country is strictly separated from that used by individuals for personal ends. Private monopoly rule has become public monopoly rule, even when in the hands of an individual as the functionary of society.

The same picture emerges if we trace the formation of the governmental apparatus as a whole. It grows out of what might be called the "private" court and domanial administration of the kings or princes. Practically all the organs of state government result from the differentiation of the functions of the royal household, sometimes with the assimilation of organs of autonomous local administration. When this governmental apparatus has finally become the public affair of the state, the household of the central ruler is at most one organ among others and finally hardly even that.

This is one of the most pronounced examples of the way in which private property becomes a public function, and the monopoly of an individual—won in contests of elimination and accumulation over several generations—is finally socialized.

It would take us too far afield to show here what is actually meant by saying that the "private" power of individuals over monopolized resources becomes "public", or "state", or "collective" power. As was said earlier, all these expressions have their full meaning only when applied to societies with extensive division of functions; only in such societies are the activities and functions of each individual directly or indirectly dependent on those of many others, and only here is the weight of these many intertwined actions and interests so great that even the few with monopoly control over immense possibilities cannot escape its pressure.

Social processes involving the monopoly mechanism are to be found in many societies, even those with relatively low division of functions and integration. There, too, every monopoly tends, from a certain degree of accumulation onwards, to escape the control of any single individual and to pass into that of entire social groups, frequently starting with the former government functionaries, the first servants of the monopolists. The process of feudalization is one example of this. It was shown earlier how, in the course of this process, control over relatively large territorial possessions and military power slips away from the monopoly ruler in successive waves, first to his former functionaries or their heirs, then to the warrior class as a whole with its own internal hierarchy. In societies with a lower degree of interdependence between social functions, this shift away from private monopoly control leads either to a kind of "anarchy", a more or less complete decay of the monopoly, or to its appropriation by an oligarchy instead of an individual dynasty. Later, such shifts in favour of the many do not lead to a disintegration of the monopoly, but only to a different form of control over it. Only in the course of a growing social interdependence of all functions does it become possible to wrest monopolies from arbitrary exploitation by a few without causing them to disintegrate. Wherever the division of functions is both high and increasing, the few who, in successive waves, claim monopoly power, sooner or later find themselves in difficulty, at a disadvantage in face of the many, through their need of their services and thus their functional dependence on them. The human web as a whole, with its increasing division of functions, has an inherent tendency that opposes increasingly strongly every private monopolization of resources. The tendency of monopolies, e.g. the monopoly of force or taxation, to turn from "private" into "public" or "state" monopolies, is nothing other than a function of social interdependence. A human web with high and increasing division of functions is impelled by its own collective weight towards a state of equilibrium where the distribution of the advantages and revenues from monopolized opportunities in favour of a few becomes impossible. If it seems self-evident to us today that certain monopolies, above all the key monopoly of government, are "public", held by the state, although this was by no means the case earlier, this marks a step in the same direction. It is entirely possible that obstructions may again and again be placed in the path of such a process by the particular conditions of a society; a particular example of such obstructions was shown earlier in the development of the old Germano–Roman Empire. And wherever a social web exceeds a certain size optimal for that particular monopoly formation, similar breakdowns will occur. But the impulsion of such a human web towards a quite definite structure, in which monopolies are administered to the advantage of the whole figuration, remains perceptible, no matter what factors may repeatedly intrude as countervailing mechanisms to arrest the process in recurrent situations of conflict.

Considered in general terms, therefore, the process of monopoly formation has a very clear structure. In it, free competition has a precisely definable place and a positive function: it is a struggle among many for resources not yet monopolized by any individual or small group. Each social monopoly is preceded by this kind of free elimination contest; each such contest tends towards monopoly.

As against this phase of free competition, monopoly formation means on one hand the closure of direct access to certain resources for increasing numbers of people, and on the other a progressive centralization of the control of these resources. By this centralization, such resources are placed outside the direct competition of the many; in the extreme case they are controlled by a single social entity. The latter, the monopolist, is never in a position to use the profit from his monopoly for himself alone, particularly in a society with a high division of functions. If he has enough social power, he may at first claim the overwhelming part of the monopoly profit for himself, and reward services with the minimum needed for life. But he is obliged, just because he depends on the services and functions of others, to allocate to others a large part of the resources he controls—and an increasingly large part, the larger his accumulated possessions become, and the greater his dependence on others. A new struggle over the allocation of these resources therefore arises among those who depend on them. But whereas in the preceding phase the competition was "free", that is, its outcome depended solely on who proved stronger or weaker at a given time, it now depends on the function or purpose for which the monopolist needs the individual to supervise his dominion. Free competition has been replaced by one that is controlled, or at any rate controllable, from a central position by human agents; and the qualities that promise success in this restricted competition, the selection it operates, the human types it produces, differ in the extreme from those in the preceding phase of free competition.

The difference between the situation of the free feudal nobility and that of the courtly nobility is an example of this. In the former, the social power of the individual house, a function of both its economic and military capacity and of the physical strength and skill of the individual, determines the allocation of resources; and in this free competition the direct use of force is indispensable. In the latter, the allocation of resources is finally determined by the man whose house or whose predecessors have emerged victoriously from the struggle by violence, so that he now possesses the monopoly of force. Owing to this monopoly, the direct use of force is now largely excluded from the competition among the nobility for the opportunities the prince has to allocate. The means of struggle have been refined or sublimated. The restraint of the affects imposed on the individual by his dependence on the monopoly ruler has increased. And individuals now waver between resistance to the compulsion to which they are subjected, hatred of their dependence and unfreedom, nostalgia for free knightly rivalry, on the one hand, and pride in the self-control they have acquired, or delight in the new possibilities of pleasure that it opens, on the other. In brief, this is a new spurt in the civilizing process.

The next step is the seizure of the monopolies of physical force and taxation, with all the other governmental monopolies based on them, by the bourgeoisie. The latter is at this stage a class which, in its totality, controls certain economic opportunities in the manner of an organized monopoly. But these opportunities are still so evenly spread among its members that relatively large numbers of them can compete freely. What this class is struggling with the princes for, and what it finally attains, is not the destruction of monopoly rule. The bourgeoisie do not aspire to re-allocate these monopolies of taxation and military and police power to their own individual members; their members do not want to become landowners each controlling his own military means and his own income from taxes. The existence of a monopoly for raising taxes and exerting physical violence is the basis of their own social existence; it is the precondition for the restriction to economic, non-violent means, of the free competition in which they are engaged with each other for certain economic opportunities.

What they are striving for in the struggle for monopoly rule, and what they finally attain is not, as noted before, a division of the existing monopolies but a different distribution of their burdens and benefits. That control of these monopolies now depends on a whole class instead of an absolute prince is a step in the direction just described; it is a step on that road which leads the opportunities given by this monopoly to be allocated less and less according to the personal favour and interests of individuals, but increasingly according to a more impersonal and precise plan in the interests of many interdependent associates, and finally in the interests of an entire interdependent human figuration.

In other words, through centralization and monopolization, opportunities that previously had to be won by individuals through military or economic force, can now become amenable to planning. From a certain point of development on, the struggle for monopolies no longer aims at their destruction; it is a struggle for control of their yields, for the plan according to which their burdens and benefits are to be divided up, in a word, for the keys to distribution. Distribution itself, the task of the monopoly ruler and administration, changes in this struggle from a relatively private to a public function. Its dependence on all the other functions of the interdependent human network emerges more and more clearly in organizational form. In this entire structure the central functionaries are, like everyone else, dependent. Permanent institutions to control them are formed by a greater or lesser portion of the people dependent on this monopoly apparatus; and control of the monopoly, the filling of its key positions, is itself no longer decided by the vicissitudes of "free" competition, but by regularly recurring elimination contests without force of arms, which are regulated by the monopoly apparatus, and thus by "unfree" competition. In other words, what we are accustomed to call a "democratic regime" is formed. This kind of regime is not—as the mere view of certain economic monopoly processes of our time might make it

114

appear—incompatible with monopolies as such and dependent for its existence on the freest possible competition. On the contrary it presupposes highly organized monopolies, and it can only come into being or survive under certain conditions, in a very specific social structure at a very advanced stage of monopoly formation.

Two main phases can thus be distinguished in the dynamics of a monopoly mechanism, as far as we are at present able to judge. First, the phase of free competition or elimination contests, with a tendency for resources to be accumulated in fewer and fewer and finally in one pair of hands, the phase of monopoly formation; secondly, the phase in which control over the centralized and monopolized resources tends to pass from the hands of an individual to those of ever greater numbers, and finally to become a function of the interdependent human web as a whole, the phase in which a relatively "private" monopoly becomes a "public" one.

Signs of this second phase are not lacking even in societies with a relatively low division of functions. But, clearly, it can only attain its full development in societies with a very high and rising division of functions.

The overall movement can be reduced to a very simple formula. Its starting point is a situation where a whole class controls unorganized monopoly opportunities and where, accordingly, the distribution of these opportunities among the members of this class is decided by free competition and open force; it is then driven towards a situation where the control of monopoly opportunities and those dependent on them by one class, is centrally organized and secured by institutions; and where the distribution of the yields of monopoly follows a plan that is not exclusively governed by the interests of single individuals or single groups, but is oriented on the overall network of interdependencies binding all participating groups and individuals to each other and on its optimal functioning. For in the long run the subordination of the quest for the optimal functioning of the overall network of interdependencies to the optimation of sectional interests invariably defeats its own end.

So much for the general mechanism of competition and monopoly formation. This schematic generalization takes on its full significance only in conjunction with concrete facts; by them it must prove its worth.

When we talk of "free competition" and "monopoly formation" we usually have present-day facts in mind; we think first of all of a "free competition" for "economic" advantages waged by people or groups within a given framework of rules through the exertion of economic power, and in the course of which some gradually increase their control of economic advantages while destroying, subjecting or restricting the economic existence of others.

But these economic struggles of our day do not only lead before our eyes to a constant restriction of the scope for really "monopoly-free" competition and to the slow formation of monopolistic structures. As has already been indicated, they actually presuppose the secure existence of certain very advanced monopolies. Without the monopoly organization of physical violence and taxation, limited at present to national boundaries, the restriction of this struggle for "economic" advantages to the exertion of "economic" power, and the maintenance of its basic rules, would be impossible over any length of time even within individual states. In other words, the economic struggles and monopolies of modern times occupy a particular position within a larger historical context. And only in relation to this wider context do our general remarks on the mechanism of competition and monopoly take on their full meaning. Only if we bear in mind the sociogenesis of these firmly established "state" monopoly institutions—which during a phase of large-scale expansion and differentiation, no doubt open the "economic sphere" to unrestricted individual competition, and thus to new private monopoly formations—only then can we distinguish more clearly amidst the multitude of particular historical facts the interplay of social mechanisms, the ordered structure of such monopoly formations.

How did these "state" monopoly organizations come to be formed? What kind of struggles gave rise to them?

It must be enough here to follow these processes in the history of the country where they took their course most undeviatingly, and which, partly as a result of this, was for long periods the foremost power in Europe, setting the example for others: France. In so doing we must not shy away from details; otherwise our general model will never take on the wealth of experience without which it remains empty—just as wealth of experience remains chaotic to those unable to perceive order and structures within it.

IV

Early Struggles within the Framework of the Kingdom

1. Within the former western Frankish territory there was a very high probability, in accordance with the inherent tendency of the monopoly mechanism, that sooner or later one of the rival warrior houses would gain predominance and finally a monopoly position; and that in this way the many smaller feudal territories would be welded into a larger unit.

That it would be this particular house, the Capetians, who emerged as victors from the elimination struggles, so becoming the executors of the monopoly mechanism, was at first far less likely, even though a number of factors favouring this house can be readily discerned. It can be said that it was only the course of the Hundred Years' War that conclusively decided whether the descendants of the Capetians or of another house were to become the monopolists or central rulers of the emerging state.

It is not unimportant to bear in mind the difference between these two questions, between the general problem of monopoly and state formation, and the more specific question why this particular house won and retained hegemony. It is with the former rather than the latter that we have been concerned and are still concerned here.

The first shift towards monopoly after the general levelling of property relationships that carries on into the tenth and even the eleventh century, has been sketched above. It involves the formation of a monopoly within the framework of a territory. Within this small area the first elimination contests are fought, and in them the balance first moves in favour of a few and finally of a single contestant. One house—for a house or family is always the social unit that asserts itself, not an individual—wins so much land that the others can no longer match its military and economic strength. As long as there is a possibility of competing with it, the relationship of liege lord to vassal is more or less nominal. With this shift in social power it takes on a new reality. A new dependence of many houses on one is established, even though, in the absence of a highly developed central apparatus, it lacks both the continuity and strength that it later has in the framework of the absolutist regime.

It is characteristic of the rigour with which this monopoly mechanism operates that analogous processes are taking place at approximately the same time in practically all the territories of the western Frankish region. Louis VI, Duke of Francia and in name the King of the whole region, is, as we have pointed out, only the representative of this stage of monopoly formation.

2. If we look at a map of France in the period about 1032, we have a clear impression of the political fragmentation of the region into a multitude of greater and lesser territories.[83] What we have in front of us is certainly not yet the France we know. This emerging France, the former western Frankish region, is bordered to the south-east by the Rhône; Arles and Lyons lie outside it in the kingdom of Burgundy; also outside it to the north lies the region of present-day Toul, Bar le Duc and Verdun, which belong, like the areas around Aachen, Antwerp and, further north, Holland, to the kingdom of Lorraine. The traditional eastern and northern frontier of the former western Frankish region runs deep within present-day France. But neither this frontier of the nominal Capetian empire nor the borders of the smaller political units within it had at that time quite the same function or fixity as present-day state frontiers. Geographical divisions, river valleys and mountain ranges, together with linguistic differences and local traditions, gave the frontiers a certain stability. But as each region, large or small, is the possession of a warrior family, what primarily decides the composition of a territorial unit is the victories and defeats, the marriages, purchases and sales of this family; and the shifts in hegemony over a given area are considerable.

Going from south to north we first see, north of the county of Barcelona, that is, north of the Pyrenees, the duchy of Gascony extending to the region of Bordeaux and the county of Toulouse. Then, to mention only the larger units, come the duchy of Guyenne, i.e. Aquitaine, the county of Anjou, the seat of the second Franco–English royal house, the counties of Maine and Blois, the duchy of Normandy, seat of the first Franco–English royal house, the counties of Troyes, Vermandois and Flanders, and finally, between the Norman dominions—the counties of Blois, Troyes and others—the small domain of the Capetians, the duchy of Francia. It has already been emphasized that this small Capetian dominion did not constitute, any more than other territories, a complete unity in the geopolitical or military sense of the word. It was made up of two or three fairly large adjoining regions, the Isle de France,

Berry and the Orléans regions, as well as scattered smaller possessions in Poitou, in the south, and in the most diverse parts of France, that had come into the possession of the Capetians in one way or another.[84]

3. In most of these territories at the time of Louis VI, therefore, a particular house has gained predominance over the others by accumulating land. Conflicts between these princely houses and the smaller nobility within the dominion are constantly flaring up, and tensions between them long remain perceptible.

But the chances of successful resistance by the smaller feudal houses are no longer great. Their dependence on the liege lord or territorial ruler of the time slowly becomes more evident in the course of the eleventh century. The monopoly position of the princely houses within their territories is now only seldom shaken. And what from now on characterizes society more and more is the struggle between these princely houses for predominance in a larger area. People are driven into these conflicts by the same compulsions as in the previous stage: when one neighbour grows larger and thus stronger, the other is threatened with being overpowered by him and made dependent; he must conquer in order not to be subjugated. And though to begin with crusades and wars of expansion to some extent reduce the internal pressure, this grows all the more intense once the chances of outward expansion have diminished. The mechanism of free competition operates from now on within a more confined circle, namely between those warrior families which have become the central houses of territories.

4. The Norman Duke's conquest of England was, as we have mentioned, one of the expansionist campaigns characteristic of this time, one among many. It too bore witness to the general hunger for land that afflicted the growing population, particularly the warriors, whether rich or poor.

But this enrichment of the Norman Duke, this enlargement of his military and financial means, was a grave disturbance to the previous equilibrium between the territorial rulers of France. The full extent of the shift did not become immediately apparent; for the Conqueror needed time to organize his power within his new dominion, and even when this had been done the threat emanating from this aggrandisement of the Norman dukes to other territorial rulers, given the low integration of the western Frankish territories, first made itself felt only in the direct vicinity of Normandy, i.e. in northern France, rather than further south. Felt it was, however, and most directly by the house with the traditional claim to predominance in the area neighbouring Normandy to the east, the house of the dukes of Francia, the Capetians. It is not unlikely that the threat from his stronger neighbour was a powerful factor impelling Louis VI in the direction that he adhered to tenaciously and energetically throughout his life, his urge to consolidate his power and defeat any possible rival within his own territory.

That he, the nominal king and liege lord of the western Frankish region was in fact, in keeping with the size of his possessions, far weaker than his vassal and neighbour, who now as ruler of England likewise wore a crown, was apparent in every conflict between them.

William the Conqueror, because he had recently conquered this island territory, had had the chance to create what was for his time a fairly centralized governmental organization. He distributed the land in a manner intended as far as possible to prevent the formation of houses and families as rich and mighty as his own, that might become rivals. The administration of the English central ruler was the most advanced of its time; even for money revenues there was already a special office.

The army with which William had conquered the island consisted only in part of his feudal retainers, the rest being mercenary knights driven by the same desire for new lands. Only now, after the conquest, was the Norman ruler's treasury large enough to engage paid soldiers; and quite apart from the size of their feudal following, this too gave the island rulers military superiority over their Continental neighbours. Louis the Fat of Francia could not afford this any more than his predecessors. He had been accused of being covetous, seeking by every means at his disposal to take possession of money. In fact it was precisely at this time, as in many periods when money is relatively scarce and the disproportion between what is available and what is needed particularly keenly felt, that an urge or "greed" for money was particularly prominent. But Louis VI did indeed find himself in particularly difficult straits in face of his richer neighbour. In this respect, as in the question of organization, centralization and the elimination of possible internal rivals, the island territory set an example that Continental rulers had to follow if they were not to succumb in the struggle for supremacy.

At the beginning of the twelfth century, therefore, the Capetian house is noticeably weaker than its rival, which controls land and people across the sea. Louis VI is defeated in practically every battle with his English rival, even though the latter does not succeed in penetrating the territory of Francia itself. This is the situation in which the ruler of Francia confines himself to enlarging the basis of his power, his family property, and to breaking the resistance of the smaller feudal lords within or between his territories. In so doing he is preparing his house for that great struggle, for those centuries of conflict for supremacy in the former western Frankish region, in the course of which more and more territories grow together in a single bloc in the hands of a single house, and in which from now on all the other territories in the region and directly or indirectly involved—the struggle for the French crown between the rulers of the Isle de France and the rulers of the English island.

5. The house that takes up the struggle with the Capetians when William the Conqueror's family becomes extinct, is that of the Plantagenets. Their family dominion is Anjou,[85] likewise a region neighbouring Francia. They make their way upwards at about the same time as the Capetians, and in almost the same manner. As in Francia under Philip I, so in neighbouring Anjou under Foulque, the Counts' actual power in relation to their vassals has become very slight. Like Philip's son, Louis VI, the Fat, Foulque's son, Foulque the Young, and his son, Geoffroi Plantagenet, slowly subdue the smaller and medium-sized feudal lords in their domain; and they, too, thus lay the foundation for further expansion.

In England itself, at first, the reverse process takes place, showing the mechanisms of this warrior society from the other side. When Henry I, William of Conqueror's grandson, dies without male heirs, Étienne of Blois, the son of one of William's daughters, lays claim to the English throne. He gains the recognition of the secular feudal lords and the Church; but he is himself no more than a medium-sized, Norman feudal lord. His personal property, the family power on which he must depend, is limited. And thus he is fairly impotent in the face of the other warriors, and also the clergy, of his region. With his accession to the throne, a disintegration of governmental power on the island immediately sets in. The feudal lords build castle upon castle, mint their own money, levy taxes from their own regions; in short, they take over all the powers that hitherto, in keeping with their superior strength, had been a monopoly of the Norman central rulers. Furthermore Étienne of Blois commits a series of blunders, alienating the Church in particular, that a stronger man might perhaps have been able to afford, but not one needing the help of others. This helps his rivals.

These rivals are the counts of Anjou. Geoffroi Plantagenet has married the daughter of the last Norman–English king. And he has the power to back the claim he bases on this marriage. He slowly gains a foothold in Normandy. His son, Henry Plantagenet, unites Maine, Anjou, Touraine and Normandy under his rule. And with this power base he can undertake to reconquer the English dominions of his grandfather as the Norman Duke had done before him. In 1153 he crosses the Channel. In 1154, at the age of twenty-two, he becomes king, and a king who, by virtue both of his military and financial power, and of his personal energy and talent, becomes a strong centralizing force. Two years previously, moreover, he had become, through his marriage with the heiress of Aquitaine, the ruler of this region in southern France. He thus combines with his English lands a territory on the mainland beside which the Capetian domain appears small indeed. The question whether the western Frankish territories are to be integrated around the Isle de France or Anjou is wide open. England itself is conquered territory and to begin with an object of politics rather than a subject.[86] It is—if one will—a semi-colonial part of the loose federation of western Frankish territories.

The distribution of power at that time bears a distant resemblance to that currently existing in the Far East. A small island territory and a dominion many times its size on the Continent are under one rule. The whole southern part of the former Capetian realm belongs to it. The chief southern area not belonging to the Plantagenet dominions is the county of Barcelona. Its rulers are caught up in a similar expansionist movement and have become kings of Aragon, likewise on grounds of marriage. Slowly, and at first almost unnoticed, they disengage themselves from the union of western Frankish territories.

Also outside the Angevin–English dominion in the south—apart from a smaller clerical territory—is the county of Toulouse. Its rulers, like smaller lords north of the Aquitainian region, begin, in face of the threatening supremacy of the Angevin realm, to incline towards the rival power centre, the

Capetians. The characteristic power balances which one encounters in figurations such as these tend to determine the conduct of people always in the same way; in the smaller sphere of the western Frankish territorial federation, their operation is little different from that determining the politics of states in modern Europe, for example, and even, incipiently, across the whole globe. As long as no absolutely dominant power has emerged, no power that has unequivocally outgrown all competition and taken up a monopoly position, units of the second rank seek to form a bloc against the one which, by uniting numerous regions, has come closest to the position of supremacy. The formation of one bloc provokes another; and however long this process may oscillate back and forth, the system as a whole tends to consolidate larger and larger regions about a centre, to concentrate real power of decision in ever fewer units and finally at a single centre.

The expansion of the Norman Duke created a bloc which displaced the balance in his favour at first in northern France. The expansion of the house of Anjou built on this and took a step further; the bloc of the Angevin realm called into question the equilibrium of the whole western Frankish region. However loosely connected this bloc may have been, however rudimentary the centralizing government within it, nevertheless the movement by which, under the pressure of the general hunger for land, one house constantly drove another to unite with it or to seek "more" land, manifests itself clearly enough in these formations. Apart from the south, a broad band comprising the whole of western France now belongs to the Plantagenets' dominion. Formerly the king of England was vassal to the Capetian kings on behalf of this mainland area. But "law" counts for little when it is not backed by corresponding social power.

When in 1177 Louis VI's successor, Louis VII of Francia, now an old and weary man, holds a meeting with the representative of the rival house, Henry II, the young King of England, he tells him:

Oh Sire, since the beginning of your reign and earlier you have heaped outrages upon me, trampling underfoot the loyalty you owed me and the homage you have done me; and of all these outrages the gravest and most flagrant is your unjust usurpation of Auvergne which you hold to the detriment of the French Crown. To be sure, old age is on my heels and robs me of the strength to recover this and other lands; but before God, before these Barons of the Realm and our loyal subjects, I publicly protest and uphold the rights of my Crown, most notably to Auvergne, Berry, and Chateauroux, Gisors and the Norman Vexin, beseeching the King of Kings who has given me an heir, to accord to him what he has denied to me.[87]

Vexin—a kind of Norman Alsace-Lorraine—was a contested borderland between the domain of the Capetians and the Norman dominion of the Plantagenets. Further south the frontier between the Capetian and Angevin dominions ran through the Berry region. The Plantagenets were clearly strong enough already to seize parts of the Capetian domain. The struggle for supremacy between Capetians and Plantagenets was in full spate; and the Angevin ruler was still far stronger than the ruler of Francia.

Accordingly, the demands the Capetian makes of his opponent are really very modest; he wants to be given back a few pieces of land that he counts among his own dominions. For the time being he can contemplate nothing more. The glory of the Angevin rule and the paucity of his own he realizes to the full. "We French," he once said, comparing himself with his rival, "have nothing but bread, wine and contentment."

6. But this manner of ruling did not yet possess great stability. It was in fact a "private enterprise"; as such it was subject to the inherent social dynamics of a struggle between freely competing units, which in any given case was much more strongly influenced by the personal capacities of the competitors—their age, their succession and similar personal factors—than were political formations of a later phase, when not only the person of the owner of the monopoly but a certain division of functions, a multiplicity of organized interests and a more stable governmental apparatus, held together larger units.

In 1189 a Capetian again confronts the Plantagenet. Almost all the contested areas have in the meantime been won back to Capetian rule. And now the Plantagenet is an old man, the Capetian younger; he is Louis VII's son, Philip II, surnamed Augustus. Age, as noted above, means much in a society where the incumbent of power is not yet able to delegate military leadership, where very much depends on his personal initiative and where he must attack or defend in person. Henry II, personally a strong ruler who still has the control of his large domains securely in his hands, is now plagued along with age by the rebellions and even the hatred of his eldest son Richard, surnamed Coeur-de-Lion, who sometimes even makes common cause against his father with the rival Capetians.

Exploiting the weakness of his adversary, Philip Augustus took back Auvergne and the parts of Berry mentioned by his father. One month after they faced each other at Tours, Henry II dies at the age of fifty-six.

In 1193—Richard the Lion Heart lies in prison—Philip seizes the long-contested Vexin. His ally is John, the younger brother of the prisoner.

In 1199 Richard dies. He, like his brother and successor John, who is soon to be John Lackland, have squandered much of the basis of their power, the family possessions and treasure of their father. Facing John as his rival, however, is a man who has felt to the quick the whole humiliation and constriction of Capetian power by the growth of the Angevin–English, and whose whole energy, stirred by this experience, is channelled in a single direction: more land, more power. More and yet more. He—like the first Plantagenet before him—is obsessed by this craving. When John Lackland enquires whether he might not have back some of the land lost to Philip for payment, Philip answers by asking if he does not know anyone else willing to sell land; he himself would rather buy more. And at this time Philip is already a man rich in land and power.

Clearly, this is not yet a struggle between states or nations. The whole history of the formation of later monopoly organizations, of nation states, remains incomprehensible until the special character of this preceding social phase of "private initiative" has been understood. This is a struggle between competing or rival houses which, following a general movement of this society, drive each other, first as small and then as larger and larger units, to expand and strive for more possessions.

The Battle of Bouvines in 1214 provisionally decides the issue. John of England and his allies are defeated by Philip Augustus. And as so often in feudal warrior society, defeat in an external battle means an internal weakening as well. Returning home John finds the barons and clergy in revolt, and their demand is the Magna Carta. Conversely, for Philip Augustus the victory in the foreign war strengthens his power within his dominion.

As his father's heir, Philip Augustus took over essentially the small inland district of Paris and Orléans, together with parts of Berry. He added—to mention only his major acquisitions—Normandy, then one of the largest and richest territories in the whole realm; the regions of Anjou, Maine and Touraine; important parts of Poitou and Saintonge; Artois, Valois, Vermandois; the region of Amiens and a large part of the region around Beauvais. "The lord of Paris and Orléans has become the greatest territorial lord in northern France."[88] He has made "the Capetian house the richest family in France".[89] His domain has gained outlets to the sea. In other territories of northern France, in Flanders, Champagne, Burgundy and Brittany, his influence is increasing in proportion to his power. And even in the south he already controls a not inconsiderable area.

This Capetian dominion is still anything but an integrated territory. Between Anjou and the Orléans region lies the domain of the Count of Blois. In the south the coastal districts around Saintes and, further east, Auvergne, are as yet scarcely connected to the northern regions. But the latter, the old family domain together with Normandy and newly conquered areas stretching beyond Arras to the north, constitute purely geographically a fairly self-contained bloc.

Even Philip Augustus did not yet have "France" in our sense in view, and his real dominion was not this France. What he aimed at above all was the territorial, military and economic expansion of his family power and the subjugation of its most dangerous competitors, the Plantagenets. In both these aims he succeeded. On Philip's death the Capetian dominions were roughly four times as large as at his accession. The Plantagenets, by contrast, who had lived hitherto more on the Continent than on the island—and whose administration in England itself was made up as much of Continental Normans and people from their other mainland possessions as of natives of the island—now controlled on the mainland merely a part of the former Aquitaine, the area north of the central and western Pyrenees along the coast as far as the Gironde estuary under the name of the duchy of Guyenne; apart from that there were a few islands in the Norman archipelago. The balance had shifted against them. Their power had decreased. But thanks to their island dominion it was not broken. After a time the balance on the mainland shifted back in their favour. The outcome of this struggle for hegemony in the former western Frankish area remained long undecided. It appears that Philip Augustus regarded as his chief rivals after the Plantagenets the counts of Flanders; and that a new power centre had indeed come into existence there is shown by the whole subsequent history of France. Philip is reputed to have once said that either Francia would become Flemish or Flanders French. He certainly did not lack awareness that in all these conflicts among the lesser territorial houses, what was at issue was supremacy or the loss of independence. But he could still imagine Flanders equally well as Francia as dominating the whole area.

7. Philip Augustus' successors at first hold firm to the course that he has set: they seek to consolidate and further extend the enlarged dominion. No sooner is Philip Augustus dead than the barons of Poitou turn back to the Plantagenets. Louis VIII, Philip Augustus' son, secures this region afresh for his own dominion, as he does Saintonge, Aunis and Languedoc, part of Picardy and the county of Perche. Partly in the form of a religious war, the struggle against the Albigensian heretics, the Capetian house begins to advance south into the sphere of the only great territorial lord in that part who could, beside the Plantagenets, rival the power of the Capetians, the domain of the counts of Toulouse.

The next Capetian, Louis IX, the Saint, has once again to protect his rapidly conglomerated possessions against every kind of internal and external attack. At the same time he goes on building, uniting parts of Languedoc north-east of the Pyrenees, the counties of Mâcon, Clermont and Mortain, and some smaller areas, with his family possessions. Philip III, the Bold, seizes the county of Guines between Calais and Saint-Omer, only to lose it twelve years later to the heirs of the Count. He acquires through purchase or promise of protection every minor possession in his vicinity that offers itself; and he prepares the assimilation of Champagne and the great territory of Toulouse into the dominions of his house.

There is by now in the whole western Frankish area scarcely a single territorial ruler who can, without allies, stand up to the Capetians, with the exception of the Plantagenets. The latter, to be sure, are no less preoccupied than the Capetians with enlarging their sphere of power. On the Continent their rule has once again extended beyond the duchy of Guyenne. Across the sea they have subdued Wales and are in the process of conquering Scotland. They still have possibilities of expansion that do not lead to a direct collision with the Capetians. The latter, too, still have scope for expansion in other directions. At the same time, under Philip the Fair, their dominion is expanding to the frontiers of the Germano–Roman Empire, on one side as far as the Maas, which at that time was usually considered as the natural and—in remembrance of the partition of the Carolingian Empire in 843—the traditional frontier of the western Frankish area; on the other side—further south—it extends as far as the Rhône and the Saône, that is, as far as the regions of Provence, Dauphiné and the county of Burgundy, which likewise do not belong to the traditional confederation of western Frankish territories. Through marriage Philip acquires Champagne and Brie with many annexed areas, some of them in the territory of the Germano–Roman Empire itself. From the Count of Flanders he obtains the dominions of Lille, Douai and Béthune; the county of Chartres and the estate of Beaugency he takes from the counts of Blois. In addition he acquires the counties of Marche and Angoulême, the ecclesiastical properties of Cahors, Mende and Puy, and further south the county of Bigorre and the viscounty of Soule.

His three sons, Louis X, Philip V and Charles IV, die one after the other without leaving a male heir; the family possessions and crown of the Capetians pass to a descendant of a younger son of the house who owns the county of Valois as an apanage.

Up to this point a continuous effort has been made in more or less the same direction throughout generations: to accumulate land. It must be enough here to summarize the results of this effort. Nonetheless, even this summary, even the mere naming of the many lands which step by step were brought together, gives an idea of the perpetual, open or concealed struggle in which the various princely houses were engaged, and in which one of these houses after another, conquered by one more powerful, disappears. Whether or not one fully realizes the meaning of these names, they give an impression of the strength of the impulse emanating from the social situation of the Capetian house, an impulse which passed in the same direction through such widely differing individuals.

At the death of Charles IV, the last Capetian who comes to the throne in direct succession, the great French Capetian dominions—i.e. the complex grouped directly around the duchy of Francia—extend from Normandy in the west to Champagne in the east and to Canche in the north; the Artois region, adjoining this to the north, has been given away as an apanage to a member of the family. Somewhat further south—separated by the apanaged region of Anjou—the county of Poitiers is part of the area directly controlled by the Paris princes; still further south the county of Toulouse belongs to them and parts of the former duchy of Aquitaine. All this already constitutes a mighty complex of lands; but it is not yet a cohesive region. It still has the typical appearance of a territorial family domain, the individual parts of which are held together less by their reciprocal dependence, or through any division of function, than by the person of the owner, through "personal union", and the common administrative centre. The separate identity of each region, the special interests and character of each territory, are still very strongly felt. However, their union under one and the same house and partly under the same administration, does remove a whole series of obstacles in the way of fuller integration. It corresponds to the tendency towards an extension of trade relations, the intensification of links beyond the local level, which is already discernible in small parts of the urban population, even though this tendency does not play remotely the same role as a driving force in the union or expansion of princely houses as it played later, in the nineteenth century, for example, at an entirely different stage in the development of urban bourgeois strata. Here, in the eleventh, twelfth and thirteenth centuries, the struggle for land, the rivalry between an ever-smaller number of warrior families, is the primary impulse behind the formation of larger territories. The initiative lies with the few rising warrior families, the princely houses; under their protection the towns and trade flourish. Both profit from the concentration of power; no doubt they also contribute to it, as will be discussed later. And quite certainly urban strata, once larger regions are united under one rule, play an important part in the consolidation of a territorial union even at this time. Without the help of the human and financial resources flowing to the princes from urban strata and growing commercialization, neither the expansion nor the governmental organization of these centuries would be conceivable. But the significance of towns and commercialization for the integration of larger areas is still mainly indirect, in so far as they are instruments or organs of the princely houses. This integration means first and foremost the conquest of one warrior house by another, that is, the absorption of one by another or at least its subjection, its dependence on the victor.

If the area is regarded from this point of view as it appears at the beginning of the fourteenth century at the extinction of the direct Capetian line, the direction of change is readily perceived. The struggle of lesser and medium warrior houses for land or more land has certainly not stopped; but these feuds no longer play remotely the part they played at the time of Louis VI, not to speak of his predecessors. At that time the lands were distributed relatively evenly among many; to be sure, there were differences between possessions which may have seemed very considerable to contemporaries. But even the possessions and thus the power of the nominal princely houses were so small that a large number of knightly families in their neighbourhood could try their arm with them as rivals for land or power. It was left to the "private initiative" of all these houses to decide how far they participated in this general struggle. Now, in the fourteenth century, these many warrior houses are no longer individually a force to be reckoned with; at most collectively, as a class, they carry a certain social weight. But the real initiative now lies with the very few warrior houses that have emerged for the time being as victors from the preceding conflicts, and have accumulated so much land that all the other houses can no longer challenge them, but act only in dependence on them. To these others, the majority of warriors, the possibility of winning new land on their own initiative in free competition is by and large foreclosed, and with it the chance of rising independently in society. Every warrior house must at most remain on the rung of the social ladder it has reached, unless one or other of its members succeeds in moving higher through the favour of one of the great lords, and thus through dependence on him.

The number of those who are still able to compete independently for land and power in the western Frankish region has steadily diminished. No independent duke or house of Nor-

130

mandy now exists and none of Aquitaine; assimilation or suppression have overtaken—to mention only the very largest—the counties of Champagne, Anjou and Toulouse. There now exist, beside the house of Francia, only four other houses that matter in this region: the duchies of Burgundy and Brittany, the county of Flanders and most powerful of all, the kings of England, dukes of Guyenne and lords of several smaller areas. A warrior society with relatively free competition has become a society where competition is restricted in the manner of a monopoly. And even out of the five great houses that still possess some degree of competitive power, and preserve a certain corresponding independence, two houses again rise as the most powerful, the Capetians and their succession, the kings of France, and the Plantagenets, kings of England. The confrontation between them must decide who will ultimately control monopoly power in the western Frankish region, and where the centre and the boundaries of the monopoly will lie.

V

The Resurgence of Centrifugal Tendencies: The Figuration of the Competing Princes

8. However, the formation of the monopoly of rule is not accomplished by any means as straightforwardly as appears merely from consideration of the accumulation of land. The larger the area becomes that is gradually united and centralized by the Capetians, the more strongly does a countervailing movement make itself felt; and the stronger, once again, grows the tendency towards decentralization. This tendency is still represented first and foremost by the closest relations and vassals of the monopoly ruler, as in the preceding phase where the barter economy was more intact, and as in the Carolingian period. But the mode of action of the decentralizing social forces has changed considerably. Money, crafts and trade now play an appreciably greater role in society than at that time; groups who concern themselves specially with all this, the burgher class, have taken on a social importance of their own. Transport has developed. All this offers the ruling organization of a large territory opportunities that were lacking earlier. The servants a

central ruler sends into the country to administrate and supervise his possessions no longer find it so easy to make themselves independent. Moreover, a growing proportion of these helpers of the central ruler now come from urban strata. The danger of such burghers developing into rivals of the ruler is incomparably less than before, when he had to take some of his aides from the warrior class, and when even bondsmen that he patronized could very rapidly acquire, thanks to the land with which he rewarded their services, the power and social rank of a warrior or noble.

However, a particular social category of people still poses a real threat to the cohesion of very large dominions under single rule, even though their power may have diminished and their mode of action changed. Even under the changed social circumstances, they become over and over again the chief exponents of decentralization. These are the closest family members of the ruler, that is, his uncles, his brothers, his sons or even, though far less so, his sisters or daughters.

A dominion and the monopoly of rule within it are not really, at this time, the possession of a single individual; they are very much a family possession, the property of a warrior house. All the closest relations of this house have and assert a claim to at least parts of this property. This is a claim which the head of the house is, for a long period, less willing or able to refuse, the larger the family possessions grow. It is certainly not a "legal claim" in the later sense of the word. In this society there are hardly more than the rudiments of a general, all-embracing "law" to which even the great warrior rulers are subject. For there is as yet no all-embracing power that could enforce such a law. It is only in conjunction with the formation of monopolies of rule, with the centralization of the ruling functions, that a common legal code is established for large areas. To provide for children is a social obligation that we often find set down in the "Coutumes". Undoubtedly it is only the better-endowed families that can adhere to this custom. For just this reason it carried prestige value. How could the richest house of the land, the royal house, have escaped this prestigious obligation?

The territorial possessions of a house continue to be, if in an increasingly restricted sense, what we would call private property. The head of the house controls it in just as unrestricted a fashion, and perhaps even more freely, than a great landowner

132

controls his property today, or the head of a major family firm its capital, income and branches. Just as the landowner can split off one or other of his estates for the benefit of a younger son or the dowry of a daughter, without asking its tenants whether their new lord is agreeable to them; as the head of the firm can withdraw capital for his daughter's dowry or install his son as director of a subsidiary, without owing his employees the slightest explanation, in the same way the princes of that earlier phase disposed of villages, towns, estates and territories of their realm. And the impulse causing the owner of large properties to provide for his sons and daughters is more or less the same in all these cases. Quite apart from a ruler's possible preference for one of his younger children, to endow them in a fitting manner is necessary for the preservation and public display of the social status of a house; and—at least apparently, at least in a short-term view—it increases the house's chances of gaining power and permanence. That this splitting up of possessions and functions of rule for the benefit of relations very often precisely endangers the power and permanence of the house, is a fact which frequently only enters the consciousness of princes after long and painful experience. In France Louis XIV was really the first to draw the full and ultimate conclusion from such experience. With implacable severity he kept all family relations—even the heir to the throne, as far as this was possible at all—far from all ruling functions and independent positions of power.

9. At the beginning of this line of development, in that early phase when the family possessions of the Capetians were scarcely larger than those of many other warrior families in the land, the danger implicit in any fragmentation of this property is immediately obvious. The direct threat from neighbouring feudal families seldom abates. This causes each family to hold its people together as well as its property. No doubt there are quarrels, fights within the household as everywhere else. But at the same time, all or at least part of the family work constantly to defend or expand the family possessions. The relatively small estates of the royal family, like those of all warrior houses, are essentially autarkic; they lack any larger social importance and have indeed very much the character of a small family enterprise. The brothers and sons, even the mothers and wives of heads of families have a say in the running of the estate which

varies with their personal qualities and circumstances. But it hardly occurs to anyone to sever any significant part from the family possessions and hand it over to a member of the family. The younger sons may receive a small estate here and there, or they may marry into a small property; but we also hear of one or other of the younger sons of a royal family leading a fairly penurious existence.

This changes completely as the royal house grows rich. Once the Capetians have become the richest family in the whole territory or indeed the entire country, it is impossible to let the younger sons of the house live like petty knights. The reputation of the royal house demands that all its members, even the younger sons and daughters of the king, receive a fitting endowment, that is to say a sizeable area over which to rule, and from which they can live. In addition, now that the Capetians far surpass most other families in the country in property and wealth, the danger from severing a portion from their possessions is no longer so keenly felt. And so the enlargement of the Capetian dominion is accompanied by the steadily increasing size of the areas passing as apanages to the younger children of the kings. Disintegration sets in on a new basis.

Louis VI, the Fat, gives his son Robert the not very extensive county of Dreux. Philip Augustus, who brought about the family's first great rise from straitened circumstances, holds together his hard-won possessions with a firm hand; the only thing he gives up is a small estate, St Riquier, as his sister's dowry.

Louis VIII, however, lays down in his will that the counties of Artois, Poitiers, Anjou and Maine, that is to say, considerable portions of the family possessions, though never its heartland, shall pass as apanages to his sons.

Louis IX gives his sons Alençon, Perche and Clermont as apanages; Philip III endows a younger son with the county of Valois. But Poitiers, Alençon and Perche return to the Capetian possession when their princely owners die without male heirs.

In 1285 five counties—Dreux, Artois, Anjou, Clermont and Valois—are split off as apanages, and on the death of Charles the Fair in 1328 the number rises to nine.

When Philip of Valois inherits the estates and crown of the Capetians, the apanages of his house, Valois, Anjou and Maine, are reunited with the larger possessions of the ruling family. The county of Chartres returns to the crown estates with the death of another Valois. Philip himself gains a few new smaller dominions as well, among them Montpellier, which he buys from the King of Majorca. Under him, however, it is above all Dauphiné that comes into Capetian hands. Thereby Capetian expansion takes a major step eastwards beyond the traditional frontiers of the western Frankish empire, into the former Lotharingian region—an expansion that Philip the Fair had begun by acquiring the archbishopric of Lyons and through a closer association with the bishoprics of Toul and Verdun.

The manner in which Dauphiné comes into the possession of the Parisian rulers, however, is less characteristic of the relation between the centralizing and decentralizing forces of this period than of the importance of apanages. Dauphiné belongs to the Arlesian or Burgundian realm that arose, following the Lotharingian interregnum, east of the Rhône and the Saône. Its last ruler, Hubert II, bequeathes or, more exactly, sells his possessions to the Capetian heir, following the death of his only son, on a number of conditions. They include the payment of his considerable debts, and also the stipulation that Philip's second son, not his eldest, shall receive Dauphiné. Clearly the Dauphiné's owner wishes to give his land to someone rich enough to pay the sums he needs; by bequeathing it to the ruler of Francia he protects it from becoming a bone of contention for other neighbours after his death, for the Paris kings are strong enough to defend their acquisitions. And this is certainly not the only example of the attraction which the immense power of the Capetians held for weaker neighbours; the need for protection of those less strong is one of the factors that furthers the process of centralization and monopolization once it has reached a certain level.

But at the same time the old ruler whose heir has died clearly wishes to prevent his land, Dauphiné, from losing its independence entirely on passing into French ownership. This is why he demands that his domain shall be given to the king's second son as apanage. This demand obviously implies an expectation that this region shall become a ruling house in its own right and so preserve an independent existence. At that time apanaged regions were indeed beginning to develop more and more clearly in that direction.

Philip of Valois, however, does not abide by this agreement. He gives Dauphiné not to his younger but to his eldest son,

John, the heir to the throne, "in recognition", so his nomination declares, "that Dauphiné lies on the frontier, that a good and strong rule in Dauphiné is necessary for the defence and security of the Kingdom, and that if we acted otherwise, great danger to the future of the Kingdom might arise".[90] The danger attending the separation of districts for younger sons is thus fairly clearly perceived at this time; this is attested by a large number of pronouncements. But the need for the king to provide fittingly for his younger sons persists. He withheld Dauphiné from his younger son for security reasons; but in its place he gives him the Orléans region as a duchy and a number of counties as well.

And his eldest son, John the Good, the very man who receives Dauphiné in this way, goes a good deal further once he is king of the entire region on his father's death: he spreads bounty unstintingly. First he gives away two counties, then four viscounties. He endows his second son Louis with Anjou and Maine, his younger son receives the county of Poitiers, then Mâcon. Still larger gifts follow.

10. John the Good came to power in 1350. Under his predecessor, the long latent tension between the two largest powers and the two mightiest warrior houses in the western Frankish region had erupted; in 1337 began the chain of military conflicts known as the "Hundred Years' War". To the Plantagenets, the island rulers, all further expansion on the mainland is blocked; even their existing mainland possessions are under constant threat until they have destroyed Capetian rule and prevented the formation of another leading power on the Continent. Equally, further expansion by the Parisian rulers is very restricted and their position permanently threatened until the island-dwellers are subdued or at least expelled from the mainland. It is the strict compulsion of genuine competition which drives these houses and their dependents against one another, and which—since for a long time neither of the antagonists can decisively defeat the other—makes the struggle so protracted.

To begin with, however, the Paris kings are for a variety of reasons at a disadvantage. John the Good is captured by the English heir, the Prince of Wales, in the Battle of Poitiers in 1356 and sent to England. Immediately the tensions latent in his territory, now ruled as regent by the Dauphin Charles, who is not yet twenty years old, break out: revolution in Paris, peasant revolts, and knights plundering the countryside. The English troops, in alliance with another descendant of the Capetian house, the owner of previously apanaged regions, the King of Navarre, occupy large areas of western France; they even reach the vicinity of Paris. John the Good, to free himself, concludes a treaty with the Plantagenets and their allies handing over to them the whole inland area that Richard the Lion Heart had last controlled at the beginning of the twelfth century. But the States General of the French dominions, summoned in 1356 by the Dauphin, declare that this treaty should be neither approved nor carried out and that the only fitting answer is a well-fought war. And this is without doubt a clear expression of how strong interdependence has become within the great dominion of the Capetian heirs, of the autonomy and self-interest of the ruled that will slowly deprive the monarchy of its private monopoly character. At this stage, however, the development was only beginning. The war is begun anew and the Treaty of Brétigny, by which it is provisionally concluded in 1359, is somewhat more favourable to the Valois than the first concluded by John himself in England. Nevertheless roughly a quarter of what Philip the Fair had possessed has to be relinquished to the Plantagenets, above all Poitou, Saintonge, Aunis, Limousin, Périgord, Quercy, and Bigorre south of the Loire, together with a few other districts making up, with the older English possession Guyenne, the kingdom of Aquitaine; and further north Calais, the counties of Guines, Ponthieu and Montreuil-sur-Mer; in addition, three million golden crowns, instead of the four million demanded by the London treaty, as ransom for the king. But the latter, a worthy and chivalrous man, returns from prison clearly oblivious of the extent of his defeat. His conduct in this situation shows clearly to what extent he is still the sole authority in control of the territory remaining to him, which is one day to become "France", a state and a nation. He feels that his house must now all the more ostentatiously demonstrate its glory. The sense of inferiority resulting from defeat leads him to overemphasize his own prestige. And he considers that the dignity and glory of his house can find no better expression than by all his sons figuring as dukes at the ratification of the peace treaty. One of his first acts after his return from prison is therefore to make duchies from parts of his dominion as apanages for his sons. His eldest is already Duke of Normandy and Dauphin, the next, Louis, he makes Duke of Anjou and Maine; to the next, John, he gives Berry and Auvergne as his duchy; and to the youngest, Philip, Touraine. This is in the year 1360.

A year later, in 1361, the young, fifteen-year-old Duke of Burgundy dies. Two years previously he had married Margaret, the daughter and sole heir of the Count of Flanders; but he dies without leaving children. It is a large region that finds itself without a ruler on the unexpected death of the young Duke; it consists not only of the duchy of Burgundy proper, but also the counties of Boulogne and Auvergne, together with the county of Burgundy, the Franche-Comté and other areas beyond the traditional frontiers of the western Frankish empire. On grounds of somewhat complex family relationships, John the Good claims this whole estate for himself. There is no one to contest it with him and in 1363 he gives it to his youngest son Philip, whom he particularly loves; Philip fought especially bravely at his side in the Battle of Poitiers and accompanied him to prison. This is to be his apanage in place of Touraine, "we being mindful," says the King, "that we are enjoined by nature to give our children enough to allow them to honour the glory of their origin, and that we must be especially generous to those who have particularly merited it".[91]

Both the fact of these apanages and their motivation show unmistakably how far French territorial power still has the character of a family possession in this period; but they also show how this promotes fragmentation. No doubt strong tendencies are already operating in the opposite direction, tendencies restricting the private or domanial character of rule; the groups representing these opposed tendencies at the court will be discussed shortly. The personal character and individual fortunes of John the Good no doubt play a part in his particular propensity for richly endowing all the royal sons for the sake of family prestige. But this tendency clearly owes no less to the heightening of competition that found expression in the Hundred Years' War and which, after the Capetians' defeat, gives rise to a particularly insistent demonstration of the wealth of their heirs. At any rate, under John a specific tendency of large family possessions is merely reinforced, a tendency which, beyond a certain point of growth, none of the preceding representatives of the Capetian house had been able to resist. Its consequences are clear.

When John the Good dies, the existence and occupancy of the central function, despite the debilitation and the defeat, are in no way in doubt. This is an indication of how firmly the power of the central ruler was already founded on social functions other than that of army leader. The Dauphin, a physically weak man, but shrewd and experienced from the trials of his youth, assumes power under the name of Charles V. He is head of all the possessions left to the Capetians by the Treaty of Brétigny, including the apanaged ones. But looking closely at the distribution of power we can see clearly how, beneath the veil of the king's sovereignty, the centrifugal tendencies have gained renewed strength. Once again, a number of territorial formations emerge within the Capetian dominion that aspire more or less obviously to autonomy, and between which there is rivalry. But what gives this rivalry within the western Frankish region its special character is the fact that almost all those involved are descendants of the Capetian house itself. With few exceptions, it is apanaged men or their offspring who now face each other as potential competitors. There are, certainly, other major territorial rulers who are not members of the royal house, or at least not directly. But in the struggle for supremacy they are no longer protagonists of the first order.

The first of these at the time of John the Good is Charles the Bad, King of Navarre. His father, Philip of Evreux, was a grandson of Philip III, a nephew of Philip the Fair and of Charles of Valois; his mother was a granddaughter of Philip the Fair, a daughter of Louis X; in addition he himself is the son-in-law of John the Good. To him belong, besides the Pyrenean territory of Navarre, a number of previously apanaged regions from the Capetian possessions, above all the county of Evreux and parts of the duchy of Normandy. His possessions thus extend dangerously close to Paris itself.

Charles the Bad of Navarre is one of the first proponents of this struggle among apanaged family members of the Capetian house for supremacy in the western Frankish region, and ultimately for the crown. He is the chief mainland ally of the Plantagenets in the first phase of the Hundred Years' War. During this war he is for a time the military commander of Paris (1358); even the burghers of the city, even Étienne Marcel, is temporarily on his side; and his dream of wresting the crown from the other Capetian heir seems close to realization. To this end his membership of the King's family gives him an impetus, powers and claims that others lack.

The Plantagenet with whom he allies himself, Edward III, is likewise, though only from the female line of descent, a close relation of the Capetians. He too is a grandson of Philip III, a nephew of Philip the Fair and of Charles of Valois; his mother is a daughter of Philip the Fair, a niece of Charles of Valois, and he is thus at least as closely related to the Capetians as the French King opposing him, John the Good, the grandson of Charles of Valois.

Adjoining the mainland territory of the Plantagenets to the north are the regions that John the Good had given his younger sons, the territories of Louis, Duke of Anjou, John, Duke of Berry, and of Philip the Bold, Duke of Burgundy, together with the land of Louis, Duke of Bourbon. He, the Duke of Bourbon, is descended from the Capetians through a brother of Philip III, Robert, Count of Clermont, who married Beatrice, the heiress of Bourbon; his mother is a Valois, his sister the wife of Charles V; and he himself is thus on his mother's side an uncle of Charles VI, as the Dukes of Anjou, Burgundy and Berry are on the paternal side. These are the main actors in the struggles of the period of John the Good, Charles V and Charles VI. Apart from the Plantagenets and the Bourbons, they are all owners of apanaged parts of the Capetian inheritance, who are now on their side struggling to increase their family's power and finally to win supremacy.

The balance within these tensions first inclines, under Charles V, to the reigning Valois. When he dies, his son and successor is only twelve years old. Here, as always, circumstances—accidents from the point of view of the whole development—favour certain tendencies already inherent in the structure of society. The youth and weakness of the ruling Valois strengthens the centrifugal forces that have long been gathering, and releases the pent-up pressures.

Charles V had absorbed Dauphiné once and for all into his family possessions; he had recovered the Norman territories of the King of Navarre as well as a number of other apanaged lands like the duchy of Orléans and the county of Auxerre. But on his death there are already seven great feudal lords in the land, descended from St Louis and thus from the Capetian house; at the time they are called "princes des fleurs de lis";

and there are now—apart from a number of smaller and medium lords who have long ceased to play an independent part in the struggles for power[92]—only two major houses besides the Plantagenets whose members are not in direct male line of descent from the Capetian house, the dukes of Brittany and the counts of Flanders. But the Count of Flanders at this time has only one child, a daughter. For her hand and the future ownership of Flanders there arises, after the death of the young Duke of Burgundy to whom she was originally betrothed, an inevitable conflict between the Plantagenets and the Capetian heirs. After much vacillation the hand of the heiress of Flanders finally goes, with the help of the head of the Valois, Charles V, to the latter's younger brother Philip, who through his father's intervention has already become Duke of Burgundy. The marriages of great feudal lords were arranged from what we would today call a purely "business" point of view, for the sake of expansion and success in the territorial competition. Philip the Bold thus unites, after the death of the Count of Flanders, the latter's possessions with Burgundy; and of the great older feudal houses on the mainland only the duchy of Brittany remains. This older stratum, however, has now been replaced by a smaller circle of territorial rulers, stemming from offshoots of the Capetian house, and these are now driven into conflict by the mechanism of territorial competition. The compulsions which—owing to the low degree of integration or division of functions in any society with a barter economy, and particularly a warrior society—threaten the existence of a monopoly of power and possessions over large regions, tending to disintegrate property and reinforce centrifugal tendencies, have begun their work anew. Once again there occurs one of those shifts towards disintegration such as had led centuries earlier to the dissolution of the Carolingian dominions and then to the feudal social order of the twelfth century. Once again people to whom the central ruler has given land from his own large possessions, tend to make themselves independent and become rivals of the weakened central house. But the possibility of entering the competition is now limited to a few descendants of the original central house, a clear indication of how far the structure of human relations has changed in this society, how far this human network has already become, at least in its agrarian sector, a system with closed opportunities.

141

11. The rivalry between the most powerful "princes des fleurs de lis" erupts immediately after the death of Charles V in the struggle for the regency and guardianship of the heir to the throne, who is still a minor. Charles V had appointed his brother Louis, Duke of Anjou, as regent, his brother Philip, Duke of Burgundy, and his brother-in-law Louis, Duke of Bourbon, as guardians of his son. This was clearly the only thing he could do to prevent power passing entirely into the hands of a single man. But it is precisely complete power that Louis of Anjou, and Philip as well, are really pursuing. They wish to unite guardianship and regency. And the conflicts between the rival members of the royal house fill the whole reign of Charles VI, who possesses little power of decision and finally succumbs to a kind of madness.

The leading figures in the struggle for supremacy among the King's relations change from time to time. The place of Louis of Anjou as the strongest rival of the Burgundian Duke, for example, is taken at a certain stage in the struggle by the younger brother of Charles VI, Louis, who rules the duchy of Orléans as his apanage. But no matter how the persons change, the net-· work of compulsions impelling them remains the same: again and again two or three people within this, by now, very small circle of competitors come face to face, none of them prepared or able—on pain of annihilation—to allow any of the others to become stronger than himself. These conflicts between relations of the King, however, necessarily become intertwined with the larger conflict of the time, which is still very far from being decided—the struggle with the Plantagenets, whose offshoots likewise become embroiled in similar rivalries by reason of analogous mechanisms.

The situation of these members of the royal house must be visualized: all their life they are second or third. Their feelings tell them often enough that they might be better and stronger monarchs than the man who happens to be the legitimate heir to the crown and the main possessions. Between them and their goal stands often only one person, often only two or three. And there is no lack of examples in history of two or more such people dying in quick succession, opening the way to power to the next in line. But even then, there are often to be hard struggles with their rivals. In this situation the less powerful man hardly ever attains the throne if he belongs to only a secondary line of the family, though he may have the best claim. There are nearly always others who contest his claim; their claim may be worse but they will win if they are stronger. So those next in line to the throne, who already rule apanaged territories of various sizes, are preoccupied with creating and extending their basis of support, increasing their possessions, their income, their power. If they have no direct access to the throne, their rule shall be at least no less rich, mighty and ostentatious than that of their rivals, if possible outshining even the King's, who after all is no more than the greatest among all the rivals or competitors.

This is the situation and attitude of the closest relations of the weak Charles VI, his uncles—not all, but some of them—and also his brother. And with certain changes, with ever-diminishing chances for the second and third in line, this attitude, this situation, these tensions around the throne are transmitted through individuals of the most diverse talents, down to the time when, with Henry of Navarre, a relatively small territorial ruler for the last time becomes King of France; and as we have said, traces of these tendencies are to be found right up to the time of Louis XIV.

The strongest contestant among the *"princes des fleurs de lis"* is Philip the Bold, the youngest son of John the Good. To begin with he has only the duchy of Burgundy as his apanage. Then he unites with it—primarily through his marriage—the counties of Flanders, the Artois region, the county of Nevers and the barony of Doncy. His second son Antoine, Duke of Brabant and Lord of Antwerp, becomes by marriage Duke of Luxembourg. His son marries the heiress of Hainaut. These are the first steps of the Burgundian lords towards expansion in their own right, towards the foundation of a secure realm lying at least in part outside the sphere of the Paris kings, in the territory of present-day Holland.

A similar course of action is adopted by Charles VI's brother, Louis, the strongest rival of Philip the Bold in the struggle for supremacy in France. Both build with considerable haste and determination on their own family power. Louis first receives as apanage the duchy of Orléans, which under Charles V, after the death of his uncle, Philip V of Orléans, had been reunited with the crown possessions.

Then Louis obtains three or four counties and large estates in Champagne. He further acquires by purchase—with the aid of a large dowry from his wife Valentina Visconti—several counties including that of Blois. Finally, through his wife, he owns the county of Asti in Italian territory, and he has the reversion of a number of other Italian territories. The Burgundian expands in the direction of Holland, the Orléans into Italy. Within the former western Frankish territory itself, relations of ownership have been consolidated; the major parts of this region belong either to the London or to the Paris kings; and between them even a "prince des fleurs de lis" can only assert himself, only compete with one or other for supremacy, if he manages in one direction or another to build up a large domestic power of his own. As the earlier elimination struggles within the large area of post-Carolingian feudality had done previously, so now analogous tensions impel members of the far narrower circle of the great Capetian territorial lords to expand their land, to crave incessantly for more possessions. But as means to expansion, marriage, inheritance and purchase now play at least as important a part as war and feud. It is not only the Habsburgs who marry into greatness. Since relatively large property units with correspondingly great military potential have by now formed in this society, individuals, and individual warrior houses who want to rise at this stage, can only hope to survive a military confrontation if they have already gained control over territorial possessions which make them militarily competitive. And this too shows, therefore, how sharply the possibilities of competing in the sphere of major territorial ownership have diminished in this phase, and how the structure of tensions between people necessarily gives rise to the formation of monopolies of rule in regions above a certain order of size.

The Franco–English area at this time is still an interdependent territorial system. Every change in social power to the advantage or disadvantage of one of the rival houses, sooner or later affects the others and thus the equilibrium of the whole system. At any given time one can say with considerable accuracy where the central and where the less central tensions lie; the balance of power and its dynamics, its developmental curve, can be traced fairly precisely. And thus the Hundred Years' War is to be considered not only as the military encounters of a number of ambitious individual princes—although it is that too—but as one of the inevitable discharges within a tension-laden society consisting of territorial possessions of a certain size, as the competitive struggles between rival houses within an interdependent system of dominions with a very unstable equilibrium. The houses of Paris and London, gradually represented by two offshoots of the earlier royal houses, Valois and Lancaster, are, through the size of their possessions and military potential, the two main rivals. Sometimes the aspirations at least of the London rulers—occasionally even those in Paris—go as far as the wish to unite the whole western Frankish area, the mainland territories and the extended island realm, under one rule. Only in the course of these struggles themselves does it become unmistakably clear how great, at this stage of social development, are the resistances to the military conquest, and above all the subsequent internal cohesion, of so large and disparate a territory under the same rule and the same governmental machinery. The question may be raised whether, at this stage of social development, the creation of a central monopoly and the permanent integration of mainland and island territories under London rule would have been possible even if the Valois had been completely defeated by the island kings and their allies. However that may be, it is at any rate the houses of Paris and London that primarily compete for supremacy in the same area, and all the other competitive tensions within this area, above all those between the different branches of the Paris house itself, crystallize about this main tension of the whole territorial system; thus the Burgundian Valois, for example, stand now on one side of this central struggle, now on the other.

But the growth of the division of functions, and of interdependence beyond the local level, not only brings the different units of the enlarged western Frankish territorial society closer together as friend and foe. Less obviously, but unmistakably nevertheless, interdependencies and shifts in the territorial balance begin at this time to be discernible over the larger area of western Europe as a whole. The Franco–English territorial society gradually becomes, in the course of this growing integration, more and more a partial system within the encompassing European one. In the Hundred Years' War this growing interdependence within larger areas, which doubtless was never entirely absent, manifests itself clearly. German and Italian princes already engage their interests and power in the struggle within the Anglo–French sector, even though they as yet play only a peripheral role. This is the first sign of what was to show itself

145

much more fully a few centuries later in the Thirty Years' War; the European Continent as a whole begins to become an interdependent system of countries with its own dynamic equilibrium, within which each shift of power directly or indirectly involves every unit, every country. A few further centuries on, in the 1914–18 war, the first "World War" as it has been called, we can see early signs of how tensions and shifts of balance within the same ever-advancing process of integration now affect units over a far wider area, countries in distant parts of the world. The nature and stages of the monopolization towards which the tensions of this worldwide interweaving are moving, like their possible outcome, the larger units of rule that may arise out of these struggles—all this appears only vaguely to us if it hardly has risen above the horizon of our consciousness at all. But it is scarcely different with the territorial houses and groups of people enmeshed in the Hundred Years' War; there, too, each unit feels only the direct threat that the size or increase of others means for it; for the larger units that slowly come into being in these struggles, France and England, as we call them, are scarcely more present in the consciousness of those forming them than "Europe" as a political unit is for us.

How the individual tensions between rival groups and houses are resolved, how the balance between the main protagonists, the English Lancasters, the French Valois and the Burgundian Valois, tilts now this way and now that, how the English seize a yet larger portion of French land and even the French kingship, and how finally, through the appearance of Joan of Arc, all the forces supporting the French Valois gather themselves in successful resistance and bring back the weak king first to Rheims for his coronation and then as victor to Paris—accounts of all this are readily available elsewhere.

What is decided in this way is the question whether London and the Anglo–Norman island, or Paris and the dominion of the rulers of Francia, are to become the centre of crystallization of the former western Frankish region. The issue is decided in favour of Paris. London's rule is confined to the island. The Hundred Years' War accelerates and makes irreversible the breach between the mainland territory, that really only now becomes "la France", that is, the domain of the rulers of Francia, and the overseas region that previously was nothing but a colonial territory of mainland rulers. The first consequence of this war is thus a disintegration. The islanders, the descendants of the Continental conquerors and the natives, have become a separate society going their own way, forming their own specific institutions of government, and developing their mixed language into a specific entity of a new kind. Neither of the contending rivals has succeeded in gaining and keeping control of the whole area. The French kings and their people have finally lost their claim to the island realm; the English kings' attempt to defeat their Paris rivals and recolonize the mainland has failed. If the people of the island need new land, new areas to colonize, new markets, they must from now on seek them further afield. The English kings are eliminated from the mainland struggles for the French crown. It is a process not unlike that which, centuries later, in the community of German territorial states, ended with the victory of Prussia over Austria. In both cases, as a result of a disintegration, integration was confined to a smaller area and thus made very much easier.

But through the repulsion of the English from the mainland, the elimination of the English kings from the struggle for supremacy there, the tension and balance within this area are altered. As long as the London and Paris kings roughly balance each other, and as long as the contest between them constitutes the main axis of tension, rivalries between the various territorial rulers on the mainland have only secondary importance. They can have considerable influence on whether the main struggle is decided in favour of the Paris or the London rulers; but they cannot directly cause any of the other competitors to take first place.

Now, with the departure of the English, the competition between the various mainland territorial rulers, above all the rivalry between different branches of the Capetian house itself, becomes the dominant tension. The outcome of the Hundred Years' War did not decide, or at any rate not finally, by which of these branches and within which frontiers the integration of the mainland territories of the former western Frankish regions was to be accomplished. In this direction, therefore, the struggles continue.

In the last years of Charles VII there are, besides the Paris house, at least eight other large houses which can pit their weight in the decisive struggles for supremacy. They are the houses of Anjou, Alençon, Armagnac, Bourbon, Burgundy,

Brittany, Dreux and Foix. Each of these houses is itself already represented by several branches; the mightiest is the house of Burgundy which, based on Burgundy and Flanders as the core of its family power, is working with great tenacity and single-mindedness to establish a major dominion, related to the earlier Lotharingia, between the empire and France. The rivalry between Burgundy and the Paris kings now forms the main axis of the system of feudal territories from which, with the latter's victory, "France" is finally to emerge. But to begin with, the houses of Bourbon and Brittany are also power-centres of major importance.

With the exception of the latter, the ducal house of Brittany, the members of all the houses named are descendants and relations of people apanaged by the Capetian house, and therefore its offshoots. Seigneurial, post-Carolingian feudality has "contracted", as one writer has put it, to a "princely", a Capetian feudality.[93] From the conflicts of the many great and small warrior houses of the western Frankish region, a single house has emerged victorious. The region has now become, by and large, the monopoly of descendants of the Capetians.

But in the course of generations the family and its accumulated territorial possessions have again become dispersed; and now the different branches of the family are struggling for supremacy. Monopoly formation does not happen in quite such a straight line as appears at first sight. What we have before us here—in the period following the Hundred Years' War—is not yet a complete concentration or centralization of power in one place and in one pair of hands, but a stage on the way to absolute monopoly.

A state of highly restricted competition has been established. For all those who do not belong to a particular family, the chance of acquiring and owning a major dominion, or enlarging their existing one, and thus taking part in further elimination struggles, has become extremely small.

VI

The Last Stages of the Free Competitive Struggle and the Final Monopoly Position of the Victor

12. What here gives the monopolizing process its special character—and what later observers, particularly those of the twentieth century, of course, must bear in mind in looking back—is the fact that social functions which have become separated in recent times were still more or less undifferentiated in that earlier phase. It has already been stressed that the social role of the great feudal lord, or prince, the function of being the richest man, the owner of the largest means of production in his region, is at first completely indistinguishable from that of being the owner of military power and jurisdiction. Functions today represented by different people and groups of people connected through the division of labour, e.g. the functions of great land-owner and of head of government, form here, inseparably bound together, a kind of private property. This is partly explained by the fact that in this society, which still had a primarily if diminishingly barter-based economy, land was the most important means of production, whereas in later society it has been supplanted in this role by money, the incarnation of the division of functions. It is explained no less, however, by the fact that in the later phase the key to all monopoly power, the monopoly of physical, of military violence, is a firmly established social institution extending over large areas, whereas in the preceding stage it only slowly develops through centuries of struggle, first of all in the form of a private, family monopoly.

We are accustomed to distinguish two spheres, "economics" and "politics", and two kinds of social function, "economic" and "political" ones. By "economic" we mean the whole network of activities and institutions serving the creation and acquisition of means of consumption and production. But we also take it for granted, in thinking of "economics", that the production and, above all, the acquisition of these means normally takes placed without threat or use of physical or military violence. Nothing is less self-evident. For all warrior societies with a barter economy—and not only for them—the sword is a frequent and indispensable instrument for acquiring means of production, and the threat of violence an indispensable means of production.

149

Only when the division of functions is very far advanced; only when, as the result of long struggles, a specialized monopoly administration has formed that exercises the functions of rule as its social property; only when a centralized and public monopoly of force exists over large areas, can competition for means of consumption and production take its course largely without the intervention of physical violence; and only then do the kind of economy and the kind of struggle exist that we are accustomed to designate by the terms "economy" and "competition" in a more specific sense.

The competitive relationship itself is a far more general and all-encompassing social fact than appears when the concept of "competition" is restricted to economic structures[94]—usually those of the nineteenth and twentieth centuries. A situation of competition arises whenever a number of people strive for the same opportunities, when demand exceeds the possibilities of satisfaction, whether these possibilities are controlled by monopolists or not. The particular kind of competition that has been discussed here, so-called "free competition", is characterized by the fact that demand is directed at opportunities not yet controlled by anyone who does not himself belong to the circle of competitors. Such a phase of "free competition" occurs in the history of many societies, if not all. A "free competitive struggle" thus arises also, for example, when land and military opportunities are so evenly distributed among several interdependent parties that none of them has clearly the best chance, the greatest social power. It arises, therefore, in that phase in the relationship between feudal warrior houses or between states, when none of the parties has clearly outgrown the rivalry of others, and when no organized, centralized monopoly of power exists. Likewise, a "free competitive struggle" arises when the financial opportunities of many interdependent people are fairly evenly distributed; in both cases, the struggle is intensified with the growth of population and demand, unless the opportunities grow at the same rate.

The course taken by these free competitive struggles, moreover, is relatively unaffected by the fact that, in one case, they are brought about by the threat and use of physical violence and, in the other, only by the threat of social decline, the loss of economic independence, financial ruin or material distress. In the struggles of the feudal warrior houses, the two forms of violence that we distinguish as physical/military and economic force, acted together more or less as one. These feudal conflicts have, indeed, a functional analogy within modern society both in free economic competition, such as the struggles of a number of firms for supremacy in the same commercial field, and in the struggles of states for predominance within a particular territorial system, conflicts that are resolved by physical violence.

In all these cases what manifests itself as struggles within the sphere not yet monopolized is only one layer of the continuous, general competition for limited opportunities pervading the whole of society. The opportunities open to those engaged in free competition, that is, competition free of monopoly, themselves constitute an unorganized monopoly from which all others are excluded who are unable to compete because they have far smaller resources. These others are thus directly or indirectly dependent on the "free" competitors, and are engaged among themselves in an unfree competition for their limited opportunities. The pressure exerted within the relatively independent section stands in the closest functional relationship to that exerted on all sides by those already dependent on monopolized opportunities.

In feudal as in modern times, free competition for chances not yet centrally organized and monopolized, tends through all its ramifications towards the subjugation and elimination of an ever-increasing number of rivals, who are destroyed as social units or fall into dependence; towards the accumulation of possibilities in the hands of an ever-diminishing number of rivals; towards domination and finally monopoly. Again, the social event of monopolization is not confined to the processes which normally come to mind today when "monopolies" are mentioned. The accumulation of possibilities that can be converted into sums of money or at least expressed as such, represents only one historical shift among many others in the process of monopolization. Functionally similar processes, that is, tendencies towards an overall structure of human relationships in which individuals or groups can by direct or indirect threat of violence, restrict and control the access of others to certain contested possibilities—such processes occur in a variety of forms at very different points in human history.

In the struggles in both these periods, the actual social existence of all the participants is at stake. That is the compulsion behind these struggles. That is what makes such struggles, and their outcome, so inescapable wherever the basic situation of free competition arises. Once a society has embarked on a movement of this kind, each social unit in the sphere not yet monopolized, whether these units are knightly families, economic enterprises, territories or states, is always confronted by the same choice.

Either they can be conquered—whether they choose to struggle or not—which in extreme cases means: imprisonment, violent death or material distress, perhaps starvation, or in the mildest: social decline, loss of independence, absorption by a larger social complex; and thereby the destruction of what gave their lives meaning, value and continuity, even if these things appear to their contemporaries, or to those coming after them, as contrary to their own meaning, social existence and "continuity", and thus as entirely deserving of destruction.

Or they may repel and conquer their nearest rivals. Then their life, their social existence, their striving attains fulfilment; they seize the contested opportunities. The mere preservation of social existence demands, in the situation of free competition, this constant enlargement. Whoever does not rise, falls back. Victory, therefore, means in the first place—whether this is intended or not—dominance of one's closest rivals and their reduction to a position of dependence. The gain of one is here necessarily the other's loss, whether in terms of land, military capacity, money or any other substance of social power. But beyond this, victory sooner or later means confrontation and conflict with a rival of the new size; once again the situation enforces the expansion of one, and the absorption, subjugation, humiliation or destruction of the other. The shift in power relationships, the establishment of domination may be accomplished by open military or economic force, or by peaceful agreement; but however it comes about, all these rivalries are impelled, whether slowly or quickly, through a series of downfalls and aggrandisements, rises and descents, fulfilments and destructions of meaning, in the direction of a new social order, a monopoly order that none of the participants has really intended or foreseen, and which replaces free competition by competition subject to monopoly. And it is only the formation of such monopolies that finally makes it possible to regulate the distribution

152

of opportunities—and thus the conflicts themselves—in the interests of the smooth-functioning collaboration to which people are bound for better or worse.

Alternatives of this kind confront the warrior families of medieval society too. And the resistance of the great feudal lords, and finally of Capetian or princely feudality, to the increase of royal power is to be understood in this sense. The king in Paris is, both in fact and in the minds of the other territorial rulers, one of themselves, not more; he is a rival, and from a certain time on the most powerful, most threatening rival. If he wins, their existence, social if not physical, is destroyed; they lose what in their eyes gives their life meaning and splendour, their independent rule, the control of their family possessions; their honour, their rank, their social standing is at worst annihilated, at best diminished. If they win, centralization, domination, monopoly, the state are for a time obstructed; Burgundy, Anjou, Brittany, and so on, remain for the time being more or less independent dominions. This may appear senseless to some contemporaries, above all the royal officials, and even to us in retrospect; for by virtue of our different state of social integration we tend not to identify with such limited geographical units. For them, the rulers of Burgundy or Brittany and a large number of their dependents, however, it is extremely worthwhile to prevent the formation of an over-mighty central government in Paris, for this means their downfall as independent social units.

But if they win, sooner or later the victors confront each other as rivals; and the ensuing tensions and conflicts cannot end until once again a clearly superior power has emerged. *Just as, in the capitalist society of the nineteenth and, above all, the twentieth century, the general impulsion towards economic monopolization shows itself clearly, regardless of which particular competitor triumphs and outgrows the others; just as, concurrently, an analogous tendency towards the clearer domination that precedes each monopolization, each larger integration, is becoming ever more apparent in the contest of "states", first of all in Europe; in the same way the struggles between medieval warrior houses and later the great feudal and territorial rulers, show a general impulsion towards monopoly formation.* The only difference is that, there, the process takes place in a sphere in which land ownership and rule form an inseparable unity, whereas later—with the increasing use of money—it takes on the combined form of centralization of taxes and of control of all the instruments that serve physical subjugation.

13. It is in an intermediate period between these two stages that, in the second half of the fifteenth century, following the death of Charles VII, the rivalry between the French branch of the Valois, the Burgundian branch together with the remainder of Capetian feudality, and the last representative of the great pre-Capetian feudality, the Duke of Brittany, comes to a head. Once again the centrifugal forces gather themselves for a common assault on the Parisian Valois, Louis XI, whose wealth and power are now particularly dangerous to them all, following the elimination of his chief opponent hitherto, the King of England. And as the centre of gravity inclined ever more threateningly towards the French ruling complex, the Burgundian Valois, Charles the Bold, once stated quite clearly what most of the King's competitors must have felt and desired in the face of this threat to their social existence: "Instead of one king I wish we had six!"[95]

Louis XI himself by no means identifies with his royal task from the first. On the contrary. As crown prince he acts very much in the same way and in the same spirit as the other great Capetian feudal lords who are working for the disintegration of the French territorial complex; and he lives for a time at the court of the strongest rival of the Paris monarchy, the Duke of Burgundy. This is certainly bound up with facts that may be called personal, above all with the peculiar hatred existing between Louis and his father. But it is also further evidence of the specific individualization of the richest house in the land, which in its turn is bound up with the apanaging of each and every prince. Whatever the earlier causes of Louis' hatred for his father may have been, the control of a territory of his own unites his feelings and actions in a common front with his father's other rivals. Even after his accession to the throne, he first thinks of avenging himself on those who had been hostile to him as Dauphin, including many loyal servants of the monarchy, and of rewarding those who had showed friendship for him then, including many opponents of the monarchy. Power is still, to a considerable extent, private property dependent on the personal inclinations of the ruler. But it also has, like any very large possession, a very strict regularity of its own that its wielder cannot contravene without destroying it. Very soon the enemies of the monarchy become the enemies of Louis; those supporting the monarchy become *his* friends and servants. His personal ambitions become one with the traditional ambitions of the central ruler in Paris, and his personal qualities—his curiosity, his almost pathological desire to penetrate all the secrets around him, his cunning, the undeviating violence of his hatred and of his affection, even the naive and intense piety that causes him to woo saints, and especially the patron saints of his enemies, with gifts, as if they were venal human beings—all this now unfolds in the direction in which he is impelled by his social position as ruler of the French territorial possessions; the struggle against centrifugal forces, against the rival feudal lords, becomes the decisive task of his life. And the house of Burgundy, the friends from his time as crown prince, become—as the immanent logic of his royal function demands—his main opponents.

The struggle thus confronting Louis XI is by no means an easy one. At times the Paris government seems on the verge of collapse. But at the end of his reign—partly through the power which his great possessions put at his disposal, partly through the skill with which he wields it, and partly through a number of accidents that come to his aid—his rivals are more or less definitively beaten. In 1476 Charles the Bold of Burgundy is defeated at Granson and Murten by the Swiss, whom Louis has incited to oppose him. In 1477 Charles is killed while attempting to conquer Nancy. Thus the chief rival of the French Valois among the competing Capetian heirs—and, after the elimination of the English, their strongest rival of all—is himself eliminated from the conflict between the western Frankish territorial lords. Charles the Bold leaves an only daughter, Marie; for her hand and inheritance Louis competes with the power which is now gradually emerging in the larger European context as the main rival of the Parisian monarchy, the house of Habsburg. As the elimination contests within the western Frankish area draw to an end with the predominance and monopoly of a single house, rivalry between this victorious house, which now begins to become the centre of the whole country, and powers of a similar magnitude outside the country, move into the foreground. In the competition for Burgundy the Habsburgs win their first victory; with the hand of Maria, Maximillian gains a large part of the

Burgundian inheritance. This creates a situation that feeds the rivalry between the Habsburgs and the Paris kings for more than two centuries. However, the duchy of Burgundy itself, and two further direct annexations from Burgundian lands, return to the crown estates of the Valois. The parts of the Burgundian inheritance that are particularly needed to round off French territory are incorporated in it.

There are now only four houses left within the western Frankish region that control territories of any significance. The most powerful or, more exactly, the most important and traditionally most independent, is the house of Brittany. But none of these houses can now match the social power of Paris; the French king's rule has now grown beyond the reach of competition from neighbouring territorial rulers. He takes up a monopoly position among them. Earlier or later, by treaty, violence or accident, they have all become dependent on him and lost their autonomy.

It is—if one will—fortuitous that towards the end of the fifteenth century a Duke of Brittany leaves an only daughter on his death, as the Duke of Burgundy had done before him. The conflict which this accident unleashes shows very exactly the existing constellation of forces. Of the remaining territorial rulers of the old western Frankish area, none is now strong enough to contest the Breton inheritance with the Paris ruler. As with the Burgundian inheritance, the rival for this also comes from outside. Here, too, the question is whether a Habsburg or a Valois shall take Brittany by marriage, whether Charles VIII, the young son of Louis XI, or Maximillian of Habsburg, the Holy Roman Emperor and lord of Burgundy, whose hand has again become free through the death of the Burgundian heiress. As in the case of Burgundy, the Habsburg again succeeds in marrying the young Anne of Brittany, at least provisionally. But after much contention—finally decided by the opinion of the Breton estates—the heiress's hand goes after all to Charles of France. The Habsburgs protest, there is war between the rivals and finally a compromise: the Franche-Comté, which lies outside French territory and does not belong to the traditional western Frankish complex of lands, is ceded to the Habsburgs; in exchange Maximillian recognizes Charles VIII's acquisition of Brittany. And when Charles VIII dies childless, his successor, Louis XII, a Valois from the Orléans branch, promptly has his existing marriage annulled by the Pope and marries the twenty-one-year-old widow of his predecessor, in order to preserve her inheritance, Brittany, for the crown estates which have now become his. When this marriage produces only daughters, the king marries his eldest, who will receive Brittany as heiress to her mother, to the heir-apparent to the throne, the nearest living descendant of the family, Count Francis of Angoulême. The danger that this important territory might fall into the hands of a rival, above all a Habsburg, always leads to the same course of action. And so, under the pressure of the competitive mechanism, the last territory in the western Frankish region that has preserved its autonomy throughout all the elimination struggles, is slowly integrated into the dominion of the Paris king. At first, when the heir to the apanage of Angoulême becomes king under the name of Francis I, Brittany retains a certain autonomy. The independent-mindedness of its Estates remains very much alive; but the military power of a single territory is now far too small to withstand the great dominions now surrounding it. In 1532 the incorporation of Brittany into the French domain is institutionally confirmed. Only the duchy of Alençon, the counties of Nevers and Vendôme, and the dominions of Bourbon and Albret[96] now remain in the former western Frankish region as independent territories, that is, areas not belonging either to the Paris kings or—like Flanders and Artois—to the Habsburgs. Even though some of their rulers, such as the lord of Albret or the house of Bourbon, may still work as best they can to enlarge their dominions, and may still dream of royal crowns,[97] their regions are really no more than enclaves within the dominions of the French kings. The wearers of the crown are now entirely beyond the competition of these other territorial lords. The houses that once existed here have lapsed into dependence or disappeared. Within the former western Frankish region the Paris kings are now finally without rivals; from now on their position takes on more and more clearly the character of an absolute monopoly. But outside the western Frankish region similar processes have been taking place, even though the monopoly process and the elimination struggles have nowhere advanced to the point they have reached in France. All the same, the Habsburgs, too, have now assembled family possessions which, in military and financial potential, far surpass most of the other dominions on the European mainland. What earlier revealed itself through the Burgundian and Breton successions now emerges, from the beginning of the sixteenth century onwards, more and more clearly: the house of the Habsburg emperors and the House of the French kings, represented at this stage by Charles V and Francis I, now stand face to face as rivals on a new scale. Both hold, to slightly varying degrees, monopoly power over a very large area; they are competing for opportunities and supremacy within a larger sphere which as yet has no monopoly ruler, and are thus in a situation of "free competition". And accordingly, the rivalry between them now becomes, for a long period, a main axis within a larger evolving European system of tensions.

14. In size the French dominion is considerably smaller than that of the Habsburgs. But it is far more centralized and, above all, self-contained, better protected militarily by "natural frontiers". Its western boundaries are the Channel and the Atlantic; the whole coastal area as far down as Navarre is now in the hands of the French kings. The southern boundary is the Mediterranean; here too the whole coast—with the exception of Roussillon and the Cerdagne—belongs to the French rulers. To the east the Rhône forms the frontier with the county of Nice and the duchy of Savoy; for the time being the frontier projects beyond the Rhône as far as the Alps only in Dauphiné and Provence. North of this, opposite the Franche-Comté, the Rhône and the Saône continue to form the frontier of the kingdom; in its middle and lower parts the Saône is somewhat overstepped. In the north and north-east the frontiers fall further short of those of present-day France; only by taking possession of the archbishoprics of Metz, Toul and Verdun does the kingdom approach the Rhine; but these are for the time being enclaves, outposts within the German Empire; the frontier with it lies only slightly to the west of Verdun and further north, roughly in the region of Sedan; like the Franche-Comté, Flanders and Artois belong to the Habsburgs. One of the first issues to be decided in the struggle for supremacy against them, is how far the frontier will move in this area. For a considerable period French rule is contained within these limits. Only in the years between 1610 and 1659 are the Artois region, together with the area between France and the three archbishoprics and—a new enclave within the empire—upper and lower Alsace, assimilated to France; only now does France approach the Rhine.[98] A great

part of the territory forming France today has now been assembled under a single rule. All that is in question is the extent of this unit's possible expansion, the question whether and where it will finally find "natural", i.e. easily defensible, frontiers within the European system of tensions.

Anyone looking back from within a state, a society with a stable and centralized monopoly of physical violence, a Frenchman living in France or a German in Germany, is apt to take for granted the existence of this monopoly of violence, and the unification of areas of this size and kind, as something natural and useful, to regard them as something consciously planned; and consequently, he tends to observe and evaluate the particular actions which led up to them in terms of their direct use to an order that seems to him self-evident and self-justifying. He is inclined to be less concerned with the actual dilemmas and necessities out of which groups and persons acted formerly, less with their direct plans, wishes and interests, than with the question whether this or that was good or bad for the thing with which he identifies. And, just as if the actors of the past already had before their eyes a prophetic vision of that future which is to him so self-evident and, perhaps, so emphatically affirmed, he praises or condemns these actors, awards them marks according to whether their actions did or did not lead directly to the desired result.

But through such censures, through such expressions of personal satisfaction, through this subjectivistic or partisan view of the past, we usually block our access to the elementary formative regularities and mechanisms, to the real structural history and sociogenesis of historical formations. These formations always develop in the struggle between opposed or, more exactly, in the resolution of ambivalent interests. What finally meets its end in such conflicts or merges into new formations, as the princely dominions merged into the royal ones and royal power into the bourgeois state, is no less indispensable to these new formations than the victorious opponent. Without violent actions, without the motive forces of free competition, there would be no monopoly of force, and thus no pacification, no suppression and control of violence over large areas.

The convolutions of the movement leading to the integration of ever-larger regions around the duchy of Francia as the centre of crystallization, illustrate how much the final integration of the western Frankish area was the outcome of a series of elimination contests in a compelling process of interweavings, and how little it resulted from a prophetic vision or a rigorous plan to which all the individual parties adhered.

"Unquestionably," Henri Hauser once said,[99] "there is always something slightly artificial in placing oneself in an *a posteriori* position and looking at history from back to front, as if the administrative monarchy and the centralized France of Henry II had been destined since the beginning of time to be born and to live within determined limits. . . ."

Only if we are transported for a moment into the landscape of the past, and see the struggles between the many warrior houses, their vital necessities, their immediate goals; only if, in a word, we have the full precariousness of their struggles and their social existence before our eyes, can we understand how probable was the formation of a monopoly within this area, but how uncertain its centre and its boundaries.

To some extent the same is true of the French kings and their representatives as was once said of the American pioneer: "He didn't want all the land; he just wanted the land next to his."[100]

This simple and precise formulation expresses very well how, from the interweaving of countless individual interests and intentions—whether tending in the same direction or in divergent and hostile directions—something comes into being that was planned and intended by none of these individuals, yet has emerged nevertheless from their intentions and actions. And really this is the whole secret of social figurations, their compelling dynamics, their structural regularities, their process character and their development; this is the secret of sociogenesis and of relational dynamics.

The representatives of the French monarchy no doubt possessed, by virtue of their more central position in the later phases of the movement, rather larger intentions and radii of action within the process of integration than the individual American pioneers. But they, too, saw distinctly only the next few steps and the next piece of land that they had to obtain to prevent it going to another, and to prevent a troublesome neighbour or rival from growing stronger than themselves. And if some among them did harbour an image of a larger realm, this image was for a long period rather the shadow of past monopolies, a reflection of the Carolingian and western Frankish monarchies;

160

more a product of memory than of prophecy or a new concept of the future. Here, as always, from the tangle of innumerable individual interests, plans and actions, a single development emerged, a regularity governing the totality of these entangled people and intended by none of them, and giving rise to a formation that none of the actors had really planned, a state: France. For this very reason the understanding of a formation of this kind requires a breakthrough to a still little-known level of reality: to the level of the immanent regularities of social relationships, the field of relational dynamics.

VII

The Distribution of Power Ratios within the Unit of Rule:
Their Significance for the Central Authority:
The Formation of the "Royal Mechanism"

15. Two main phases have been distinguished in the development of monopolies: the phase of free competition tending to the formation of private monopolies, and the gradual transformation of "private" into "public" monopolies. But on closer consideration this movement does not consist of a simple succession of tendencies. Even though the "opening-up" of monopolies in the course of such change only reaches its full extent and becomes a dominant phenomenon at a late stage, the structures leading up to it have already been present and active in the phase in which, through numerous struggles, the power monopoly slowly emerged in the form of a private possession.

Certainly the French Revolution, for example, represents a massive step on the way to the opening-up of the monopoly of taxation and physical force in France. Here, these monopolies do indeed pass into the power, or at least the institutionally secured control, of broad social classes. The central ruler, whatever title he may bear, and all those exercising monopoly power, become more unequivocally than before functionaries among others within the whole web of a society based on the division of functions. Their functional dependence on the representatives of other social functions has become so great that it is clearly expressed in the organization of society. However, this functional dependence of the monopolies and their incumbents on other functions of society was already present in the preceding phases. It was merely less developed, and for this reason was not expressed in a direct and unconcealed way in the organization and institutional structure of society. And for this reason the power of the monopoly ruler had at first more or less the character of a "private possession".

16. As noted above tendencies towards a kind of "opening-up" of the monopoly of a single family show themselves under certain conditions—namely, when the area it controls or its possessions begin to grow very large—even in societies with a barter economy. What we call "feudalism", what was described above as the action of centrifugal forces, is no more than an expression of such tendencies. They indicate that the functional dependence of a lord on his servants or subjects, that is, on broader strata, is increasing; they lead to the transfer of control of land and military power from the hands of a single warrior family and its head, first to the hierarchy of its closest servants and relations, and then in some cases to the whole warrior society. It has already been pointed out that in feudal society the "opening-up", as a result of the peculiarities of land-ownership and the instruments of violence, means a dissolution of the centralized—even if only loosely centralized—monopoly; it leads to the transformation of a single large monopoly possession into a number of smaller ones, and so to a decentralized and less organized form of monopoly. As long as land ownership remains the dominant form of ownership, new shifts in this or that direction can take place: the establishment of supremacy within free competition, the assembly of large areas of land and masses of warriors under a single central lord; waves of decentralization under his successors, new struggles in different strata of their servants, their relations or their subjects, new attempts to gain supremacy. And this whole ebb and flow of centralization and decentralization can sometimes—depending on geographical or climatic factors, on particular economic forms, on the kind of animals and plants on which the life of people depends, and always in conjunction with the traditional structure of organized religion—all this can lead to a complex medley of social deposits from the various shifts. The history of other, non-European, feudal societies everywhere follows the same pattern in this respect. But however much this kind of ebb and flow is detectable in the development of France, in comparison with

most other societies the movement here follows a relatively straight path.

This rhythm that over and over again threatens the dissolution of the great monopolies of power and possessions is modified and finally broken only to the extent that, with the growing division of functions in society, money rather than land becomes the dominant form of property. Only then is the large centralized monopoly, in passing from the hands of one ruler or a small circle into the control of a larger circle, not broken up into numerous smaller areas as was the case in each advance of feudalization; instead, it slowly becomes, centralized as it is, an instrument of functionally divided society as a whole, and so first and foremost a central organ of what we call the state.

The development of money and exchange, together with the social formations carrying them, stands in a permanent reciprocal relationship to the form and development of monopoly power within a particular area. These two series of developments, constantly intertwining, drive each other upwards. The form and development of power monopolies are influenced on all sides by the differentiation of society, the advance of money use and the formation of classes earning and possessing money. On the other hand, the success of the division of labour itself, the securing of routes and markets over large areas, the standardization of coinage and the whole monetary system, the protection of peaceful production from physical violence and an abundance of other measures of co-ordination and regulation, are highly dependent on the formation of large centralized monopoly institutions. The more, in other words, the work processes and the totality of functions in a society become differentiated, the longer and more complex the chains of individual actions which must interlock for each action to fulfil its social purpose, the more clearly one specific characteristic of the central organ emerges: *its role as supreme co-ordinator and regulator for the functionally differentiated figuration at large.* From a certain degree of functional differentiation onward, the complex web of intertwining human activities simply cannot continue to grow or even to function without co-ordinating organs at a correspondingly high level of organization. Their role is certainly not entirely lacking in the central institutions of more simply organized and less differentiated societies. Even a society as loosely bound together as that of the many autarkic estates of the ninth and tenth centuries needed a supreme co-ordinator under certain conditions. If a powerful enemy threatened from outside, necessitating war, someone was needed to ensure the collaboration of the many knights, to co-ordinate their activity and to take the final decisions. In this situation the interdependence of the many scattered rulers re-emerged more clearly. Each individual was threatened if the whole army failed to co-operate. And as, in this situation, the dependence of all on a central ruler, the king, increased considerably, so too did his importance, his social power—provided he fulfilled his social function, provided he was not beaten. But when the external threat or possibility of expansion lapsed, the dependence of individuals and groups on a supreme co-ordinating and regulating centre was relatively slight. This function only emerges as a permanent, specialized task of the central organ when society as a whole becomes more and more differentiated, when its cellular structure slowly but incessantly forms new functions, new professional groups and classes. Only then do regulating and co-ordinating central organs for maintaining the whole social network become so indispensable that while alterations in the power structure can change their occupants and even their organization, they cannot dissolve them, as happened earlier in the course of feudalization.

17. The formation of particularly stable and specialized central organs for large regions is one of the most prominent features of Western history. As we have said, there are central organs of some sort in every society. But as the differentiation and specialization of social functions have attained a higher level in the West than in any other society on earth—and as they begin to reach this level elsewhere only through an impetus coming from the West—it is in the West that specialized central organs first attain a hitherto unknown degree of stability. However, the central organs and their functionaries do not necessarily gain social power corresponding to their rising importance as supreme social co-ordinators and regulators. One might suppose that, with advancing centralization and the stricter control and supervision of the whole social process by stable authorities, the rift between rulers and ruled would be deepened. The actual course of history shows a different picture. Western history is certainly not lacking in phases when the powers of the central authority are so great and wide that we may speak with some

justice of the hegemony of single central rulers. But precisely in the more recent history of many Western societies there are also phases when, despite their centralization, the control of the centralized institutions themselves is so dispersed that it is difficult to discern clearly who are the rulers and who the ruled. The scope for decision vested in the central functions varies. Sometimes it increases; then the people exercising these functions take on the aspect of "rulers". Sometimes it diminishes, without centralization, or the importance of the central organs as the highest centre of co-ordination and regulation, being reduced. In other words, in the case of the central organs as of all other social formations, two characteristics must be distinguished: *their function within the human network to which they belong, and the social power that is vested in this function*. What we call "rule" is, in a highly differentiated society, no more than the special social power with which certain functions, above all the central functions, endow their occupants in relation to the representatives of other functions. Social power, however, is determined, in the case of the highest central functions of a highly differentiated society, in exactly the same way as with all others: it corresponds—if these functions are not allied to permanent control of individual hereditary monopoly power—solely to the degree of dependence of the various interdependent functions on one another. Growth in the "power" of the central functionaries is, in a society with a high division of functions, an expression of the fact that the dependence of other groups and classes within this society on a supreme organ of co-ordination and regulation is rising; a fall in the latter appears to us as a limitation of the former. Not only the earlier stage in the formation of states which is central to the present study, but also the contemporary history of the Western figuration of states, offers examples enough of such changes in the social power of the central functionaries. They are all sure indications of specific changes in the system of tensions within the society at large. Here again, beneath all the differences between the social structures, we find certain mechanisms of social interweaving which—at least in more complex societies—tend very generally towards either a reduction or an increase in the social power of the central authorities. Whether it is the nobility and the bourgeoisie, or the bourgeoisie and the proletariat, whether, in conjunction with these larger divisions, it is smaller ruling circles, such as compet-

165

ing cliques within a princely court or within the supreme military or party apparatus, that form the two poles of the decisive axis of tension at a given time within society, it is always a quite definite set of social power relationships which strengthens the position of the authority at their centre, and a different set that weakens it.

It is necessary to deal here briefly with the figurational dynamics which determine the power of the central authority. The process of social centralization in the West, particularly in the phase when "states" were formed, remains incomprehensible, like the civilizing process itself, as long as the elementary regularities of figurational dynamics are disregarded as a means of orientation and as a guide to both thought and observation. This "centralization" or state-formation, has been shown in the preceding sections from the point of view of the power-struggle between various princely houses and dominions, i.e. from the point of view of what we would today call the "foreign affairs" of such dominions. Now the complementary problem poses itself; we face the task of tracing the figurational processes *within* one of the units which give the central authority—as compared with the preceding phase—a special power and durability, and thus endow the whole society with the form of an "absolutist state". In historical reality these two processes—shifts in power between classes *within* a unit and displacements in the system of tensions *between* different units—constantly intertwine.

In the course of the struggle between different territorial dominions *one* princely house—as we have shown—slowly outgrows all the others. It thus assumes the function of supreme regulator for a larger unit; but it did not create this function. It appropriates it by virtue of the size of its possessions accumulated in the course of the struggles, and its monopoly control of army and taxes. The function itself derives its form and power from the increasing differentiation of functions within society at large. And from this aspect it seems, at first sight, thoroughly paradoxical that the central ruler in this early phase of state-formation should attain such enormous social power. For, from the end of the Middle Ages onwards, with the rapid advance of the division of functions, the monarchy becomes more and more perceptibly dependent on the other functions. At precisely this time the chains of action based on division of functions take on ever wider scope and ever greater durability. The autonomy of social processes, the central authority's character as a functionary, which gradually receives clearer institutional expression after the French Revolution, are by this time far more prominent than in the Middle Ages. The dependence of the central lords on the revenues from their dominions is a clear indication of this. Beyond doubt, Louis XIV is incomparably more tightly bound to this vast and autonomous network of chains of actions, than, for example, Charlemagne. How, therefore, did the central ruler in this phase have, to begin with, such scope for decision and such social power that we are accustomed to call him an "absolute" ruler?

It was not only the prince's monopoly control of military power which held the other classes within his territory, and especially the powerful leading groups, in check. Owing to a peculiar social constellation, the dependence of precisely these groups on a supreme co-ordinator and regulator of the tension-ridden structure was so great at this phase that, willingly or not, they renounced for a long period the struggle for control and participation in the highest decisions.

This peculiar constellation cannot be understood unless we take account of a special quality of human relationships which was likewise emerging with the increasing division of functions in society: *their open or latent ambivalence*. In the relations between individuals, as well as in those between different functional strata, a specific *duality or even multiplicity of interests* manifests itself more strongly, the broader and denser the network of social interdependence becomes. Here, all people, all groups, estates or classes, are in some way dependent on one another; they are potential friends, allies or partners; and they are at the same time potential opponents, competitors or enemies. In societies with a barter economy there are sometimes unambiguously negative relationships, of pure, unmoderated enmity. When migrant nomads invade a settled region, there need be in their relations with the settlers no trace of mutual functional dependence. Between these groups exists pure enmity to the death. Far greater, too, in such societies, is the chance of a relationship of clear and uncomplicated mutual dependence, unmixed friendships, alliances, relationships of love or service. In the peculiar black-and-white colouring of many medieval books, which often know nothing but good friends or villains, the greater susceptibility of medieval reality to relationships of this kind is clearly expressed. No doubt, at this stage the chains of functional interdependencies are relatively short; hence rapid switches from one extreme to another, an easy changeover from firm friendship into violent enmity also occur more frequently. As social functions and interests become increasingly complex and contradictory, we find more and more frequently in the behaviour and feelings of people a peculiar split, a co-existence of positive and negative elements, a mixture of muted affection and muted dislike in varying proportions and nuances. The possibilities of pure, unambiguous enmity grow fewer; and, more and more perceptibly, every action taken against an opponent also threatens the social existence of its perpetrator; it disturbs the whole mechanism of chains of action of which each is a part. It would take us too far afield to explore in detail this fundamental *ambivalence of interests*, its consequences in political life or psychological make-up, and its sociogenesis in relation to the advancing division of functions. But the little that has already been said shows it to be one of the most important structural characteristics of more highly developed societies, and a chief factor moulding civilized conduct.

Increasingly ambivalent, with the growing division of functions, are the relations between different units of power. The relations between the states of our own time, above all in Europe, offer a clear example of this. Even if integration and the division of functions *between* them have not yet advanced as far as the division of functions *within* them, nevertheless every military exchange so threatens this highly differentiated network of nations as a whole, that in the end the victor himself finds himself in a seriously shaken position. He is no longer able—or willing—to depopulate and devastate the enemy country sufficiently to settle a part of his own population in it. He must, in the interests of victory, destroy as far as possible the industrial power of the enemy, and at the same time, in the interests of his own peace, try within limits to preserve or restore this industrial apparatus. He can win colonial possessions, frontier revisions, export markets, economic or military advantages, in short, a general advance of his power; but just because, in the struggles of highly complex societies, each rival and opponent is at the same time a partner at the production line of the same machinery, every sudden and radical change in one sector of this network inevitably leads to disruption and changes in another. To be sure, the mechanism of competition and monopoly does not for this reason cease to operate. But the inevitable conflicts grow increasingly risky for the whole precarious system of nations. However, through these very tensions and discharges the figuration moves slowly towards a more unequivocal form of hegemony, and towards an integration, perhaps at first of a federative kind, of larger units around specific hegemonial centres.

And the relationship between different social classes *within* a dominion becomes, with the advancing division of functions, more and more ambivalent in the same way. Here, too, within a far more restricted space, groups whose social existence is mutually dependent through the division of functions, are struggling for certain opportunities. They too are at once opponents and partners. There are extreme situations in which the existing organization of a society functions so badly, and the tensions within it grow so large, that a large portion of the people and classes within it "no longer care". In such a situation the negative side of the ambivalent relationships, the opposition of interests, may so gain the upper hand over the positive side, the community of interests arising from the interdependence of functions, that there are violent discharges of tensions, abrupt shifts in the social centre of gravity, and reorganization of society on a changed social basis. Up to this revolutionary situation, the classes bound together by the division of functions are cast back and forth between their split and contradictory interests. They oscillate between the desire to win major advantages over their social opponents and their fear of ruining the whole social apparatus, on the functioning of which their actual social existence depends. And this is the constellation, the form of relationships, that harbours the key to an understanding of the changes in the social power of the central functionaries. If the co-operation of the powerful functional classes gives rise to no special difficulties, if their conflicts of interest are not great enough to conceal from them their mutual dependence and to threaten the functioning of the entire social apparatus, the scope of the central authority is restricted. It tends to increase when the tension between certain leading groups of society grows. And it attains its optimum level when the majority of the various functional classes are still so concerned to preserve their social existence in the established form that they fear any major disturbance of the total apparatus and the concomitant upheaval within their own existence, while at the same time the structural conflict of interests between powerful groups is so great that an ordered voluntary compromise can scarcely be reached, and troublesome social skirmishes without a decisive outcome become a permanent feature of social life. This is most acutely the case in phases when different groups or classes of a society have attained roughly the same power, and hold each other in balance, even though, like the nobility and the bourgeoisie, or the bourgeoisie and the proletariat, they may be institutionally on a quite unequal footing. He who, in this constellation, in a society wearied and disturbed by inconclusive struggles, can attain power over the supreme organs of regulation and control, has the chance of enforcing a compromise between the divided interests in order to preserve the existing social distribution of power. The various interest groups can move neither apart nor together; this makes them dependent on the supreme central co-ordinator for their social existence to a quite different degree than when the interdependent interests are less divergent and direct agreements between them more easily reached. When the situation of the bulk of the various functional classes, or at least their active leading groups, is not yet so bad that they are willing to put their social existence at risk, and they yet feel themselves so threatened by each other, and power is so evenly distributed between them, that each fears the slightest advantage of the other side, they tie each other's hands: this gives the central authority better chances than any other constellation within society. It gives those invested with this authority, whoever they may be, the optimal scope for decision. The variations on this configuration in historical reality are manifold. That it only emerges in a clearly delineated form in more highly differentiated societies, and that in less interdependent societies with lower division of functions it is above all military success and power that form the basis of a strong central authority over large areas, has already been stated. And even in more complex societies, success in war or conflicts with other powers undoubtedly plays a decisive part for strong central authorities. But if for the time being we disregard these external relations of a society and their influence of the internal balance, and ask how a strong central authority is possible in a richly differentiated society, despite the high and evenly distributed interdependence of all functions, we always find ourselves confronted with that specific constellation which can now be stated as a general principle: *the hour of the strong central authority within a highly differentiated society strikes when the ambivalence of interests of the most important functional groups grows so large, and power is distributed so evenly between them, that there can be neither a decisive compromise nor a decisive conflict between them.*

It is a figuration of this kind to which here the term "royal mechanism" is applied. In fact the central authority attains the optimal social power of an "absolute" monarchy in conjunction with such a constellation of social forces. But this balancing mechanism is certainly not only the sociogenetic motive force of a powerful monarchy; we find it in more complex societies as the foundation of every strong one-man rule, whatever its name might be. The man or men at the centre are always balanced on a tension between greater or lesser groups who keep each other in check as interdependent antagonists, as opponents and partners at once. This kind of figuration may appear at first sight extremely fragile. Historical reality shows, however, how compellingly and inescapably it can hold in bondage the individuals who constitute it—until finally the continuous shift of its centre of gravity that accompanies its reproduction through generations makes possible more or less violent changes in the mutual bonds of people, so giving rise to new forms of integration.

18. The regularities of social dynamics place the central ruler and apparatus in a curious situation, the more so the more specialized this apparatus and its organs become. The central ruler and his staff may have reached the top of the central administration as proponents of a particular social formation; or they may be recruited primarily from a certain class of society. But once someone has attained a position in the central apparatus and held on to it for any time, it imposes its own regularities upon him. It distances him in varying degrees from all the other groups and classes of society, even the one which has brought him to power and from which he originates. His specific function gives the central ruler of a differentiated society specific interests. It is his function to superintend the cohesion and security of the whole of society as it exists, and he is thus concerned to balance the interests of the other functional

171

groups. And this task, with which he is simply confronted by daily experience and which conditions his whole view of society —this task itself distances him from all the other groups of functionaries. But he must also, like any other person, be concerned for his own social survival. He must work to ensure that his social power is not reduced, but, if anything, increased. In this sense he, too, is a party within the play of social forces. Insofar as his interests, through the peculiarity of his function, are bound up with the security and smooth functioning of the whole social structure, he must favour some individuals within this structure, he must win battles and enter alliances within it with a view to strengthening his personal position. But in this the interests of the central ruler never become *quite* identical with those of any other class or group. They may sometimes converge with those of one group or another, but if he identifies too strongly with one of them, if the distance between himself and any group diminishes too far, his own social position is sooner or later threatened. For its strength depends, as noted above, on the one hand on the preservation of a certain balance between the different groups, and a certain degree of co-operation and cohesion between the different interests of society; but it also depends on the persistence of sharp and permanent tensions and conflicts of interest between them. The central ruler undermines his own position in using his power and support to make one group clearly superior to others. Dependence on a supreme co-ordinator, and thus his own functional dominance, necessarily shrink when a single group or class of society unequivocally has the upper hand over all others, unless this group is itself torn by internal tensions. And the central ruler's position is no less weakened and undermined if the tensions between the leading groups of society are so reduced that they can settle their differences between themselves and unite in common actions. This is true at least for relatively peaceful times. In time of war, when an external enemy of the whole of society, or at least of its most important groups, must be repulsed, a reduction of internal tensions can be harmless and useful even to the central ruler.

To put the matter in a few words, the central ruler and his apparatus form within his society a centre of interests of its own. His position often urges an alliance with the second most powerful group rather than identification with the most powerful; and his interest requires both a certain co-operation and a certain tension between society's parts. Thus, his position not only depends on the nature and strength of the ambivalence between the different formations making up society; his relationship to each of these formations is itself ambivalent.

The basic pattern of society that emerges in this way is very simple. The single ruler, the king, is always as an individual incomparably weaker than the whole society whose ruler or first servant he is. If this whole society, or even a considerable part of it, stood together against him, he would be powerless as every individual is powerless in face of pressure from a whole network of interdependent people. The unique position, the abundance of power inhering in a single person as the central ruler of a society is to be explained, as we have said, by the fact that the interests of people in this society are partly alike and partly opposed, that their actions are both adjusted to and contrary to each other's needs; it is explained by the fundamental ambivalence of the social relationships within a complex society. There are conditions in which the positive side of these relationships grows dominant or is at least not smothered by the negative side. But on the way towards dominance of the negative side there are transitional phases in which antagonisms and conflicts of interest grow so strong that the continuing interdependence of actions and interests is obscured to the consciousness of the participants without quite losing its importance. The constellation that thus comes into being has already been described: different parts of society hold each other roughly in balance in terms of social strength; the tensions between them find expression in a chain of major or minor skirmishes; but neither side can conquer or destroy the other; they cannot settle their differences because any strengthening of one side will threaten the social existence of the other; they cannot split wholly apart because their social existence is interdependent. This is a situation that gives the king, the man at the top, the central ruler, optimal power. It shows unmistakably where his specific interests lie. Through this interplay of strong interdependencies and strong antagonisms there arises a social apparatus which might be considered a dangerous invention, at once significant and cruel, were it the work of a single social engineer. Like all social formations in these phases of history, however, this "royal mechanism" which gives a single man extraordinary power as supreme co-ordinator, arises very gradually and unintentionally in the course of social processes.

This apparatus can be brought to mind most vividly and simply by the image of the tug-of-war. Groups, social forces, that hold each other roughly in check, stretch a rope. One side pits itself with all its might against the other; both heave incessantly; but neither side can dislodge the other appreciably from its position. If in this situation of utmost tension between groups pulling the same rope in opposite directions and yet bound together by this rope, there is a man who belongs entirely to neither of the two contending groups, who has the possibility of interposing his individual strength now on the side of one group, now of the other, while taking great care not to allow the tension itself to be reduced or either of the sides to obtain a clear advantage, then he is the one who actually controls this whole tension; the minimal power at the disposal of a single man, who alone could set neither of the groups in motion and quite certainly not both combined, is sufficient, with this arrangement of social forces, to move the whole. The reason why it is sufficient is clear. Within this balanced apparatus enormous forces are latent but bound; without someone to release them they can have no effect. At the touch of a finger an individual releases the forces of one side; he unites himself with the latent forces operating in one direction so that they gain a slight advantage. This enables them to become manifest. This type of social organization represents as it were a power-station which automatically multiplies the smallest effort of the person in control. But an extremely cautious manipulation of this apparatus is called for if it is to function for any length of time without disruption. The man in control is subject to its regularities and compulsions to exactly the same degree as everyone else. His scope for decision is greater than theirs, but he is highly dependent on the structure of the apparatus; his power is anything but absolute.

This is no more than a schematic outline of the arrangement of social forces that gives the central ruler optimal power. But this sketch shows clearly the fundamental structure of his social position. Not by chance, not whenever a strong ruling personality is born, but when a specific social structure provides the opportunity, does the central organ attain that optimal power which usually finds expression in a strong autocracy. The relatively wide scope for decision left open in this way to the central ruler of a large and complex society comes about through his standing in the crossfire of social tensions, so being able to play on the variously directed interests and ambitions counterpoised in his dominion.

Of course, this outline simplifies the actual state of affairs to a certain extent. Equilibrium in the field of tensions making up every society always arises in differentiated human networks through the collaboration and collision of a large number of groups and classes. But the importance of this multi-polar tension for the central ruler's position is no different from that of the bi-polar tension outlined above.

The antagonism between different parts of society certainly does not only take the form of conscious conflict. Plans and consciously adopted goals are far less decisive in producing tensions than anonymous figurational dynamics. To give one example, it is the dynamics of advancing monetarization and commercialization far more than the conscious attacks of bourgeois–urban circles, which push the bulk of the knightly feudal lords downhill at the end of the Middle Ages. But however the antagonisms arising with the advance of the money network may be expressed in the plans and goals of individual people or groups, with them grows the tension between the urban classes who are gaining strength and the functionally weakening lords of the land. With the growth of this network and this tension, however, grows the room to manoeuvre of those who, having won the struggle between initially freely competing units, have become the central rulers of the whole—the kings, until finally, balanced between the bourgeoisie and the nobility, they attain their optimal strength in the form of the absolute monarchy.

19. We asked earlier how it is possible at all for a central authority with absolute power to evolve and survive within a differentiated society, despite the fact that this central ruler is no less dependent on the working of the entire mechanism than the occupants of other positions. The pattern of the royal mechanism provides the answer. It is no longer his military power or the size of his possessions and revenues *alone* that can explain the social power of the central ruler in this phase, even though no central authority can function without these two components.

For the central rulers of a complex society to attain such optimal power as they had in the age of absolutism requires, in addition, a special distribution of forces within their society.

In fact the social institution of the monarchy attains its greatest power at that phase in history when a weakening nobility is already forced to compete in many ways with rising bourgeois groups, without either side being able decisively to defeat the other. The quickening monetarization and commercialization of the sixteenth century gives bourgeois groups increased impetus; it appreciably pushes back the bulk of the warrior class, the old nobility. At the end of the social struggles in which this violent transformation of society finds expression, the interdependence between parts of the nobility and parts of the bourgeoisie has grown considerably. The nobility, whose social function and form is itself undergoing a decisive transformation, now has to contend with a third estate, whose members have become, in part, far stronger and more socially ambitious than hitherto. Many families of the old warrior nobility die out, many bourgeois families take on aristocratic character and within a few generations their descendants themselves uphold the interests of the transformed nobility against those of the bourgeoisie, interests which now, in keeping with the closer integration, are more inescapably opposed.

But the objective of this bourgeois class, or at least of its leading groups, is not—like that of substantial parts of the bourgeoisie in 1789—to eliminate the nobility as a social institution. The highest goal of individual bourgeois is, as we have mentioned, to obtain for themselves and their family an aristocratic title with the attendant privileges. The representative leading groups of the bourgeoisie as a whole set out to seize the privileges and prestige of the military nobility; they do not want to remove the nobility as such, but at most to take their place as a new nobility supplanting or merely supplementing the old. Incessantly, this leading group of the third estate, the *noblesse de robe*, emphasize in the seventeenth and above all in the eighteenth century, that their nobility is just as good, important and genuine as that won by the sword. And the rivalry thus expressed certainly does not manifest itself only in words and ideologies. Behind it is a continuous, if more or less concealed and indecisive struggle for power positions and advantages between the representatives of the two estates.

As has been stressed above, it is to block understanding of this social constellation to start from the presupposition that the bourgeoisie of this phase is roughly the same formation as today or at least yesterday—if, in other words, we regard the "independent merchant" as the most typical and socially most important representative of the bourgeoisie. The most representative and socially influential example of the bourgeois in the seventeenth and eighteenth centuries is, at least in the larger Continental countries, the middle-class servant of princes or kings, that is, a man whose nearer or more distant forefathers were indeed craftsmen or merchants, but who himself now occupies a quasi-official position within the governmental apparatus. Before merchant classes themselves form the leading groups of the bourgeoisie, there are at the top of the third estate—to speak in our language—bureaucrats.

The structure and character of official posts varies widely in particular countries. In old France the most weighty representative of the bourgeoisie is a peculiar mixture of *rentier* and official; he is a man who has bought a position in the state service as his personal and, as it were, private property, or, which comes to the same thing, has inherited one from his father. Through this official position he enjoys a number of quite specific privileges; for example, many of these posts carry exemption from taxes; and the capital invested bears interest in the form of fees, a salary or other income which the post brings in.

It is men of this kind, men of the "robe", who during the *ancien régime* represent the bourgeoisie at the assemblies of the estates, and are in general, even outside these assemblies, its spokesmen, the exponents of its interests *vis-à-vis* the other estates and the kings. And whatever social power the third estate possesses is expressed in the demands and political tactics of this leading group. Undoubtedly, the interests of this bourgeois upper class are not always identical with those of the other bourgeois groups. Common to them, however, is one interest above all others: the preservation of their various privileges. For it is not only the social existence of the noble or official which is distinguished by special rights and privileges; the merchant of this time is likewise dependent on them; so, too, are the craft guilds. Whatever these privileges may consist of in particular cases, the bourgeoisie, as far as it carries any social weight, is, up to the second half of the eighteenth century, a social formation characterized and maintained by special rights in exactly the same way as the nobility itself. And here, therefore, we come upon a particular aspect of the machinery by virtue of which this bourgeoisie is never able to deliver a decisive blow against its antagonist, the nobility. It may contest this or that particular privilege of the nobility; but it can and will never eliminate the social institution of privilege as such, which makes the nobility a class apart; for its own social existence, the preservation of which is its main concern, is likewise maintained and protected by privileges. It is only when bourgeois forms of existence no longer based on class privileges emerge more and more in the tissue of society, and when as a result an ever-larger sector of society recognizes these special rights guaranteed or created by the government as a serious impediment to the whole functionally divided network of processes, only then are social forces in existence which can decisively oppose the nobility, which strive to eliminate not only particular noble privileges, but the social institution of noble privileges itself.

But the new bourgeois groups who now oppose privileges as such thereby lay hands, knowingly or otherwise, on the foundation of the old bourgeois formations, the bourgeois estate. Its privileges, its whole organization as an estate, have a social function only as long as a privileged nobility exists in opposition to it. The estates are hostile or, more precisely, ambivalent siblings, interdependent cells of the same social order. If one is destroyed as an institution, the other automatically falls, and with it the whole order.

In fact, the Revolution of 1789 is not simply a struggle of the bourgeoisie against the nobility. By it the middle-class estate, particularly that of the robe, the privileged officials of the third estate and also those of the old craft guilds, is destroyed no less than the nobility. And this common end illuminates at a stroke the whole social entanglement, the specific constellation of forces of the preceding phase. It illustrates what was said earlier in general terms about the interdependence and ambivalence of the interests of certain social classes, about the balanced mechanism that arises with them, and about the social power of the central authority. The politically relevant parts of the bourgeoisie which did not constitute an estate and emerged very slowly from the earlier one, these older bourgeois groups are bound in their interests, their actions and thoughts, entirely to the existence and the specific equilibrium of an order based on estates. For this reason, in all their conflicts with the nobility and also, of course, with the first estate, the clergy, they are always being caught, like the latter, in the trap of their ambivalent interests. They never dare advance too far in their struggle with the nobility without cutting into their own flesh; any decisive blow against the nobility as an institution would shake the whole state and social structure and thus knock down like skittles the social existence of this privileged bourgeoisie. All the privileged classes are equally concerned not to push the struggle between them too far; they all fear nothing more than a profound upheaval and shift of weight within the social structure as a whole.

But at the same time they cannot entirely avoid conflict with each other; for their interests, parallel in one direction, are diametrically opposed in many others. Social power is so distributed between them and their rivalry so great, that one side feels threatened by the slightest advantage of the other and by anything that might give the other the least superiority of power. Accordingly, there is on the one hand no lack of courteous and even friendly relationships between members of the different groups; but on the other their relations, above all between the leading groups, remain extremely strained throughout the whole of the *ancien régime*. Each fears the other; each observes the other's steps with constant if concealed mistrust. Moreover, this main axis of tension between the nobility and bourgeoisie is embedded in a multitude of others no less ambivalent. The official hierarchy of the secular governmental apparatus is in constant open or latent competition for power and prestige with the clerical hierarchy. The clerics in turn are forever colliding for one reason or another with this or that circle of the nobility. So this multi-polar system of equilibrium constantly gives rise to minor explosions and skirmishes, to social trials of strength in various ideological disguises and for the most diverse and often quite incidental reasons.

The king or his representatives, however, steers and controls this whole mechanism by pitting his weight now in one direction, now another, and his social power is so great precisely because the structural tension between the main groups in the social network is too strong to allow them to reach direct agreement in their affairs and thus to make a determined common stand against the king.

As we know, it was in only one country during this period that bourgeois and noble groups took such a stand successfully against the king—in England. Whatever may be the special structural characteristics of English society that permit the tension between the estates to relax and stable contacts between them to be established—the social constellation which, after considerable tribulations, leads in England to a restriction of the central ruler's powers, makes clear to us once more the different basic constellation which in other countries maintains the social power and the absolutist form of the central authority.

During the sixteenth and even the early seventeenth century, there is no lack, in France too, of attempts by people of the most different social origins to combine against the menacing increase in royal power. They all fail. These civil wars and revolts reveal quite nakedly how strong even in France is the desire among the various estates to restrict the powers of the kings and their representatives. But they show no less clearly how strong are the rivalries and conflicts of interest between these groups, which impede a common pursuit of this objective. Each of them would like to limit the monarchy in its own favour, and each is just strong enough to prevent others from doing so. They all hold each other in check, and so they finally find themselves resigned to their common dependence on a strong king.

There is, in other words, within that great social transformation which makes bourgeois groups functionally stronger and aristocratic ones weaker, a phase when both groups—despite all the tensions both between them and third parties and within themselves—by and large balance each other out in social power. Thus is established for a greater or lesser period that apparatus that was described above as the "royal mechanism": the antitheses between the two main groups are too great to make a decisive compromise between them likely; and the distribution of power, together with their close interdependence, prevents a decisive struggle or the clear predominance of one or the other. So, incapable of uniting, incapable of fighting with all their strength and winning, they must leave to a central ruler all the decisions that they cannot bring about themselves.

This apparatus is formed, as we have said, in a blind, unplanned way in the course of social processes. Whether it is controlled well or badly, however, depends very much on the person exercising the central function. Reference to a few particular historical facts must be enough here to show how the apparatus is formed, and to illustrate what has been said in general terms about the absolutist royal mechanism.

20. In the society of the ninth and tenth centuries there are two classes of free men, the clerics and the warriors. Below them, the mass of the more or less unfree, who are generally excluded from bearing arms, have no active part in social life, even though the existence of society depends on their activities. We have noted that under the special conditions of the western Frankish area, the dependence of the warriors, practically autarkic lords on their estates, on the co-ordinating activity of a central ruler is only slight. The dependence of the clerics on the king, for the most diverse reasons, is far greater. The Church in the western Frankish area never attained major secular power as it did in the empire. Archbishops did not here become dukes. The ecclesiastical peers remain by and large outside the system of competing territorial lords. Thus their centrifugal interests directed at weakening the central ruler are not particularly strong. The possessions of the clerics lie scattered amongst the dominions of secular lords. They are constantly exposed to attacks and encroachment by the latter. The Church therefore desires a central ruler, a king, who has enough power to protect her against secular violence. The feuds, the major and minor wars that are incessantly flaring up across the whole region, are often highly unwelcome to the monks and other clerics who, while certainly more militarily competent and even bellicose than later, at any rate did not live on or for war. These feuds and wars often enough take place at their expense. And over and again priests and abbeys throughout the country, mistreated, injured, deprived of their rights, appeal to the king as judge.

The strong, only occasionally troubled, association between the first Capetian kings and the Church is in no way fortuitous; nor does its cause lie solely in the strong personal faith of these first Capetians. It also expresses an obvious constellation of interests. The dignity of the monarchy in this phase, whatever else it may be, is always an instrument of the priests in their conflict with the warrior class. The royal consecration, anointment and coronation are influenced more and more by Church investiture and ceremony. The monarchy takes on a kind of sacral character; it becomes in a certain sense an ecclesiastical function. That this link, unlike what happens in other societies, does not go beyond these mere beginnings of a merging of worldly and ecclesiastical central authority, and is very soon broken off, results not least from the structure of the Christian Church itself. This Church is older and its organization more firmly established than most secular dominions of the time; and it has its own head, who aspires more and more clearly to combine spiritual pre-eminence with worldly supremacy, a central authority transcending all others. Sooner or later, therefore, a competitive situation arises, a struggle for supremacy between the Pope and the worldly central lord of a given area. This struggle everywhere ends with the Pope being thrown back on his spiritual predominance, with the worldly character of emperor and king re-emerging more clearly, and with the latters' incipient assimilation to the Church hierarchy and ritual regressing without entirely disappearing. But the fact that there are even the beginnings of such an assimilation in the West is worthy of note—especially in comparing historical structures and in explaining differences between social processes in various parts of the world.

The western Frankish kings, for their part, at first collaborate quite closely with the Church, in keeping with the structural regularity governing their function, discussed earlier. They take support for the second strongest group in their conflict with the stronger and more dangerous. They are nominally the liege lords over all warriors. But in the domains of the other great lords they are, to begin with, virtually powerless, and even within their own territory their power is sharply restricted. The close association of royal house and Church turns the monasteries, abbeys and bishoprics in the lands of other territorial lords into bastions of the monarchy; it puts a part of the Church's spiritual influence throughout the country at their disposal. And the kings derive numerous advantages from the writing skills of the clergy, the political and organizational experience of the Church bureaucracy, and not least its finance. It is an open question whether the kings of the early Capetian period receive, over and above the revenues from their own territory, any actual "royal income", that is, duties from the whole western Frankish kingdom. If they have such income, it is hardly a significant addition to what they receive from their own domestic estates. But one thing is certain: they receive duties from Church institutions in regions outside their own territory, for example the income of a vacant diocese or occasional subsidies in extraordinary situations. And if anything gives the traditional royal house an advantage in power over the competing houses, if anything contributes to the fact that in these early elimination struggles beginning within their own territory, the Capetians are the first to begin to rebuild their power, it is this alliance of the nominal central rulers with the Church. From this alliance above all, in a phase of powerful centrifugal tendencies, spring those social forces which work independently of the individual kings for the continuity of the monarchy, and in the direction of centralization. The importance of the clergy as a motive force of centralization recedes, without entirely disappearing, in proportion as the third estate advances. But even in this phase it is apparent how the tensions between different social groups, beginning with that between the priestly class and the warrior class, benefit the central ruler; but it is clear, too, how he is bound by these tensions, imprisoned by them. The excessive power of the many military lords drives king and Church together, even though minor conflicts between them are not lacking. But the first major difference between king and Church, the first real power struggle between them, occurs only when more abundant human and financial resources are beginning to flow to the king from the bourgeois camp, in the period of Philip Augustus.

21. With the formation of a third estate, the network of tensions becomes more complex and the axis of tension within society moves. Just as in an interdependent system of competing countries or territories, particular tensions become predominant at different times, all the other antagonisms being subordinated to them until one of the main power centres establishes preponderance, similarly there are, within each dominion, certain central tensions about which numerous smaller ones crystallize, and which gradually shift in favour of one side or the other. If these central tensions include, up to the eleventh and twelfth centuries, the ambivalent relationship between the warriors and the clergy, from then on the antagonism between the warriors and the urban–bourgeois groups slowly but steadily moves into the foreground as the central internal tension. With it, and the

183

whole differentiation of society that it expresses, the central ruler gains new importance: the dependence of all parts of society on a supreme co-ordinator grows. The kings who, in the course of the struggles for predominance, detach themselves more and more from the rest of the warrior class as their dominions expand, also distance themselves from the other warriors through their position within the tension between the latter and the urban classes. In this tension they are not by any means unequivocally on the side of the warriors, to whom they belong by origin. Rather, they apply their weight now to one side of the scales, now to the other.

The towns' attainment of communal rights is the first milestone on this road. The kings of this phase, above all Louis VI and VII, like their representatives and all the other feudal lords, regard the growing communes with mistrust and, to say the least, "partial hostility",[101] particularly within their own domain. Only gradually do the kings grasp the uses of these unfamiliar formations. As always, a certain time is needed for them to perceive that the emergence of a third estate within the fabric of society means an immense enlargement of their own scope. But from then on they promote the interests of this third estate with the utmost consistency, as far as these accord with their own. Above all they foster the financial, taxable power of the bourgeoisie. But they emphatically oppose, whenever they have the power to do so, the towns' claims to governmental functions, claims which cannot fail to arise with the growing economic and social power of the urban classes. The rise of the monarchy and that of the bourgeoisie are connected in the closest functional interdependence; partly consciously, partly unwittingly, these two social positions elevate each other; but their relations remain always ambivalent. There is no lack of animosity and conflict between them nor, at first, of occasions when the nobility and bourgeoisie attempt jointly to restrict the sovereign powers of the kings. Throughout the entire Middle Ages, the kings find themselves repeatedly in situations where they have to seek the approval of the assembled representatives of the estates for certain measures; and the course taken by these assemblies, both the smaller regional ones and the larger ones representing broad areas of the kingdom, shows clearly how different the structure of tensions in society still is, despite all its fluctuations, from that existing in the absolutist period.[102] The

184

parliaments of the estates—to use their English name—are able to function, not unlike the party parliaments of bourgeois–industrial society, as long as direct agreement between the representatives of different classes over particular objectives is possible. They function less well the more difficult direct compromise becomes, and the greater the tensions within society; and to the same degree the potential power of the central ruler rises. Given the low degree of monetary and commercial integration in the medieval world, at first neither the interdependence nor the antagonisms between the land-owning warrior class and the urban bourgeois class were such that they needed to hand over the regulation of their relations to the central ruler. Each estate, the knights and the burghers, like the clergy, despite their contacts, live far more within their own confines than later. The different estates do not yet compete so frequently or directly for the same social opportunities; and the leading bourgeois groups are still far from being strong enough to challenge the social pre-eminence of the nobility, the warriors. Only at one point in society do rising bourgeois elements, with the help of the monarchy, gradually displace knights and clergy directly from their positions: within the governmental apparatus, as officials.

22. The functional dependence of the monarchy on what went on in society at large is manifested particularly clearly in the development of the machinery of government, in the splitting-off of all those institutions which first of all were not much more than parts of the royal domestic and domanial administration. When the society of free men consists essentially only of knights and clergy, the government apparatus, too, is made up above all of knights and clergy; the clergy or clerks, as already mentioned, usually being loyal servants and proponents of royal interests, while the feudal lords, even at court and within the royal administration, are often enough rivals of the king, more concerned with developing their own power positions than with consolidating his. Then, as the warrior class outside the governmental apparatus becomes more complex, as in the course of the elimination struggles major and minor feudal lords are more sharply differentiated, this constellation is mirrored in the structure of a growing governmental machine: clerics and members of minor warrior houses form its staff while major feudal lords find themselves confined to very few positions, for

example, as members of the great assembly or the smaller council.

Even in this phase men from the stratum below the warriors and priests are certainly not lacking in the royal administration, even if elements of unfree origin do not play the same role in the development of the French central apparatus as they do in the development of the German. Perhaps that is connected with the fact that in the former case, urban communities, and thus a third estate of freedmen, have risen somewhat earlier to independent significance than in the latter. In France the participation of urban groups in the royal administration rises with the growth of the towns, and as early as the Middle Ages members of these groups gradually permeate the governmental apparatus to an extent that is not reached in the majority of German territories until well into the modern period.

They enter this apparatus by two main routes:[103] first through their growing share of secular posts, that is, positions previously filled by nobles, and secondly through their share of ecclesiastical posts, that is as clerks. The term *clerc* begins slowly to change its meaning from about the end of the twelfth century onwards; its ecclesiastical connotation recedes and it refers more and more to a man who has studied, who can read and write Latin, though it may be that the first stages of an ecclesiastical career are for a time a prerequisite for this. Then, in conjunction with the extension of the administrative apparatus, both the term *clerc* and certain kinds of university study are increasingly secularized. People no longer learn Latin exclusively to become members of the clergy, they also learn it to become officials. To be sure, there are still bourgeois who enter the king's council simply on account of their commercial or organizational competence. But the majority of bourgeois attain the higher regions of government through study, through knowledge of canon and Roman law. Study becomes a normal means of social advancement for the sons of leading urban strata. Bourgeois elements slowly push back the noble and ecclesiastical elements in the government. The class of royal servants, of "officials", becomes—in contrast to the situation in Germany—an exclusively bourgeois formation.

From the time of Philip Augustus onwards at the latest . . . the lawyers, true "knights of law" (*chevaliers ès lois*) appear:

they were to take on the task of amalgamating feudal with canon and Roman law to make up monarchic law. ... A small army of thirty scribes in 1316, 104 or 105 in 1359, about sixty in 1361, these chancellery clerks gained numerous advantages from constantly swelling their ranks in the proximity of the king. The broad mass was to become privileged notaries; the élite (three under Philip the Fair, twelve before 1388, sixteen in 1406, eight in 1413) would give birth to the privy clerks or financial secretaries. ... The future was theirs. Unlike the grand officers of a palatinate, they had no ancestors, but were themselves to be ancestors.[104]

With the growth of the royal possessions a class of specialists is formed whose social position depends first and foremost on their place in royal service, and whose prestige and interests are largely identical with those of the monarchy and the governmental apparatus. As the Church had done earlier, and still did to some extent, members of the third estate now uphold the interests of the central function. They do so in the most diverse capacities, as scribes and councillors to the king, as tax administrators, as members of the highest courts. And it is they who seek to ensure the continuity of royal policy beyond the life of a particular king and often enough against his personal inclinations. Here too, bourgeois classes elevate the monarchy, and the monarchs elevate the bourgeois classes.

23. With this almost total expulsion of the nobility from the governmental apparatus, the bourgeoisie attains in the course of time a power position which is of the utmost importance to the overall balance of power in society. In France, as already mentioned, it is not, almost till the end of the *ancien régime*, the rich merchants or the guilds who directly represent the bourgeoisie in conflicts with the nobility; it is the bureaucracy in its various formations. The weakening of the social position of the nobility, the strengthening of the bourgeoisie, is most clearly expressed in the fact that the upper bureaucracy lays claim, at least from the beginning of the seventeenth century onwards, to equal social status with the nobility. At this time the interweaving of interests and the tensions between nobility and bourgeoisie have indeed reached a level which secures exceptional power for the central ruler.

This permeation of the central apparatus by sons of the urban bourgeoisie is one of the strands within that process indicating most clearly the close functional interdependence between the rise of the monarchy and of the bourgeoisie. The bourgeois upper stratum, which gradually evolves from the families of the higher "royal servants", attains in the sixteenth and seventeenth centuries such increased social power that the central ruler would have been at its mercy, had it not counterweights in the nobility and clergy, whose resistance neutralizes their strength; and it is not difficult to observe how the kings, above all, Louis XIV, play constantly on this system of tensions. In the preceding phase, however, the nobility and clergy—despite all the ambivalence already inhering in their relationship—are still, at first, far stronger opponents of the central authority than the urban bourgeoisie. For this very reason the bourgeois eager for social advancement are as welcome helpers of the king as they are willing. The kings allow the central apparatus to become a monopoly of people from the third estate, because this is still socially weaker than the first and second estates.

This interdependence between the growth of the power of king and bourgeoisie, and the weakening of nobility and clergy, is seen from a different aspect if we consider the financial connections between the social existence of the various parties. That this shift to the disadvantage of the nobility is to be attributed only in small part to conscious and systematic actions by bourgeois circles has already been stressed. It is, on the one hand, a consequence of the competitive mechanism by which the bulk of the nobility sink into dependence on a single noble house, the royal house, and thus in a sense to the same level as the bourgeoisie. On the other, it is a consequence of advancing monetary integration. Hand in hand with the rise in the volume of money goes a constant devaluation. This increase and devaluation of money accelerates in the sixteenth century to an extraordinary extent. And the nobility who live on the income from their estates, which they cannot increase to keep pace with devaluation, are impoverished.

The religious wars—to mention only this final act—have the same significance for the weakening nobility as civil wars so often have for declining classes: they conceal from them, for a time, the inevitability of their fate. The uproar and unrest, the self-assertion in fighting, the possibility of pillage and the facility of gain, all this encourages the nobility to believe they can maintain their threatened social position and save themselves from downfall and impoverishment. Of the economic upheavals whirling them back and forth, those embroiled in them have scarcely an inkling. They see that money is increasing, prices rising, but they do not understand it. Brantôme, one of the courtly warriors of the period, has captured this mood:

... far from having impoverished France, this (civil) war has positively enriched her, in so far as it has uncovered and placed in full view an infinity of treasures previously hidden underground, where they served no purpose. ... It has placed them so well in the sun, and turned them into such quantities of good money, that there were more millions of gold to be seen shining in France than there had been millions of silver pounds before, and there appeared more new, subtle silver coins, forged from these fine hidden treasures, than there had been coppers before. ... And that is not all: the rich merchants, usurers, bankers and other niggards down to the priests, kept their coin locked in their coffers and neither enjoyed it themselves nor lent it except at gross interest and with excessive usury, or by the purchase or mortgage of land, goods or houses at a wretched price; so that the noble who had been impoverished during the foreign wars and had pawned or sold his goods, was at his wits' end, without even the wood to keep himself warm, for these scamps of usurers had pocketed everything—this good civil war restored them to their rightful place. So I have seen gentlemen of high birth who, before the civil war, went about with two horses and a footman, recover to such effect that during and after it they were seen travelling the country with six or seven good horses. ... *And that is how the honest nobility of France has been restored by the grace or, one might say, by the grease of this good civil war.*[105]

In reality the majority of the French nobility, on their return from this "good" civil war, find themselves debt-ridden and ruined once more. Life grows more expensive. Creditors, along with rich merchants, usurers and bankers, and above all high officials, men of the robe, clamour for repayment of the money they have lent. Wherever they can, they possess themselves of the noble estates, and often enough the titles too.

The nobles who hold on to their estates very soon find their income no longer sufficient to cover the increased cost of living:

> The lords who had ceded land to their peasants against duties in cash, continued to collect the same revenue but without the same value. What had cost five sous in the past cost twenty at the time of Henry III. The nobles grew poor without knowing it.[106]

24. The picture of the distribution of social power that presents itself here is fairly unambiguous. The change in the social structure which had long been working against the warrior nobility in favour of bourgeois classes, accelerates in the sixteenth century. The latter gain in social weight what the former lose. Antagonisms in society grow. The warrior nobility do not understand the process forcing them out of their hereditary positions, but they see it embodied in these men of the third estate with whom they must now compete directly for the same opportunities, above all for money, but also, through money, for their own land and even their social pre-eminence. Thereby the equilibrium is slowly established which gives optimal power to one man, the central ruler.

In the struggles of the sixteenth and seventeenth centuries we come across bourgeois corporations which have become wealthy, numerous and powerful enough to confront the warrior nobility's claims to dominance and power with firm resistance, but neither able nor strong enough to make the warriors, the military class, directly dependent on them. We find a nobility still strong and belligerent enough to represent a constant threat to the rising bourgeois classes, but already too weak, above all economically, to control directly the town-dwellers and their taxes. The fact that at this time the nobility has already entirely lost the functions of administration and jurisdiction, these being now in the hands of bourgeois corporations, contributes in no small way to the nobility's weakness. Nevertheless, no part of society is yet able to attain a lasting and decisive preponderance over the others. In this situation the king again and again appears to each class or corporation as an ally against the threats from other groups which they cannot master on their own.

Of course, the nobility and bourgeoisie themselves consist of various groups and strata whose interests do not always run in the same direction. Into the primary tension between these two classes are woven numerous other tensions, whether within these groups or between one or other of them and the clergy. But at the same time all these groups and strata are more or less dependent for their existence on the others; none is at this stage strong enough to overthrow the established order as a whole. The leading groups, the only ones which can exert a certain political influence within the framework of the existing institutions, are the least disposed to radical change. And this multiplicity of tensions strengthens all the more the potential power of the kings.

Of course, each of these leading groups, the highest nobles, the "great ones" at court, as much as of the bourgeoisie, the parliaments, would like to restrict the royal power in their own favour. Efforts or at least ideas tending in this direction recur throughout the whole of the *ancien régime*. These social groups with opposed interests and wishes are also divided in their attitude to the monarchy. There is no lack of occasions on which this becomes clear; there are even a number of temporary alliances between noble and urban–bourgeois groups, above all the parliaments, against the representatives of the monarchy. But if anything shows up the difficulty of such direct reconciliation, and the strength of the tensions and rivalries existing between the parties, it is the fate of such occasional alliances.

Take, for example, the *Fronde*. Louis XIV is still a minor. Mazarin is governing. Once more, for the last time for a long period, the most disparate social groups unite to assail royal omnipotence represented by the Minister. Parliaments and broad nobility, urban corporations and men of the high nobility, all try to exploit the monarchy's moment of weakness, the regency of the Queen exercised by the Cardinal. But the picture presented by this rising shows clearly enough how tense are relationships between all these groups. The *Fronde* is a kind of social experiment. It exposes once again the structure of tensions which gives the central authority its strength, but which remains concealed from view as long as this authority is firmly established. No sooner does one of the competing allies seem to gain the slightest advantage than all the others feel threatened, desert the alliance, make common cause with Mazarin against their erstwhile ally, and then partly switch back to his side. Each of these people and groups wants to curtail royal power; but each wants to do it to his own advantage. Each fears that another's power might grow at the same time. Finally—not least thanks to the skill with which Mazarin takes advantage of this mechanism of tensions—the old equilibrium is re-established in favour of the existing royal house. Louis XIV never forgot the lesson of these days; far more consciously and carefully than all his predecessors, he nurtured this equilibrium and maintained the existing social differences and tensions.

25. For a long period of the Middle Ages the urban classes, through their social position, are decidedly weaker than the warrior nobility. In this period the community of interests between the king and the bourgeois section of society is considerable, if not so great that friction and even conflicts between towns and the central ruler are entirely absent. One of the most visible consequences of this community of interests, as we have noted, is the expulsion of the nobility from the monarchy's governmental organization, and its permeation by people of bourgeois origin.

Then, as the relative social power of the nobility diminishes with the advance of monetary integration and monopolization, the kings shift some of their weight back to the side of the nobility. They now secure the existence of the nobility as a privileged class against the bourgeois assault, and they do so to just the degree necessary to preserve the social differences between nobility and bourgeoisie and thus the equilibrium of tensions within the realm. So, for example, they secure for the bulk of the nobility exemption from taxes, which the bourgeoisie would like to see abolished or at least reduced. But this is certainly not enough to give the economically weak landowners a sufficient basis on which to satisfy their claim to be the upper class and their need to cultivate a demonstratively affluent mode of life. Despite their tax exemption, the mass of the landed nobility lead throughout the *ancien régime* a thoroughly restricted life. They can hardly compete in material prosperity with the upper strata of the bourgeoisie. *Vis-à-vis* the authorities, above all the courts, their position is far from favourable; for the posts in the latter are held by people of bourgeois origin. In addition, the kings, supported by a section of aristocratic opinion, uphold the rule that a noble who engages directly in commerce should renounce both his title and all his noble privileges, at least for the duration of this activity. This rule certainly serves to maintain the existing differences between bourgeoisie and nobility, which the kings no less than the nobles themselves are concerned to preserve. But at the same time it blocks the nobility's only direct access to greater prosperity. Only indirectly, through marriage, can a noble profit from the wealth that stems from commerce and official posts. The nobility would have had nothing of the splendour and social prestige they still enjoyed in the seventeenth and eighteenth centuries; they would unfailingly have succumbed to the increasingly prosperous bourgeoisie and perhaps to a new bourgeois nobility, had they not—or at least a small section of them—obtained with the king's help a new monopoly position at court. This both permitted them a mode of life adequate to their social station, and preserved them from involvement in bourgeois activities. The court offices, the many and various official positions within the royal household, are reserved to the aristocracy. In this way hundreds and finally thousands of nobles find relatively highly paid posts. Royal favour, attested by occasional gifts, is added for good measure; and proximity to the king gives these posts high prestige. And so from the broad mass of the landed aristocracy there arises a stratum of nobles which can counterbalance the upper bourgeoisie in wealth and influence, the courtly nobility. Just as earlier, when the bourgeoisie was weaker than the aristocracy, posts in the royal administration had been made a bourgeois monopoly with the king's help, now that the nobility is weakening, the court positions, likewise with royal assistance, become a preserve of the nobility.

The exclusive filling of court posts by nobles does not happen at one stroke or by the design of a particular king, any more than the reservation of all the other state posts to the bourgeoisie had been earlier.

Under Henry IV, and still under Louis XIII, court positions, like the majority of military appointments and, still more, like administrative and judicial offices, are purchasable and thus the property of their occupant. This is even true of the post of *gouverneur*, the military commanders of particular regions of the kingdom. To be sure, on occasions the occupant of such a post can only exercise his office with the king's approval, and it naturally happens, too, that this or that position is awarded solely through royal favour. But in general the purchase of offices had by this time gained the upper hand over their nomination through favour. And since the majority of the nobility are no match for the upper bourgeoisie in terms of wealth, the third estate, or at least families sprung from it and only recently ennobled, slowly but visibly take over the court and military posts as well. Only the great noble families still have enough revenue, partly thanks to the size of their lands and partly through pensions paid to them by the king, to hold on to positions of this kind in face of such competition.

Nevertheless, a willingness to help the nobility in this situation is quite unmistakable in Henry IV, just as it is in Louis XIII and Richelieu. None of them forgets for a moment that they are themselves aristocrats. Moreover, Henry IV attained the throne at the head of an army of nobles. But apart from the fact that even they are largely impotent in face of the economic processes working against the nobility, the royal function has necessities of its own, and its relation to the nobility is ambivalent. Henry IV, Richelieu and all their successors, in order to secure their own position, are anxious to keep the nobility as far as possible from positions of political influence; but at the same time they are obliged to preserve the nobility as an independent social factor in the internal balance of forces.

The double face of the absolutist court corresponds exactly to this split relationship of king to nobility. This court is at the same time an instrument for controlling the nobility and a means of sustaining it. In this direction it gradually develops.

Even Henry IV takes it for granted that the king lives within an aristocratic circle. But it is not yet his strict policy to demand permanent residence at court of those members of the nobility who wish to remain in royal favour. No doubt he also lacks the means to finance as enormous a court, and to distribute court offices, favours and pensions as lavishly, as Louis XIV was able to do later. At his time, moreover, society is still in an extreme state of flux. Noble families are declining, bourgeois rising. The estates are surviving, but their occupancy is being drastically transformed. The wall dividing the estates is riddled with holes. Personal qualities or lack of them, personal fortune or misfortune, often play as large a part in a family's destiny as its origin in this or that estate. Even the gates to the court and court offices are still fairly wide open to people of bourgeois origin.

This the nobility deplores. It is they who desire and propose that these offices be reserved to them. And not only these offices. They desire a share in many others; they seek to win back their lost positions in the governmental machine. In 1627 they address to Louis XIII, under the title "Requests and Articles for the Restoration of the Nobility", a petition with precise proposals to this effect.[107]

The petition begins by saying that, after divine help and the sword of Henry IV, it is the nobility who are to be thanked for the preservation of the crown at a time when the majority of other classes had been incited to insurrection; yet the nobility were "in the most pitiable state they had ever known . . . crushed by poverty . . . rendered vicious by idleness . . . reduced by oppression almost to despair."

Here, in a few words, a picture of the declining class is sketched. It corresponds closely to reality. Most landed estates are overburdened with debt. Many noble families have lost all their possessions. The youth of the aristocracy is without hope; the unrest and social pressure emanating from these displaced people is felt everywhere in the life of this society. What is to be done?

Among the reasons for this state of affairs, express mention is made of the mistrust which a number of noblemen had aroused in the king through their arrogance and ambition. This had finally led the kings to believe it necessary to reduce the power of such nobles by excluding them from official positions which they had perhaps misused, and by elevating the third estate; so that since that time the nobles had been stripped of their judicial and fiscal duties, and expelled from the king's councils.

Finally, in twenty-two articles, the nobility demand, among other things, the following: in addition to the military command of the various *gouvernements* of the kingdom, the civil and military functions of the royal house—that is, the skeleton of what was later to make the court a sinecure for the nobility—should cease to be purchasable and become reserved to the nobility.

In addition, the nobility demand a certain influence on provincial administration and access for a number of particularly eligible aristocrats to the high courts, the parliaments, at least in an advisory capacity and without emoluments; and they demand, finally, that a third of the membership of the financial and military councils, and other parts of the royal government, should come from their ranks.

Of all these demands, if we disregard a few minor concessions, only one was fulfilled: court posts are closed to the bourgeoisie and reserved to the nobility. All the others, insofar as they involve participation by the nobility, however modest, in government or administration, remain unfulfilled.

In many German territories, nobles seek and receive administrative and judicial offices as well as military ones; at least since the Reformation, they are therefore to be found in the universities.[108] Most of the higher offices of state remain virtually a monopoly of the nobility; elsewhere, nobles and bourgeois normally balance each other *within* many state offices according to a precise formula of allocation.

In the French central government, as we have mentioned, the tension and the constant open or latent struggle between the two estates is expressed in the fact that the whole administration remains a monopoly of the bourgeoisie, while the whole court in the narrower sense, which had always been largely staffed by nobles but was threatened by bourgeoisification when offices were made purchasable, becomes in the seventeenth century once and for all a noble monopoly.

Richelieu, in his will, had recommended that the court should be closed to all those who "have not the good fortune of a noble origin".[109] Louis XIV then restricted access to court offices by bourgeois to the utmost; but even he did not completely close them. Thus, after many preparatory movements in which the social interests of the nobility and the monarchy were, as it were, feeling each other out, the court is given its clear role as an asylum for the nobility on one hand, and a means of controlling and taming the old warrior class on the other. The untrammelled knightly life is gone forever.

For the majority of the nobility, not only are their economic circumstances from now on straitened, but their horizons and scope for action are narrowed. With their meagre revenues they are restricted to their country seats. Escape from this in military campaigns is, to a large extent, blocked. Even in war they no longer fight for themselves as free knights, but as officers in a strict organization. And special luck or connections are needed to escape permanently from the landed nobility to the wider horizons and greater prestige of the noble circle at court.

This smaller part of the nobility finds at court, and in and around Paris, a new, more precarious homeland. Up to the time of Henry IV and Louis XIII it is not difficult for a noble belonging to the court circle to spend time at his country seat or that of another noble. There is, to be sure, a courtly nobility distinct from the broad country gentry; but this society is still relatively decentralized. Louis XIV, having learned his lesson early through the *Fronde*, exploits the nobility's dependence on him to the full. He wants "to unite directly under his eyes all those who are possible leaders of risings, and whose *châteaux* could serve as focal points for rebellion . . .".[110]

The construction of Versailles corresponds perfectly to both the intertwined tendencies of the monarchy: to provide for and visibly elevate parts of the nobility while controlling and taming them. The king gives liberally, particularly to his favourites. But he demands obedience; he keeps the nobles constantly aware of their dependence on the money and other opportunities he has to distribute.

> The King [Saint-Simon records in his *Mémoires*[111]] not only saw that the high nobility were present at his court, he demanded it also of the petty nobles. At his *Lever* and his *Coucher*, at his meals, in his gardens at Versailles, he was always looking about him, noticing everyone. He took it amiss if the most distinguished nobles did not reside permanently at court, and if the others came only seldom, and total disgrace awaited those who showed themselves hardly or not at all. If one of these had a request, the king would say proudly: "I do not know him." And his judgement was irrevocable. He did not mind if a person enjoyed living in the country, but he had to show moderation in this and take precautions before longer absences. Once in my youth when I went to Rouen on some legal business, the king had a minister write to enquire my reasons.

This surveillance of everything that went on is very characteristic of the structure of this monarchy. It shows clearly how strong were the basic tensions which the king had to observe and master in order to maintain his rule, not only within his society but outside it as well. "The art of governing is not at all difficult or unpleasant", Louis XIV once said in his instructions to his heir. "It consists quite simply in knowing the real thoughts of all the princes in Europe, knowing everything that people try to conceal from us, their secrets, and keeping close watch over them."[112]

The king's curiosity to know what was going on around him [Saint-Simon writes in another place[113]] grew more and more intense; he charged his first valet and the governor of Versailles to enroll a bodyguard. These received the royal livery, were dependent only on those just mentioned, and had the clandestine task of wandering the corridors by day and night, secretly observing and following people, seeing where they went and when they came back, overhearing their conversations and reporting everything exactly.

Hardly anything is as characteristic of the peculiar structure of the society which makes possible a strong autocracy, as this necessity of minutely supervising everything that goes on within the realm. This necessity shows up both the immense tensions and the precariousness of the social apparatus without which the co-ordinating function would not endow the central ruler with so high a power ratio. The tension and equilibrium between the various social groups, and the resulting highly ambivalent attitude of all these groups to the central ruler himself, was certainly not created by any king. But once this constellation had been established, it is vitally important for the ruler to preserve it in all its precariousness. This task demands exact supervision of his subjects.

For good reasons Louis XIV had a particularly watchful eye on people closest to him in rank. The division of labour and the interdependence of everyone, including dependence of the central ruler on the masses, were not yet so advanced that pressure from the common people was the greatest threat to the king, even though popular unrest, above all in Paris, was certainly not without danger; one of the reasons for the removal of his court from Paris to Versailles lies here. But whenever, under Louis' predecessors, dissatisfaction among the masses leads to uprisings, it is members of the royal family or the high nobility who place themselves at their head and use the factions and discontent for their own ambitions. Here, in his closest circle, the monarch's most dangerous rivals are still to be found.

It was shown earlier how, in the course of monopolization, the circle of people able to compete for the chance to rule is gradually reduced to the members of the royal house. Louis XI finally conquered these princely feudal lords and restored their territories to the crown; but in the religious wars different parties are still headed by branches of the royal family. With Henry

IV, after the extinction of the main branch, a member of a secondary one again comes to the throne. And the blood princes, the "great ones", the dukes and peers of France, continue to wield considerable power. The basis of this power is fairly clear. It is primarily their position as *Gouverneurs*, military commanders of provinces, and their fortresses. Slowly, with the consolidation of monopoly rule, these possible rivals of the kings take on the character of functionaries in a powerful government apparatus. But they resist this change. The natural brother of Louis XIII, the Duke of Vendôme, Henry IV's bastard son, rises against the central authority at the head of a faction. He is governor of Brittany and believes he has a hereditary right to this province on grounds of marriage. Then it is the governor of Provence from whom the resistance comes, then the governor of Languedoc, the Duke of Montmorency; and even the Huguenot nobility's attempts at resistance have their basis in a similar power position. The army is not yet completely centralized; the commanders of fortresses and captains of strongholds still have a high degree of independence. The governors of provinces regard their purchased and salaried positions as their property. So there are renewed flickerings of centrifugal tendencies in the land. Under Louis XIII they are still perceptible. The king's brother, Gaston, Duke of Orléans, rises, like many royal brothers before him, against the king. He formally renounces friendship for the Cardinal after taking over the leadership of the faction hostile to him, and goes to Orléans to begin his struggle against Richelieu and the King from a strong military position.

Richelieu finally won all these battles, not least with the aid of the bourgeoisie and the superior financial means they put at his disposal. The resisting lords die vanquished, some in prison, some in exile, some in battle; even the king's mother Richelieu lets die abroad.

> The belief that as sons or brothers of the King, or princes of his blood, they may disturb the realm with impunity, is mistaken. It is far more judicious to secure the realm and monarchy than to respect impunity endowed by rank.

So he writes in his memoirs. Louis XIV reaps the benefit of these victories; but a sense of threat from the nobility, particularly the high nobility closest to him, is second nature to him. The lesser nobility he forgives an occasional absence from court if reasons are given. Towards the "great ones" he is implacable. And the court's role as a place of detention emerges particularly clearly in relation to them. "The surest place for a son of France is the heart of the King", he replies when his brother asks him for a governorship and a fortress, a *place de sûreté*. That his eldest son holds separate court at Meudon he views with the utmost displeasure. And when the heir to the throne dies, the king hastily has the furniture of his *château* sold in case the grandson who inherits Meudon should make the same use of it and once again "divide the court".[114]

This fear, says Saint-Simon, was quite groundless. For none of the king's grandsons would have dared to displease him. But when it is a matter of maintaining his prestige and securing his personal rule, the king's severity makes no distinction between his relations and other persons.

Monopoly rule, centred on the monopolies of taxation and physical violence, has thus attained, for this particular stage as the personal monopoly of an individual, its consummate form. It is protected by a fairly efficient organization of surveillance. The land-owning king distributing land or tithes has become a money-owning king distributing salaries: this gives centralization a power and solidity unattained hitherto. The strength of the centrifugal social forces has been finally broken. All possible rivals of the monopoly ruler have been brought into an institutionally secured dependence on him. No longer in free competition but in one restricted by monopoly, only a section of the nobility, the courtly section, competes for the opportunities distributed by the monopoly ruler, and is at the same time under constant pressure from a reserve army of country aristocracy and rising bourgeois elements. The court is the organizational form of this restricted competition.

But even if at this stage the king's personal control of the monopolized opportunities is great, it is anything but unlimited. In the structure of this relatively private monopoly there are already unmistakable elements which will finally lead from personal control of the monopolies to public control by ever-broader sections of society. For Louis XIV the statement: "L'État c'est moi" has, indeed, a measure of truth, whether or not he himself uttered it. Institutionally, the monopoly organization still has to a considerable extent the character of a personal possession. Functionally, however, the monopoly ruler's dependence on other strata, on the entire network of differentiated social functions, is already very great, and is constantly increasing with the advance of the commercial and monetary integration of society. Only the particular situation of society, the peculiar balance of tensions between the rising bourgeois and the declining aristocratic groups, and then between the many major and minor groups throughout the land, gives the central ruler his immense powers of control and decision. The independence with which earlier kings ruled their domains, an expression of lower social interdependence, has vanished. The vast human network that Louis XIV rules has its own momentum and its own centre of gravity which he must respect. It costs immense effort and self-control to preserve the balance of people and groups and, by playing on the tensions, to steer the whole.

The central functionary's ability to govern the whole human network largely in his personal interest is only seriously restricted when the balance on which he is poised tilts sharply in favour of the bourgeoisie, and a new social balance with new axes of tension is established. Only then do personal monopolies begin to become public monopolies in an institutional sense. In a long series of elimination contests, in a gradual centralization of the means of physical violence and taxation, in conjunction with a constantly increasing division of functions and the rise of professional bourgeois classes, French society is organized step by step in the form of a state.

VIII

On the Sociogenesis of the Monopoly of Taxation

26. A certain aspect of this monopolization, and thus of the whole process of state-formation, easily escapes the retrospective observer because he usually has a clearer picture of the later stages, of the results of the process, than of developments lying further back. He can hardly conceive that this absolutist monarchy and centralized government emerged quite gradually from the medieval world as something new and extraordinary in the eyes of its contemporaries. Nevertheless, only an attempt to

reconstruct this aspect gives us the possibility of understanding what really happened.

The main outlines of the transformation are clear. From a particular central point it can be described in a few words: *the territorial property of one warrior family, its control of certain lands and its claim to tithes or services of various kinds from the people living on this land, is transformed with the advancing division of functions and in the course of numerous struggles, into a centralized control of military power and of regular duties or taxes over a far larger area.* Within this area no one may now use weapons and fortifications or physical violence of any kind without the central ruler's permission. That is something very novel in a society in which originally a whole class of people could use weapons and physical violence according to their means and their inclinations. And everyone of whom the central ruler requires it is now bound to pay a certain portion of his income or his wealth to the central ruler. This is even more novel, measured by what was customary in medieval society. In the barter economy of that time, where money was relatively rare, demands by princes or kings for money payments—leaving aside certain occasions fixed by tradition—were regarded as something quite unprecedented; such measures were regarded in much the same way as pillaging or the levying of tributes.

"Constituti sunt reditus terrarum, ut ex illis viventes a spoliatione subditorum abstineant";[115] the revenues of the land are intended to prevent those living on them from plundering their subjects, said St Thomas Aquinas. In this he certainly expresses not only the opinion of ecclesiastical circles, even though church institutions are probably particularly exposed to such measures on account of their wealth. The kings themselves do not think very differently, even if, with the general shortage of money, they cannot refrain from repeatedly demanding such compulsory duties. Philip Augustus, for example, arouses so much unrest and opposition through a series of taxes, particularly the contribution for the Crusades in 1188, the famous *dîme saladine*, that in 1189 he declares that no such taxes will ever again be levied. In order, his decree runs, that neither he nor his successors shall ever fall into the same error, he forbids with his royal authority and the whole authority of all the churches and barons of the realm, this damnable effrontery. If anyone, whether the king or anyone else, should attempt "by audacious temperity" to revert to it, he wants them disobeyed.[116] It may be that in the formulation of this decree his pen was guided by agitated notables. But when he is preparing for the Crusade in 1190, he himself expressly orders that in the event of his death during the Crusade, a part of the war treasury shall be distributed among those who have been impoverished by the levies. Duties demanded by the kings in this society with its relative scarcity of money, are indeed something different from taxes in a more commercialized society. No one takes them for granted as a permanent institution; market transactions and the whole level of prices are in no way adjusted to them; they come like a bolt from the blue, ruining large numbers of people. The kings or their representatives, as we can see, are somettimes aware of this. But with the limited revenues they receive directly from their domanial estates, they are constantly faced with the choice of either using all the threats and force at their disposal to raise money by levies, or succumbing to rival powers. All the same, the agitation over the "Saladin tithe" and the opposition it unleashed seem to be long remembered. It is only after seventy-nine years that a king again demands a special tax, an *aide féodale* for his Crusade.

The general belief of kings themselves is that the rulers of a territory and their government should support themselves on the income from their domanial possessions in the narrower sense, that is, on the income from their own estates. To be sure, the kings and a number of other great feudal lords, in the course of monopolization, already rise considerably above the mass of the feudal lords, and we can see in retrospect that new functions are evolving. But these new functions develop only slowly, by small steps and in constant conflict with the representatives of other functions, into solid institutions. For the time being, the king is a great warrior among many other greater or lesser warriors. Like them, he lives on the produce of his estates; but like them he also has a traditional right to raise taxes from the inhabitants of his region on certain extraordinary occasions. Every feudal lord demands and receives certain duties when his daughter is married, when his son is knighted, and to pay his ransom if he is made a prisoner-of-war. These are the original *aides féodales*; and the kings demand them like every other feudal lord.

Demands for money over and above these have no basis in custom; this is why they have a similar repute to pillage and extortion.

Then, in about the twelfth and thirteenth centuries, a new form of princely revenue begins to establish itself. In the twelfth century the towns are slowly growing. According to ancient feudal custom, only men of the warrior class, the nobles, are entitled to bear arms; but the burghers have now fought sword in hand for civic freedom or are about to do so; and about the time of Louis VI it becomes customary to enrol the town-dwellers, the "bourgeois", for war duties. Very soon, however, the town-dwellers prefer to offer the territorial lords money instead of war services so that he can hire warriors. They commercialize war service; and to the kings and the other great feudal lords this is not unwelcome. The supply of war services by indigent warriors is usually greater than the purchasing power of the rival feudal lords. So these civic payments for exemption from war service quite quickly become an established custom or an institution. The king's representatives demand from each town community such and such a number of men or the payment of a corresponding sum for a particular campaign, and the towns agree or negotiate a reduction. But even this custom is still seen as only a further form of the feudal *aides* in extraordinary cases; it is called the *aide de l'ost* and these aids are taken together as the "aids in the four cases".

It would take us too far afield to show how the town communities themselves gradually begin to form a kind of internal taxation system for the various communal tasks. Suffice it to say that the king's demands serve to develop this, just as, conversely, the urban taxation institutions that begin to be consolidated about the end of the twelfth century have an importance for the organization of royal taxation that should not be underestimated. Here, too, the bourgeoisie and the royal house—usually involuntarily—propel each other. But this is certainly not to say that the burghers or any other social class pay willingly and without resistance. As is the case with regular taxation later, no one pays these occasional taxes unless he feels directly or indirectly forced to do so. Both cases indicate exactly the nature of the mutual dependence of groups in society at a given stage and of the prevailing power balances.

The kings do not wish and cannot afford to provoke excessive opposition; the social power of the royal function is clearly not yet strong enough for this. On the other hand, they need for their function and self-assertion, above all to finance the constant struggles with rivals, continual and gradually increasing sums of money that they can only obtain by such *aides*. Their measures change. Under the pressure of this situation the royal representatives grope for one solution after another; they shift the main burden now onto this urban or other class, now that. But in all this twisting and turning the social power of the monarchy is constantly growing, and with this growth, each furthering the other, taxes gradually take on a new character.

In 1292 the king demands a duty of one "denier" in the pound for all wares sold, the duty being payable by both buyer and seller. "An exaction of a kind unheard-of in the French realm"—a chronicler of the time calls it. In Rouen the counting-house of the royal tax-collectors is plundered. Rouen and Paris, the two most important towns in the kingdom, finally buy themselves free for a fixed sum.[117] But this tax remains long in the popular memory under the ominous name *mal-tôte*; and the opposition it arouses remains long in the minds of the royal officials. Accordingly, the king attempts in the following year to raise compulsory loans from the wealthy bourgeois. When this too meets with violent resistance, he reverts in 1295 to the *aide* in its original form; the levy is demanded from all estates, not only the third. One hundredth of the value of all goods is to be paid. But the yield of this tax is clearly not enough. The following year the duty is raised to a fiftieth. And now, of course, the feudal lords also affected by the tax are extremely angry. The king therefore declares himself willing to return to the religious and secular feudal lords a part of the sum he raises from their dominions. He gives them, so to speak, a share of the booty. But this no longer reassures them. Above all, the secular feudal lords, the warriors, feel increasingly threatened in their traditional rights, their independent rule and perhaps even in their whole social existence, by this central governmental apparatus. The king's men are intruding everywhere; they appropriate rights and duties which earlier were the exclusive prerogative of the individual feudal lord. And here, as so often, it is money duties that are the last straw. When, in 1314, shortly before the death of Philip the Fair, high taxes for a campaign in Flanders are once again levied, unrest and discontent, reinforced by the mismanagement of the war, become open resistance. "We cannot tolerate the levying of these 'aides'", says one of those affected,[118] "we cannot bear them with a quiet conscience; they would cost us our honour, our rights and our freedom." "A new kind of unjustified extortion, of unseemly money-raising, unknown in France and particularly in Paris," another man of the time records, "was used to cover expenses; it was said to be intended for the Flanders war. The servile councils and ministers of the King wanted buyers and sellers to pay six deniers for each pound of the selling price. Nobles and commoners . . . united under oath to maintain their freedom and that of the fatherland."

The unrest is indeed so great and general that towns and feudal lords form an alliance against the king. It is one of those historical experiments from which we can read off the degree of divergence of their interests, the strength of the tension between them. Under the common threat from the fiscal demands of the royal representatives, and the high feelings it arouses on all sides, a league between bourgeoisie and nobility is still possible. Will it last, will it be effective? It has already been pointed out that in other countries, above all in England, on the basis of a different social structure, a rapprochement and concerted action between certain urban and rural classes gradually comes into being which—despite all the tensions and hostility between them—finally contributes in no small way to the curtailment of royal power. The fate of such alliances in France, as can be seen here in embryonic form and far more clearly later, with the growing interdependence of the estates, is very different. The unanimity of the estates does not survive long; the impact of their combined actions is broken by their mutual mistrust. "Anger and discontent bring them together, but their interests admit no unity."[119]

> Il sont lignée deslignée
> Contrefaite et mal alignée

runs a song of the time about the allies. All the same, this violent reaction to wilfully levied taxes leaves a strong impression, not least on the royal officials. Such upheavals within the dominion are not without danger for the struggle with external rivals. The social position of the central ruler is not yet strong enough for him alone to determine the duties and their level; power is still distributed in such a way that he must negotiate on each occasion with the estates whom he is taxing and gain their approval. And as yet the *aides* are no more than occasional and extraordinary payments to assist in a particular concrete purpose. This is only gradually to change in the course of the Hundred Years' War. As war becomes permanent, so also do the duties needed by the central ruler for its conduct.

27. "The struggle facing the monarchy in seeking to establish and develop its fiscal power can only be appreciated if we are aware of the social forces and interests it encountered as obstacles to its designs."[120] This statement does indeed point to the basic feature of the sociogenesis of the taxation monopoly. To be sure, the kings themselves cannot foresee, any more than their adversaries in this struggle, the new institution to which it will give rise. They do not really have any general intention to "increase their fiscal power". To begin with they and their representatives want quite simply to extract as much money as possible from their dominion on one occasion after another, and the tasks and expenses necessitating this are always quite specific and immediate. No single man created taxes or the taxation monopoly; no individual, or series of individuals throughout the century in which this institution was slowly formed, worked towards this goal by any deliberate plan. Taxation, like any other institution, is a product of social interweaving. It arises—as from a parallelogram of forces—from the conflicts of the various social groups and interests, until sooner or later the instrument which has developed in the constant social trials of strength becomes more and more consciously understood by the interested parties and more deliberately constructed into an organization or institution. In this way, in conjunction with a gradual transformation of society and a shift of the power relationships within it, the occasional aids to the lords of estates or territories, levied for specific campaigns or ransom or dowries or the provision of sons, are transformed into regular payments. As the money and trade sector of the economy slowly increases, as a particular house of feudal lords gradually becomes a house of kings over an ever-larger area, the feudal *aide aux quatre cas* turns step by step into taxation.

From 1328 onwards, and more strongly from 1337, this transformation of the extraordinary aid into regular duties accelerates. In 1328 a direct tax for the war with Flanders is again levied in certain parts of the kingdom; in 1335 there is an indirect tax in a number of western towns, a duty on each sale, for equipping a fleet; in 1338 all royal officials have something deducted from their pay; in 1340 the tax on the sale of wares is re-introduced and made general; in 1341 there is an additional tax on the sale of salt, the *gabelle du sel*. In 1344, 1345 and 1346 these indirect taxes continue to be raised. After the Battle of Crécy, the royal officials again try a personal direct tax, and in 1347 and 1348 they revert once more to the indirect form, the tax on sales. All this is to some degree experimental; all these levies are regarded, as we have said, as temporary assistance from society in the conduct of the king's war; they are *les aides sur le fait de la guerre*. The king and his officials declare over and over again that the demands for money will cease with the hostilities.[121] And whenever the estates' representatives have the chance, they underline this; they try to ascertain that the money coming from the *aides* is actually used for military purposes. The kings themselves, however, at least from Charles V on, never adhere very strictly to this demand. They control the funds from the *aides* and continue, when they think it necessary, to meet their own household costs or to reward their favourites from this money. This whole development, this inflow of money to the king's treasury as well as the establishment of a military force paid from this money, slowly but surely leads to an extraordinary strengthening of the central function. Each of the estates, the nobility above all, opposes the central authority's increase in power to the best of its ability. But here, too, their divergence of interests weakens their resistance. They are far too much affected by the war, far too directly interested in a successful repulsion of the English, to be able to refuse the king funds. In addition, the strength of the antagonism between them, together with local differences, not only undermines any common front to limit the king's financial demands or to supervise the use of this income, but prevents a direct organization of the war by the estates. The threat from outside makes the people of this society, which still has relatively little unity and interdependence, particularly dependent on the king as supreme co-ordinator and on his governmental machine. So they have to put up year after year with the levying in the king's name of "extraordinary aids" for a war that does not end.

Finally, after King John is taken prisoner in the Battle of

Poitiers, in order to pay the enormous ransom demanded by the English, a tax is levied for the first time not just for one year but for six. Here, as so often, a major but fortuitous event merely accelerates something that had long been prepared in the structure of society. In reality this tax is raised continuously not for six years but for twenty, and we may suppose that by this time a certain adaptation of the market to such payments is taking place. Moreover, apart from this purchase-tax for the king's ransom there are continual taxes for other purposes as well; in 1363 a direct tax to cover the immediate costs of war, in 1367 another to combat pillage by the soldiery, in 1369, on the resumption of war, new direct and indirect taxes including the specially hated house-tax, the *fouage*.

"All these are still, no doubt, feudal 'aides', but generalized, made uniform and levied not only in the king's domain but throughout the kingdom under the supervision of a special, centralized administrative machine."[122] In fact, in this phase of the Hundred Years' War when the *aides* are slowly becoming permanent, there gradually evolve specialized official functions devoted to collecting and legally enforcing these "extraordinary payments", as they are still called. First of all they are represented simply by a few *Généraux sur le fait des finances*, who supervise the army of those responsible for the *aides* throughout the land. Then, in 1370, there are already two supreme administrators, one of whom specializes in the financial and the other in the legal questions arising from the collection of *aides*. This is the first form of what later, throughout the whole *ancien régime*, remains one of the most important organs of fiscal administration, the *Chambre* or *Cour des Aides*. But here, in the years 1370 to 1380, this institution is still in the process of formation; it lacks a definite form; it is one more attempt in the open or silent struggle in which the different social power-centres are constantly testing each other's strength. And its presence does not, as often happens with solidly established institutions, obliterate the memory of the social conflicts from which it has resulted. Each time the monarchy, meeting resistance in different parts of the population, has to limit its taxation demands, these official functions also recede. Their level and the curve of their growth is a fairly exact indicator of the social strength of the central function and the apparatus for ruling in relation to the nobility, the clergy and the urban classes.

Under Charles V, as has been mentioned, the *aides sur le fait de la guerre* become as permanent as the war itself. They weigh upon a people that is being impoverished in this war by devastation, fire, trade difficulties and not least by continuous raids by troops who want to be fed and feed themselves by force. All the more oppressive are the taxes demanded by the king; and the more strongly their becoming the rule instead of the exception is felt as a contravention of tradition. As long as Charles V is alive all this finds no visible expression. Distress grows unseen, and with it discontent. But it seems that the king is to some extent aware of this growing tension in the country, of the suppressed feelings, particularly against the taxes. He probably realizes the danger to which this mood must give rise if, in his place, in place of an old, experienced king, a child, his son who is still a minor, comes to the throne under the guardianship of rival relations. And perhaps this fear of the future is coupled to pangs of conscience. Certainly the taxes that his government has brought in year after year seem to the king inevitable and indispensable. But even for him, the beneficiary, these taxes clearly still have a tinge of injustice about them. At any rate, a few hours before his death, on 16 September 1380, he signs a decree repealing above all the most oppressive and unpopular tax, the house-tax which weighs equally on rich and poor. How appropriate this decree is to the situation created by the king's death very quickly becomes apparent. The central function weakened, the repressed tensions in the country break out. The competing relations of the dead king, above all Louis of Anjou and Philip the Bold of Burgundy, contest predominance and not least control of the royal treasury. The towns begin to revolt against the taxes. The people put the royal tax-collectors to flight. And the agitation of the lower urban strata is at first not unwelcome to the richer bourgeoisie. The desires of both run parallel. The urban notables who in November 1380 meet representatives of the other estates in Paris, demand the abolition of the royal taxes. Probably the Duke of Anjou, the king's Chancellor, promises to fulfil the demand under this direct pressure. On 16 November 1380 a decree is issued in the king's name by which "henceforth for ever, all 'fouage' impositions, salt taxes, fourths and eights, by which our subjects have been so much aggrieved, all aids and subsidies of any kind which have been imposed on account of the said wars . . .", are abolished.

"The whole financial system of the last ten years, all the conquests made in the years 1358/59 and 1367/68, are sacrificed. The monarchy is thrown back almost a century. It finds itself at almost the same point as at the beginning of the Hundred Years' War."[123]

Like a system of forces that has not yet reached equilibrium, society sways back and forth between the various poles in the struggle for power. It speaks for the social power already possessed by the central government and the royal function at this time, that they are able to make up the lost ground with extraordinary speed, although the king himself is a child and wholly dependent on the administrators and servants of the monarchy. What later manifests itself once more under Charles VIII with particular clarity, emerges fairly clearly even at this time: the opportunities open to the royal function in this structure of French society and in this situation, are already so great that the monarchy can increase its social power even when the king is personally weak or insignificant. The dependence of the groups and classes in this society on a supreme co-ordinator who maintains co-operation between the various social functions and districts, grows with their interdependence, and grows even more under the pressure of military danger. And so, willingly or not, they very quickly restore the means needed to conduct the war to the men who represent their common interests, above all in conflicts with external enemies: the king and his representative. But in so doing they also give the monarchy the means to control them. In 1382/83 the monarchy, i.e. the king together with all the relations, councils and servants who in any way belong to the government machine, is again in a position to dictate to the towns, the chief centres of resistance, the taxes it considers necessary.

The question of taxes is at the centre of the urban risings of 1382. But in the struggle over taxes and the distribution of their burden by the central apparatus, the question of the whole distribution of power, as so often, is tested and decided. The objective of gaining a voice in the raising and distribution of taxes, that is, of supervising from a central position the working of the government machine, is pursued quite consciously by the urban notables of the time, and not only by them. At assemblies, representatives of the other estates sometimes push in the same direction. The horizons of the lower and middle urban classes are generally narrower; what they want above all is release from their oppressive burdens, nothing more. Even in this direction the goals of the various urban groups are not always the same, even if—in their relation to the central apparatus of the country—they are not necessarily mutually hostile. In the smaller circle of the towns themselves matters are very different. Here the interests of the different strata, despite all their interweaving and indeed precisely because of it, are often diametrically opposed.

The urban communities of this time are already highly complex formations. There is in them a privileged upper stratum, the bourgeoisie proper, whose monopoly position is expressed in its control of the civic offices and therefore of finances. There is a middle stratum, a kind of petty bourgeoisie, the less wealthy craftsmen and tradesmen; and finally there is a mass of journeymen and workers, the "people". And here, too, the taxes form the nodal point where both the interdependence and the antitheses emerge particularly clearly. If clear demands are expressed at all, the middle and lower groups seek direct, progressive taxes which each pays according to his means, while the urban upper stratum prefers indirect or flat-rate taxes. As so often, the agitation of the people over taxes and the first wave of unrest are to begin with not unwelcome to the urban upper stratum. It favours this movement as long as it reinforces its own opposition to the monarchy or even to the local feudal lords. But very quickly the insurrection turns against the wealthy town-dwellers themselves. It becomes in part a struggle for urban administration between the ruling bourgeois patriciate and the middle strata, who demand their share in the civic offices as the urban notables demand theirs in the larger sphere of the government of the country. The urban upper strata take flight or defend themselves; and they are usually saved at this stage of the struggle by the arrival of royal troops.

It would take us too far afield to follow these struggles and the risings in different towns in detail. They end with a further shift of power in favour of the central apparatus and the monarchy. The ringleaders of the revolt, particularly those who had refused to pay taxes, are punished by death, others with heavy fines. On the towns as a whole large payments are imposed. In Paris, the fortified royal castles or bastilles are reinforced and new ones built, manned by royal men-at-arms, *gens d'armes*. And urban liberties are restricted. From now on local town administrations are increasingly placed under royal officials until they too are essentially organs of the royal apparatus for ruling. In this way the hierarchy of the central government apparatus, whose occupants are the leading bourgeois, extends from ministerial posts and the highest judicial offices to the positions of mayor and guild-master. And the question of taxes as a whole is decided in the same way. They are now dictated by the central organization.

If we examine the reasons why this trial of strength was so quickly decided in favour of the central function, we again encounter the fact already mentioned so often: it is the antagonisms between the various groups of this society that give the central function its strength. The bourgeois upper class has a tense relationship not only to the secular and clerical feudal lords, but also to the lower urban strata. Here, it is above all the disunity of the urban classes themselves which favours the central ruler. No less important is the fact that as yet scarcely any close association exists between the different towns of the kingdom. There are weak tendencies towards a collaboration of several cities. But integration is not yet nearly close enough to permit concerted action. The different towns still confront each other to some extent like foreign powers; between them too there is more or less intense competition. So the royal representatives first conclude a truce with Paris in order to have a free hand against the towns of Flanders. Thus secured, they break the urban resistance in Flanders; then they break it in Rouen, then in Paris. They defeat each town singly. Not only social but regional fragmentation as well—within certain limits and not excluding a certain degree of interdependence—favours the central function. In face of the combined opposition of all parts of the population, the monarchy would necessarily be defeated. But in face of each individual class or region the central function, drawing its power from the whole country, is the stronger.

Nevertheless, sections of society continue to try to limit or break the growing power of the central function. Each time, in accordance with the same structural regularities, the disturbed balance is restored after a time in the monarch's favour, and each of these trials of strength further advances its power. Taxes paid to the king still disappear now and then or are briefly restricted, but they are always very soon revived. In exactly the same way offices concerned with the administration and collection of taxes vanish and reappear. The history of the *Chambre des Aides*, for example, is full of such upheavals and sudden reversals. There are several successive resurrections between 1370 and 1390. Then again in 1413, 1418, 1425, 1462, 1464 and 1474 it undergoes, as its historian writes, "excesses of life and death, unpredictable resurrections",[124] until finally it becomes a firmly established institution in the royal governmental machine. And while these fluctuations do not, of course, reflect only the great social trials of strength, they nevertheless give a certain picture of the sociogenesis of the royal function, the growth of the monopoly organization in general. They make it clear how little all these functions and formations result from the long-term conscious plans of individuals, and how much they arise by small, tentative steps from a multitude of intertwining and conflicting human efforts and activities.

28. The individual kings themselves are, in the deployment of their personal power, wholly dependent on the situation in which they find the royal function. This seldom shows itself so clearly as in the case of Charles VII. As an individual he is certainly not especially strong; he is not a great or powerful person. Yet, after the English have been expelled from his territory, during his reign the monarchy grows stronger and stronger. The king now stands before his people as a victorious army leader, however little he may be inclined to this role by personal predisposition. In the war all the financial and human resources of the country have been collected in the hands of the central authority. The centralization of the army, the monopoly control of taxation have advanced a good distance. The external foe has been driven out, but the army, or at least a good part of it, is still present. It gives the king such internal preponderance that resistance to his wishes by the estates is as good as hopeless, particularly as the exhausted population wants one thing above all else: peace. In this situation the king declares in 1436 that the nation has approved the *aides* for an unlimited period, that he has been asked not to assemble the estates in future to decide on taxes; the costs of the journey to the estates' assemblies, he says, place far too heavy a burden on the people.

This justification is, of course, wholly without substance. The measure itself, the suppression of the estates' assemblies, is simply an expression of the social power of the monarchy. This power has become so great that the *aides*, which during the war have in practice become more or less continuous, can now be openly declared a permanent institution. And this power is already so unquestionable that the king no longer thinks it necessary to agree the amount and kind of taxes with those who pay them. As has been mentioned, the estates still repeatedly attempt to resist. The suppression of their parliament and the dictatorial powers of the kings are not consolidated without a series of trials of strength. But each of these shows yet again, and more and more clearly, how inexorably, in this phase of the advancing differentiation and integration of society, the power of the central function is growing. Again and again it is the military power concentrated in the hands of the central authority which secures and increases his control of taxes, and it is this concentrated control of taxes which makes possible an ever-stronger monopolization of physical and military power. Step by step these two means drive each other upwards until, at a certain point, the total superiority attained by the central function in this process is revealed nakedly to the eyes of its astonished and embittered contemporaries. Here again a voice from that time is better than any description in conveying to us how all this broke upon people as something new, without their knowing how or why.

When, under Charles VII, the central government begins quite openly to announce and collect taxes permanently without the estates' agreement, Juvenal des Ursines, the Archbishop of Rheims, writes a letter to the king. It includes, freely translated, the following:[125]

When your predecessors intended to go to war, it was their custom to assemble the three estates; they invited people from the Church, the nobility and the common people to meet them in one of their good cities. Then they came and explained how things stood and what was needed to resist the enemy and they required that the people took counsel on how the war was to be conducted in order to help the king with taxes decided in this discussion. You yourself always maintained this procedure until you realized that God and Fortune—which is changeable—have so helped you that you feel such discussions to be beneath your dignity. You now impose the "Aides" and other duties, and suffer them to be levied like duties from your domain, without the agreement of your three estates.

Earlier ... this kingdom could rightly be called "Royaume France", for it used to be free [franc] and had all liberties [franchises et libertés]. Today the people are no more than slaves, wilfully taxed [taillables à voulenté]. If we look at the population of the kingdom we find only a tenth of those who were formerly there. I would not wish to diminish your power, but rather to increase it to the best of my small ability. There is no doubt that a prince, and particularly Your Highness, may in certain cases cut off [tailler] something from your subjects and levy the "Aides", particularly to defend the kingdom and the public cause [chose publique]. But this he must agree in a reasonable manner. His task is not mine. It may be that you are sovereign in matters of justice, and that this is your authority. But as far as domanial revenues are concerned, you have your domain and each private person his [N.B. in other words the king should kindly support himself on his estates and domanial revenues, and not usurp control of the revenues of the whole country]. And today the subjects do not merely have their wool sheared, but their skin, their flesh and blood down to the bones.

In another passage the archbishop gives free rein to his indignation: "He deserves to be stripped of his rule who uses it wilfully and not one half to the advantage of his subjects. . . . Take care, therefore, that the surfeit of money flowing to you from the 'Aides', which you draw from the body, does not destroy your soul. You are also the head of this body. Would it not be great tyranny if the head of a human creature destroyed the heart, the hands, and feet [N.B. probably symbolizing clergy, warriors and common people]."

From now on, and for a long period, it is the subjects who point to the public character of the royal function. Expressions like "public cause", "fatherland" and even "state" are first used generally in opposition to the princes and kings. The central rulers themselves control the monopolized opportunities in this phase, above all the revenue from their dominions—as Juvenal des Ursines says—like private property. And it is in this sense, too, as a reply to the opposition's use of such words as fatherland or state, that we should understand the saying attributed to the king: "I am the state." Amazement at this whole development is not, however, confined to the French. The régime that is emerging in France, the strength and solidity of the central apparatus and function, that subsequently appear, sooner or later, on the basis of analogous structures, in almost every country in Europe, is in the fifteenth century something even more surprising and novel to observers outside France. We need only read reports of Venetian envoys of this time to have an impression of how a foreign observer, who undoubtedly has wide experience in such matters, encounters in France an unknown form of government.

In 1492 Venice sends two envoys to Paris, officially to congratulate Charles VIII on his marriage to Anne of Brittany, but in reality, no doubt, to find out how and where France intends to use her power in Italy, and in general, how things stand in France, what is the financial situation, what kind of people the king and government are, what products are imported and exported, what factions exist; in a word, the envoys have to discover everything worth knowing to enable Venice to take the correct political action. And these embassies, which now gradually change from an occasional to a permanent institution, are themselves a sign of how in this period Europe is slowly becoming interdependent over larger areas.

Accordingly, we find in their report, among other things, an exact depiction of the French finances and of financial procedure in the country. The envoy estimates the king's income at approximately 3,600,000 francs per annum—including "1,400,000 franchi da alcune imposizioni che se solevano metter *estraordinarie* . . . le quali si sono continuate per tal modo che al presente sono fatte *ordinarie*" (1,400,000 francs from impositions which used to be *extraordinary* but have become *ordinary*). The ambassador estimates the king's expenses at 6,600,000 or 7,300,000 francs. The resultant deficit, he reports, is raised in the following way:

Every year, in January, the directors of the financial administration of each region—that is, those of the royal domain proper, Dauphiné, Languedoc, Brittany and Burgundy—meet to calculate incomes and expenses to meet the needs of the following year. And they *begin* by considering expenses [prima mettono tutta la spesa], and to cover the deficit between the expenses and the expected revenues they fix a general tax for all the provinces of the Kingdom. Of these taxes neither prelates nor nobles pay anything, but only the people. In this way the ordinary revenues and this tax bring in enough to cover the expenditure of the coming year. If, during the year, a war breaks out or there is any other unexpected cause of expenditure, so that the estimates are no longer enough, another tax is levied or stipends are cut so that under all circumstances the necessary sum is obtained.[126]

Up to now a good deal has been said about the formation of the taxation monopoly. Here, in the Venetian envoys' account, we are given a clear picture of its form and functioning at this stage of development. We also find one of the most important structural features of absolutism and—to a certain extent—of the "state" in general: the primacy of expenditure over income. For the individual members of society, particularly in bourgeois society, it becomes more and more a habit and a necessity to determine expenditure strictly by income. In the economy of a social whole, by contrast, expenses are the fixed point; on them income, i.e. the sums demanded from the individual members of society through the tax monopoly, are made dependent. This is another example of how the totality arising from the interdependence of individuals possesses structural characteristics and is subject to regularities different from those of individuals, and not to be understood from the individual's point of view. The only limit set to the financial needs of a central social agency of this time is the taxable capacity of society as a whole, and the social power of individual groups in relation to the controllers of the tax monopoly. Later, when the monopoly administration has come under the control of broader bourgeois strata, the economy of society as a whole is sharply divided from that of the individual people administrating the central monopoly. Society as a whole, the state, can and must continue to make taxes, income, essentially dependent on the socially necessary expenditure; but the kings, the individual central rulers, must now behave like all other individuals; they have precisely fixed stipends and manage their expenses accordingly.

Here, in the first phase of full monopoly, things are different. The royal and public economies are not yet separate. The kings set taxes in accordance with the expenses they consider necessary, whether these are for wars or castles or gifts to their favourites. The key monopolies of rule still have the character of personal monopolies. But what from our point of view is only the first stage on the way to the formation of societal or public monopolies, appears to these Venetian observers of about 1500 as a novelty which they regard with curiosity, as one is apt to consider the unknown manners and customs of strange peoples. Where they come from things are quite different. The power of the supreme Venetian authorities, like that of medieval princes, is restricted to a high degree by the local government of different regions and estates. Venice, too, is the centre of a major dominion. Other municipalities have placed themselves voluntarily or otherwise under its rule. But even in the case of communes subjugated by force, the conditions on which they are incorporated into the Venetian dominion nearly always includes a provision "that no new taxes may be introduced without the agreement of the majority of the council".[127]

In the dispassionate reports of the non-partisan Venetian envoys, the transformation that has taken place in France is perhaps more vividly expressed than in the indignant words of the Archbishop of Rheims.

In 1535 the report of the Venetian envoys contains the following:

> Apart from the fact that the king is militarily powerful, he obtains money through his people's obedience. I say that his Majesty usually has an income of two and a half million. I say "usually"; for, if he so wishes, he can increase the taxes on his people. Whatever burdens he places on them, they pay without restriction. But I must say in this regard that the section of the population which bears the major part of his burden is very poor, so that any increase in the burden however small, would be unbearable.

In 1546, finally, the Venetian Ambassador Marino Cavalli gives an exact and detailed report on France in which the peculiarities of the government of that country, as it appears to an impartial contemporary with wide horizons, emerge particularly clearly:

> Many kingdoms are more fertile and richer than France, for example, Hungary and Italy, many are larger and more powerful, for example, Germany and Spain. But none is as united and obedient. I do not believe that her prestige has any other cause than these two things: unity and obedience [unione e obbedienza]. To be sure, freedom is the most cherished gift in the world; but not all are worthy of it. For this reason some peoples are usually born to obey, others to command. If it is

the other way round we have a situation like the present one in Germany, or earlier in Spain. The French, however, perhaps feeling unsuited to it, have handed over their freedom and will entirely to the king. So it is enough for him to say: I want such-and-such, I approve such-and-such, I decide such-and-such, and all this is promptly executed as if they had all decided it. Things have gone so far that today one of them who has more wit than the others, says: Earlier their kings had called themselves "reges Francorum", today they can call themselves "reges servorum". So they not only pay the king whatever he demands, but all other capital is likewise open to his grasp.

Charles VII increased this obedience of the people, after he had freed the country from the yoke of the English; and after him Louis XI and Charles VIII, who conquered Naples, did likewise. Louis XII made his own contribution. But the ruling King (Francis I) can boast of having greatly outdone his predecessors: he has his subjects pay extraordinary sums, as much as he wants; he unites new possessions with the Crown Estates without giving anything in return. And if he does give anything away, this is valid only for the lifetime of the giver or of the recipient. And if one or the other lives too long, the whole gift is withdrawn as something due to the Crown. It is true that some are afterwards made permanent. And their practice is the same with regard to the leaders and the various grades of the military. So that if someone enters your service and says he has had such-and-such reward, titles and provisions from the French, Your Serenity will know of what kind these provisions, titles and gifts are. Many never attain them, or on only one occasion in their lives, some remain two, three years without receiving any reward. Your Serenity, who give away quite definite things, but to some extent hereditary ones, should certainly not be influenced by the example of what is done elsewhere. In my judgement the custom of giving only for the duration of a lifetime ... is excellent. It always gives the king the opportunity of rewarding those who are deserving; and there is always something left to give away. If the gifts were hereditary, we would now have an impoverished Francia and the present kings would have nothing more to give away; but in this way they are served by people of more merit than the heirs of some earlier recipient. Your Serenity might reflect, if France acts in this way, on what other princes ought to do who do not rule such a large country. If we do not carefully consider where these hereditary gifts lead—to the preservation of the family, it is said—it will happen that there are no sufficient rewards left for truly deserving people, or new burdens will have to be placed on the people. Both things are unjust and harmful enough. If gifts are made only for lifetime, then only those who deserve it are rewarded. Estates circulate and after a time revert to the fisc. . . . For eighty years new agreements have continually been made with the Crown without giving anything away, through confiscation, reversion on inheritance or purchase. In this way the Crown has absorbed everything, to the extent that there is not a single prince in the whole realm who has an income of 20,000 scudi. Moreover, those who possess incomes and land are not ordinary owners; for the king retains supreme rule by virtue of the appeals, taxes, garrisons and all the other new and extraordinary burdens. The Crown becomes more and more wealthy and unified and attains immense prestige; and that secures it from civil war. For as there are nothing but poor princes, they have neither reason nor the possibility to take action against the king, as the dukes of Brittany, Normandy, Burgundy and many other great lords of Gascony did earlier. And if anyone does anything ill-considered and tries to bring about some change, like the Bourbons, this only gives the king an even earlier opportunity to enrich himself through that man's ruin.[128]

Here, compressed into a single view, we have a summary of the decisive structural features of emergent absolutism. One feudal lord has won predominance over all his competitors, supreme rule over all land. And this control of land is increasingly commercialized or monetarized. The change is expressed on the one hand by the fact that the king possesses a monopoly in collecting and fixing taxes throughout the country, so that he controls by far the largest income. A king owning and distributing land becomes more and more a king owning money and distributing income. This is precisely what enables him to break out of the vicious circle which trapped the rulers of countries with barter economies. He pays no longer for the services he needs, military, courtly or administrative, by giving away parts of his property as the hereditary property of his servants, as is clearly still in part the case in Venice. At most he gives land or salaries for life, and then withdraws them so that the crown possessions are not reduced; and in an increasingly large number of cases he rewards services only with money gifts, with salaries. He centralizes the taxation of the whole country and distributes the inflowing money at his own discretion and in the interests of his rule, so that an immense and ever-growing number of people throughout the country are directly or indirectly dependent on the king's favour, on payments by the royal financial administration. It is the more or less private interests of the kings and their closest servants which veer toward exploitation of their social opportunities in this direction; but what emerges in the conflicts of interest between the various social functions, is the form of social organization which we call the "state". The tax monopoly, together with the monopoly of physical force, are the backbone of this organization. We can understand neither the genesis nor the existence of "states" unless we are aware—even from the example of a single country—how one of these central institutions of the "state" develops step by step in accordance with relational dynamics, as a result of a very specific regularity arising from the structure of interwoven interests and actions. Even at this stage—as we see from the Venetian's report—the central organ of society takes on a hitherto unknown stability and strength because its ruler, thanks to the monetarization of society, no longer needs to pay for services from his own possessions, which without expansion would sooner or later be exhausted, but with sums of money from the regular inflow of taxation. Finally, the peculiarity of money exempts him from the necessity first taken over from the procedure of rewarding with land, of repaying services with a possession to be held for life and hereditary. It makes it possible to reward the service or a number of services by a single payment, by a fee or salary. The numerous and far-reaching consequences of this change must be left aside here. The astonishment of the Venetian envoy is enough to show how this custom, which is now commonplace and taken for granted, appeared then as something new. His account also once again shows particularly clearly why it is only the monetarization of society that makes possible stable central organs: money payment keeps all recipients permanently dependent on the central authority. Only now can the centrifugal tendencies be finally broken.

And it is also from this wider context that we must understand what is happening to the nobility at this time. In the preceding period, when the rest of the nobility were stronger, the king exerted his power as central ruler, within certain limits, in favour of the bourgeoisie. His apparatus for ruling thus became

222

a bastion of the bourgeoisie. Now that, as a result of monetary integration and military centralization, the warriors, the land-owners, the nobility are declining further and further, the king begins to pit his weight and the opportunities he has to distribute somewhat more on the side of the nobility. He gives a part of the nobility the possibility of continuing to exist as a stratum elevated above the bourgeoisie. Slowly, after the last fruitless resistance by elements of the estates in the religious wars and then in the *Fronde*, court offices become a privilege and thus a bastion of the nobility. In this way the kings protect the nobility's pre-eminence; they distribute their favour and the money they control in such a way that the balance endangered by the nobility's decline is preserved. But thereby the relatively free warrior nobility of earlier times becomes a nobility in lifelong dependence on, and in the service of, the central ruler. Knights become courtiers. And if we ask what social functions these courtiers really have, the answer lies here. We are accustomed to refer to the courtly nobility of the *ancien régime* as a "functionless" class. And indeed, this nobility had no function in terms of the division of labour, and thus in the understanding of the nations of the nineteenth and twentieth centuries. The configuration of functions in the *ancien régime* is different. It is primarily determined by the fact that the central ruler still is to a high degree the personal owner of the power monopoly, that there is not yet any division between the central ruler as a private individual and as a functionary of society. The courtly nobility has no direct function in the division of labour, but it has a function for the king. It is one of the indispensable foundations of his rule. It enables the king to distance himself from the bourgeoisie just as the bourgeoisie enables him to distance himself from the nobility. It is the counterweight to the bourgeoisie in society. That, together with a number of others, is its most important function for the king; without this tension between nobility and bourgeoisie, without this marked difference between the estates, the king would lose the major part of his power. The existence of the courtly aristocracy is indeed an expression of how far monopoly government here is still the personal property of the central ruler, and how far the country's income can still be allocated in the special interests of the central function. The possibility of a kind of planned distribution of national revenue is already created with monopolization. But this possibility of planning is used here to prop up declining strata or functions.

A clear picture of the structure of absolutist society emerges from all this. The secular society of the French *ancien régime* consists, more markedly than that of the nineteenth century, of two sectors: a larger rural agrarian sector, and an urban–bourgeois one which is smaller, but steadily if slowly gaining in economic strength. In both there is a lower stratum, in the latter the urban poor, the mass of journeymen and workers, in the former the peasants. In both there is a lower middle stratum, in the latter the small artisans and probably the lowest officials too, in the former the poorer landed gentry in provincial corners; in both an upper middle stratum, in the latter the wealthy merchants, the high civic officials and even in the provinces the highest judicial and administrative officials, and in the former the more well-off country and provincial aristocracy. In both sectors, finally, there is a leading stratum extending into the court, in the latter the high bureaucracy, the *noblesse de robe*, and the courtly nobility, the élite of the *noblesse d'épée* in the former. In the tensions within and between these sectors, complicated by the tensions and alliances of both with a clergy structured on a similar hierarchy, the king carefully maintains equilibrium. He secures the privileges and social prestige of the nobles against the growing economic strength of bourgeois groups. And, as has been mentioned, he uses part of the social product that he has to distribute by virtue of his control of the financial monopoly to provide for the highest nobility. When, not long before the Revolution, after all attempts at reform have failed, the demand for the abolition of noble privileges moves into the foreground among the watchwords of the opposing bourgeois groups, this implies a demand for a different management of the tax monopoly and tax revenue. The abolition of noble privileges means on the one hand the end of the nobility's exemption from taxes and thus a redistribution of the tax burden; and on the other the elimination or reduction of many court offices, the annihilation of what was—in the eyes of this new professional bourgeoisie—a useless and functionless nobility, and thus a different distribution of tax revenue, no longer in the interests of the king but in those of society at large, or at least, to begin with, of the upper bourgeoisie. Finally, however, the removal of noble privileges means the destruction of the position of the central ruler as the balance maintaining the two estates in their existing order of precedence. The central rulers of the subsequent period are indeed balanced on a different network of tensions. They and their function accordingly have a different character. Only one thing remains the same: even in this new structure of tensions, the power of the central authority is relatively limited as long as the tensions remain relatively low, as long as direct agreement is possible between the representatives of the opposed poles, and it grows in phases when these tensions are growing, as long as none of the competing groups has attained a decisive preponderance.

Towards a Theory of Civilizing Processes

I

The Social Constraint towards Self-Constraint

What has the organization of society in the form of "states",
what have the monopolization and centralization of taxes and
physical force over a large area, to do with "civilization"?

The observer of the civilizing process finds himself confronted
by a whole tangle of problems. To mention a few of the most
important at the outset, there is, first of all, the most general
question. We have seen—and the quotations in the first volume
served to illustrate this with specific examples—that the civilizing process is a change of human conduct and sentiment in a
quite specific direction. But, obviously, individual people did not
at some past time intend this change, this "civilization", and
gradually realize it by conscious, "rational", purposive measures.
Clearly, "civilization" is not, any more than rationalization, a
product of human "ratio" or the result of calculated long-term
planning. How would it be conceivable that gradual "rationalization" could be founded on pre-existing "rational" behaviour and
planning over centuries? Could one really imagine that the
civilizing process had been set in motion by people with that
long-term perspective, that specific mastery of all short-term
affects, considering that this type of long-term perspective and
self-mastery already presuppose a long civilizing process?

229

In fact, nothing in history indicates that this change was brought about "rationally", through any purposive education of individual people or groups. It happened by and large unplanned; but it did not happen, nevertheless, without a specific type of order. It has been shown in detail above how constraints through others from a variety of angles are converted into self-restraints, how the more animalic human activities are progressively thrust behind the scenes of men's communal social life and invested with feelings of shame, how the regulation of the whole instinctual and affective life by steady self-control becomes more and more stable, more even and more all-embracing. All this certainly does not spring from a rational idea conceived centuries ago by individual people and then implanted in one generation after another as the purpose of action and the desired state, until it was fully realized in the "centuries of progress". And yet, though not planned and intended, this transformation is not merely a sequence of unstructured and chaotic changes.

What poses itself here with regard to the civilizing process is nothing other than the general problem of historical change. Taken as a whole this change is not "rationally" planned; but neither is it a random coming and going of orderless patterns. How is this possible? How does it happen at all that formations arise in the human world that no single human being has intended, and which yet are anything but cloud formations without stability or structure?

The preceding study, and particularly those parts of it devoted to the problems of social dynamics, attempts to provide an answer to these questions. It is simple enough: plans and actions, the emotional and rational impulses of individual people, constantly interweave in a friendly or hostile way. *This basic tissue resulting from many single plans and actions of men can give rise to changes and patterns that no individual person has planned or created. From this interdependence of people arises an order sui generis, an order more compelling and stronger than the will and reason of the individual people composing it.*[129] It is this order of interweaving human impulses and strivings, this social order, which determines the course of historical change; it underlies the civilizing process.

This order is neither "rational"—if by "rational" we mean that it has resulted intentionally from the purposive deliberation of individual people; nor "irrational"—if by "irrational" we mean that it has arisen in an incomprehensible way. It has occasionally been identified with the order of "Nature"; it was interpreted by Hegel and some others as a kind of supra-individual "Spirit", and his concept of a "cunning of reason" shows how much he too was preoccupied by the fact that all the planning and actions of people give rise to many things that no one actually intended. But the mental habits which tend to bind us to opposites such as "rational" and "irrational", or "spirit" and "nature", prove inadequate here. In this respect, too, reality is not constructed quite as the conceptual apparatus of a particular standard would have us believe, whatever valuable services it may have performed in its time as a compass to guide us through an unknown world. *The immanent regularities of social figurations are identical neither with regularities of the "mind", of individual reasoning, nor with regularities of what we call "nature", even though functionally all these different dimensions of reality are indissolubly linked to each other.* On its own, however, this general statement about the relative autonomy of social figurations is of little help in their understanding; it remains empty and ambiguous, unless the actual dynamics of social interweaving are directly illustrated by reference to specific and empirically demonstrable changes. Precisely this was one of the tasks to which Part One of this volume was devoted. It was attempted there to show what kind of interweaving, of mutual dependence between people, sets in motion, for example, processes of feudalization. It was shown how the compulsion of competitive situations drove a number of feudal lords into conflict, how the circle of competitors was slowly narrowed, and how this led to the monopoly of one and finally—in conjunction with other mechanisms of integration such as processes of increasing capital formation and functional differentiation— to the formation of an absolutist state. This whole reorganization of human relationships went hand in hand with corresponding changes in men's manners, in their personality structure, the provisional result of which is our form of "civilized" conduct and sentiment. The connection between these specific changes in the structure of human relations and the corresponding changes in the structure of the personality will be discussed again shortly. But consideration of these mechanisms of integration is also relevant in a more general way to an understanding of the

231

civilizing process. Only if we see the compelling force with which a particular social structure, a particular form of social intertwining, veers through its tensions to a specific change and so to other forms of intertwining,[130] can we understand how those changes arise in human mentality, in the patterning of the malleable psychological apparatus, which can be observed over and again in human history from earliest times to the present. And only then, therefore, can we understand that the psychological change involved by civilization is subject to a quite specific order and direction, although it was not planned by individual people or produced by "reasonable", purposive measures. Civilization is not "reasonable"; not "rational",[131] any more than it is "irrational". It is set in motion blindly, and kept in motion by the autonomous dynamics of a web of relationships, by specific changes in the way people are bound to live together. But it is by no means impossible that we can make out of it something more "reasonable", something that functions better in terms of our needs and purposes. For it is precisely in conjunction with the civilizing process that the blind dynamics of men intertwining in their deeds and aims gradually leads towards greater scope for planned intervention into both the social and individual structures—intervention based on a growing knowledge of the unplanned dynamics of these structures.

But which specific changes in the way people are bonded to each other mould their personality in a "civilizing" manner? The most general answer to this question too, an answer based on what was said earlier about the changes in Western society, is very simple. From the earliest period of the history of the Occident to the present, social functions have become more and more differentiated under the pressure of competition. The more differentiated they become, the larger grows the number of functions and thus of people on whom the individual constantly depends in all his actions, from the simplest and most commonplace to the more complex and uncommon. As more and more people must attune their conduct to that of others, the web of actions must be organized more and more strictly and accurately, if each individual action is to fulfil its social function. The individual is compelled to regulate his conduct in an increasingly differentiated, more even and more stable manner. That this involves not only a conscious regulation has already been stressed. Precisely this is characteristic of the psychological changes in the course of civilization: the more complex and stable control of conduct is increasingly instilled in the individual from his earliest years as an automatism, a self-compulsion that he cannot resist even if he consciously wishes to. The web of actions grows so complex and extensive, the effort required to behave "correctly" within it becomes so great, that beside the individual's conscious self-control an automatic, blindly functioning apparatus of self-control is firmly established. This seeks to prevent offences to socially acceptable behaviour by a wall of deep-rooted fears, but, just because it operates blindly and by habit, it frequently indirectly produces such collisions with social reality. But whether consciously or unconsciously, the direction of this transformation of conduct in the form of an increasingly differentiated regulation of impulses is determined by the direction of the process of social differentiation, by the progressive division of functions and the growth of the interdependency chains into which, directly or indirectly, every impulse, every move of an individual becomes integrated.

A simple way of picturing the difference between the integration of the individual within a complex society and within a less complex one is to think of their different road systems. These are in a sense spatial functions of a social integration which, in its totality, cannot be expressed merely in terms of concepts derived from the four-dimensional continuum. One should think of the country roads of a simple warrior society with a barter economy, uneven, unmetalled, exposed to damage from wind and rain. With few exceptions, there is very little traffic; the main danger which man here represents for other men is an attack by soldiers or thieves. When people look around them, scanning the trees and hills or the road itself, they do so primarily because they must always be prepared for armed attack, and only secondarily because they have to avoid collision. Life on the main roads of this society demands a constant readiness to fight, and free play of the emotions in defence of one's life or possessions from physical attack. Traffic on the main roads of a big city in the complex society of our time demands a quite different moulding of the psychological apparatus. Here the danger of physical attack is minimal. Cars are rushing in all directions; pedestrians and cyclists are trying to thread their way through the *mêlée* of cars; policemen stand at the main crossroads to regulate the traffic with varying success. But this external control is founded on the assumption that every individual is himself regulating his behaviour with the utmost exactitude in accordance with the necessities of this network. The chief danger that people here represent for others results from someone in this bustle losing his self-control. A constant and highly differentiated regulation of one's own behaviour is needed for the individual to steer his way through traffic. If the strain of such constant self-control becomes too much for an individual, this is enough to put himself and others in mortal danger.

This is, of course, only an image. The tissue of chains of action into which each individual act within this complex society is woven, is far more intricate, and the self-control to which he is accustomed from infancy far more deeply rooted, than this example shows. But at least it gives an impression of how the great formative pressure on the make-up of "civilized" man, his constant and differentiated self-constraint, is connected to the growing differentiation and stabilizing of social functions and the growing multiplicity and variety of activities that continuously have to be attuned to each other.

The pattern of self-constraints, the template by which drives are moulded, certainly varies widely according to the function and position of the individual within this network, and there are even today in different sectors of the Western world variations of intensity and stability in the apparatus of self-constraint that seem at face value very large. At this point a multitude of particular questions are raised, and the sociogenetic method may give access to their answers. But when compared to the psychological make-up of people in less complex societies, these differences and degrees within more complex societies become less significant, and the main line of transformation, which is the primary concern of this study, emerges very clearly: as the social fabric grows more intricate, the sociogenic apparatus of individual self-control also becomes more differentiated, more all-round and more stable.

But the advancing differentiation of social functions is only the first, most general of the social transformations which we observe in enquiring into the change in psychological make-up known as "civilization". Hand in hand with this advancing division of functions goes a total reorganization of the social fabric. It was shown in detail earlier why, when the division of functions is low, the central organs of societies of a certain size are relatively unstable and liable to disintegration. It has been shown how, through specific figurational pressures, centrifugal tendencies, the mechanisms of feudalization, are slowly neutralized and how, step by step, a more stable central organization, a firmer monopolization of physical force, are established. The peculiar stability of the apparatus of mental self-restraint which emerges as a decisive trait built into the habits of every "civilized" human being, stands in the closest relationship to the monopolization of physical force and the growing stability of the central organs of society. Only with the formation of this kind of relatively stable monopolies do societies acquire those characteristics as a result of which the individuals forming them get attuned, from infancy, to a highly regulated and differentiated pattern of self-restraint; only in conjunction with these monopolies does this kind of self-restraint require a higher degree of automaticity, does it become, as it were, "second nature".

When a monopoly of force is formed, pacified social spaces are created which are normally free from acts of violence. The pressures acting on individual people within them are of a different kind than previously. Forms of non-physical violence that always existed, but hitherto had always been mingled or fused with physical force, are now separated from the latter; they persist in a changed form internally within the more pacified societies. They are most visible so far as the standard thinking of our time is concerned as types of economic violence. In reality, however, there is a whole set of means whose monopolization can enable men as groups or as individuals to enforce their will upon others. The monopolization of the means of production, of "economic" means, is only one of those which stand out in fuller relief when the means of physical violence become monopolized, when, in other words, in a more pacified state society the free use of physical force by those who are physically stronger is no longer possible.

In general, the direction in which the behaviour and the affective make-up of people change when the structure of human relationships is transformed in the manner described, is as follows: societies without a stable monopoly of force are always societies in which the division of functions is relatively slight and the chains of action binding individuals together are comparatively short. Conversely, societies with more stable monopolies of force, always first embodied in a large princely or royal court,

235

are societies in which the division of functions is more or less advanced, in which the chains of action binding individuals together are longer and the functional dependencies between people greater. Here the individual is largely protected from sudden attack, the irruption of physical violence into his life. But at the same time he is himself forced to suppress in himself any passionate impulse urging him to attack another physically. And the other forms of compulsion which now prevail in the pacified social spaces pattern the individual's conduct and affective impulses in the same direction. The closer the web of interdependence becomes in which the individual is enmeshed with the advancing division of functions, the larger the social spaces over which this network extends and which become integrated into functional or institutional units—the more threatened is the social existence of the individual who gives way to spontaneous impulses and emotions, the greater is the social advantage of those able to moderate their affects, and the more strongly is each individual constrained from an early age to take account of the effects of his own or other people's actions on a whole series of links in the social chain. The moderation of spontaneous emotions, the tempering of affects, the extension of mental space beyond the moment into the past and future, the habit of connecting events in terms of chains of cause and effect—all these are different aspects of the same transformation of conduct which necessarily takes place with the monopolization of physical violence, and the lengthening of the chains of social action and interdependence. It is a "civilizing" change of behaviour.

The transformation of the nobility from a class of knights into a class of courtiers is an example of this. In the earlier sphere, where violence is an unavoidable and everyday event, and where the individual's chains of dependence are relatively short, because he largely subsists directly from the produce of his own land, a strong and continuous moderation of drives and affects is neither necessary, possible nor useful. The life of the warriors themselves, but also that of all others living in a society with a warrior upper class, is threatened continually and directly by acts of physical violence; thus, measured against life in more pacified zones, it oscillates between extremes. Compared to this other society, it permits the warrior extraordinary freedom in living out his feelings and passions, it allows savage joys, the uninhibited satisfaction of pleasure from women, or of hatred in destroying and tormenting anything hostile. But at the same time it threatens the warrior, if he is defeated, with an extraordinary degree of exposure to the violence and the passions of others, and with such radical subjugation, such extreme forms of physical torment as are later, when physical torture, imprisonment and the radical humiliation of individuals has become the monopoly of a central authority, hardly to be found in normal life. With this monopolization, the physical threat to the individual is slowly depersonalized. It no longer depends quite so directly on momentary affects; it is gradually subjected to increasingly strict rules and laws; and finally, within certain limits and with certain fluctuations, the physical threat when laws are infringed is itself made less severe.

The greater spontaneity of drives and the higher measure of physical threat, that are encountered wherever strong and stable central monopolies have not yet formed are, as can be seen, complementary. In this social structure the victorious have a greater possibility of giving free rein to their drives and affects, but greater too is the direct threat to one man from the affects of another, and more omnipresent the possibility of subjugation and boundless humiliation if one falls into the power of another. This applies not only to the relationship of warrior to warrior, for whom in the course of monetarization and the narrowing of free competition an affect-moderating code of conduct is already slowly forming; within society at large the lesser measure of restraint impinging upon seigneurs initially stands in sharper contrast than later to the confined existence of their female counterparts and to the radical exposure to their whims of dependents, defeated, and bondsmen.

To the structure of this society with its extreme polarization, its continuous uncertainties, corresponds the structure of the individuals who form it and of their conduct. Just as in the relations between man and man danger arises more abruptly, the possibility of victory or liberation more suddenly and incalculably before the individual, so he is also thrown more frequently and directly between pleasure and pain. The social function of the free warrior is indeed scarcely so constructed that dangers are long foreseeable, that the effects of particular actions can be considered three or four links ahead, even though his function is slowly developing in this direction throughout the Middle Ages with the increasing centralization of armies. But for the time being it is the immediate present that provides the impulse. As the momentary situation changes, so do affective expressions; if it brings pleasure this is savoured to the full, without calculation or thought of the possible consequences in the future. If it brings danger, imprisonment, defeat, these too must be suffered more desolately. And the incurable unrest, the perpetual proximity of danger, the whole atmosphere of this unpredictable and insecure life, in which there are at most small and transient islands of more protected existence, often engenders even without external cause, sudden switches from the most exuberant pleasure to the deepest despondency and remorse. The personality, if we may put it thus, is incomparably more ready and accustomed to leap with undiminishing intensity from one extreme to the other, and slight impressions, uncontrollable associations are often enough to induce these immense fluctuations.[132]

As the structure of human relations changes, as monopoly organizations of physical force develop and the individual is held no longer in the sway of constant feuds and wars but rather in the more permanent compulsions of peaceful functions based on the acquisition of money or prestige, affect-expressions too slowly gravitate towards a middle line. The fluctuations in behaviour and affects do not disappear, but are moderated. The peaks and abysses are smaller, the changes less abrupt.

We can see what is changing more clearly from its obverse. Through the formation of monopolies of force, the threat which one man represents for another is subject to stricter control and becomes more calculable. Everyday life is freer of sudden reversals of fortune. Physical violence is confined to barracks; and from this store-house it breaks out only in extreme cases, in times of war or social upheaval, into individual life. As the monopoly of certain specialist groups it is normally excluded from the life of others; and these specialists, the whole monopoly organization of force, now stand guard only in the margin of social life as a control on individual conduct.

Even in this form as a control organization, however, physical violence and the threat emanating from it have a determining influence on individuals in society, whether they know it or not. It is, however, no longer a perpetual insecurity that it brings into the life of the individual, but a peculiar form of security. It no longer throws him, in the swaying fortunes of battle, as the physical victor or vanquished, between mighty outbursts of pleasure and terror; a continuous, uniform pressure is exerted on individual life by the physical violence stored behind the scenes of everyday life, a pressure totally familiar and hardly perceived, conduct and drive economy having been adjusted from earliest youth to this social structure. It is in fact the whole social mould, the code of conduct which changes; and accordingly with it changes, as has been said before, not only this or that specific form of conduct but its whole pattern, the whole structure of the way individuals steer themselves. The monopoly organization of physical violence does not usually constrain the individual by a direct threat. A strongly predictable compulsion or pressure mediated in a variety of ways is constantly exerted on the individual. This operates to a considerable extent through the medium of his own reflection. It is normally only potentially present in society, as an agency of control; the actual compulsion is one that the individual exerts on himself either as a result of his knowledge of the possible consequences of his moves in the game in intertwining activities, or as a result of corresponding gestures of adults which have helped to pattern his own behaviour as a child. The monopolization of physical violence, the concentration of arms and armed men under one authority, makes the use of violence more or less calculable, and forces unarmed men in the pacified social spaces to restrain their own violence through foresight or reflection; in other words it imposes on people a greater or lesser degree of self-control.

This is not to say that every form of self-control was entirely lacking in medieval warrior society or in other societies without a complex and stable monopoly of physical violence. The agency of individual self-control, the super-ego, the conscience or whatever we call it, is instilled, imposed and maintained in such warrior societies only in direct relation to acts of physical violence; its form matches this life in its greater contrasts and more abrupt transitions. Compared to the self-control agency in more pacified societies, it is diffuse, unstable, only a slight barrier to violent emotional outbursts. The fears securing socially "correct" conduct are not yet banished to remotely the same extent from the individual's consciousness into his so-called "inner life". As the decisive danger does not come from failure or relaxation of self-control, but from direct external physical threat, habitual fear predominantly takes the form of fear of

239

external powers. And as this fear is less stable, the control apparatus too is less encompassing, more one-sided or partial. In such a society extreme self-control in enduring pain may be instilled; but this is complemented by what, measured by a different standard, appears as an extreme form of freewheeling of affects in torturing others. Similarly, in certain sectors of medieval society we find extreme forms of asceticism, self-restraint and renunciation, contrasting to a no less extreme indulgence of pleasure in others, and frequently enough we encounter sudden switches from one attitude to the other in the life of an individual person. The restraint the individual here imposes on himself, the struggle against his own flesh, is no less intense and one-sided, no less radical and passionate than its counterpart, the fight against others and the maximum enjoyment of pleasures.

What is established with the monopolization of physical violence in the pacified social spaces is a different type of self-control or self-constraint. It is a more dispassionate self-control. The controlling agency forming itself as part of the individual's personality structure corresponds to the controlling agency forming itself in society at large. The one like the other tends to impose a highly differentiated regulation upon all passionate impulses, upon men's conduct all around. Both—each to a large extent mediated by the other—exert a constant, even pressure to inhibit affective outbursts. They damp down extreme fluctuations in behaviour and emotions. As the monopolization of physical force reduces the fear and terror one man must have for another, but at the same time reduces the possibility of causing others terror, fear or torment, and therefore certain possibilities of pleasurable emotional release, the constant self-control to which the individual is now increasingly accustomed seeks to reduce the contrasts and sudden switches in conduct, and the affective charge of all self-expression. The pressures operating upon the individual now tend to produce a transformation of the whole drive and affect economy in the direction of a more continuous, stable and even regulation of drives and affects in all areas of conduct, in all sectors of his life.

And it is in exactly the same direction that the unarmed compulsions operate, the constraints without direct physical violence to which the individual is now exposed in the pacified spaces, and of which economic restraints are an instance. They too are less affect-charged, more moderate, stable and less erratic than

240

the constraints exerted by one person on another in a monopoly-free warrior society. And they, too, embodied in the entire spectrum of functions open to the individual in society, induce incessant hindsight and foresight transcending the moment and corresponding to the longer and more complex chains in which each act is now automatically enmeshed. They require the individual incessantly to overcome his momentary affective impulses in keeping with the longer-term effects of his behaviour. Relative to the other standard, they instil a more even self-control encompassing his whole conduct like a tight ring, and a more steady regulation of his drives according to the social norms. Moreover, as always, it is not only the adult functions themselves which immediately produce this tempering of drives and affects; partly automatically, partly quite consciously through their own conduct and habits, adults induce corresponding behaviour-patterns in children. From earliest youth the individual is trained in the constant restraint and foresight that he needs for adult functions. This self-restraint is ingrained so deeply from an early age that, like a kind of relay-station of social standards, an automatic self-supervision of his drives, a more differentiated and more stable "super-ego" develops in him, and a part of the forgotten drive impulses and affect inclinations is no longer directly within reach of the level of consciousness at all.

Earlier, in warrior society, the individual could use physical violence if he was strong and powerful enough; he could openly indulge his inclinations in many directions that have subsequently been closed by social prohibitions. But he paid for this greater opportunity of direct pleasure with a greater chance of direct and open fear. Medieval conceptions of hell give us an idea of how strong this fear between man and man was. Both joy and pain were discharged more openly and freely. But the individual was their prisoner; he was hurled back and forth by his own feelings as by forces of nature. He had less control of his passions; he was more controlled by them.

Later, as the conveyor belts running through his existence grow longer and more complex, the individual learns to control himself more steadily; he is now less a prisoner of his passions than before. But as he is now more tightly bound by his functional dependence on the activities of an ever-larger number of people, he is much more restricted in his conduct, in his chances of directly satisfying his drives and passions. Life becomes in a sense less dangerous, but also less emotional or pleasurable, at least as far as the direct release of pleasure is concerned. And for what is lacking in everyday life a substitute is created in dreams, in books and pictures. So, on their way to becoming courtiers, the nobility read novels of chivalry; the bourgeois contemplate violence and erotic passion in films. Physical classes, wars and feuds diminish, and anything recalling them, even the cutting up of dead animals and the use of the knife at table, is banished from view or at least subjected to more and more precise social rules. But at the same time the battlefield is, in a sense, moved within. Part of the tensions and passions that were earlier directly released in the struggle of man and man, must now be worked out within the human being. The more peaceful constraints exerted on him by his relations to others are mirrored within him; an individualized pattern of near-automatic habits is established and consolidated within him, a specific "super-ego", which endeavours to control, transform or suppress his affects in keeping with the social structure. But the drives, the passionate affects, that can no longer directly manifest themselves in the relationships *between* people, often struggle no less violently *within* the individual against this supervising part of himself. And this semi-automatic struggle of the person with himself does not always find a happy resolution; not always does the self-transformation required by life in this society lead to a new balance between drive-satisfaction and drive-control. Often enough it is subject to major or minor disturbances, revolts of one part of the person against the other, or a permanent atrophy, which makes the performance of social functions even more difficult, or impossible. The vertical oscillations, if we may so describe them, the leaps from fear to joy, pleasure to remorse are reduced, while the horizontal fissure running right through the whole person, the tension between "super-ego" and "unconscious"—the wishes and desires that cannot be remembered—increases.

Here too the basic characteristics of these patterns of intertwining, if one pursues not merely their static structures but their sociogenesis, prove to be relatively simple. Through the interdependence of larger groups of people and the exclusion of physical violence from them, a social apparatus is established in which the constraints between people are lastingly transformed into self-constraints. These self-constraints, a function of the perpetual hindsight and foresight instilled in the individual from childhood in accordance with his integration in extensive chains of action, have partly the form of conscious self-control and partly that of automatic habit. They tend towards a more even moderation, a more continuous restraint, a more exact control of drives and affects in accordance with the more differentiated pattern of social interweaving. But depending on the inner pressure, on the condition of society and the position of the individual within it, these constraints also produce peculiar tensions and disturbances in the conduct and drive economy of the individual. In some cases they lead to perpetual restlessness and dissatisfaction, precisely because the person affected can only gratify a part of his inclinations and impulses in modified form, for example in fantasy, in looking-on and overhearing, in daydreams or dreams. And sometimes the habituation to affect-inhibition goes so far—constant feelings of boredom or solitude are examples of this—that the individual is no longer capable of any form of fearless expression of the modified affects, or of direct gratification of the repressed drives. Particular branches of drives are as it were anaesthetized in such cases by the specific structure of the social framework in which the child grows up. Under the pressure of the dangers that their expression incurs in the child's social space, they become surrounded with automatic fears to such an extent that they can remain deaf and unresponsive throughout a whole lifetime. In other cases certain branches of drives may be so diverted by the heavy conflicts which the rough-hewn, affective and passionate nature of the small human being unavoidably encounters on its way to being moulded into a "civilized" being, that their energies can find only an unwanted release through bypasses, in compulsive actions and other symptoms of disturbance. In other cases again, these energies are so transformed that they flow into uncontrollable and eccentric attachments and repulsions, in predilections for this or that peculiar hobby-horse. And in all these cases a permanent, apparently groundless inner unrest shows how many drive energies are dammed up in a form that permits no real satisfaction.

Until now the individual civilizing process, like the social, runs its course by and large blindly. Under the cover of what adults think and plan, the relationships that forms between them and the young has functions and effects in the latter's personalities which they do not intend and of which they scarcely know. Unplanned in that sense are those results of social patterning of individuals to which one habitually refers as 'abnormal'; psychological abnormalities which do not result from social patterning but are caused by unalterable hereditary traits need not be considered here. But the psychological make-up which keeps within the social norm and is subjectively more satisfying comes about in an equally unplanned way. It is the same social mould from which emerge both more favourably and more unfavourably structured human beings, the "well-adjusted" as well as the "mal-adjusted", within a very broad spectrum of varieties. The automatically reproduced anxieties which, in the course of each individual civilizing process and in connection with the conflicts that form an integral part of this process, attach themselves to specific drives and affect impulses sometimes lead to a permanent and total paralysis of these impulses, and sometimes only to a moderate regulation with enough scope for their full satisfaction. Under present conditions it is from the point of view of the individuals concerned more a question of their good or bad fortune than that of anybody's planning whether it is the one or the other. In either case it is the web of social relations in which the individual lives during his most impressionable phase, during childhood and youth, which imprints itself upon his unfolding personality where it has its counterpart in the relationship between his controlling agencies, super-ego and ego, and his libidinal impulses. The resulting balance between controlling agencies and drives on a variety of levels determines how an individual person steers himself in his relations with others; it determines that which we call, according to taste, habits, complexes or personality structure. However, there is no end to the intertwining, for although the self-steering of a person, malleable during early childhood, solidifies and hardens as he grows up, it never ceases entirely to be affected by his changing relations with others throughout his life. The learning of self-controls, call them 'reason' or 'conscience', 'ego' or 'super-ego', and the consequent curbing of more animalic impulses and affects, in short the civilizing of the human young, is never a process entirely without pain; it always leaves scars. If the person is lucky—and as no one, no parent, no doctor, and no counsellor, is at present able to steer this process in a child according to a clear knowledge of what is best for its future, it is still largely a question of luck—the wounds of the civilizing conflicts incurred during childhood heal; the scars left by them are not too deep. But in less favourable cases the conflicts inherent in the civilizing of young humans—conflicts with others and conflicts within themselves—remain unsolved, or, more precisely, though perhaps buried for a while, open up once more in situations reminiscent of those of childhood; the suffering, transformed into an adult form, repeats itself again and again, and the unsolved conflicts of a person's childhood never cease to disturb his adult relationships. In that way, the interpersonal conflicts of early youth which have patterned the personality structure continue to perturb or even destroy the interpersonal relationships of the grown-up. The resulting tensions may take the form either of contradictions between different self-control automatisms, sunk-in memory traces of former dependencies and needs, or of recurrent struggles between the controlling agencies and the libidinal impulses. In the more fortunate cases, on the other hand, the contradictions between different sections and layers of the controlling agencies, especially of the super-ego structure, are slowly reconciled; the most disruptive conflicts between that structure and the libidinal impulses are slowly contained. They not only disappear from waking consciousness, but are so thoroughly assimilated that, without too heavy a cost in subjective satisfaction, they no longer intrude unintentionally in later interpersonal relationships. In one case the conscious and unconscious self-control always remains diffuse in places and open to the breakthrough of socially unproductive forms of drive energy; in the other this self-control, which even today in juvenile phases is often more like a confusion of overlapping ice-floes than a smooth and firm sheet of ice, slowly becomes more unified and stable in positive correspondence to the structure of society. But as this structure, precisely in our times, is highly mutable, it demands a flexibility of habits and conduct which in most cases has to be paid for by a loss of stability.

Theoretically, therefore, it is not difficult to say in what lies the difference between an individual civilizing process that is considered successful and one that is considered unsuccessful. In the former, after all the pains and conflicts of this process, patterns of conduct well adapted to the framework of adult social functions are finally formed, an adequately functioning set of

245

habits and at the same time—which does not necessarily go hand-in-hand with it—a positive pleasure balance. In the other, either the socially necessary self-control is repeatedly purchased, at a heavy cost in personal satisfaction, by a major effort to overcome opposed libidinal energies, or the control of these energies, renunciation of their satisfaction is not achieved at all; and often enough no positive pleasure balance of any kind is finally possible, because the social commands and prohibitions are represented not only by other people but also by the stricken self, since one part of it forbids and punishes what the other desires.

In reality the result of the individual civilizing process is clearly unfavourable or favourable only in relatively few cases at each end of the scale. The majority of civilized people live midway between these two extremes. Socially positive and negative features, personally gratifying and frustrating tendencies, mingle in them in varying proportions.

The social moulding of individuals in accordance with the structure of the civilizing process of what we now call the West is particularly difficult. In order to be reasonably successful it requires with the structure of Western society, a particularly high differentiation, an especially intensive and stable regulation of drives and affects, of all the more elementary human impulses. It therefore generally takes up more time, particularly in the middle and upper classes, than the social moulding of individuals in less complex societies. Resistance to adaptation to the prevailing standards of civilization, the effort which this adaptation, this profound transformation of the whole personality costs the individual, is always very considerable. And later, therefore, than in less complex societies the individual in the Western world attains with his adult social function the psychological make-up of an adult, the emergence of which by and large marks the conclusion of the individual civilizing process.

But even if in the more differentiated societies of the West the modelling of the individual self-steering apparatus is particularly extensive and intense, processes tending in the same direction, social and individual civilizing processes, most certainly do not occur only there. They are to be found wherever, under competitive pressures, the division of functions makes large numbers of people dependent on one another, wherever a monopolization of physical force permits and imposes a co-operation less charged with emotion, wherever functions are established that demand constant hindsight and foresight in interpreting the actions and intentions of others. What determines the nature and degree of such civilizing spurts is always the extent of inter-dependencies, the level of the division of functions, and within it, the structure of these functions themselves.

II

Spread of the Pressure for Foresight and Self-Constraint

What lends the civilizing process in the West its special and unique character is the fact that here the division of functions has attained a level, the monopolies of force and taxation a solidity, and interdependence and competition an extent, both in terms of physical space and of numbers of people involved, unequalled in world history.

Hitherto extensive networks of money or trade, with fairly stable monopolies of physical force at their centres, had developed almost exclusively on waterways, that is, above all, on riverbanks and seacoasts. The large areas of the hinterland remained more or less at the level of a barter economy, that is, people remained largely autarkic and their interdependence chains were short, even when a few trade arteries crossed the areas and a few major markets existed. With Western society as its starting point, a network of interdependence has developed which not only encompasses the oceans further than any other in the past, but extends to the furthest arable corners of vast inland regions. Corresponding to this is the necessity for an attunement of human conduct over wider areas, and foresight over longer chains of actions, than ever before. Corresponding to it, too, is the strength of self-control and the permanence of compulsion, affect-inhibition and drive-control, which life at the centres of this network imposes. One of the characteristics which make this connection between the size of and pressure within the network of interdependence on the one hand, and the psychological make-up of the individual on the other particularly clear, is what we call the "tempo"[133] of our time. This "tempo" is in fact nothing other than a manifestation of the multitude of intertwining chains of interdependence which run through every single social function people have to perform, and of the competitive pressure permeating this densely populated network and affecting, directly or indirectly, every single act of individuals. This may show itself in the case of an official or businessman in the profusion of his appointments or meetings, and in that of a worker by the exact timing and duration of each of his movements; in both cases the tempo is an expression of the multitude of interdependent actions, of the length and density of the chains composed by the individual actions, and of the intensity of struggles that keep this whole interdependent network in motion. In both cases a function situated at a junction of so many chains of action demands an exact allocation of time; it makes people accustomed to subordinating momentary inclinations to the overriding necessities of interdependence; it trains them to eliminate all irregularities from behaviour and to achieve permanent self-control. This is why tendencies in the individual so often rebel against social time represented by his own super-ego, and why so many people come into conflict with themselves when they wish to be punctual. From the development of chronometric instruments and the consciousness of time—as from that of money and other instruments of social integration—it is possible to read off with considerable accuracy how the division of functions, and with it the self-control imposed on the individual, advances.

Why, within this network, patterns of affect-control vary in some respects, why, for example, sexuality is surrounded by stronger restrictions in one country than in another, is a question in its own right. But however these differences may arise in particular cases, the general direction of the change in conduct, the "trend" of the movement of civilization, is everywhere the same. It always veers towards a more or less automatic self-control, to the subordination of short-term impulses to the commands of an ingrained long-term view, and to the formation of a more complex and secure "super-ego" agency. And broadly the same, too, is the manner in which this necessity to subordinate momentary affects to more distant goals is propagated; everywhere small leading groups are affected first, and then broader and broader strata of Western society.

It makes a considerable difference whether someone lives in a world with dense and extensive bonds of dependence as a mere passive object of these interdependencies, being affected by dis-

248

tant events without being able to influence or even perceive them—or whether someone has a function in society which demands for its performance a permanent effort of foresight and steady control of conduct. To begin with in Western development it is certain upper- and middle-class functions that require of their incumbents such steadily active self-discipline in long-term interests: courtly functions at the political centres of large societies, and commercial functions at the centres of long-distance trade networks which are under the protection of a fairly stable monopoly of force. But it is one of the peculiarities of social processes in the West that with the extension of inter-dependence, the necessity for such long-term thinking and the active attunement of individual conduct to some larger entity remote in time and space, spreads to ever-broader sections of society. Even the functions and the whole social situation of the lower social strata demand and make more and more possible a certain foresight, and produce a corresponding transformation or restraint of all those inclinations that promise immediate or short-term satisfactions at the cost of remoter ones. In the past the functions of the lower strata of manual workers were gener-ally involved in the interdependent network only to the extent that their members felt the effect of remote actions and—if they were unpleasant—responded with unrest and rebellion, with short-term affective discharges. But their functions were not so constructed that within themselves the "alien" constraints were constantly converted into "self"-restraints; their daily tasks made them only little capable of restraining their immediate desires and affects in favour of something not tangible here and now. And so such outbursts hardly ever had lasting success.

Here a number of different nexuses are interlocking. Within every large human network there are some sectors which are more central than others. The functions of these central sectors, for example, the higher co-ordinating functions, impose more steady and strict self-control not only because of their central position and the large number of chains of action meeting in them; owing to the large number of actions depending on their incumbents, they carry major social power. What gives Western development its special character is the fact that in its course the dependence of all on all becomes more evenly balanced. To an increasing degree, the complex functioning of Western societies, with their high division of labour, depends on the lower agrarian and urban strata controlling their conduct increasingly through insight into its more long-term and more remote connections. These strata are ceasing to be merely "lower" social strata. The highly differentiated social apparatus becomes so complex, and in some respects so vulnerable, that disturbances, at one point of the interdependency chains which pass through all social positions inevitably affect many others, thus threatening the whole social tissue. Established groups engaged in competitive struggles among themselves are at the same time compelled to take into consideration the demands of the broad mass of outsiders. But as the social functions and power of the masses take on greater importance in this way, these functions require and permit greater foresight in their execution. Usually under heavy social pressure, members of the lower strata grow more accustomed to restraining momentary affects, and disciplining their whole conduct from a wider understanding of the total society and their position within it. Thereby their behaviour is forced increasingly in a direction originally confined to the upper strata. Their social power in relation to the latter increases; but at the same time they are increasingly trained to take a long-term view, no matter by whom and on what models their training is conducted. They, too, are increasingly subject to the kind of external compulsions that are transformed into individual self-restraint; in them, too, the horizontal tension between a self-control agency, a "super-ego", and libidinal energies that are now more or less successfully transformed, controlled or suppressed, increases. In this way civilizing structures are constantly expanding within Western society; both upper and lower strata are tending to become a kind of upper stratum and the centre of a network of interdependencies spreading over further and further areas, both populated and unpopulated, of the rest of the world. And only this vision of a comprehensive movement, of the progressive expansion, often in spurts and counter-spurts, of certain functions and patterns of conduct towards more and more outsider groups and outsider regions—only this vision, and the realization that we ourselves are in the midst of this up and down of a civilizing process and its crises, not at its end, places the problem of "civilization" in its proper perspective. If one steps back from the present into the past, what patterns, what structures does one discover in the successive waves of this movement, if one looks not from us to them, but from them to us?

III

Diminishing Contrasts, Increasing Varieties

The civilizing process moves along in a long sequence of spurts and counter-spurts. Again and again a rising outsider stratum or a rising survival unit as a whole, a tribe or a nation state, attains the functions and characteristics of an establishment in relation to other outsider strata or survival units which, on their part, are pressing from below, from their position as oppressed outsiders, against the current establishment. And again and again, as the grouping of people which has risen and has established itself is followed by a still broader, and more populous grouping attempting to emancipate itself, to free itself from oppression, one finds that the latter, if successful, is forced in turn into the position of an established oppressor. The time may well come when the former oppressed groups, freed from oppression, do not become oppressors in turn; but it is not yet in sight.

There are, of course, many unsolved problems raised by this vista. In the present context it may be enough to draw attention to the fact that by and large the lower strata, the oppressed and poorer outsider groups at a given stage of development, tend to follow their drives and affects more directly and spontaneously, that their conduct is less strictly regulated than that of the respective upper strata. The compulsions operating upon the lower strata are predominantly of a direct, physical kind, the threat of physical pain or annihilation by the sword, poverty or hunger. That type of pressure, however, does not induce a stable transformation of constraints through others, or "alien" constraints, into "self"-restraints. A medieval peasant who goes without meat because he is too poor, because beef is reserved for the lord's table, i.e. solely under physical constraint, will give way to his desire for meat whenever he can do so without external danger, unlike the founders of religious orders from the upper strata who deny themselves the enjoyment of meat in consideration of the after-life and the sense of their own sinfulness. A totally destitute person who works for others under constant threat of hunger or in penal servitude, will stop working once the threat of external force ceases, unlike the wealthy merchant who goes on and on working for himself although he probably has enough to live on without this work. He is compelled to do it not by simple need but by the pressure of the competition for power and prestige, because his profession, his elevated status, provide the meaning and justification of his life; and for him constant self-constraint has made work such a habit that the balance of his personality is upset if he is no longer able to work.

It is one of the peculiarities of Western society that in the course of its development this contrast between the situation and code of conduct of the upper and lower strata decreases considerably. Lower-class characteristics are spreading to all classes. The fact that Western society as a whole has gradually become a society where every able person is expected to earn his living through a highly regulated type of work is a sympton of this: earlier, work was an attribute of the lower classes. And at the same time, what used to be distinguishing features of the upper classes are likewise spreading to society at large. The conversion of "alien" social constraints into self-restraints, into a more or less habitual and automatic individual self-regulation of drives and affects—possibly only for people normally protected from external, physical threat by the sword or starvation—is taking place in the West increasingly among the broad masses, too.

Seen at close quarters, where only a small segment of this movement is visible, the differences in social personality structure between the upper and lower classes in the Western world today may still seem considerable. But if the whole sweep of the movement over centuries is perceived, one can see that the sharp contrasts between the behaviour of different social groups—like the contrasts and sudden switches within the behaviour of individuals—are steadily diminishing. The moulding of drives and affects, the forms of conduct, the whole psychological make-up of the lower classes in the more civilized societies, with their growing importance in the entire network of functions, is increasingly approaching that of other groups, beginning with the middle classes. This is the case even though a part of the self-constraints and taboos among the latter, which arise from the urge to "distinguish themselves", the desire for enhanced prestige, may initially be lacking in the former, and even though the type of social dependence of the former does not yet necessitate or permit the same degree of affect-control and steadier foresight as in the upper classes of the same period.

This reduction in the contrasts within society as within individuals, this peculiar commingling of patterns of conduct deriving from initially very different social levels, is highly characteristic of Western society. It is one of the most important peculiarities of the "civilizing process". But this movement of society and civilization certainly does not follow a straight line. Within the overall movement there are repeatedly greater or lesser counter-movements in which the contrasts in society and the fluctuations in the behaviour of individuals, their affective outbreaks, increase again.

What is happening under our eyes, what we generally call the "spread of civilization" in the narrower sense, that is, the spread of our institutions and standards of conduct beyond the West, constitutes, as we have said, the last wave so far within a movement that first took place for several centuries within the West, and whose trend and characteristic patterns, including science, technology, and other manifestations of a specific type of self-restraint, established themselves here long before the concept of "civilization" existed. From Western society—as a kind of upper class—Western "civilized" patterns of conduct are today spreading over wide areas outside the West, whether through the settlement of Occidentals or through the assimilation of the upper strata of other nations, as models of conduct earlier spread within the West itself from this or that upper stratum, from certain courtly or commercial centres. The course taken by all these expansions is only slightly determined by the plans or desires of those whose patterns of conduct were taken over. The classes supplying the models are even today not simply the free creators or originators of the expansion. This spread of the same patterns of conduct from the "white mother-countries or fatherlands" follows the incorporation of the other areas into the network of political and economic interdependencies, into the sphere of elimination struggles between and within the nations of the West. It is not "technology" which is the cause of this change of behaviour; what we call "technology" is itself only *one* of the symbols, one of the last manifestations of that constant foresight imposed by the formation of longer and longer chains of actions and the competition between those bound together by them. "Civilized" forms of conduct spread to these other areas because and to the extent that in them, through their incorporation into the network whose centre the West still

253

constitutes, the structure of their societies and of human relationships in general, is likewise changing. Technology, education—all these are facets of the same overall development. In the areas into which the West has expanded, the social functions with which the individual must comply are increasingly changing in such a way as to induce the. same constant foresight and affect-control as in the West itself. Here, too, the transformation of the whole of social existence is the basic condition of the civilization of conduct. For this reason we find in the relation of the West to other parts of the world the beginnings of the reduction in contrasts which is peculiar to every major wave of the civilizing movement.

This recurrent fusion of patterns of conduct of the functionally upper classes with those of the rising classes, is not without significance regarding the curiously ambivalent attitude of the upper classes in this process. The habituation to foresight, and the stricter control of behaviour and the affects to which the upper classes are inclined through their situation and functions, are important instruments of their dominance, as in the case of European colonialism, for example. They serve as marks of distinction and prestige. For just this reason such a society regards offences against the prevailing pattern of drive and affect control, any "letting go" by their members, with greater or lesser disapproval. This disapproval increases when the social power and size of the lower, rising group increase, and concomitantly, the competition for the same opportunities between the upper and lower groups becomes more intense. The effort and foresight which it costs to maintain the position of the upper class is expressed in the internal commerce of its members with each other by the degree of reciprocal supervision they practise on one another, by the severe stigmatization and penalties they impose upon those members who breach the common distinguishing code. The fear arising from the situation of the whole group, from their struggle to preserve their cherished and threatened position, acts directly as a force maintaining the code of conduct, the cultivation of the super-ego in its members. It is converted into individual anxiety, the individual's fear of personal degradation or merely loss of prestige in his own society. And it is this fear of loss of prestige in the eyes of others, instilled as self-compulsion, whether in the form of shame or sense of honour, which assures the habitual reproduction of distinctive conduct, and the strict drive-control underlying it, in individual people.

But while on the one hand these upper classes—and in some respects, as noted above, the Western nations as a whole have an upper-class function—are thus driven to maintain at all costs their special conduct and drive-control as marks of distinction, on the other their situation, together with the structure of the general movement carrying them along, forces them in the long run to reduce more and more these differences in standards of behaviour. The expansion of Western civilization shows this double tendency clearly enough. This civilization is the characteristic conferring distinction and superiority on Occidentals. But at the same time the Western people, under the pressure of their own competitive struggle, bring about in large areas of the world a change in human relationships and functions in line with their own standards. They make large parts of the world dependent on them and at the same time, in keeping with a regularity of functional differentiation that has been observed over and again, become themselves dependent on them. On the one hand they build, through institutions and by the strict regulation of their own behaviour, a wall between themselves and the groups they colonize and whom they consider their inferiors. On the other, with their social forms, they also spread their own style of conduct and institutions in these places. Largely without deliberate intent, they work in a direction which sooner or later leads to a reduction in the differences both of social power and of conduct between colonists and colonized. Even in our day the contrasts are becoming perceptibly less. According to the form of colonization and the position of an area in the large network of differentiated functions, and not least to the region's own history and structure, processes of commingling are beginning to take place in specific areas outside the West similar to those sketched earlier on the example of courtly and bourgeois conduct in different countries within the West itself. In colonial regions too, according to the position and social strength of the various groups, Western standards are spreading downwards and occasionally even upwards from below, if we may adhere to this spatial image, and fusing to form new unique entities, new varieties of civilized conduct. *The contrasts in conduct between the upper and lower groups are reduced with the spread of civilization; the varieties or nuances of civilized conduct are increased.*

This incipient transformation of Oriental or African people in the direction of Western standards represents the last wave of the continuing civilizing movement that we are able to observe. But as this wave rises, signs of new and further waves in the same direction can already be seen forming in it; for until now the groups approaching the Western upper class in colonial areas as the lower, rising class, are primarily the upper classes within those nations.

One step further back in history one can observe in the West itself a similar movement: the assimilation of the lower urban and agrarian classes to the standards of civilized conduct, the growing habituation of these groups to foresight, to a more even curbing and more strict control of the affects, and a higher measure of individual self-constraint in their case too. Here too, according to the structure of the history of each country, very diverse varieties of affect-formation emerge within the framework of civilized conduct. In the conduct of workers in England, for example, one can still see traces of the manners of the landed gentry and of merchants within a large trade network, in France the airs of courtiers and a bourgeoisie brought to power by revolution. In the workers too, we find a stricter regulation of conduct, a type of courtesy more informed by tradition in colonial nations which have for a long period had the function of an upper class within a large interdependent network, and less polished control of the affects in nations that achieved colonial expansion late or not at all, because strong monopolies of force and taxation, a centralization of national power—preconditions for any lasting colonial expansion—developed later in them than in their competitors.

Further back, in the seventeenth, eighteenth and nineteenth centuries—earlier or later according to the structure of each nation—we find the same pattern in a still smaller circle: the interpenetration of the standards of conduct of the nobility and the bourgeoisie. In accordance with the power-relationship, the product of interpenetration is dominated first by models derived from the situation of the upper class, then by pattern of conduct of the lower, rising classes, until finally an amalgam emerges, a new style of unique character. Here, too, the same dualism in the position of the upper class is visible that can be observed today in the vanguard of "civilization". The courtly nobility, the vanguard of "*civilité*", is gradually compelled to exercise a strict restraint of the affects and an exact moulding of conduct through its increasing integration in a network of interdependencies, represented here by the pincer formed of monarchy and bourgeoisie in which the nobility is trapped. For the courtly nobility, too, the self-restraint imposed on them by their function and situation serves at the same time as a prestige value, a means of distinguishing themselves from the lower groups harrying them, and they do everything within their power to prevent these differences from being effaced. Only the initiated member should know the secrets of good conduct; only within good society should this be learned. Gratian deliberately wrote his treatise on "savoir-vivre", the famous "Hand Oracle", in an obscure style, a courtly princess once explained,[134] so that this knowledge could not be bought by anyone for a few pence; and Courtin does not forget, in the introduction to his treatise on "Civilité", to stress that his manuscript was really written for the private use of a few friends, and that even printed it is intended only for people of good society. But even here the ambivalence of the situation is revealed. Owing to the peculiar form of interdependence in which they lived, the courtly aristocracy could not prevent—indeed, through their contacts with rich bourgeois strata whom they needed for one reason or another, they assisted—the spreading of their manners, their customs, their tastes and their language to other classes. First of all in the seventeenth century, these manners passed to small leading groups of the bourgeoisie—the "Excursus on the Modelling of Speech at Court" gives a vivid example[135]—and then, in the eighteenth century, to broader bourgeois strata; the mass of civilité-books that appeared at that time shows this clearly. Here too the force of the current of interweaving as a whole, the tensions and competition leading within it to ever-greater complexity and functional differentiation, to the individual's dependence on an ever-larger number of others, to the rise of broader and broader classes, proved stronger than the barricade the nobility had been seeking to build around themselves.

It is at small functional centres that the foresight, more complex self-discipline, more stable super-ego formation enforced by growing interdependence, first becomes noticeable. Then more and more functional circles within the West change in the same direction. Finally, in conjunction with pre-existing forms of civilization, the same transformation of social functions and thus of conduct and the whole personality, begins to take place in countries outside Europe. This is the picture which emerges if we attempt to survey the course followed up to now by the Western civilizing movement in social space as a whole.

IV

The Courtization of Warriors

The courtly society of the seventeenth and eighteenth centuries, and above all the courtly nobility of France that forms its centre, occupies a specific position within this whole movement of interpenetration of the patterns of conduct of ever-wider circles. As noted above, the courtiers did not originate or invent the muting of affects and the more even regulation of conduct. They, like everyone else in this movement, were bending to the constraints of interdependence that were not planned by any individual person or group of persons. But it is in this courtly society that the basic stock of models of conduct is formed which then, fused with others and modified in accordance with the position of the groups carrying them, spread, with the compulsion to exercise foresight, to ever-wider circles of functions. Their special situation makes the people of courtly society, more than any other Western group affected by this movement, specialists in the elaboration and moulding of social conduct. For, unlike all succeeding groups in the position of an established upper class, they have a social function but no profession.

Not only in the Western civilizing process, but in others such as that of eastern Asia, the moulding which behaviour receives at the great courts, the administrative centres of the key monopolies of taxation and physical force, is of equal importance. It is first here, at the seat of the monopoly ruler, that all the threads of a major network of interdependence run together; here, at this particular social nexus, more and longer chains of action intersect than at any other point in the web. Even long-distance trade links, into which urban–commercial centres are interwoven here and there, never prove lasting and stable unless they are protected for a considerable period by strong central authorities. Correspondingly, the provident long-term view, the strict control of conduct which this central organ demands of its functionaries and of the prince himself or his representatives and servants, are greater than at any other point. Ceremony and etiquette give this situation clear expression. So much presses directly and indirectly on the central ruler and his close entourage from the whole dominion, each of his steps, each of his gestures may be of such momentous and far-reaching importance, precisely because the monopolies still have a strongly private and personal character, that without this exact timing, these complex forms of reserve and distance, the tense balance of society on which the peaceful operation of the monopoly administration rests would rapidly lapse into disorder. And, if not always directly, then at least through the persons of the central ruler and his ministers, every movement or upheaval of any significance in the whole dominion reacts on the bulk of the courtiers, on the whole narrower and wider entourage of the prince. Directly or indirectly, the intertwining of all activities with which everyone at court is inevitably confronted, compels him to observe constant vigilance, and to subject everything he says and does to minute scrutiny.

The formation of monopolies of tax and physical force, and of great courts around these monopolies, is certainly no more than one of several interdependent processes of which the civilizing process forms a part. But it certainly provides one of the keys by which we can gain access to the driving forces of these processes. The great royal court stands for a period at the centre of the social networks which set and keep the civilizing of conduct in motion. In tracing the sociogenesis of the court, we find ourselves at the centre of a civilizing transformation that is both particularly pronounced and an indispensable precondition for all subsequent spurts and counter-spurts in the civilizing process. We see how, step by step, a warrior nobility is replaced by a tamed nobility with more muted affects, a courtly nobility. Not only within the Western civilizing process, but as far as we can see within every major civilizing process, one of the most decisive transitions is that of *warriors to courtiers*. But it need scarcely be said that there are widely differing stages and degrees of this transition, this inner pacification of a society. In the West the transformation of the warriors proceeds very gradually from the eleventh or twelfth centuries until it slowly reaches its conclusion in the seventeenth and eighteenth centuries.

How it comes to pass has already been described in detail: first, the wide landscape with its many castles and estates; the degree of integration is slight; the everyday dependence and thus the horizon of the bulk of the warriors, like that of the peasants, is restricted to their immediate district:

"Localism was writ large across the Europe of the early Middle Ages, the localism at first of the tribe and the estate, later shaping itself into those feudal and manorial units upon which medieval society rested. Both politically and socially these units were nearly independent, and the exchange of products and ideas was reduced to a minimum."[136] Then, from the profusion of castles and estates in every region, arise individual houses whose rulers have attained, in many battles and through the growth of their possessions and military power, a position of predominance over the other warriors in a more extended area. Their residences become, as a result of the greater confluence of goods arriving at them, the homes of a larger number of people, "courts" in a new sense of the word. The people who come together here in search of opportunities, always including a number of poorer warriors, are no longer as independent as the free warriors ensconced in their more or less self-sufficient estates; they are all placed in a kind of monopolistically controlled competition. And even here, in a circle of people that is still small compared to the absolutist courts, the co-existence of a number of people whose actions constantly intertwine, compels even the warriors who find themselves thus in closer interdependence to observe some degree of consideration and foresight, a more strict control of conduct and—above all towards the mistress of the house on whom they depend—a greater restraint of the affects, a transformation of the drive economy. The *courtois* code of conduct gives us an idea of the regulation of manners, and the *minnesang*[137] an impression of the drive-control, that become necessary and normal at these major and minor territorial courts. They bear witness to a first spurt in the direction which finally leads to the complete transformation of the nobility into courtiers, and a permanent "civilizing" of their conduct. But the web of interdependence into which the warrior enters at first is not yet very extensive or tight. If he must adopt a certain reserve at court, there are still countless people and situations in respect of which he need observe no special restraint. He may escape the lord and the lady of one court in the hope of finding lodgings at another. The country road is full of sought and unsought encounters which require no very great control of impulses. At court, towards the mistress, he may deny himself violent acts and affective outbursts; but even the *courtois* knight is first and foremost still a warrior, and his life an almost uninterrupted chain of wars, feuds and violence. The more peaceful constraints of social intertwining which tend to impose a profound transformation of drives, do not yet bear constantly and evenly on his life; they intrude only intermittently, are constantly breached by belligerence which neither tolerates nor requires any restraint of the affects. So the self-restraint which the *courtois* knights observe at court is only slightly consolidated into half-unconscious habits, into the almost automatic pattern characteristic of a later stage. The *courtois* precepts—as noted above—are mostly addressed, in the heyday of knightly courtly society, to adults and children alike; conformity to them by adults is never taken so much for granted that one may cease to speak about them. The opposed impulses never disappear from consciousness. The structure of self-constraints, especially the "super-ego", is not yet very strongly or evenly developed.

In addition, one of the main motive forces which later, in absolutist–courtly society, especially consolidates polite manners in the individual and continuously refines them, is as yet still lacking. The rise of urban–bourgeois strata against the nobility is still relatively slight, as therefore is the competitive tension between the two estates. To be sure, at the territorial courts themselves, warriors and town-dwellers sometimes compete for the same opportunities. There are bourgeois as well as noble *minnesänger*; in this respect too the *courtois* court shows incipiently the same structural regularities which later appear, fully developed, in the absolutist court: it brings people of bourgeois and noble origin into constant contact. But later, in the era of fully developed monopolies of rule, the functional integration of nobility and bourgeoisie, and thus the possibility of constant contacts as well as permanent tensions, is already quite highly developed even outside the court. Contacts between bourgeois and warriors such as occur at the *courtois* courts, are still relatively rare. In general, the intertwining of dependencies between bourgeoisie and nobility is still slight compared to the later period. The towns and the feudal lords in their immediate or wider neighbourhood still stand opposed as alien political and social units. How little the division of functions is developed, and how great the relative independence of the different estates still is, is clearly demonstrated by the fact that the spread of customs and ideas between town and town, court and court, monastery and monastery, i.e. relationships within the same social stratum, even over long distances, is often greater than contacts between castle and towns in the same district.[138] This is the social structure which—by way of contrast—we must keep in mind in order to understand the different structure, the different social processes in which gradually an increasing "civilization" of the way the individual steers himself emerges.

Here, as in every society with a barter economy, exchange and thus mutual dependence and integration between different classes is still slight as compared to the following phases. Society's whole mode of life is therefore less uniform. Military potential and property are here extremely closely and directly related. Thus the unarmed peasant lives in an abject condition. He is at the mercy of the armed lord to a degree that no person was exposed to others in the everyday life of later phases, when public or state monopolies of force had developed. The lord and master, on the other hand, the warrior, is functionally so little dependent on his inferiors (though of course not independent of them), he is, through the overwhelming physical threat normally emanating from him, untrammelled in relation to them to an extent which surpasses by far the relative power surplus of any upper class in relation to lower classes at the later stages of social development. Similarly with the standard of living: here, too, the contrast between the highest and lowest classes of this society is extremely great, particularly in the phase when a decreasing number of especially mighty and wealthy lords is emerging from the mass of the warriors. We encounter similar contrasts today in areas where the social structure is nearer to that of Western medieval society than that of the West today, for example in Peru or Saudi Arabia. Members of a small élite have an immense income of which a far larger part than is the case with high incomes in the West today, is used for the personal consumption of its owner, luxuries of his "private life", robes and jewellery, residence and stables, utensils and meals, feasts and other pleasures. The members of the lowest class, the peasants, by contrast, live wretchedly under the constant threat of bad harvests and starvation; even under normal circumstances

262

the produce of their work just suffices to provide them with a subsistence; their standard of living is considerably lower than that of any class in "civilized" societies. And only when these contrasts are reduced, when through the competitive pressure affecting this society from top to bottom the division of functions and interdependence over large areas gradually increases, when the functional dependence of the upper classes grows while the social power and living standards of the lower class rise, only then do we find the constant foresight and self-control in the upper classes, the continuous upward movement of the lower ones, and all the other changes which one can observe in any civilizing spurt encompassing broader strata.

To begin with—at the starting point of this movement as it were—the warriors live their own lives and the burghers and peasants theirs. Even in spatial proximity the gulf between the estates is deep; customs, gestures, clothes or amusements differ, even if mutual influences are not entirely lacking. On all sides social contrast—or, as people in a more uniform world like to call it, the variety of life—is greater. The upper class, the nobility, does not yet feel any appreciable social pressure from below; even the bourgeoisie scarcely contest their function and prestige. They do not yet need to hold themselves constantly in check and on the alert in order to maintain their position as the upper class. They have their land and their swords: the primary danger for each warrior is other warriors. And so the mutual control the nobles impose on their conduct as a means of class distinction is less, so that from this side too the individual knight is subjected to a lower degree of self-control. He occupies his social position far more securely and as a matter of course than the courtly noble. He does not need to banish coarseness and vulgarity from his life. The thought of the lower classes has nothing disturbing for him; they are not permanently associated with anxiety, and thus there is no social taboo on anything recalling the lower classes in upper-class life, as happened later. No repugnance or embarrassment is aroused by the sight of the lower classes and their behaviour, but a feeling of *contempt*, which is expressed openly, untroubled by any reserve, uninhibited and unsublimated. The "Scenes from the Life of a Knight" included earlier in this study,[139] give a certain impression of this attitude, although the documentation was taken from a later, courtly period of knightly existence.

How the warriors are drawn step by step into the vortex of

increasingly stronger and closer interdependencies with other classes and groups, how an increasing part of them falls into functional and finally institutional dependence on others, has already been described in detail from various aspects. These are processes acting in the same direction over centuries: loss of military and economic self-sufficiency by all warriors, and the conversion of a part of them into courtiers.

One can detect the operation of these forces of integration as early as the eleventh and twelfth centuries, when territorial dominions consolidate themselves and a number of people, particularly less favoured knights, are forced to go to the greater and lesser courts to seek service.

Then, slowly, the few great courts of princely feudality rise above all the others; only members of the royal house now have the chance to compete freely with one another. And above all the richest, most brilliant court of this period of competing feudal princes, the Burgundian court, gives an impression of how this transformation of warriors into courtiers gradually advances.

Finally, in the fifteenth and above all the sixteenth century, the whole movement underlying this transformation, the differentiation of functions, the increasing interdependence and integration of ever-larger areas and classes, accelerates. This is seen particularly clearly in the movement of a social instrument the use and changes of which indicate most accurately the degree of division of functions, and the extent and nature of social interdependence: the movement of money. The volume of money grows more quickly, and at a corresponding rate the purchasing power or value of money falls. This movement, too, that is, the devaluation of minted metal, begins, like the transformation of warriors into courtiers, early in the Middle Ages. What is new at the transition from medieval to modern times is not monetarization, the decrease in the purchasing power of minted metal as such, but the pace and extent of this movement. Here, as so often, what first appears as merely a quantitative change, is on closer inspection an expression of qualitative changes, transformations in the structure of human relationships, of society.

Certainly, this accelerating devaluation of money is not by itself the cause of the social changes that emerge more and more clearly at this time; it is part of a larger process, a lever in a more complex system of intertwining trends. Under the pressure of competitive struggles of a particular stage and structure, the demand for money increases at this time; to satisfy it new ways and means are sought and found. But, as was pointed out earlier,[140] this movement has a very different meaning for different sectors of society; precisely this shows how great the functional interdependence of different strata has become. Favoured by this movement are all those groups whose functions permit them to compensate for the falling purchasing power of money by acquiring more money, i.e., above all bourgeois groups and the controllers of the tax monopoly, the kings; disadvantaged are groups of warriors or nobles who have an income which nominally remains the same but in purchasing power constantly diminishes with the accelerating devaluation of money. It is the pull of this movement that in the sixteenth and seventeenth centuries draws more and more warriors to the court and thus into direct dependence on the king, while conversely the kings' tax revenues grow to such an extent that they can maintain an ever-larger number of people at their court.

If one contemplates the past as a kind of aesthetic picture book, if one's gaze is directed above all at changes of "styles", one may easily have the impression that from time to time the tastes or minds of people changed abruptly through a kind of inner mutation: now we have "Gothic people" before us, now "men of the Renaissance", and now "Baroque people". If we try to gain an idea of the structure of the whole network of relationships in which all the individual people of a certain epoch are enmeshed, if we try to follow the changes in the institutions under which they live, or in the functions on which their social existence is based, our impression that at some moment the same mutation suddenly and inexplicably took place in many minds independent of each other, is increasingly dispelled. All these changes take place quite slowly over a considerable period, in small steps and to a large extent noiselessly for ears capable of perceiving only the great events heard far and wide. The explosions in which the existence and attitudes of individual people are changed abruptly and therefore especially perceptibly, are nothing but particular events within these slow and often almost imperceptible social shifts, whose effects are grasped only by comparing different generations, by placing side by side the social destinies of fathers, sons and grandsons. Such is the case with the transformation of the warriors into courtiers, the change whereby an upper class of free knights was replaced by one of courtiers. Even in the last phases of this process, many individuals may still have seen the fulfilment of their existence, of their wishes, affects and talents, in the life of a free knight. But all these talents and affects are now becoming increasingly impossible to put into practice because of the gradual transformation of human relations; the functions that give them scope are disappearing from the fabric of society. And the case is no different, finally, with the absolutist court itself. It too was not suddenly conceived or created at some moment by individuals, but was formed gradually on the basis of a specific transformation of social power-relationships. All individuals are driven by a particular dependence on others into this specific form of relationship. Through their interdependence they hold each other fast within it, and the court is not only generated by this interweaving of dependencies, but creates itself over and again as a form of human relationships outlasting individuals, as a firmly established institution, as long as this particular kind of mutual dependence is continuously renewed on the basis of a particular structure of society at large. Just as, for example, the social institution of a factory is incomprehensible unless we try to explain why the entire social structure continuously generates factories, why people in them are obliged to perform services as employees or workers for an employer, and why the employer is in turn dependent on such services, the social institution of the absolutist court is likewise incomprehensible unless we know the formula of needs, the nature and degree of mutual dependence, by which people of different kinds were bound together in this way. Only thus does the court appear before our eyes as it really was; only thus does it lose the aspect of a fortuitously or arbitrarily created grouping, about which it is neither possible nor necessary to ask the reason for its existence, and takes on meaning as a network of human relationships which, for a period, continuously reproduced itself in this way, because it offered many individual people opportunities of satisfying certain needs generated over and again in their society.

The constellation of needs out of which the "court" constantly reproduced itself as an institution over generations has been shown above: the nobility, or at least parts of it, needed the king because, with advancing monopolization, the function of free warrior was disappearing from society; and because, with increasing monetary integration, the produce from their estates—measured against the standards of the rising bourgeoisie—no longer allowed them more than a mediocre living and frequently not even that, and certainly not a social existence that could maintain the nobility's prestige as the upper class against the growing strength of the bourgeoisie. Under this pressure a part of the nobility—whoever could hope to find a place there—entered the court and thus direct dependence on the king. Only life at court opened to individual nobles within this social space access to economic opportunities and prestige that could in any way satisfy their claims to a demonstratively upper-class existence. Had the nobles been concerned solely or even primarily with economic opportunities, they would not have needed to go to the court; many of them could have acquired wealth more successfully through commercial activity—such as a rich marriage. But to gain wealth through commercial activity they would have had to renounce their noble rank; they would have degraded themselves in their own eyes and those of other nobles. It was this very distance from the bourgeoisie, their character as nobles, their membership of the upper class of the country, that gave their lives meaning and direction. The desire to preserve their class prestige, to "distinguish" themselves, motivated their actions far more than the desire to accumulate money. They therefore not only remained at court because they were dependent on the king, but they remained dependent on the king because only life amid courtly society could maintain the distance from others and the prestige on which depended their salvation, their existence as members of the upper class, the establishment or the "Society" of the country. No doubt, at least a part of the courtly nobility could not have lived at court had they not been offered many kinds of economic opportunities there. But what they sought were not economic possibilities as such—they were, as noted above, to be had elsewhere—but possibilities of existence that were compatible with the maintenance of their distinguishing prestige, their character as a nobility. And this double bond through the necessity for both money and prestige is to varying degrees characteristic of all upper classes, not only the bearers of "civilité" but also of "civilization". The compulsion that membership of an upper class and the desire to retain it exert on the individual, is no less strong and formative than that arising from the simple necessity of economic subsistence. Motives of both kinds are wound as a double and invisible chain about the individual members of such classes, and the first bond, the craving for prestige and fear of its loss, the struggle against the obliteration of social distinction, is no more to be explained solely by the second, as a masked desire for more money and economic advantages, than it is ever to be found lastingly in classes or families that live under heavy external pressure on the borderline of hunger and destitution. A compulsive desire for social prestige is to be found as the primary motive of action only among members of classes whose income under normal circumstances is substantial and perhaps even growing, and at any rate is appreciably over the hunger threshold. In such classes the impulse to engage in economic activity is no longer the simple necessity of satisfying hunger, but a desire to preserve a certain high, socially expected standard of living and prestige. This explains why, in such elevated classes, affect-control and self-constraint are generally more highly developed than in the lower classes: fear of loss or reduction of social prestige is one of the most powerful motive forces in the transformation from constraints through others into self-restraints. Here, too, as in many other instances, the upper-class characteristics of "good society" are particularly highly developed in the courtly aristocracy of the seventeenth and eighteenth centuries, precisely because, within its framework, money was indispensable and wealth desirable as a means of living, but certainly not, as in the bourgeois world, the basis of prestige as well. Membership of courtly society means to those belonging to it more than wealth; for just this reason they are so entirely and inescapably bound to the court; for just this reason the pressure of courtly life shaping their conduct is so strong. There is no other place where they could live without loss of status; and this is why they are so dependent on the king.

The king for his part is dependent on the aristocracy for a large number of reasons. For his own conviviality he needs a society whose manners he shares; the fact that the people who serve him at table, on going to bed or while hunting belong to the highest nobility of the land, serves his need to be distinguished from all the other groups in the country. But above all he needs the nobility as a counterweight to the bourgeoisie, just as he needs the bourgeoisie to counterbalance the nobility, if his scope to manipulate the key monopolies is not to be reduced. It is the inherent regularities of the "royal mechanism" that place the absolutist ruler in dependence on the nobility. To maintain the nobility as a distinguishing class, and thus to preserve the balance and tension between nobility and bourgeoisie, to allow neither estate to grow too strong or too weak: these are the fundamentals of royal policy.

The nobility—and the bourgeoisie, too—is not only dependent on the king; the king depends on the existence of the nobility. But without doubt the dependence of the individual noble on the king is incomparably greater than that of the king on any individual noble; this is very clearly manifested in the relation between king and nobility at court.

The king is not only the nobility's oppressor, as part of the courtly nobility feel; nor is he only their preserver, as large sections of the bourgeoisie believe; he is both. And the court, therefore, is likewise both: an institution for taming and preserving the nobility. "If a noble," La Bruyère says in a passage on the court, "lives at home in the provinces, he is free, but without support; if he lives at Court, he is protected, but a slave." In many respects this relationship resembles that between a small independent businessman and a high employee in a powerful family concern. At court a part of the nobility find the possibility of living in accordance with their status; but the individual nobles are not now, as the knights were earlier, in free military competition with each other: they are in monopoly-bound competition for the opportunities the monopoly ruler has to allocate. And they not only live under the pressure of this central lord; they are not only subjected to the competitive pressure which they, together with a reserve army of country aristocracy, exert on each other; they are above all under pressure from rising bourgeois strata. With the latters' growing social power the noblemen at court have constantly to contend; they live from the duties and taxes that come primarily from the third estate. The interdependence and integration of different social functions, above all between nobility and bourgeoisie, is very much tighter than in preceding phases. All the more omnipresent, therefore, are the tensions between them. And as the structure of human relationships is changed in this way, as the individual is now embedded in the human network quite differently from before

269

and moulded by the web of his dependencies, so too changes the structure of individual consciousness and affects, of the interplay between drives and drive-controls, between conscious and unconscious levels of the personality. The closer interdependence on every side, the heavy and continuous pressure from all directions, demands and instils a more even self-control, a more stable super-ego and new forms of conduct between people: warriors become courtiers.

Wherever we encounter civilizing processes of any scope, we also find structural similarities within the wider socio-historical context in which these changes in mentality occur. They may take place more or less quickly, they may advance, as here, in a single sweep or in several spurts with strong counter-spurts; but as far as we can see today, a more or less decisive courtization of warriors, whether permanent or transitory, is one of the most elementary social preconditions of every major movement of civilization. And however little importance the social formation of the court may at first sight have for our present life, a certain understanding of the structure of the court is indispensable in comprehending civilizing processes. Some of its structural characteristics may also throw light on the life at centres of power in general.

V

The Muting of Drives: Psychologization and Rationalization

"Life at court", La Bruyère writes,[141], "is a serious, melancholy game, which requires of us that we arrange our pieces and our batteries, have a plan, follow it, foil that of our adversary, sometimes take risks and play on impulse. And after all our measures and meditations we are in check, sometimes checkmate."

At the court, above all at the great absolutist court, there was formed for the first time a kind of society and human relationships having structural characteristics which from now on, over a long stretch of Western history and through many variations, again and again play a decisive part. In the midst of a large populated area which by and large is free of physical violence, a "good society" is formed. But even if the use of physical viol-

270

ence now recedes from human intercourse, if even duelling is now forbidden, people now exert pressure and force on each other in a wide variety of different ways. Life in this circle is in no way peaceful. Very many people are continuously dependent on each other. Competition for prestige and royal favour is intense. "Affaires", disputes over rank and favour, do not cease. If the sword no longer plays so great a role as the means of decision, it is replaced by intrigue, conflicts in which careers and social success are contested with words. They demand and produce other qualities than did the armed struggles that had to be fought out with weapons in one's hand. Continuous reflection, foresight, and calculation, self-control, precise and articulate regulation of one's own effects, knowledge of the whole terrain, human and non-human, in which one acts, become more and more indispensable preconditions of social success.

Every individual belongs to a "clique", a social circle which supports him when necessary; but the groupings change. He enters alliances, if possible with people ranking high at court. But rank at court can change very quickly; he has rivals; he has open and concealed enemies. And the tactics of his struggles, as of his alliances, demand careful consideration. The degree of aloofness or familiarity with everyone must be carefully measured; each greeting, each conversation has a significance over and above what is actually said or done. They indicate the standing of a person; and they contribute to the formation of court opinion on his standing:

"Let a favourite pay close heed to himself: for if he does not keep me waiting as long as usual in his antechamber; if his face is more open, if he frowns less, if he listens to me more willingly and accompanies me a little further when showing me out, I shall think that he is beginning to fall, and I shall be right."[142]

The court is a kind of stock exchange; as in every "good society", an estimate of the "value" of each individual is continuously being formed. But here his value has its real foundation not in the wealth or even the achievements or ability of the individual, but in the favour he enjoys with the king, the influence he has with other mighty ones, his importance in the play of courtly cliques. All this, favour, influence, importance, this whole complex and dangerous game in which physical force and direct affective outbursts are prohibited and a threat to existence, demands of each participant a constant foresight and an exact knowledge of every other, of his position and value in the network of courtly opinion; it exacts precise attunement of his own behaviour to this value. Every mistake, every careless step depresses the value of its perpetrator in courtly opinion; it may threaten his whole position at court.

"A man who knows the court is master of his gestures, of his eyes and his expression; he is deep, impenetrable. He dissimulates the bad turns he does, smiles at his enemies, suppresses his ill-temper, disguises his passions, disavows his heart, acts against his feelings."[143]

The transformation of the nobility in the direction of "civilized" behaviour is unmistakable. Here, it is not yet in all respects so profound and all-embracing as later in bourgeois society; for it is only towards their peers that the courtier and the court lady need to subject themselves to such constraint, and far less so towards their social inferiors. Quite apart from the fact that the pattern of drive- and affect-control is different in courtly from that in bourgeois society, the awareness that this control is exercised for social reasons is more alive. Opposing inclinations do not yet wholly vanish from waking consciousness; self-constraint has not yet become so completely an apparatus of habits operating almost automatically and including all human relationships. But it is already quite clear how human beings are becoming more complex, and internally split in a quite specific way. Each man, as it were, confronts himself. He "conceals his passions", "disavows his heart", "acts against his feelings". The pleasure or inclination of the moment is restrained in anticipation of the disagreeable consequences of its indulgence; and it is, indeed, the same mechanism as that by which adults— whether parents or other persons—increasingly instil a stable "super-ego" in children. The momentary drive and affect impulses are, as it were, held back and mastered by the foreknowledge of the later displeasure, by the fear of a future pain, until this fear finally opposes the forbidden behaviour and inclinations by force of habit, even if no other person is directly present, and the energy of such inclinations is channelled into a harmless direction not threatened by any displeasure.

In keeping with the transformation of society, of interpersonal relationships, the affective make-up of the individual is also reconstructed: as the series of actions and the number of people on whom the individual and his actions constantly depend are increased, the habit of foresight over longer chains grows stronger. And as the behaviour and personality structure of the individual change, so does his manner of considering others. His image of them becomes richer in nuances, freer of spontaneous emotions: it is "psychologized".

Where the structure of social functions allows the individual greater scope for actions under the influence of momentary impulses than is the case at court, it is neither necessary nor possible to consider very deeply the nature of another person's consciousness and affects, or what hidden motives may underlie his behaviour. If at court calculation meshes with calculation, in simpler societies affect directly engages affect. This strength of the immediate affects, however, binds the individual to a smaller number of behavioural options: someone is friend or foe, good or evil; and depending on how one perceives another in terms of these black and white affective patterns, so one behaves. Everything seems directly related to feeling. That the sun shines, or lightning flashes, that someone laughs or knits his brow, all this appeals more directly to the affects of the perceiver. And as it excites him here and now in a friendly or unfriendly way, he takes it as if it were meant this way especially for him. It does not enter his head that all this, a flash of lightning that almost strikes him, a face that offends him, are to be explained by remote connections that have nothing directly to do with himself. People only develop a more long-sighted view of nature and other people to the extent that the advancing division of functions and their daily involvement in long human chains accustom them to such a view and a greater restraint of the affects. Only then is the veil which the passions draw before the eyes slowly lifted, and a new world comes into view—a world whose course is friendly or hostile to the individual person without being intended to be so, a chain of events that need to be contemplated dispassionately over long stretches if their connections are to be disclosed.*

Like conduct generally, the perception of things and people also becomes affectively more neutral in the course of the civilizing process. The "world picture" gradually becomes less directly determined by human wishes and fears, and more

*See in this context Norbert Elias, "Problems of Involvement and Detachment", *British Journal of Sociology*, 7 (1956), pp. 226–52. [*Author's note to the translation*]

273

strongly oriented to what we call "experience" or "the empirical", to sequences with their own immanent regularities. Just as today, in a further spurt in this direction, the course of history and society is gradually emerging from the mists of personal affects and involvement, from the haze of collective longings and fears, and beginning to appear as a relatively autonomous nexus of events, so too with nature and—within smaller confines—with human beings. It is particularly in the circles of court life that what we would today call a "psychological" view of man develops, a more precise observation of others and oneself in terms of longer series of motives and causal connections, because it is here that vigilant self-control and perpetual observation of others are among the elementary prerequisites for the preservation of one's social position. But this is only one example of how what we call the "orientation to experience", the observation of events within a lengthening and broadening nexus of interdependence, slowly begins to develop at exactly the point where the structure of society itself compels the individual to restrain his momentary affects and transform his libidinal energies to a higher degree.

Saint-Simon in one place observes someone with whom he is on an uncertain footing. He describes his own behaviour in this situation as follows: "I soon noticed that he was growing colder; I closely followed his conduct towards me to avoid any confusion between what might be accidental in a man burdened with prickly affairs, and what I suspected. My suspicions were confirmed, causing me to withdraw from him entirely without in the slightest appearing to do so."[144]

This courtly art of human observation—unlike what we usually call 'psychology" today—is never concerned with the individual in isolation, as if the essential features of his behaviour were independent of his relations to others, and as if he related to others, so to speak, only retrospectively. The approach here is far closer to reality, in that the individual is always seen in his social context, *as a human being in his relations to others, as an individual in a social situation.*

It was pointed out above[145] that the precepts on behaviour of the sixteenth century differ from those of the preceding centuries less in terms of their content than in their tone, their changed affective atmosphere; psychological insights, personal observations, begin to play a larger part. A comparison between the precepts of Erasmus or Della Casa and the corresponding medieval rules shows this clearly. Investigation of the social changes of this time, the transformation of human relationships that took place, provides an explanation. This "psychologization" of rules of conduct, or, more precisely, their greater permeation by observation and experience, is an expression of the accelerated courtization of the upper class and of the closer integration of all parts of society in this period. Signs of a change in this direction are certainly not to be found only in writings recording the standard of "good behaviour" of the time; we find them equally in works devoted to the entertainment of this class. The observation of people that life in the courtly circle demands finds its literary expression in an art of human portraiture.

The increased demand for books within a society is itself a √ sure sign of a pronounced spurt in the civilizing process; for the transformation and regulation of drives that is demanded both to write and read books is always considerable. But in courtly society the book does not yet play quite the same part as in bourgeois society. In the former social intercourse, the market of prestige values, forms the centre of existence for each individual; books, too, are intended less for reading in the study or in solitary leisure hours wrung from one's profession, than for social conviviality; they are a part and continuation of conversation and social games, or, like the majority of court memoirs, they are substitute conversations, dialogues in which for some reason or other the partner is lacking. The high art of human portraiture in court memoirs, letters or aphorisms thus gives a good impression of the complex human observation instilled by courtly life. And here, as in many other respects, bourgeois society in France develops the courtly heritage with a singular continuity. The persistence of a Parisian "good society" as beneficiary and further developer of the instruments of prestige evolved in courtly society long beyond the Revolution and up to the present day, may have contributed to this. At any rate, we can say that from the courtly human portraits of Saint-Simon and his contemporaries to the portrayal of the "high society" of the nineteenth century by Proust—by way of Balzac, Flaubert, Maupassant and many others—and finally to the depiction of the life of broader classes by writers such as Jules Romains or André Malraux, and by a large number of French films, there is

275

a direct line of tradition, characterized by precisely this lucidity of human observation, this capacity to see people in their entire social context and to understand them through it. The individual figure is never artificially isolated from the fabric of his social existence, his simple dependence on others. This is why the atmosphere and plasticity of real experience is never lost in the descriptions.

And much the same that can be said of this "psychologization" applies also to the "rationalization" which slowly becomes increasingly perceptible from the sixteenth century onwards in the most varied aspects of society. This, too, is not an isolated fact; it is only *one* expression of the change in the *whole* personality that emerges at this time, and of the growing foresight that is from now on required and instilled by an ever-increasing number of social functions.

Here, as in many other instances, the understanding of socio-historical developments requires a suspension of the habits of thinking with which we have grown up. This often-noted historical rationalization is not something that arose from the fact that numerous unconnected individual people simultaneously developed from "within", as if on the basis of some pre-established harmony, a new organ or substance, an "understanding" or "reason" which had not existed hitherto. What changes is the way in which people are bonded to each other. This is why their behaviour changes, and why their consciousness and their drive–economy, and, in fact, their personality structure as a whole, change. The "circumstances" which change are not something which comes upon men from "outside": they are the relationships between people themselves.

Man is an extraordinarily malleable and variable being. The changes of human attitude discussed here are examples of this malleability. It is by no means confined to what we generally distinguish as the "psychological" from the "physiological". The "physis", too, indissolubly linked to what we call the "psyche", is variously moulded in the course of history in accordance with the network of dependencies that extend throughout a human life. One might think, for example, of the moulding of the facial muscles and thus of facial expression during a person's lifetime, or of the formation of reading or writing centres in the brain. The same applies to what we refer to by the reifying terms "reason", "ratio" or "understanding". All that does not exist—though our use of words suggests otherwise—relatively untouched by socio-historical change, in the way that, for example, the heart or stomach exists. Rather, these terms express a particular moulding of the whole personality; they are aspects of a moulding which takes place very gradually, repeatedly advancing and slipping back, and which emerges more strongly the more clearly and totally the spontaneous impulses of the individual threaten to bring about, through the structure of human dependencies, loss of pleasure, decline and inferiority in relation to others, or even the ruin of one's social existence. They are aspects of that moulding by which the libidinal centre and the ego-centre are more and more sharply differentiated, until finally a comprehensive, stable and highly differentiated agency of self-constraint is formed. There is not actually a "ratio", there is at most "rationalization".

Our habits of thinking incline us to look for "beginnings"; but there is nowhere in the development of people a "point" before which one could say: hitherto there was no "ratio" and now it has "arisen"; hitherto there were no self-compulsions and no "super-ego" and now, in this or that century, they are suddenly there. There is no zero-point of all these data. But it does no more justice to the facts to say: everything was always there as it is now. The habits of self-constraint, the conscious and affective make-up of "civilized" people, clearly differ *in their totality* from those of so-called "primitives"; but both are, in their structure, different yet clearly explainable mouldings of largely the same natural functions.

Traditional habits of thinking continually confront us with static alternatives; they are schooled, in a sense, on Eleatic models: we can imagine only numerous individual points, separate abrupt changes, or no change at all. And it is clearly still very difficult to see ourselves as situated in a gradual, continuous change with a particular structure and regularity, a change which is lost to our gaze in the darkness of the more distant past, and as part of a movement which, as far as is possible, should be seen as a whole, like the flight of an arrow or the flow of a river, not as the recurrence of always the same thing at different points or as something that jumps from point to point. What changes in the course of the process which we call history are, to reiterate, the mutual relationships, the figurations, of people and the moulding the individual undergoes within them. But at the very moment when this fundamental historicity of man is clearly seen, we also perceive the regularity, the structural characteristics of human existence which remain constant. Each single aspect of human social life is comprehensible only if seen in the context of this perpetual movement; no particular detail can be isolated from it. It is formed within this moving context—which may seem slow, as in the case of many primitive peoples, or rapid, as in our own—and must be grasped within it, as a part of a particular stage or wave. Thus social drive-controls and restrictions are nowhere absent among people, nor is a certain foresight; but these qualities have a different form and degree among simple herdsmen or in a warrior class than among courtiers, state officials or members of a mechanized army. They grow more powerful and more complete the greater the division of functions and thus, the greater the number of people to whom the individual has to attune his actions. Likewise, the nature of "understanding" or "thinking" to which an individual is accustomed resembles or differs from that of other people in his society to the same extent as his own social situation and function and those of his parents or the most important influences moulding him resemble or differ from those of others. The foresight of the printer or the fitter is different from that of the book-keeper, the engineer's from that of the sales director, the finance minister's from that of the army commander, even though all these different surface mouldings are to an extent equalized by the interdependence of functions. At a deeper level, the rationality and affect-moulding of someone who has grown up in a working-class family are different from those of someone who grew up in secure, well-to-do surroundings. And finally, the rationality and affect-patterns, the self-images and drive economy of the Germans, the English, the French and Italians differ in keeping with their different histories of interdependence, and the social moulding of people in the West as a whole differs from that of Orientals. But all these differences are comprehensible precisely because the same human and social regularities underly them. The individual differences *within* all these groups, such as those of "intelligence", are merely nuances within a framework of very specific historical forms, differentiations for which a society offers greater or lesser scope depending on its structure. Thus, for example, the venture of highly individualized independent thought, the stance by which a person proves himself to be a "creative intelligence", not only has a very special individual "natural talent" as a precondition. It is only possible at all within a particular structure of power balances; its precondition is a quite specific *social structure*. And it depends further on the access which the individual has, within a society so structured, to the kind of schooling, and to the not very numerous social functions, which alone permit his capacity for independent individual thought to develop.

Thus the foresight or "thought" of the knight is different from that of the courtier. A scene described by Ranke[146] gives a good impression of how the typical personality structure of knights was doomed by the growing monopolization of force. More generally, it provides an example of the way in which a change in the structure of social functions enforces a change of conduct. The Duke of Montmorency, the son of a man who had played a major part in the victory of Henry IV, had rebelled. He was a knightly, princely man, generous and brilliant, brave and ambitious. And he served the king; but that power and the right to rule should be confined to the latter or, more precisely, to Richelieu, he neither understood nor approved. So, with his followers, he began to fight against the king, as in old times knights, feudal lords, had often fought against each other. There was a confrontation. The king's general, Schomberg, was in a tactically weak position. This, however, Ranke tells us:

was an advantage to which Montmorency paid but little attention; seeing the enemy army, he suggested to his friends that they should attack without delay. For he understood war primarily as a brave cavalry charge. An experienced companion, Count Rieux, begged him to wait until a few guns that were being drawn up had shaken the enemy's position. But Montmorency was already gripped by a belligerent frenzy. There was no more time to lose, he said, and his advisor, though foreseeing disaster, did not dare to oppose the clear will of the knightly leader. "Lord", he cried, "I shall die at your feet."

Montmorency was recognizable by a stallion splendidly adorned with red blue and dun feathers. It was only a small group of followers who leapt with him over the ditch. They cut down everyone who was in their way, battling forward until they finally arrived in front of the enemy's actual position. There they were met by close and rapid musket fire: horses and men were wounded and killed. Count Rieux and most of the others fell; the Duke of Montmorency, wounded, fell from his stricken horse and was taken prisoner.

Richelieu had him tried, certain of the outcome, and soon afterwards the last Montmorency was beheaded in the courtyard of the town hall of Toulouse.

To give way directly to impulses and not to take thought of the further consequences was, in the preceding phases when warriors could compete more freely with each other, a mode of behaviour which—even if it led to the downfall of the individual—was adequate to the social structure as a whole and therefore to "reality". Martial fervour was a necessary precondition of success and prestige for a man of the nobility. With advancing monopolization and centralization all that changed.

The different structure of sociey now punishes affective outbursts and actions lacking the appropriate forethought with certain ruin. And anyone who does not agree with the existing state of affairs, with the omnipotence of the king, must change his ways. Let us listen to Saint-Simon. He, too, scarcely more than a generation after Montmorency, is and remains throughout his life a duke in opposition. But all he can do is form a kind of faction at court; if he is skilful he can hope to win over the king's successor, the Dauphin, to his ideas. But this is a dangerous game at the court of Louis XIV, demanding utmost caution. The prince must first be very carefully sounded out and then gradually guided in the desired direction:

My principal intention [thus Saint-Simon describes his tactics in a conversation with the Dauphin] was to sound his opinion on everything that concerned our dignity. I thus took care gently to break off all discussion that led away from this goal, to draw the conversation back and conduct it through all the different chapters . . . the Dauphin, eagerly attentive, appreciated all my arguments . . . became heated . . . and groaned at the ignorance and lack of reflection of the King. I did little more than mention all these different subjects in presenting them successively to the Dauphin, and then followed after him, leaving him the pleasure of talking, showing me that he was educated. I let him persuade himself, work himself up, grow angry, while I was able to see his feelings, his way of

thinking, and to gain impressions from which I could profit
. . . I sought less to press my arguments and parentheses
than . . . gently and firmly to imbue him with my feelings and
views on each of these subjects. . . .

This brief sketch of the attitude of these two men, the dukes of
Montmorency and Saint-Simon, when giving expression to their
opposition to the king's omnipotence, helps to complete our picture. The former, one of the last knights, seeks to reach his goal
by physical combat; the latter, the courtier, by conversation.
The former acts from impulse with little thought of others; the
latter perpetually adjusts his behaviour to his interlocutor. Both,
not only Montmorency but Saint-Simon too, are in a highly
dangerous situation. The Dauphin can always break the rules of
courtly conversation; he can, if he so wishes, break off the conversation and the relationship for any reason he chooses, and
lose very little; if Saint-Simon is not very careful, he can divine
the duke's seditious thoughts and inform the king. Montmorency
hardly registers the danger; he is wholly bound by the straightforward behaviour his passion dictates; he seeks to overcome
danger precisely by the fury of his passion. Saint-Simon perceives the exact compass of the danger; he thus goes to work
with utmost self-control and forethought. He seeks to attain
nothing by force; he works with a longer view. He holds back,
in order to "imbue" the other imperceptibly but enduringly with
his feelings.

What we have in this autobiographical anecdote is a very
revealing piece of that *courtly rationality* which—though this is
not generally appreciated—played a no less important part, and
at first an even more important one, than the urban–commercial rationality and foresight instilled by functions in the trade
network, in the development of what we call the "Enlighten-
ment". But, certainly, these two forms of foresight, rationalization and psychologization—in the courtly group of the nobility
and in the leading middle-class groups—however different in
their pattern, developed in close conjunction with each other.
They indicate an increasing intertwining of nobility and
bourgeoisie; they spring from a transformation of human relationships throughout the whole of society: they are connected in
the closest possible way to the change by which the relatively
loosely knit estates of medieval society gradually become sub-

ordinate formations in a more centralized society, an absolute state.

The historical process of rationalization is a prime example of a kind of process which hitherto has been hardly or only vaguely grasped by systematic thought. It pertains—if we adhere to the traditional pattern of academic disciplines—to a science that does not yet exist, historical psychology. In the present structure of scholarly research a sharp dividing line is generally drawn between the work of the historian and of the psychologist. Only Western people living at present appear in need of or accessible to psychological investigation, or at most also so-called primitive peoples living today. The path leading, in Western history itself, from the simpler, more primitive psychological structure to the more differentiated one of our day remains in the dark. Precisely because the psychologist thinks unhistorically, because he approaches the psychological structures of present-day people as if they were something without evolution or change, the results of his investigations are in general of little use to the historian. And because the historian, preoccupied by what he calls facts, avoids psychological problems, he on his side has little to say to the psychologist.

The situation is little better with sociology. As far as it is concerned at all with historical problems, it accepts entirely the dividing line drawn by the historian between the seemingly immutable psychological structure of man and its different manifestations in the form of arts, ideas or whatever. That a historical social psychology, a study at once psychogenetic and sociogenetic, is needed to draw the connections between all these different manifestations of social human beings, remains unrecognized. Those concerned with the history of society, like those concerned with the history of mind, perceive "society" on the one hand and the world of "ideas" on the other as two different formations that can be meaningfully separated. Both seem to believe that there is either a society outside ideas and thoughts, or ideas outside society. And they merely dispute which of the two realms is more "important": some say that it is society-less ideas which set society in motion, and the others that it is an idea-less society that moves "ideas".

The civilizing process and, within it, such trends as psychologization and rationalization, do not fit into this kind of scheme. Even in thought they simply cannot be severed from the historical change in the structure of interpersonal relationships. It is quite pointless to ask whether the gradual transition from less to more rational modes of thought and conduct changes society; for this process of rationalization, like the more all-embracing process of civilization, is itself both a psychological and a social event. But it is equally meaningless to explain the civilizing process as a "superstructure" or "ideology", i.e. solely from its function as a weapon in the struggle between particular social groups and interests.

The gradual rationalization and, further, the whole civilizing process, undoubtedly takes place in constant conjunction with the struggles of different social strata and other groupings. The totality of European society, the sub-stratum of what is hitherto the last and strongest civilizing spurt, is certainly not the peaceful unity it sometimes appears in harmonistic edifices of thought. It is not an originally harmonious whole into which—as if by the ill-will or incomprehension of particular people—conflicts are accidentally introduced. Rather, tensions and struggles—as much as the mutual dependencies of people—are an integral part of its structure; they decisively affect the direction in which it changes. Undoubtedly, a civilizing movement can take on considerable importance as a weapon in these struggles. For habituation to a higher degree of foresight and greater restraint of momentary affects—to recall only these two facets—can give one group a significant advantage over another. But a higher degree of rationality and drive inhibition can also, in certain situations, have a debilitating and adverse effect. "Civilization" can be a very two-edged weapon. And whatever its effect may be in particular cases, at any rate the spurts in the civilizing process take place by and large independently of whether they are pleasant or useful to the groups involved. They arise from powerful dynamics of intertwining group activities the overall direction of which any single group on its own is hardly able to change. They are not open to conscious or half-conscious manipulation or deliberate conversion into weapons in the social struggle, far less so, indeed, than for instance, ideas. Just as the personality structure characteristic of a particular stage of social development, so specific traits of civilized conduct are at the same time a product of and a lever in the workings of the larger social process within which individual classes and interests form and transform themselves. Civilization, and therefore rationalization, for example, is not a process within a separate sphere of "ideas" or "thought". It does not involve solely changes of "knowledge", transformations of "ideologies", in short alterations of the *content* of consciousness, but changes in the whole human make-up, within which ideas and habits of thought are only a single sector. We are here concerned with changes in the whole personality throughout all its zones, from the steering of the individual by himself at the more flexible level of consciousness and reflection to that at the more automatic and rigid level of drives and affects. And to grasp changes of this kind, the pattern of thought summoned to mind by the concepts of "super-structure" or "ideology" is not enough.

The idea that the human "psyche" consists of different zones functioning independently of each other and capable of being considered independently, has become deeply rooted in human consciousness over a long period. It is common, in thinking about the more differentiated personality structure, to sever one of its functional levels from the others as if this were really the "essential" factor in the way men steer themselves in their encounter with their human fellows and with non-human nature. Thus the humanities and the sociology of knowledge stress above all the aspect of knowledge and thought. Thoughts and ideas appear in these studies as it were as that which is the most important and potent aspect of the way men steer themselves. And the unconscious impulses, the whole field of drive and affect structures, remains more or less in the dark.

But every investigation that considers only the consciousness of men, their "reason" or "ideas", while disregarding the structure of drives, the direction and form of human affects and passions, can be from the outset of only limited value. Much that is indispensable for an understanding of men escapes this approach. The rationalization of men's intellectual activity itself, and beyond that the whole structural changes of the ego and super-ego functions, all these interdependent levels of men's personality—as has been shown above and will be shown in more detail later—are only very imperfectly accessible to thought as long as enquiries are confined to changes in the intellectual aspects of men, to changes of ideas, and pay little regard to the changing balance and the changing pattern of the relationships between drives and affects on the one hand and drive- and affect-control on the other. A real understanding, even of the changes of ideas and forms of cognition, can be gained only if one takes into account too the changes of human interdependencies in conjunction with the structure of conduct and, in fact, the whole fabric of men's personality at a given stage of social development.

The inverse accentuation, with a corresponding limitation, is to be found often enough in psycho-analytical research today. It frequently tends, in considering human beings, to extract something "unconscious", conceived as an "id" without history, as the most important thing in the whole psychological structure. Although recently this image may have undergone corrections in therapeutic practice, these corrections have not yet led to theoretical elaboration of the data supplied by practive into more adequate conceptual tools. On the theoretical level it still usually appears as if the steering of the individual by unconscious libidinal impulses has a form and structure of its own, independently of the figurational destiny of the individual, the changing fortunes of his relationships with others throughout his life, and independently too of the pattern and structure of the other self-steering functions of his personality, conscious and unconscious. No distinction is made between the natural raw material of drives, which indeed perhaps changes little throughout the whole history of mankind, and the increasingly more firmly wrought structures of control, and thus the paths into which the elementary energies are channelled in each person through his or her relations with other people from birth onward. But nowhere, except perhaps in the case of madmen, do men in their encounter with each other find themselves face to face with psychological functions in their pristine state, in a state of nature that is not patterned by social learning, by a person's experience of other persons who satisfy or frustrate his or her needs in accordance with a specific social setting. The libidinal energies which one encounters in any living human being are always already socially processed; they are, in other words, sociogenetically transformed in their function and structure, and can in no way be separated from the corresponding ego and super-ego structures. The more animalic and automatic levels of men's personality are neither more nor less significant for the understanding of human conduct than their controls. What matters, what determines conduct, are the balances and conflicts between men's malleable drives and the built-in drive-controls.

Decisive for a person as he appears before us is neither the "id" alone, nor the "ego" or "super-ego" alone, but always *the relationship* between these various sets of psychological functions, partly conflicting and partly co-operating in the way an individual steers himself. It is they, these relationships *within* man between the drives and affects controlled and the built-in controlling agencies, whose structure changes in the course of a civilizing process, in accordance with the changing structure of the relationships *between* individual human beings, in society at large. In the course of this process, to put it briefly and all too simply, "consciousness" becomes less permeable by drives, and drives become less permeable by "consciousness". In simpler societies elementary impulses, however transformed, have an easier access to men's reflections. In the course of a civilizing process the compartmentalization of these self-steering functions, though in no way absolute, becomes more pronouned.

In accordance with the sociogenetic ground rule (see Volume 1, p. xiii) one can observe processes in the same direction directly in every child. One can see that, in the course of human history and again and again in that of each individual civilizing process, the self-steering in the form of ego and super-ego functions on the one hand and that through drives on the other become more and more firmly differentiated. Hence it is only with the formation of conscious functions less accessible to drives that the drive automatisms take on more and more that specific character which one today commonly diagnoses as "ahistoric", as a peculiarity of man throughout the ages which is purely natural, and independent of the developmental condition of human societies. However, the peculiarity of man discovered by Freud in men of our own time and conceptualized by him as a strict division between unconscious and conscious mental functions, far from being part of man's unchanged nature is a result of a long civilizing process in the course of which the wall of forgetfulness separating libidinal drives and "consciousness" or "reflection" has become harder and more impermeable.*

*To understand this fact is not only of theoretical but also of practical significance. Differences in the extent to which thinking is charged with affects make themselves felt again and again in the relationships between states at different stages of social development. As a rule, however, the leading statesmen of highly differentiated societies devise their strategies on the assumption that the level of restraint, the code of conduct, represented by the foreign policy of all countries is the same. Without an understanding of the different stages of a

In the course of the same transformation, the conscious mental functions themselves develop in the direction of what one calls increasing "rationalization": only with the sharper and firmer differentiation of the personality do the outward-directed psychological functions take on the character of a more rationally functioning consciousness less directly coloured by drive impulses and affective fantasies. Thus the form and structure of the more conscious and more unconscious psychological self-steering functions can never be grasped if they are imagined as something in any sense existing or functioning in isolation from one another. Both are equally fundamental to the existence of a human being; both together form a single great functional continuum. Nor can their structure and changes be understood if observation is confined to individual human beings. They can only be comprehended in connection with the structure of relationships *between* people, and with the long-term changes in that structure.

Therefore in order to understand and explain civilizing processes one needs to investigate—as has been attempted here—the transformation of both the personality structure and the entire social structure. This task demands, within a smaller radius, *psychogenetic* investigations aimed at grasping the whole field of individual psychological energies, the structure and form of the more elementary no less than of the more self-steering functions. Within a larger radius, the exploration of civilizing processes demands a long-range perspective, *sociogenetic* investigations of the overall structure, not only of a single state

---

civilizing process interstate policy must necessarily be somewhat unrealistic. However, to work out foreign policy based on the knowledge of these differentials in affectivity is far from easy. It will need a good deal of experimenting—and of wisdom—before an effective political dialogue and co-operation between societies at different levels of development can be worked out. The same applies to those cases in which, under stress, the affectivity and the fantasy character of the foreign policy of one of the more developed countries increases again to a higher level than that regarded at present as normal in the interstate relations of the leading industrial nation states. Nor are these levels in the degree of affectivity entirely dependent on the differentials of the economic or industrial development of countries. Thus, in the political strategies of China, for instance, one can discover a level of self-restraint at least on a par with that of the most highly developed industrial nations. Although in terms of its own economic development China still lags behind, its state formation process in terms of duration and continuity surpasses that of most other existing state societies of our time. [*Author's note to the translation*]

society but of the social field formed by a specific group of inter-dependent societies, and of the sequential order of its evolution.

But for an adequate enquiry into such social processes a similar correction of traditional habits of thinking is needed to the one that proved necessary earlier to obtain an adequate basis for psychogenetic enquiry. To understand social structures and processes, it is never enough to study a single functional stratum within a social field. To be really understood, these structures and processes demand a study of the *relationships between the different functional strata* which are bound together within a social field, and which, with the slower or more rapid shift of power-relationships arising from the specific structure of this field, are for a time reproduced over and over again. Just as in every psychogenetic enquiry it is necessary to take account not only of the "unconscious" or the "conscious" functions alone, but of the continuous circulation of impulses from the one to the other, it is equally important in every sociogenetic study to consider from the first the whole *figuration* of a social field which is more or less differentiated and charged with tensions. It is only possible to do this because the social fabric and its historical change are not chaotic but possess, even in phases of greatest unrest and disorder, a clear pattern and structure. To investigate the totality of a social field does not mean to study each individual process within it. It means first of all to discover the basic structures which give all the individual processes within this field their direction and their specific stamp. It means asking oneself in what way the axes of tension, the chains of functions and the institutions of a society in the fifteenth century differ from those in the sixteenth or seventeenth centuries, and why the former change in the direction of the latter. To answer these questions knowledge of a wealth of particular facts is of course necessary. But beyond a certain point in the accumulation of material facts, historiography enters the phase when it ought no longer to be satisfied with the collection of further particulars and with the description of those already assembled, but should be concerned with those problems which facilitate penetration of the underlying regularities by which people in a certain society are bound over and over again to particular patterns of conduct and to very specific functional chains, for example as knights and bondsmen, kings and state officials, bourgeois and nobles, and by which these relationships and institutions change in a very specific

288

direction. Beyond a certain point of factual knowledge, in a word, a more solid framework, a structural nexus can be perceived in the multitude of particular historical facts. And all further facts that can be discovered serve—apart from the enrichment of the historical panorama they may offer us—either to revise the insight already gained into these structures, or to extend and deepen it. The statement that every sociogenetic study should be aimed at the *totality* of a social field does not mean that it should be directed at the sum of all particulars, but at its structure within the entirety of its interdependencies. In the last resort the boundaries of such a study are determined by the boundaries of the interdependencies, or at least by the immanent articulation of the interdependencies.

It is in this light that what was said above about rationalization is to be understood. The gradual transition to more "rational" behaviour and thought, like that to a more differentiated, a more comprehensive type of self-control, is usually associated today only with bourgeois functions. We often find firmly lodged in the minds of our contemporaries the idea that the bourgeoisie was the "originator" or "inventor" of more rational thought. Here, for the sake of contrast, certain rationalization processes in the aristocratic camp have been described. But one should not deduce from this that the courtly aristocracy was the social "originator" of this spurt of rationalization. Just as the courtly aristocracy or the bourgeoisie in the age of manufacture did not have "originators" in any other social class, so this rationalization equally lacked an originator. The very transformation of the whole social structure, in the course of which these figurations of bourgeois and nobles come into being, is itself, considered from a certain aspect, a rationalization. What becomes more rational is not just the individual products of men, nor, above all, merely the systems of thought set down in books. What is rationalized is, primarily, the modes of conduct of certain groups of people. "Rationalization" is nothing other—think, for example, of the courtization of warriors—than an expression of the direction in which the moulding of people in specific social figurations is changed during this period. Changes of this kind, however, do not "originate" in one class or another, but arise in conjunction with the tensions *between* different functional groups in a social field and *between* the competing people within them. Under the pressure of tensions

289

of this kind which permeate the whole fabric of society, the latter's whole structure changes, during a particular phase, in the direction of an increasing centralization of particular dominions and a greater specialization, a tighter integration of the individual people within them. And with this transformation of the whole social field, the structure of social and psychological functions is also changed—first in small, then in larger and larger sectors—in the direction of rationalization.

The slow defunctionalization of the first estate and the corresponding diminution of its power potential, the pacification of the second estate and the gradual rise of the third, none of these can be understood independently of the others any more than, for example, the development of trade in this period is comprehensible independently of the formation of powerful monopolies of physical force and the rise of mighty courts. All these are levers in the comprehensive process of increasing differentiation and extension of all chains of action, which has played such a decisive role in the whole course of Western history. In this process—as was shown from particular aspects—the functions of the nobility are transformed, and with them bourgeois functions and the form of the central organs. And hand in hand with this gradual change in the totality of social functions and institutions, goes a transformation of individual self-steering—first in the leading groups of both the nobility and the bourgeoisie—in the direction of greater foresight and a stricter regulation of libidinal impulses.

In perusing the traditional accounts of the intellectual development of the West, one often has the impression of a vague conception in the minds of their authors that the rationalization of consciousness, the change from magical–traditional to rational forms of thinking in the history of the West, had its cause in the emergence of a number of geniuses and ousstanding individuals. These enlightened individuals, such accounts appear to suggest, taught Western man how to use his innate reason properly.

Here, a different picture emerges. What the great thinkers of the West have achieved is certainly considerable. They gave to what their contemporaries experienced in their daily actions without being able to grasp it clearly in thought, comprehensive and exemplary expression. They tried to articulate the more reality-oriented or in their own language, more rational forms of thinking which had gradually developed along with the overall changes in the structure of social interdependencies, and with their help to clarify the problems of human existence. They gave other people a clearer view of their world and themselves. And so they also acted as levers within the larger workings of society. They were to a greater or lesser degree, depending on their talent and personal situation, interpreters and spokesmen of a social chorus. But they were not on their own the originators of the type of thought prevalent in their society. They did not create what we call "rational thought".*

This expression itself evidently is somewhat too static and insufficiently differentiated for what it is intended to express. Too static, because the structure of psychological functions changes at the same rate as that of social functions. Insufficiently differentiated because the pattern of rationalization, the structure of more rational habits of thinking, was and is very different in different social classes—for instance, in the courtly nobility or the leading bourgeois strata—in accordance with their different social functions and their overall historical situation. And finally, the same is true of rationalization as was said above of changes of consciousness in general: in it only *one* side of a more comprehensive change in the whole social personality is manifested. It goes hand in hand with a corresponding transformation of drive structures. It is, in brief, *one* manifestation of civilization among others.

*The waning supremacy of the Church, the changing balance of power between religious and secular rulers—between priests and warriors—in favour of the latter opened the way to, was, in other words, the *conditio sine qua non* of the secularization of thought without which all that one means if one speaks of "rationalization" could not have come into its own. The emergence not only of one but of a whole group of tightly organized and competing large territorial states ruled by secular princes which is one of the major distinguishing characteristics of the European development was one of its factors; the growth of large urban markets and long-distance trade and the growth of capital indispensable for it was another. A whole complex of social levers—levers of "rationalization"—worked in the direction towards a strengthening of less affective, less fantasy-oriented modes of thought and experience. The great intellectual pioneers, above all the philosophical pioneers of rational thought, thus worked from within a powerful process of social change which gave them direction, but they themselves were also active levers within this movement, not merely its passive objects. In fact one has to take into consideration the whole concourse of basic processes forming the core of the overall development of society—basic processes such as the long-term process of state formation, of capital formation, of differentiation and integration, of orientation, of civilization, and others. [*Author's note to the translation*]

VI

Shame and Repugnance

No less characteristic of a civilizing process than "rationalization" is the peculiar moulding of the drive economy that we call "shame" and "repugnance" or "embarrassment". Both these, the strong spurt of rationalization and the (for a time) no less strong advance of the threshold of shame and repugnance that becomes more and more perceptible in the make-up of Western men broadly speaking from the sixteenth century onwards, are different sides of the same transformation of the social personality structure. The feeling of shame is a specific excitation, a kind of anxiety which is automatically reproduced in the individual on certain occasions by force of habit. Considered superficially, it is fear of social degradation or, more generally, of other people's gestures of superiority. But it is a form of displeasure or fear which arises characteristically on those occasions when a person who fears lapsing into inferiority can avert this danger neither by direct physical means nor by any other form of attack. This defencelessness against the superiority of others, this total exposure to them does not arise directly from a threat from the physical superiority of others actually present, although it doubtless has its origins in physical compulsion, in the bodily inferiority of the child in face of its parents or teachers. In adults, however, this defencelessness results from the fact that the people whose superiority one fears are in accord with one's own super-ego, with the agency of self-constraint implanted in the individual by others on whom he was dependent, who possessed power and superiority over him. In keeping with this, the anxiety that we call "shame" is heavily veiled to the sight of others; however strong it may be, it is never directly expressed in noisy gestures. Shame takes on its particular coloration from the fact that the person feeling it has done or is about to do something through which he comes into contradiction with people to whom he is bound in one form or another, and with himself, with the sector of his consciousness by which he controls himself. The conflict expressed in shame—fear is not merely a conflict of the individual with prevalent social opinion; the individual's behaviour has brought him into conflict with the part of himself that represents this social opinion. It is a conflict within

292

his own personality; he himself recognizes himself as inferior. He fears the loss of the love or respect of others, to which he attaches or has attached value. Their attitude has precipitated an attitude within him that he automatically adopts towards himself. This is what makes him so defenceless against gestures of superiority by others which somehow trigger off this automatism within him.

This also explains why the fear of transgression of social prohibitions takes on more clearly the character of shame the more completely alien constraints have been turned into self-restraints by the structure of society, and the more comprehensive and differentiated the ring of self-restraints have become within which a person's conduct is enclosed. The inner tension, the excitement that is aroused whenever a person feels compelled to break out of this enclosure in any place, or when he has done so, varies in strength according to the gravity of the social prohibition and the degree of self-constraint. In ordinary life we call this excitement shame only in certain contexts and above all when it has a certain degree of strength; but in terms of its structure it is, despite its many nuances and degrees, always the same event. Like self-constraints, it is to be found in a less stable, less uniform and less all-embracing form even at simpler levels of social development. Like these constraints, tensions and fears of this kind emerge more clearly with every spurt of the civilizing process, and finally predominate over others—particularly the physical fear of others. They predominate the more, the larger the areas that are pacified, and the greater the importance in the moulding of people of the more even constraints that come to the fore in society when the representatives of the monopoly of physical violence normally only exercise their control as it were standing in the wings—the further, in a word, the civilization of conduct advances. Just as we can only speak of "reason" in conjunction with advances of rationalization and the formation of functions demanding foresight and restraint, we can only speak of shame in conjunction with its sociogenesis, with spurts in which the shame-threshold advances or at least moves, and the structure and pattern of self-constraints are changed in a particular direction, reproducing themselves thenceforth in the same form over a greater or lesser period. Both rationalization and the advance of the shame and repugnance thresholds are expressions of a reduction in the direct physical fear of other beings, and of a consolidation of the automatic inner anxieties, the compulsions which the individual now exerts on himself. In both, the greater, more differentiated foresight and long-term view which become necessary in order that larger and larger groups of people may preserve their social existence in an increasing differentiated society, are equally expressed. It is not difficult to explain how these seemingly so different psychological changes are connected. Both, the intensification of shame like the increased rationalization, are different aspects of the growing split in the individual personality that occurs with the increasing division of functions; they are different aspects of the growing differentiation between drives and drive-controls, between "id" and "ego" or "super-ego" functions. The further this differentiation of individual self-steering advances, the more clearly that sector of the controlling functions which in a broader sense is called the "ego" and in a narrower the "super-ego", takes on a twofold function. On the one hand this sector forms the centre from which a person regulates his relations to other living and non-living beings, and on the other it forms the centre from which a person, partly consciously and partly quite automatically and unconsciously, controls his "inner life", his own affects and impulses. The layer of psychological functions which, in the course of the social transformation that has been described, is gradually differentiated from the drives, the ego or super-ego functions, has, in other words, a twofold task within the personality: they conduct at the same time a domestic policy and a foreign policy—which, moreover, are not always in harmony and often enough in contradiction. This explains the fact that in the same socio–historical period in which rationalization makes perceptible advances, an advance in the shame and repugnance threshold is also to be observed. It also explains the fact that here, as always—in accordance with the sociogenetic ground rule—a corresponding process is to be observed even today in the life of each individual child: the rationalization of conduct is an expression of the foreign policy of the same super-ego formation whose domestic policy is expressed in an advance of the shame threshold.

From here many large trains of thought lead off in different directions. It remains to be shown how this increased differentiation within the personality is manifested in a transformation of particular drives. Above all, it remains to be shown how it leads to a transformation of sexual impulses and an advance of shame feelings in the relations of men and women.* It must be enough here to indicate some of the main connections between the social processes described above and this advance of the frontier of shame and repugnance.

Even in the more recent history of the West itself, shame feelings have not always been built into the personality in the same way. To mention only one difference, the manner in which they are built in is not the same in a hierarchical society made up of estates as in the succeeding bourgeois industrial order.

The examples quoted earlier, above all those showing differences in the development of shame on the exposure of certain bodily parts,[148] give a certain impression of such changes. In courtly society shame on exposing certain parts is, in keeping with the structure of this society, still largely restricted within estate or hierarchical limits. Exposure in the presence of social

*This particular problem, important as it is, must be left aside for the time being. Its elucidation demands a description and an exact analysis of the changes which the structure of the family and the whole relationship of the sexes have undergone in the course of Western history. It demands, furthermore, a general study of changes in the upbringing of children and the development of adolescents. The material which has been collected to elucidate this aspect of the civilizing process, and the analyses it made possible have proved too extensive; they threatened to dislocate the framework of this study and will find their place in a further volume.

The same applies to the middle-class line of the civilizing process, the change it produced in bourgeois–urban classes and the non-courtly landed aristocracy. While this transformation of conduct and of the structure of psychological functions is certainly connected in these classes, too, with a specific historical restructuring of the *whole* Western social fabric, nevertheless—as already pointed out on a number of occasions—the non-courtly middle-class line of civilization follows a different pattern to the courtly one. Above all, the treatment of sexuality in the former is not the same as in the latter—partly because of a different family structure, and partly because of the different kind of foresight which middle-class professional functions demand. Something similar emerges if the civilizing transformation of Western religion is investigated. The change in religious feeling to which sociology has paid most attention hitherto, the increased inwardness and rationalization expressed in the various Puritan and Protestant movements, is obviously closely connected to certain changes in the situation and structure of the middle classes. The corresponding change in Catholicism, as shown, for example, in the formation of the power position of the Jesuits, appears to take place in closer touch with the absolutist central organs, in a manner favoured by the hierarchical and centralist structure of the Catholic Church. These problems, too, will only be solved when we have a more exact overall picture of the intertwining of the non-courtly, middle-class and the courtly lines of civilization, leaving aside for the time being the civilizing movement in worker and peasant strata which emerges more slowly and much later.

inferiors, for example by the king in front of a minister, is placed under no very strict social prohibition, any more than the exposure of a man before the socially weaker and lower-ranking woman was in an earlier phase. Given his minimal functional dependence on those of lower rank, exposure as yet arouses no feeling of inferiority or shame; it can even be taken, as Della Casa states, as a sign of benevolence towards the inferior. Exposure by someone of lower rank before a superior, on the other hand, or even before people of equal rank, is banished more and more from social life as a sign of lack of respect; branded as an offence, it becomes invested with fear. And only when the walls between estates fall away, when the functional dependence of all on all increases and all members of society become several degrees more equal, does such exposure, except in certain narrower enclaves, become an offence in the presence of any other person. Only then is such behaviour so profoundly associated with fear in the individual from an early age, that the social character of the prohibition vanishes entirely from his consciousness, shame appearing as a command coming from within himself.

And the same is true of embarrassment. This is an inseparable counterpart of shame. Just as the latter arises when someone infringes the prohibitions of his own self and of society, the former occurs when something outside the individual impinges on his danger zone, on forms of behaviour, objects, inclinations which have early on been invested with fear by his surroundings until this fear—in the manner of a conditioned reflex—is reproduced automatically in him on certain occasions. Embarrassment is displeasure or anxiety which arises when another person threatens to breach, or breaches, society's prohibitions represented by one's own super-ego. And these feelings too become more diverse and comprehensive the more extensive and subtly differentiated the danger zone by which the conduct of the individual is regulated and moulded, the further the civilization of conduct advances.

It was shown earlier by a series of examples how, from the sixteenth century onwards, the frontier of shame and embarrassment gradually begins to advance more rapidly. Here, too, the chains of thought begin slowly to join up. This advance coincides with the accelerated courtization of the upper class. It is the time when the chains of dependence intersecting in the individual grow denser and longer, when more and more people are being bound more and more closely together and the compulsion to self-control is increasing. Like mutual dependence, mutual observation of people increases; sensibilities, and correspondingly prohibitions, become more differentiated; and equally more subtle, equally more manifold become the reasons for shame and for embarrassment aroused by the conduct of others.

It was pointed out above that with the advancing division of functions and the greater integration of people, the major contrasts between different classes and countries diminish, while the nuances, the varieties of their moulding within the framework of civilization multiply. Here one encounters a corresponding trend in the development of individual conduct and sentiment. The more the strong contrasts of individual conduct are tempered, the more the violent fluctuations of pleasure or displeasure are contained, moderated and changed by self-control, the greater becomes the sensitivity to shades or nuances of conduct, the more finely attuned people grow to minute gestures and forms, and the more complex becomes their experience of themselves and their world at levels which were previously hidden from consciousness through the veil of strong affects.

To clarify this by an obvious example, "primitive" people experience human and natural events within the relatively narrow circle which is vitally important to them—narrow, because their chains of dependence are relatively short—in a manner which is in some respects far more differentiated than that of "civilized" people. The differentiation varies, depending on whether we are concerned with farmers or hunters or herdsmen, for example. But however this may be, it can be stated generally that, insofar as it is of vital importance to a group, the ability of primitive people to distinguish things in forest and field, whether it be a particular tree from another, or sounds, scents or movements, is more highly developed than in "civilized" people. But among more primitive people the natural sphere is still far more a danger zone; it is full of fears which more civilized men no longer know. This is decisive for what is or is not distinguished. The manner in which "nature" is experienced is fundamentally affected, slowly at the end of the Middle Ages and then more quickly from the sixteenth century onwards, by the pacification of larger and larger populated areas. Only now do forests, meadows and mountains gradually cease to be danger zones of the first order, from which anxiety and fear constantly intrude into individual life. And now, as the network of roads becomes, like social interdependence in general, more dense; as robber-knights and beasts of prey slowly disappear; as forest and field cease to be the scene of unbridled passions, of the savage pursuit of man and beast, wild joy and wild fear; as they are moulded more and more by intertwining peaceful activities, the production of goods, trade and transport; now, to pacified men a correspondingly pacified nature becomes visible, and in a new way. It becomes—in keeping with the mounting significance which the eye attains as the mediator of pleasure with the growing moderation of the affects—to a high degree an object of visual pleasure. In addition, people—more precisely the town-people for whom forest and field are no longer their everyday background but a place of relaxation—grow more sensitive and begin to see the open country in a more differentiated way, at a level which was previously screened off by danger and the play of unmoderated passions. They take pleasure in the harmony of colour and lines, become open to what is called the beauty of nature; their feelings are aroused by the changing shades and shapes of the clouds and the play of light on the leaves of a tree.

And, in the wake of this pacification, the sensitivity of people to social conduct is also changed. Now, inner fears grow in proportion to the decrease of outer ones—the fears of one sector of the personality for another. As a result of these inner tensions, people begin to experience each other in a more differentiated way which was precluded as long as they constantly faced serious and inescapable threats from outside. Now a major part of the tensions which were earlier discharged directly in combat between man and man, must be resolved as an inner tension in the struggle of the individual with himself. Social life ceases to be a danger zone in which feasting, dancing and noisy pleasure frequently and suddenly give way to rage, blows and murder, and becomes a different kind of danger zone if the individual cannot sufficiently restrain himself, if he touches sensitive spots, his own shame-frontier or the embarrassment-threshold of others. In a sense, the danger zone now passes through the self of every individual. Thus people become, in this respect too, sensitive to distinctions which previously scarcely entered consciousness. Just as nature now becomes, far more than earlier, a source of pleasure mediated by the eye, people too become a source of visual pleasure or, conversely, of visually aroused displeasure, of different degrees of repugnance. The direct fear inspired in men by men has diminished, and the inner fear mediated through the eye and through the super-ego is rising proportionately.

When the use of weapons in combat is an everyday occurrence, the small gesture of offering someone a knife at table (to recall one of the examples mentioned earlier) has no great importance. As the use of weapons is restricted more and more, as external and internal pressures make the expression of anger by physical attack increasingly difficult, people gradually become more sensitive to anything reminiscent of an attack. The very gesture of attack touches the danger zone; it becomes distressing to see a person passing someone else a knife with the point towards him.[149] And from the most highly sensitized small circles of high courtly society, for whom this sensitivity also represents a prestige value, a means of distinction cultivated for that very reason, this prohibition gradually spreads throughout the whole of civilized society. Thus aggressive associations, infused no doubt with others from the layer of elementary urges, combine with status tensions in arousing anxiety.

How the use of a knife is then gradually restricted and surrounded, as a danger zone, by a wall of prohibitions, has been shown through a number of examples. It is an open question how far, in the courtly aristocracy, the renunciation of physical violence remains an external compulsion, and how far it has already been converted into an inner constraint. Despite all restrictions, the use of the table knife, like that of the dagger, is still quite extensive. Just as the hunting and killing of animals is still a permitted and commonplace amusement for the lords of the earth, the carving of dead animals at table remains within the zone of the permitted and is as yet not felt as repugnant. Then, with the slow rise of bourgeois classes, in whom pacification and the generation of inner constraints by the very nature of their social functions is far more complete and binding, the cutting up of dead animals is pushed back further behind the secenes of social life (even if in particular countries, particularly England, as so often, some of the older customs survive incorporated in the new) and the use of the knife, indeed the mere holding of it, is avoided wherever it is not entirely indispensable. Sensitivity in this direction grows.

This is one example among many of particular aspects of the

structural transformation of society that we denote by the catchword "civilization". Nowhere in human society is there a zero-point of fear of external powers, and nowhere a zero-point of automatic inner anxieties. Although they may be experienced as very different, they are finally inseparable. What takes place in the course of a civilizing process is not the disappearance of one and the emergence of the other. What changes is merely the proportion between the external and the self-activating fears, and their whole structure. People's fears of external powers diminish without ever disappearing; the never-absent, latent or actual anxieties arising from the tension between drives and drive-control functions become relatively stronger, more comprehensive and continuous. The documentation for the advance of the shame and embarrassment frontiers found in the first volume of this study, consists in fact of nothing but particularly clear and simple examples of the direction and structure of a change in the human personality which could be demonstrated from many other aspects too. A very similar structure is exhibited, for example, by the transition from the medieval–Catholic to the Protestant super-ego formation. This, too, shows a pronounced shift towards the internalization of fears. And one thing certainly should not be overlooked in all this: the fact that today, as formerly, all forms of adult inner anxieties are bound up with the child's fears of others, of external powers.

VII

Increasing Constraints on the Upper Class: Increasing Pressure from Below

It was pointed out earlier that in certain pictures[150] attributed to the knightly-courtly upper class of the late Middle Ages, the depiction of lower-class people and their gestures was not yet felt as particularly repugnant, whereas the stricter selection corresponding to the structure of repugnance of the absolutist-courtly upper class permits the expression only of large, calm, refined gestures in art, while everything reminiscent of lower classes, everything vulgar, is kept at a distance.

This repulsion of the vulgar, this increasing sensitivity to anything corresponding to the lesser sensibility of lower-ranking classes, permeates all spheres of social conduct in the courtly upper class. It has been shown in more detail[151] how this is expressed, for example, in the courtly moulding of speech. One does not say, a court lady explains, "un mien ami" or "le pauvre deffunct"; all that "smells of the bourgeois". And if the bourgeois protests, if he replies that after all a large number of people of good society use these expressions themselves, he is told: "It is quite possible that there are a number of decent people who do not have sufficient feeling for the delicacy of our tongue. This 'delicacy' . . . is entrusted to but a few."

This is categorical, like the demands of this sensitivity themselves. The people who select in this way are neither able, nor do they attempt, to justify further why in a particular case this form of a word is pleasing and that displeasing. Their particular sensitivity is very closely bound up with the heightened regulation and transformation of libidinal impulses imposed on them by their specific social situation. The certitude with which they are able to say: 'This combination of words sounds well; those colours are ill-chosen", the sureness of their taste, in a word, derives rather from a more or less unconsciously operating psychological self-steering agency than from conscious reflection. But it is clear, here too, how it is first of all small circles of courtly society who listen with growing sensitivity to nuances of rhythm, tone and significance, to the spoken and written word, and how this sensitivity, this "good taste", also represents a prestige value for such circles. Anything that touches their embarrassment-threshold smells bourgeois, is socially inferior; and inversely: anything bourgeois touches their embarrassment-threshold. It is the necessity to distinguish themselves from anything bourgeois that sharpens this sensitivity; and the particular structure of court life, by which it is not professional competence or even the possession of money, but polished social conduct, that is the main instrument in the competition for prestige and favour, provides the occasion for the sharpening of taste.

In the course of this study it was indicated by means of a number of examples how from the sixteenth century onwards the standard of social conduct is caught up in a quicker movement, how it remains in motion during the seventeenth and eighteenth centuries in order, during the eighteenth and nineteenth centuries, to spread, transformed in some respects, throughout the whole of Western society. This advance of restrictions and libidinal transformations sets in with the conversion of the knightly into a courtly nobility. It is very closely bound up with the change already discussed in the relationship of the upper class to other functional groups. The *"courtois"* warrior society is not remotely under the same pressure, does not live in anything like the same interdependence with bourgeois strata, as the courtly aristocracy. This courtly upper class is a formation within a much denser network of interdependencies. It is held in a pincer comprising the central lord of the court on whose favour it depends on the one hand, and the leading bourgeois groups with their economic advantages on the other, groups which are forcing their way upwards and contesting the aristocracy's position. Tensions between courtly aristocratic and bourgeois circles do not increase only at the end of the eighteenth or the beginning of the nineteenth century; from the first the existence of the courtly aristocracy is strongly and constantly threatened by the aspiring bourgeois classes. Indeed, the courtization of the nobility takes place only in conjunction with an increased upward thrust by bourgeois strata. The existence of a high degree of interdependence and tension between nobles and bourgeois is a basic constituent of the courtly character of the leading groups of the nobility.

We should not be deceived by the fact that it took centuries for this continuous tug of war between noble and bourgeois groups to be decided in favour of some of the latter. Nor should we be misled by the fact that the constraints on the upper class, the functional interdependence and latent tension between different strata in the absolutist society of the seventeenth and eighteenth centuries were less than in the various national societies of the nineteenth and twentieth centuries. As compared with the functional constraints on the free medieval warrior nobility, those on the courtly aristocracy are already very great. Social tensions, particularly between the nobility and bourgeoisie, take on a different character with increasing pacification.

As long as control of the instruments of physical violence—weapons and troops—is not very highly centralized, social tensions lead again and again to warlike actions. Particular social groups, artisan settlements and their feudal lords, towns and knights, confront each other as units of power which—as only states do later—must always be ready to settle their differences of interest by force of arms. The fears aroused in this structure of social tensions can still be discharged easily and frequently in military action and direct physical force. With the gradual consolidation of power monopolies and the growing functional interdependence of nobility and bourgeoisie, this changes. The tensions become more even. They can be resolved by physical violence only at infrequent climaxes or turning points. And they therefore express themselves in a continuous pressure that each individual member of the nobility must absorb within himself. With this transformation of social relationships, social fears slowly cease to resemble flames that flare rapidly, burn intensely and are quickly extinguished, only to be rekindled just as quickly, becoming instead like a permanently smouldering fire whose flame is hidden and seldom breaks out directly.

From this point of view as well, the courtly aristocracy represents a type of upper class different from the free warriors of the Middle Ages. It is the first of the more constrained upper classes, which is followed in modern times by even more heavily fettered ones. It is threatened more directly and strongly than the free warriors by bourgeois classes in the whole basis of its social existence, its privileges. As early as the sixteenth and seventeenth centuries there is in France, among certain leading bourgeois groups, particularly the high judicial and administrative courts, a strong desire to establish themselves in place of, or at least alongside, the nobility of the sword as the upper class of the country. The policy of these bourgeois strata is largely aimed at increasing their own privileges at the expense of the old nobility, even though they are at the same time—and this gives their relationship its peculiarly ambivalent character—bound to the old nobility by a number of common social fronts. For just this reason the fears that such continuous tensions bring with them express themselves, in these leading bourgeois strata, only in a concealed form controlled by strong super-ego impulses. And this applies all the more to the genuine nobility who now find themselves on the defensive, and in whom the shock of the defeat and loss they have suffered with pacification and courtization, long shows its aftereffects. The courtly aristocrats too must contain more or less within themselves the agitation aroused by the constant tug of war with bourgeois groups. With this structure of interdependencies, the social tension produces a strong *inner* tension in the members of the threatened upper class. These fears sink down in part, though never entirely, into the unconscious zones of the personality and re-emerge from them only in changed form, as specific automatisms of self-control. They show themselves, for example, in the special sensitivity of the courtly aristocracy to anything that remotely touches the hereditary privileges on which their existence is based. They manifest themselves in the affect-laden gestures of revulsion from anything that "smells bourgeois". They are partly responsible for the fact that the courtly aristocracy is so much more sensitive to lower-class gestures than were the warrior nobility of the Middle Ages, that they strictly and emphatically exclude everything "vulgar" from their sphere of life. Finally, this permanently smouldering social fear also constitutes one of the most powerful driving forces of the social control that every member of this courtly upper class exerts over himself and other people in his circle. It is expressed in the intense vigilance with which members of courtly aristocratic society observe and polish everything that distinguishes them from people of lower rank: not only the external signs of status, but also their speech, their gestures, their social amusements and manners. The constant pressure from below and the fear it induces above are, in a word, one of the strongest driving forces—though not the only one—of that specifically civilized refinement which distinguishes the people of this upper class from others and finally becomes second nature to them.

For it is precisely the chief function of the courtly aristocracy—their function for the mighty central ruler—to distinguish themselves, to maintain themselves as a distinct formation, a social counterweight to the bourgeoisie. They are completely free to spend their time elaborating the distinguishing social conduct of good manners and good taste. The rising bourgeois strata are less free to elaborate their conduct and taste; they have professions. Nevertheless, it is at first their ideal, too, to live like the aristocracy exclusively on annuities and to gain admittance to the courtly circle; this circle is still the model for a large part of the ambitious bourgeoisie. They become "Bourgeois Gentilhommes". They ape the nobility and its manners. But precisely this makes modes of conduct developed in courtly circles continually become useless as means of distinction, and the noble groups are forced to elaborate their conduct still further. Over and again customs that were once "refined" become "vulgar". Manners are polished and polished and the embarrassment-threshold constantly advances, until finally, with the downfall of absolutist-courtly society in the French Revolution, this spiral movement comes to an end or at least loses its force. The motor which, in the courtly phase, drives forward the civilizing transformation of the nobility—and with it the shame and repugnance frontier, as the examples in the first volume showed—is propelled both by the increased competition for the favour of the most powerful within the courtly stratum itself, and by the constant pressure from below. In this phase the *circulation of models* procccds, as a result of the greater interdependence and therefore closer contact and more constant tension between different classes, far more quickly than in the Middle Ages. The "good societies" that come after the courtly one are all interwoven directly or indirectly, into the network of professional occupations, and even though "courtly" orientations are never entirely lacking in them, these no longer have remotely the same influence; from now on profession and money are the primary sources of prestige, and the art, the refinement of social conduct ceases to have the decisive importance for the reputation and success of the individual that it had in courtly society.

In every social stratum that area of conduct which is functionally of most vital importance to its members is the most carefully and intensively moulded. The exactitude with which, in courtly society, each movement of the hands while eating, each piece of etiquette and even the manner of speech is fashioned, corresponds to the importance which all these functions have for courtly people both as means of distinction from below, and as instruments in the competition for royal favour. The tasteful arrangement of house or park, the ostentatious or intimate—depending on the fashion—ornamentation of rooms, the witty conduct of a conversation or even a love affair, all these are in the courtly phase not only the private pleasures of individuals, but vital demands of their social position. They are preconditions for the respect of others, for the social success which here plays the same role as professional success in bourgeois society.

In the nineteenth century, with the gradual ascendency of

305

economic, of commercial and industrial bourgeois strata, and their increasing pressure for access to the highest power positions in the state, all these skills cease to hold the central place in the social existence of people; they cease to be of primary significance for success or failure in their status and power struggles. Other skills take their place as primary skills on which success or failure in life depends—skills such as occupational proficiency, adeptness in the competitive struggle for economic chances, in the acquisition or control of capital wealth, or the highly specialized skill needed for political advancement in the fierce though regulated party struggles characteristic of an age of increasing functional democratization. While the aristocratic courtiers' personality structure is to a large extent determined by the need to compete for status and power chances within one of the ruling court establishments of their age, the social personality structure of the rising bourgeois strata is determined by the competition for a greater share of the growing capital wealth, or else for jobs or for positions which endow their occupants with greater political or administrative chances of power. These and related competitive struggles now become the main factors of constraint which leave their imprint upon the personality of individuals. Even though certain strata of the new economic and political bourgeoisie again and again form "good Societies" of their own, and thus develop, or take over, some of the skills more highly cultivated in aristocratic societies, the pattern of social constraints acting upon the members of bourgeois "good Societies" is in one decisive respect different from that acting upon aristocratic courtiers and gentlemen. The social existence of the latter is not only *de facto* founded upon unearned income of one kind or another, but living on unearned income and thus without any occupational work, in these circles, has a very high value. It is an almost indispensable condition for those who wish to "belong". With the rise of the economic and political bourgeoisie this aristocratic ethos changes. Its members, or at least its male members, are expected to work for a living, even if they form "good Societies" of their own. Forms of sociability, the ornamentation of one's house, visiting etiquette or the ritual of eating, all are now relegated to the sphere of private life. They preserve their vital function most strongly in that national society where, despite the rise of bourgeois elements, aristocratic social formations remained longest and most vigorously alive: in England. But even in the peculiar amalgam that developed here from the interpenetration over centuries of aristocratic and bourgeois models of conduct, middle-class traits gradually move into the foreground. And generally in all Western societies, with the decline of the purer aristocracy, whenever and however this takes place, the modes of conduct and affective forms which are developed are those necessary to the performance of money-earning functions and the execution of precisely regulated work. This is why professional bourgeois society, in everything that concerns social conduct, takes over the ritual of courtly society without developing it with the same intensity. This is why the standard of affect-control in this sphere advances only slowly with the rise of the professional bourgeoisie. In courtly society, and partly in English society too, this division of human existence into professional and private spheres does not exist. As the split becomes more general a new phase begins in the civilizing process; the pattern of drive-control that professional work necessitates is distinct in many respects from that imposed by the function of courtier and the game of courtly life. The exertion required by the maintenance of bourgeois social existence, the stability of the super-ego functions, the intensity of drive-control and drive-transformation demanded by bourgeois professional and commercial functions, are in sum considerably greater, despite a certain relaxation in the sphere of social manners, than the corresponding social personality structure required by the life of a courtly aristocrat. Most obvious is the difference in the regulation of sexual relationships. However, the courtly-aristocratic moulding of the personality passes over in this or that form into the professional bourgeois one and is propagated further by it. We find this impregnation of broader strata by behavioural forms and drive-controls originating in courtly society particularly in regions where the courts were great and wealthy and their influence as style-building centres correspondingly strong. Paris and Vienna are examples of this. They are the seats of the two great rival absolutist courts of the eighteenth century. An echo of this can still be heard in the present day, not only in their reputation as centres of "good taste" or of luxury industries whose products are intended particularly for the use of "ladies", but even in the cultivation of sexual relationships, the erotic character of the population, even though reality in this respect may no longer

307

quite match the reputation so frequently exploited by the film industry.

In one form or another, however, the models of conduct of courtly-aristocratic *bonne compagnie* have penetrated industrial society at large even where the courts were less rich, powerful and influential. That the conduct of the ruling Western groups, the degree and kind of their affect-control, show a high degree of uniformity despite all national variations, is certainly, in general terms, a result of the closely knit and long-ranging chains of interdependence linking the various national societies of the West. But within this general framework the phase of the semi-private power monopolies and of courtly–aristocratic society, with its high interdependence all over Europe, plays a special part in the moulding of Western civilized conduct. This courtly society exercised for the first time, and in a particularly pure form, a function which was afterwards transmitted in differing degrees and with various modifications to broader and broader strata of Western society, the function of a "good society", an upper class under pressure from many sides, from the organized monopolies of taxation and physical force on the one hand, and from the rising middle and lower classes on the other. Courtly society was indeed the first representative of the particular form of upper class which emerged more clearly the more closely, with the advancing division of functions, the different social classes became mutually dependent, and the larger the number of people and the geographical areas that were placed in such interdependence. It was a highly constricted upper class, whose situation demanded constant self-restraint and intense drive-control. Precisely this form of upper class from now on predominated in Western regions. And the models of this self-restraint, first developed in courtly-aristocratic society for the sphere of sociability, were passed on from class to class, adjusted and modified, like the upper-class function itself. The heritage of aristocratic society had greater or lesser importance depending on whether its character as "good society" played a greater or lesser role for a class or a nation. As we have said, this was the case to a greater or lesser degree with increasingly broad classes and finally entire nations in the West, particularly nations which, having early developed strong central institutions, early became colonial powers. In such nations there was an increase—under the pressure of social integration embodied both in the intensity of competition within the upper class itself and in the necessity of preserving its higher living standard and prestige *vis-à-vis* lower strata—in the strength of a particular kind of social control, in sensitivity to the behaviour of other members of one's own class, in individual self-control and in the strength of the individual "super-ego". In this way modes of conduct of a courtly–aristocratic upper class were amalgamated with those of various bourgeois strata as these rose to the position of upper classes; *civilité* was incorporated and perpetuated—with certain modifications depending on the situation of its new host—in what was now called "civilization" or, more precisely, "civilized conduct". So, from the nineteenth century onwards, these civilized forms of conduct spread across the rising lower classes of Western society and over the different classes in the colonies, amalgamating with indigenous patterns of conduct. Each time this happens upper-class conduct and that of the rising groups interpenetrate. The standard of conduct of the rising class, its pattern of commands and prohibitions, reflects in its structure the history of the rise of this class. So it comes about that the typical "drive- and conduct-pattern" of the different industrial nation states, their "national character", still represents the nature of the earlier power-relationships between nobility and bourgeoisie and the course of the century-long struggles between them, from which a specific type of middle-class groups in the end emerged for a time as the dominant establishment. Thus, to give one out of many examples, the national code of conduct and affect-control in the United States has to a higher extent middle-class characteristics than—in spite of many similarities—the corresponding English code. In the making of this English code features of aristocratic descent fused with those of middle-class descent—understandably, for in the development of English society one can observe a continuous assimilating process in the course of which upper-class models (especially a code of good manners) were adopted in a modified form by middle-class people, while middle-class features (as for instance elements of a code of morals) were adopted by upper-class people. Hence, when, in the course of the nineteenth century, most of the aristocratic privileges were abolished, and England with the rise of the industrial working classes became a nation state, the English national code of conduct and affect-control showed very clearly the gradualness of the resolution of conflicts between upper and middle classes in the form, to put it briefly, of a peculiar blend between a code of good manners and a code of morals. Analogous processes were shown in Chapter One of Volume 1 of this study by the example of the differences between the German and French national characters. And it would not be difficult to add further illustrations relating to the national characters of the other European nations.

In each case, the waves of expansion of the standards of civilized conduct to a new class go hand in hand with an increase in the social power of that class, and a raising of its standard of living to that of the class above it, or at least in that direction. Classes living permanently in danger of starving to death or of being killed by enemies can hardly develop or maintain those stable restraints characteristic of the more civilized types of conduct. To instil and maintain a more stable super-ego agency, a relatively high standard of living and a fairly high degree of security are necessary.

However complex the leverage of intertwining processes within which the civilization of conduct and experience in European societies takes place may at first sight appear, the basic connections are clear enough. All the individual trends mentioned so far, e.g. the slow rise in the living standards of broad sections of population, the greater functional dependence of the upper class, or the increasing stability of the central monopolies, all these are parts and consequences of a division of functions advancing now more rapidly, now more slowly. With this division of functions the productivity of work increased; this greater productivity is the precondition for the rise of the living standards of ever-larger classes; with this division of functions the functional dependence of the upper classes increases; and only at a very advanced point in the division of functions, finally, is the formation of more stable monopolies of physical force and taxation with highly specialized administrations possible, i.e. the formation of states in the Western sense of the word, through which the life of the individual gradually gains greater "security". But this rise in the division of functions also brings more and more people, larger and larger populated areas, into dependence on one another; it requires and instils greater restraint in the individual, more exact control of his affects and conduct; it demands a stricter regulation of drives and—from a particular stage on—more even self-restraint. This is the price, if we may call it so, which we pay for our greater security and related advantages.

Moreover—and this is of decisive importance for the standard of civilization in our day—the restraint and self-control characteristic of all phases of civilization up to now, result not merely from the necessity for each individual to co-operate constantly with many others; they are no less determined by the split of society into upper and lower classes. The kind of restraint and drive patterning produced in people of the upper classes takes its special stamp primarily from the tensions running through society. The ego and super-ego formation of these people reflects both the competition within their own class and the constant pressures from below, produced in ever-changing forms by the advancing division of functions. The strength of the social constraints and the many contradictions within it, to which the behaviour of each individual member of the upper class, the establishment, is subject and which are represented by his own "super-ego", are not determined solely by the fact that it is a control exerted by competitors, some of them even in free competition, but above all by the fact that the competing members of the established groups at the same time have to make common cause in their endeavour to preserve their distinguishing prestige and their higher status from those pressing from below—still more or less as outsiders. Often enough, under these conditions, the preservation of the higher status and the distinguishing personality characteristics requires a form of foresight, self-restraint and prudence beset by anxieties.

If the outline of these processes is followed over centuries, we see a clear tendency for standards of living and conduct to be equalized and contrasts levelled out. In each of the waves of expansion which occur when the mode of conduct of a small circle spreads to larger rising classes, two phases can be clearly distinguished: a phase of colonization or assimilation in which the lower and larger outsider class is still clearly inferior and governed by the example of the established upper group which, intentionally or unintentionally, permeates it with its own pattern of conduct, and a second phase of repulsion, differentiation or emancipation, in which the rising group gains perceptibly in social power and self-confidence, and in which the upper group is forced into increased restraint and isolation, and the contrasts and tensions in society are increased.

Here, as always, both tendencies, equalization and distinction, attraction and repulsion, are certainly present in both of these phases; these relationships too are fundamentally ambivalent. But in the first phase, which is usually that in which people rise individually from the lower to the upper class, the tendency for the upper class to colonize the lower and for the lower to copy the upper is more pronounced. In the second phase, when the social power of the lower group is increasing while that of the upper group declines, the self-consciousness of both groups increases with their rivalry, with a tendency to emphasize differences and—as far as the upper class is concerned—to consolidate them. Contrasts between the classes increase, the walls grow higher.

In phases of the first kind, phases of assimilation, many individuals in the rising outsider class are, however reluctantly, very dependent on the upper class, not only in their social existence but also in their conduct, their ideas and ideals. They are frequently, though not always, still unformed in many areas in which members of the upper class are highly developed, and they are so impressed, in their social inferiority, by the affect-control and code of conduct of the upper class, that they try to control their own affects according to the same pattern. Here we come upon one of the most remarkable characteristics of this civilizing process: the people of the rising class develop within themselves a "super-ego" modelled on the superior, colonizing upper class. But on closer inspection this super-ego is in many respects very different from its model. It is less balanced and therefore often much more severe. It always reveals the immense effort which individual social advancement requires; and it shows equally the constant threat from below as from above, the crossfire from all sides to which individuals are exposed in their social rise. Total assimilation to a higher established group succeeds only very exceptionally in one generation. In most people from the aspiring outsider groups the effort to rise inevitably leads to specific deformations of consciousness and attitude. These are known in the Orient and colonies as "Levantinism"; and in the petty-bourgeois circles of Western societies they are often enough to be found in the form of "half-education", the pretension to be what one is not, insecurity of taste and conduct, "vulgarity" not only of furniture and clothing but also of the mind: all this expresses a social situation which gives rise to an urge to imitate models of a higher social group. The attempt does not succeed. It remains clearly an imitation of alien models. The education, standards of living and fears of the rising groups and the upper class are in this phase still so different that the attempt to achieve the poise of the upper class leads in most cases to a peculiar falseness and incongruity of behaviour which nevertheless conceals a genuine distress, a desire to escape the pressure from above and the sense of inferiority. And this shaping of the super-ego on upper-class models also brings about in the rising class a specific form of shame and embarrassment. These are very different from the sensibilities of lower groups with no chance of individual rise. Their behaviour may be coarser, but it is more uniform and in a way more of a piece. They live more vigorously in their own world without any claim to upper-class prestige, and therefore with greater scope for discharge of the affects; they live more fully in accordance with their own manners and customs. Their inferiority *vis-à-vis* the upper class, their gestures both of subordination and resistance, are clear and relatively unconcealed like their affects, bound by clear, definite forms. In their consciousness they and the other classes have for better or worse their clearly defined positions.

By contrast, the feelings and gestures of inferiority in people rising socially as individuals take on their particular coloration from the fact that these people identify to a certain extent with the upper class. They have the same structure as was described earlier in the case of shame feelings; people in this situation acknowledge in one part of their consciousness the upper-class norms and manners as binding on themselves, without being able to adopt them with the same ease and matter-of-factness. It is this peculiar contradiction between the upper class within themselves, represented by their own super-ego, and their incapability of fulfilling its demands, it is this constant inner tension that gives their affective life and their conduct its particular character.

At the same time their predicament shows, from a new angle, the importance which a strict code of manners has for the upper class. It is a prestige instrument, but it is also—in a certain phase—an instrument of power. It is not a little characteristic of the structure of Western society that the watchword of its colonizing movement is "civilization". For the people of a society with a high division of functions it is not enough simply to rule subject people and countries by force of arms like a warrior caste, although the old, simple goals of most of the earlier expansionist movements, the expulsion of other peoples from their land, the acquisition of new soil for cultivation and settlement, doubtless play no small part in Western expansion. But it is not only the land that is needed but the people; these must be integrated, whether as workers or consumers, into the web of the hegemonial, the upper-class country, with its highly developed differentiation of functions. This in turn requires both a certain raising of living standards and the cultivation of self-control or super-ego functions in the subject peoples on the Western models; it demands a "civilization" of the colonized. Just as it was not possible in the West itself, from a certain stage of interdependence onwards, to rule people solely by force and physical threats, so it also became necessary, in maintaining an empire that went beyond mere plantation-land and plantation-labour, to rule people in part through themselves, through the moulding of their super-egos. In established-outsiders relationships of this type one can observe figurational characteristics akin to, though of course not identical with, those to be observed in established-outsiders relationships between social classes at a comparable stage of development. One can observe, for instance, characteristics of an early form of rise, not yet of the outsider groups as a whole but of some of its individual members. They absorb the code of the established groups and thus undergo a process of assimilation. Their own affect-control, their own conduct, obeys the rules of the established groups. Partially they identify themselves with them, and even though the identification may show strong ambivalencies, still their own conscience, their whole super-ego apparatus, follows more or less the pattern of the established groups. People in that situation attempt to reconcile and fuse that pattern, the pattern of occidentally civilized societies, with the habits and traditions of their own society with a higher or lesser degree of success.*

*While going over the translation with my friend Johan Goudsblom I repeatedly had to resist the temptation to change the original text in accordance with the present state of my knowledge. The temptation was particularly strong when we came to the problems of ascending social units discussed in these pages and of the influence which social rise or, alternatively, social hegemony, has on their social code, especially on the restraints inherent in such a code. The problems discussed above now form part of an established-outsiders theory. Not all forms

But to observe such processes we do not need to go far afield. A very similar phase is to be found in the rise of the Western bourgeoisie itself: the courtly phase. Here too it was initially the highest aspiration of many individuals from leading bourgeois groups to behave and live like nobles. They inwardly acknowledged the superiority of courtly-aristocratic conduct; they sought to mould and control themselves according to that model. The conversation on correct speech of a bourgeois in a courtly circle, quoted earlier, is one example of this. And in the history of the German language, this courtly phase of the bourgeoisie is clearly marked by the well-known tendency of speakers or writers to insert a French word after every three or four German ones, if they did not prefer simply to use French, the court language of Europe. Nobles and even bourgeois members of courtly circles often enough made fun at this time of other bourgeois unsuccessfully trying to act in a "refined" or courtly manner.

As the social power of the bourgeoisie grows, this mockery disappears. Sooner or later all the characteristics of the second phase of social elevation move into the foreground. Bourgeois groups emphasize more and more their specifically bourgeois self-image; they oppose their own codes and manners more and more confidently to the courtly-aristocratic ones. Depending on their particular situation, they contrast work to aristocratic idleness, "nature" to etiquette, the cultivation of knowledge and morals to that of good manners and conversation, not to mention the special bourgeois demands for control of the central key monopolies, for a new structure for the administration of taxation and the army. Above all they counterpose "virtue" to "courtly frivolity". The regulation of sexual relations, the fences surrounding the sexual sphere of libidinal life, are far stronger in middle and rising bourgeois classes, in keeping with their profes-

of social oppression of one group by another have the form of class relations. At present one often tries to use the conceptual apparatus developed in connection with class relations for all forms of group oppression or, alternatively, group emancipation. However, the class model is too narrow; one needs a broader overall concept to deal with the varieties of group oppression and group rise. I have found it helpful to use the term established-outsiders relationships as a more comprehensive concept in that sense. With its help one can work out more clearly the common features of group domination and group subjection as well as the distinguishing characteristics of each particular type. [*Author's note to the translation*] sional position, than in the courtly-aristocratic upper class; and later it is repeatedly stronger here than in high bourgeois groups which have already reached the social summit and taken on an upper-class character. But however sharp this opposition may be during the phase of social struggle, however great the emancipation of the bourgeoisie from the models and predominance of the nobility, the code of conduct which the leading bourgeois groups develop when they finally take over the function of the upper class is, because of the preceding phase of assimilation, the product of an amalgamation of the codes of the old and new upper classes.

The main line of this movement of civilization, the successive rises of larger and larger groups, is the same in all Western countries, and incipiently so in increasingly large areas elsewhere. And similar, too, is the structural regularity underlying it, the increasing division of functions under the pressure of competition, the tendency to more equal dependence of all on all, which in the long run allows no group greater social power than others and nullifies hereditary privileges. Processes of free competition also follow a similar course: they veer toward the formation of monopolies controlled by a few and may finally lead to the passing of control into the hands of broader classes. All this emerges very clearly, at this stage in the struggle of the bourgeoisie against noble privileges, in the "nationalization" of the monopolies of taxation and force previously administered in the interests of very small circles; all this takes the same course, earlier or later, by one path or another, in all the interdependent countries of the West. But within this common framework of basic similarities each country develops structural characteristics of its own; and corresponding to the different social structures are the specific patterns of affect regulation, the structure of the drive economy and the super-ego, which finally emerge in the various nations.

Thus in England, where the courtly-absolutist phase was relatively short, and where contacts and alliances between urban-bourgeois circles and the landed nobility came about early on, the amalgamation of upper and middle-class behaviour patterns took place gradually over a long period. Germany, on the other hand—which, through its lack of centralization and the Thirty Years' War resulting from this, remained a relatively poor land with a low standard of living for far longer than its Western neighbours—had an extraordinary long phase of absolutism with a large number of small, far from luxurious, courts, and, likewise through its lack of centralization, reached the phase of external, colonial expansion only relatively late and incompletely. For all these reasons, internal tensions, the isolation of the aristocracy from the bourgeoisie, were strong and enduring there, and access by bourgeois groups to the central monopolies difficult. In the Middle Ages urban-bourgeois groups had for a time been politically and economically more powerful, more independent and self-confident than in any other country in Europe. The shock of their political and economic decline was therefore particularly keenly felt. If specifically bourgeois traditions had earlier developed in a particularly pure form in many German regions because the urban formations were so rich and independent, they now persisted as specifically bourgeois traditions because their bearers were particularly poor and socially impotent. And accordingly, it was only very late that bourgeois and noble circles interpenetrated and their modes of conduct were amalgamated. For a long period the codes of both classes persisted disconnectedly side by side; and because throughout this period the key positions of the tax monopoly and the police and army administration were monopolies of the nobility, habituation to a strong external state authority became deeply ingrained in the bourgeoisie. Whereas in England, owing to its island situation,[152] for a long period neither the army nor a centralized police force played any major role in moulding the population, though the navy did to some extent, in Prussia/Germany, with its long, vulnerable land frontiers, the army led by the nobility, by privileged classes, was, like the powerful police force, of the utmost significance for the social personality structure of its people. This structure of the monopoly of physical force did not, however, compel individual people to adopt the same kind of self-control as in England. It did not force individuals to become integrated in relations of "teamwork" based on a high degree of individual self-control and self-attunement to others; instead, it habituated the individual from childhood on to a very much higher extent to a strict order of superiority and inferiority, an order of obedience and command on many levels. Understandably, this type of state control and the use made within it of the monopoly of physical force was less conducive to a transformation of controls through others, or alien controls, into self-controls. Also lacking in Germany for a long period was a particular function which in some other countries, especially England, enhanced in both noble and bourgeois classes a common foresight, and a similar pattern of firmly differentiated self-control: the central function in a very extensive network of interdependencies, as the upper class of a colonial empire. Thus the drive-control of the individual remained in Germany highly dependent on strong external state power. The emotional balance, the self-control of the individual, was endangered if this external power was lacking. From generation to generation a super-ego was reproduced in the bourgeois masses which was disposed to relinquish to a separate, higher social circle the specific kind of foresight demanded by the ruling and organization of society at large. It was shown at the beginning of this study how this situation led, at an early phase of the rise of the bourgeoisie, to a very specific kind of bourgeois self-image, a turning away[153] from everything to do with the administration of the power monopolies, and to a cultivation of inwardness, and the elevation of spiritual and cultural achievements to a special place in the table of values.

It was also shown how the corresponding movement took a different course in France. Here, more continuously than in any other country in Europe and from the early Middle Ages on, courtly circles were formed, first by *courtois* groups and then by larger and larger courts, until finally the competition between the many lords culminated in the formation of a single powerful and wealthy royal court to which flowed the taxes from the entire territory. Accordingly, a centrally controlled protectionist economic policy was adopted at an early stage. Although this primarily served the interests of the monopoly ruler and his desire to maximize his fiscal income, nevertheless it also promoted the development of trade and the emergence of wealthy bourgeois classes. Thus there were early contacts between rising bourgeois and court aristocrats with their constant need of money. Unlike the many relatively small and poorly endowed absolutist dominions in Germany, the rich, centralized, absolutist regime in France furthered both a comprehensive transformation of alien constraints into self-restraints and the amalgamation of courtly-aristocratic and bourgeois patterns of conduct. And when at the end of this stage, the rise from below was completed, and with it the levelling and equalization of social standards characteristic of this whole phase of the civilizing process; when the nobility had lost its hereditary rights and its status as a separate upper class and bourgeois groups took over the upper-class function, they continued, as a result of the long preceding interpenetration, the models, the drive patterns and the forms of conduct of the courtly phase more undeviatingly than any other bourgeois class in Europe.

VIII

Conclusion

If we survey these past movements in their entirety, it is a change in a quite definite direction that we see. The deeper we penetrate the wealth of particular facts to discover the structure and regularities of the past, the more clearly emerges a firm framework of processes within which the scattered facts are taken up. Just as in past times people observing nature, after following many blind alleys in thought, gradually saw a more coherent vision of nature take shape before them, in our time the fragments of the human past gathered in our minds and books by the work of many generations, are beginning slowly to fall into place in a cohesive picture of history and of the human universe in general. The contribution made here to this picture will be briefly summarized by presenting it from a particular point of view, that of our own day. For the profile of past changes in the social fabric becomes most sharply visible when seen against the events of one's own time. Here, too, as so often, present events illuminate the understanding of the past, and immersion in the past illuminates the present. In many respects, the dynamics of intertwining to be observed in our own day, with their numerous ups and downs, represent a continuation in the same direction of the moves and countermoves of former changes in the structure of Occidental societies.

At the point of utmost feudal disintegration in the West, as was shown above,[154] certain dynamics of social intertwining come into play which tend to integrate larger and larger units. Out of the competition of small dominions, the territories, themselves formed in the struggles of even smaller survival units, a few, and finally a single unit slowly emerges victorious.

The victor forms the centre about which a new larger dominion is integrated; he forms the monopoly centre of a state organization within the framework of which many of the previously freely competing regions and groups gradually grow together into a more or less unified and well-balanced society of a higher order of magnitude.

Today these states in turn form analogous power balances of freely competing survival units. These states too, under the pressure of the tensions of competition that keep our whole society in a perpetual ferment of conflicts and crises, are now in their turn gradually being forced more and more clearly into mutual opposition. Again, many rivalling dominions are so closely intertwined that any that stands still, that does not grow stronger, runs the risk of growing weaker and becoming dependent on other states. As in every system of balances with growing competition and without a central monopoly, the powerful states forming the primary axes of tensions in the system force each other in an incessant spiral to extend and strengthen their power. The struggle for supremacy and thus, knowingly or otherwise, for the formation of monopolies over still larger areas, is already in full swing. And if at present it is supremacy over continents that is at issue, there are already clear signs, concomitant with the interdependence of larger and larger areas, of struggles for supremacy over a system embracing the entire inhabited earth.

In the present no less than in the past, the dynamics of interdependencies which have been so often mentioned in these enquiries, keep men moving and press towards changes in their institutions and indeed in the overall structure of their figurations. The experiences of our day, too, refute the notion which has now dominated men's thinking for more than a century, the idea that a balanced system of freely competing units—states, concerns, craftsmen or whatever else—can be maintained indefinitely in this state of precarious equilibrium. Now, as of old, this state of monopoly-free competition finds itself driven towards monopoly formation. Why this equilibrium is so exceedingly unstable, and the probability of its breakdown so high, has been shown in the analysis of the dynamics of competition and monopolization given earlier.[155]

And today, no more than formerly, is it "economic" goals and pressures *alone*, or *only* political motives, which are the primary driving forces of these changes. Neither the acquisition of "more" money or "more" economic power is the actual goal of state rivalry and the extension of state rule, nor the acquisition of greater political and military power merely a mask, a means to an economic end. Monopolies of physical violence and of the economic means of consumption and production, whether coordinated or not, are inseparably connected, without one ever being the real base and the other merely a "superstructure". Both together produce specific tensions at particular points in the development of the social structure, tensions pressing towards a transformation of this structure. *Both together form the lock joining the chain by which men are mutually bound.* And in both spheres of human bonding, the political and the economic, the same mechanisms, in permanent interdependence, are at work. Just as the tendency of the big merchant to enlarge his enterprise springs finally from tension within the *whole* human network of which he is a part, and above all from the danger of diminished control and loss of independence if rival concerns grow larger than his, likewise competing states drive each other further and further up the competitive spiral under the pressure of tensions immanent in the entire structure which they constitute. Many individual people may wish to put a stop to this spiral movement, the breakdown of equilibrium between "free" competitors, and to the struggles and changes this breakdown brings with it. In the course of history so far the constraints of human bonding have always proved stronger in the long run than such wishes. And so today international relationships, not yet regulated by an encompassing monopoly of force, are again driven towards such monopolies and thus to the formation of dominions of a new order of magnitude.

Precursors of such hegemonial units such as united states, empires or leagues of nations, certainly already exist. They are all still relatively unstable. As earlier, in the centuries of struggle between territorial dominions, it is as yet unresolved in the struggle of states today, and impossible to resolve, where the centres and frontiers of the larger hegemonial units of the future will lie. As earlier, it is impossible to predict how long it will take for this struggle, with its many spurts and counter-spurts, to be finally decided. And like the members of the smaller units whose struggles slowly produced the states, we too nave scarcely more than a vague idea of the structure, organization and institutions of the larger units towards which the actions of today tend, whether the actors know or not.[156] Only one thing is certain: the direction in which the integration of the modern world is veering. The competitive tension between states, given the pressures which our social structure brings with it, can be resolved only after a long series of violent or non-violent trials of strength have established monopolies of force, and central organizations for larger dominions, within which many of the smaller ones, "states", can grow together in a more balanced unity. Here, indeed, the compelling forces of social interweaving have led the transformation of Western society in one and the same direction from the time of utmost feudal disintegration to the present.

And the case is very similar with many other movements of the "present". They are all seen in a new light when viewed as moments in that stream that we variously call "the past" or "history". Even *within* the different hegemonial units of today we see a number of monopoly-free competitive struggles. But this free competition is in many places nearing its final phase. Everywhere in these struggles fought with economic weapons, private monopoly organizations are already forming. And as earlier, in the formation of monopolies of taxation and physical force in the hands of single dynasties, compelling forces were already discernible that finally led to a broadening of control, whether by subordinating the monopoly executive to an elected public legislator or by any other form of "nationalization", in our day we already see the immanent figurational dynamics at work curtailing the possibility of private control of the recent "economic" monopolies and bringing their structure closer to the older ones, so that eventually they are likely to veer towards an integration of both.

The same can be said of the other tensions leading towards changes within the different hegemonial units, the tensions between those people directly controlling certain instruments of monopoly as a hereditary possession, and those excluded from such control and who engage in unfree competition, all being dependent on opportunities distributed by the monopoly rulers. Here too we find ourselves in the midst of a historical spurt which, like a great wave of an advancing tide, takes up the smaller ones preceding it and carries them further in the same direction. In the analysis of the monopoly mechanism, it was shown in more general terms[157] how and why, in the tension between monopoly rulers and monopoly servants at a certain degree of overall pressure, the balance tends to be more or less quickly overturned. It was shown that spurts in this direction already take place in an early period of Western society. We find them, for example, in the process of feudalization even though this involves only a shift within the upper class itself; moreover, this change in favour of the many at the expense of the few led, as a result of the low degree of division of functions, to the disintegration of control over monopolized opportunities and the decay of the monopoly centres.

As the division of functions, and with it the mutual interdependence of all functions, advances, this kind of change in the balance of power is no longer expressed by a tendency to disperse monopolized opportunities among many individuals, but by a tendency to control the monopoly centres and the opportunities they allocate in a different way. The first great transitional phase of this kind, the struggle of bourgeois classes for control of the old monopoly centres, controlled by the kings and, partly, by the aristocracy, as a hereditary possession—the first complete monopolies of modern times—shows this clearly enough. For many reasons, the pattern of rising classes in our day is more complex. One reason is that it is now necessary to struggle not only for the old monopoly centres of taxation and physical violence, or only for the recent economic monopolies still in the process of formation, but for control of both at once. But the elementary pattern of forces at work here is very simple even in this case: every monopoly opportunity restricted by heredity to particular families leads to specific tensions and disproportions in the society concerned. Tensions of this kind tend towards a change of relationships and thus of institutions in all societies, though when differentiation is low and, particularly, when the upper class consists of warriors, they often remain unresolved. Societies with a highly developed division of functions are far more sensitive to the disproportions and malfunctions caused by such tensions, the effects of which are permanently felt throughout the whole society. And though in such societies there may be more than one way in which such tensions might be resolved and removed, the *direction* in which they tend towards transcending themselves is predetermined by the mode of their becoming, by their genesis. The tensions, disproportions and malfunctions resulting from monopoly control of opportunities in the interests of a few can only be resolved by breaking this control. What cannot be decided in advance, however, is how long the ensuing struggle will take.

And something very similar, finally, is happening in our time to the conduct of people and to their whole personality structure. In the course of this study it has been attempted to show in detail both that and how the structure of psychological functions, the particular standard of behavioural controls at a given period, is connected to the structure of social functions and the change in relationships between people. To trace these connections in detail in our own time is a task yet to be undertaken. The most general points can be quickly made. The structural forces working so perceptibly today towards a more or less rapid change of institutions and of interpersonal relationships, are leading no less clearly to corresponding changes in the personality structure. Here, too, we only gain a clear picture of what is happening by comparing it, as a spurt in a particular direction, with the past movements of which it is a continuation. In the birth pains of other social upheavals the dominant standard of conduct of the upper classes was finally loosened to a greater or lesser extent. A period of uncertainty preceded the consolidation of a new standard. Behaviour patterns were transmitted not only from above to below but, in line with the shift in the social centre of gravity, from below to above. Thus, in the course of the rise of the bourgeoisie, for example, the courtly-aristocratic code of conduct lost some of its hold. Social forms became more relaxed and in some ways more coarse. The stricter taboos placed in middle-class circles on certain spheres, above all those of money and sexuality, pervaded broader circles in varying degrees until finally, as this specific balance of tensions disappeared, in alternating waves of relaxation and renewed severity, elements of the behaviour patterns of both classes were fused into a new, more stable code of conduct.

The upheavals in the midst of which we live are different in structure from all those preceding them, however much they may continue these earlier movements and be based upon them. Nevertheless, certain structural similarities with the change just described are encountered in our own time. Here too we find a relaxation of traditional patterns of behaviour, the rise of certain modes of conduct from below, and increased interpenetration of the standards of different classes; we see an increased severity in some spheres and a certain coarsening in others.

Periods like this, periods of transition, give a particular opportunity for reflection: the older standards have been called into question but solid new ones are not yet available. People become more uncertain in their conduct. The social situation itself makes "conduct" an acute problem. In such phases—and perhaps only in such phases—much is open to scrutiny in conduct that previous generations took for granted. The sons begin to think further where their fathers brought their reflection to a halt; they begin to ask for reasons where their fathers saw no reason to ask: why must "one" behave in this way here and that way there? Why is this permitted and that forbidden? What is the point of this precept on manners and that on morals? Conventions that have long gone untested from generation to generation, become problems. In addition, as a result of increased mobility and more frequent meetings with different human types, people are learning to see themselves from a greater distance: why is the code of conduct different in Germany from that in England, different in England from that in America, and why is the conduct of all these countries different from that of the Orient or of more primitive societies?

The preceding investigations attempt to bring some of these questions closer to resolution. They really raise only problems that are "in the air". They try, as far as one person's knowledge permits, to clarify the questions and to prepare a way which, in the crossfire of discussion, may lead enquiry forward in collaboration with many others. The behaviour patterns of our society, imprinted on the individual from early childhood as a kind of second nature and kept alert in him by a powerful and increasingly strictly organized social control, are to be explained, it has been shown, not in terms of general, ahistorical human purposes, but as something which has evolved from the totality of Western history, from the specific forms of behaviour that develop in its course and the forces of integration which transform and propagate them. These patterns, like the whole control of our behaviour, like the structure of our psychological functions in general, are many-layered: in their formation and reproduction emotional impulses play their part no less than rational ones, drives and affects no less than ego functions. It has long been customary to explain the control to which individual behaviour is subject in our society as something essentially rational, founded solely on logical considerations. Here it has been seen differently.

Rationalization itself, and with it the more rational shaping and explanation of social taboos has been shown[158] to be only one side of a transformation affecting the *whole* personality, the level of drives and affects no less than the level of consciousness and reflection. The motive force of this change of individual self-steering is provided, it was shown, by pressures arising out of the manifold intertwining of human activities, pressures operating in a particular direction, and bringing about shifts in the form of relationships and in the whole social fabric. This rationalization goes hand in hand with a tremendous differentiation of functional chains and a corresponding change in the organization of physical force. Its precondition is a rise in the standard of living and in security, or, in other words, increased protection from physical attack or destruction and thus from the uncontrollable fears which erupt for more powerfully and frequently into the lives of individuals in societies with less stable monopolies of force and lower division of functions. At present we are so accustomed to the existence of these more stable monopolies of force and the greater predictability of violence resulting from them, that we scarcely see their importance for the structure of our conduct and our personality. We scarcely realize how quickly what we call our "reason", this relatively farsighted and differentiated steering of our conduct, with its high degree of affect-control, would crumble or collapse if the anxiety-inducing tensions within and around us changed, if the fears affecting our lives suddenly became much stronger or much weaker or, as in many simpler societies, both at once, now stronger, now weaker.

It is only when we penetrate these connections that we gain access to the problem of conduct and its control by the social code valid at a particular time. The degree of anxiety, like the whole pleasure economy, is different in every society, in every class and historical phase. To understand the control of conduct which a society imposes on its members, it is not enough to know the rational goals that can be adduced to explain its commands and prohibitions; we must trace to their source the fears which induce the members of this society, and above all the custodians of its precepts, to control conduct in this way. We therefore only gain a better understanding of the changes of conduct and sentiment in a civilizing direction if we are aware of the changes in the structure of inbuilt fears to which they are connected. The direction of this change was sketched earlier:[159] the direct fear of one person for others diminishes; indirect or internalized fears increase proportionately; and both kinds become more even; the waves of anxiety no longer rise so fre*quently or steeply, only to fall away just as sharply; with some oscillation, slight by comparison with the earlier phase, they normally remain at a middle level. When this is the case, as has been seen, conduct takes on—by degrees and stages—a more "civilized" character. Here as everywhere, the structure of fears and anxieties is nothing other than the psychological counterpart of the constraints which people exert on one another through the intertwining of their activities. Fears form one of the channels—and one of the most important—through which the structure of society is transmitted to individual psychological functions. The driving force underlying the change in drive economy, in the structure of fears and anxieties, is a very specific change in the social constraints acting on the individual, a specific transformation of the whole web of relationships, above all the organization of force.

Often enough it seems to people as if the codes regulating their conduct towards one another, and thus also the fears moving them, are something from outside the human sphere. The more deeply we immerse ourselves in the historical processes in the course of which prohibitions, like fears and anxieties, are formed and transformed, the stronger grows an insight which is not without importance for our actions as well as for our understanding of ourselves: *we realize to what degree the fears and anxieties that move people are men-made*. To be sure, the possibility of feeling fear, just like that of feeling joy, is an unalterable part of human nature. But the strength, kind and structure of the fears and anxieties that smoulder or flare in the individual never depend solely on his own "nature" nor, at least in more complex societies, on the "nature" in the midst of which he lives. They are always determined, finally, by the history and the actual structure of his relations to other people, by the structure of society; and they change with it.

Here, indeed, is one of the indispensable keys to all the problems posed by the steering of human conduct and the social codes of commandments and "taboos". The child and adolescent would never learn to control his behaviour without the fears instilled by other people. Without the lever of these men-made fears the young human animal would never become an adult deserving the name of a human being, any more than someone's humanity matures fully if life denies him sufficient joy and pleasure. The fears which grown-ups consciously or unconsciously induce in the child are precipitated in him and henceforth reproduce themselves more or less automatically. The malleable personality of the child is so fashioned by fears that it learns to act in accord with the prevailing standard of behaviour, whether these fears are produced by direct physical force or by deprivation, by the restriction of food or pleasure. And men-made fears and anxieties from within or without finally hold even the adult in their power. Shame, fear of war and fear of God, guilt, fear of punishment or of loss of social prestige, man's fear of himself, of being overcome by his own affective impulses, all these are directly or indirectly induced in him by other people. Their strength, their form and the role they play in the individual's personality depend on the structure of his society and his fate within it.

No society can survive without a channelling of individual drives and affects, without a very specific control of individual behaviour. No such control is possible unless people exert constraints on one another, and all constraint is converted in the person on whom it is imposed into fear of one kind or another. We should not deceive ourselves: the constant production and reproduction of human fears by people is inevitable and indispensable wherever people live together, wherever the desires and actions of a number of people interact, whether at work, in leisure or in love-making. But one should not believe or attempt to be persuaded that the commands and fears which *today* set their stamp on human conduct have as their "purpose" simply and fundamentally these basic necessities of human co-existence, or that they are restricted in our world to those constraints and fears necessary to a stable equilibrium between the desires of many and for the maintenance of social collaboration. Our codes of conduct are as riddled with contradictions and as full of disproportions as are the forms of our social life, as is the structure of our society. The constraints to which the individual is subjected today, and the fears corresponding to them, are in

328

their character, their strength and structure decisively determined by the particular forces engendered by the structure of our society just discussed: by its power and other differentials and the immense tensions created by them.

It is clear in what turmoils and dangers we live, and the structural forces determining their direction have been discussed. It is these forces, far more than the simple constraint of working together, it is tensions and entanglements of this kind which at present constantly expose the individual to fear and anxiety. The tensions between states arising from the compelling dynamics of their contests for supremacy over larger and larger dominions find their expression in the make-up of the individual people, in specific frustrations and restraints; they impose upon these individuals a mounting work-pressure and also a profound insecurity which never ceases. All this, the frustrations, the restlessness, the pressure of work, no less than the never-ending threat to life, inherent in these inter-state tensions, produces anxieties and fears. The same holds true of the tensions within each of the different state societies. The uncontrollable, monopoly-free competition between people of the same class on the one hand, and the tensions between different classes and groups on the other, likewise give rise, for the individual, to continuous anxiety and particular prohibitions or restrictions. They too engender their own specific fears: the fears of dismissal, of unpredictable exposure to those in power, of falling below the subsistence level, which prevail in the lower classes; and the fears of social degradation, of the reduction of possessions or independence, of loss of prestige and status, which play so great a part in the life of the middle and upper classes. And it is precisely fears and anxieties of this kind, fears of the loss of distinguishing hereditary prestige, as was pointed out earlier,[160] that have had to this day a decisive part in shaping the prevailing code of conduct. Precisely these fears, it was also seen, are particularly disposed to internalization; they, far more than the fear of poverty, hunger or direct physical danger, become rooted in the individual member of such classes, through his upbringing, as inner anxieties which bind him to a learned code almost automatically, under the pressure of a strong super-ego, even independently of any control by others. The continuous concern of parents whether their child will attain the standard of conduct of their own or even a higher class, whether it will maintain or increase the prestige of the family, whether it will hold its own in the competition within their own class, fears of this kind surround the child from its earliest years, and they do so in the middle classes, in those ambitious to rise, far more than in the upper class. Fears of this kind play a considerable part in the control to which the child is subject from the beginning, in the prohibitions placed on him. Perhaps only partly conscious in the parents, and partly already automatic, they are transmitted to the child as much by gestures as by words. They continuously add fuel to the fiery circle of inner anxieties, which holds the behaviour and feelings of the growing child permanently within definite limits, binding him to a certain standard of shame and embarrassment, to a specific accent, to particular manners, whether he wishes or not. Even the rules imposed on sexual life and the automatic anxieties now surrounding it to such a high degree, stem not only from the elementary necessity of controlling and balancing the desires of many who live together. They likewise have their origins to a considerable extent in the pressures and tensions in which the upper and particularly the middle classes of our society live. They too are very closely related to the fear of losing opportunities or possessions and prestige, of social degradation, of reduced chances in the harsh struggle of life, induced from early on in the child by the behaviour of parents and educators. And even though these parental constraints and anxieties may sometimes bring about precisely what they are supposed to prevent, even though the child might be made incapable, by such blindly instilled automatic anxieties, of succeeding in the struggle of life and attaining social prestige—whatever the outcome, it is always the tensions of their society that are projected by the parental gestures, prohibitions and fears on to the child. The hereditary character of monopolized chances and of social prestige finds direct expression in the parents' attitude to their child; and so the child is made to feel the dangers threatening these chances and this prestige, to feel the entire tensions of his society, even before he knows anything about them.

This connection between the external fears of the parents directly conditioned by their social position, and the inner, automatic anxieties of the growing child, is certainly a fact of far more general significance than can be shown here. We shall only gain a fuller understanding of the personality structure of the individual, and of the historical changes in its moulding over successive generations, when we are better able to observe and analyse long chains of generations than is possible today. But one thing has become clear enough even here: how deeply the stratification, the pressures and tensions of our own time penetrate the structure of the individual personality.

We cannot expect of people who live in the midst of such tensions, who are thus driven guiltlessly to incur guilt upon guilt against each other, that they should behave to each other in a manner representing—as seems so often to be believed today—an ultimate pinnacle of "civilized" conduct. The continuous intertwining of human activities again and again acts as a lever which over the centuries produces changes in human conduct in the direction of our standard. The same pressures quite clearly operate within our own society towards changes transcending present standards of conduct and sentiment in the same direction—although, today as in the past, these trends can go at any time into reverse gear. No more than our kind of social structure, is our kind of conduct, our level of constraints, prohibitions and anxieties, something definitive, still less a pinnacle.

To begin with, there is the constant danger of war. War, to repeat the point in different words, is not the opposite of peace. Through a necessity the reasons of which have become clear, wars between smaller units have been, in the course of history up to now, inevitable stages and instruments in the pacification of larger ones. Certainly, the vulnerability of the social structure, and so the risks and upheavals brought on all concerned by the explosive violence of wars, increase the further the division of functions advances, the greater the mutual dependence of the rivals. We therefore feel in our own time a growing disposition to resolve future interstate conflicts by less dangerous means. But the fact that, in our day, just as earlier, the dynamics of increasing interdependence are impelling the figuration of state societies towards such conflicts, to the formation of monopolies of physical force over larger areas of the earth and thus, through all the terrors and struggles, towards their pacification, is clear enough. And as mentioned above, beyond the tensions between continents and partly involved in them, the tensions of the next stage are already emerging. One can see the first outlines of a worldwide system of tensions composed by alliances and suprastate units of various kinds, the prelude of struggles embracing

331

the whole globe, which are the precondition for a worldwide monopoly of physical force, for a single central political institution and thus for the pacification of the earth.

The case is no different with economic struggles. Free economic competition, too, as we have seen, is not just the opposite of a monopolistic order. It is constantly veering beyond itself towards this opposite. From this aspect too our epoch is anything but a final point or pinnacle, no matter how many partial downfalls, as in structurally similar transitional periods, it may contain. In this respect too it is full of unresolved tensions, of unconcluded processes of integration the duration and exact course of which are not predictable and whose direction alone is clear: the tendency of free competition or, which means the same thing, the unorganized ownership of monopolies, to be reduced and abolished; the change in human relationships by which control of opportunities gradually ceases to be the hereditary and private preserve of an established upper class and becomes a function under social and public control. And here, too, beneath the veil of the present tensions, those of the next stage are becoming visible, the tensions between the upper and middle functionaries of the monopoly administration, between the "bureaucracy" on the one hand and the rest of society on the other.

Only when these tensions between and within states have been mastered can we expect to become more truly civilized. At present many of the rules of conduct and sentiment implanted in us as an integral part of one's conscience, of the individual super-ego, are remnants of the power and status aspirations of established groups, and have no other function than that of reinforcing their power chances and their status superiority. They help members of these groups to such distinction not simply through their own achievement—which in moderation is justified—but through the monopolistic appropriation of power chances the access to which is blocked for other interdependent groups. Only when the tensions between and within states have been mastered is there a chance that the regulation of men's affects and conduct in their relations with each other can be confined to those instructions and prohibitions which are necessary in order to keep up the high level of functional differentiation and interdependence without which even the present levels of civilized conduct in men's co-existence with each other could not be maintained, let alone surpassed. Only then is there a chance, too, that the common pattern of self-control expected of men can be confined to those restraints which are necessary in order that men can live with each other and with themselves with a high chance of enjoyment and a low chance of fear—be it of others, be it of themselves. Only with the tensions and conflicts between men can those within men become milder and less damaging to their chances of enjoyment. Then it need no longer be the exception, then it may even be the rule that an individual person can attain the optimal balance between his imperative drives claiming satisfaction and fulfilment and the constraints imposed upon them (and without which man would remain a brutish animal and a danger as much to himself as to others)—that condition to which one so often refers with big words such as "happiness" and "freedom": a more durable balance, a better attunement, between the overall demands of man's social existence on the one hand, and his personal needs and inclinations on the other. If the structure of human figurations, of men's interdependencies, has these characteristics, if the co-existence of men with each other, which after all is the condition of the individual existence of each of them, functions in such a way that it is possible for all those bonded to each other in this manner to attain this balance, then and only then can humans say of themselves with some justice that they *are* civilized. Until then they are at best in the process of becoming civilized. Until then they may at best say: the civilizing process is under way, or, with the old Holbach: "la civilisation . . . n'est pas encore terminée."

NOTES

1. James Westfall Thompson, *Economic and Social History of Europe in the Later Middle Ages (1300–1530)* (New York and London, 1931), pp. 506–7.

2. This is exemplified by the consequences resulting from the Carolingian estates or fisc. These were perhaps not as extreme as they appear from the following quotation; but undoubtedly the situation of the Carolingian fisc played a part in the formation of the national frontiers:

The widespread character of the Carolingian fisc . . . made the fisc like a vast net in which the Empire was held. The division and dissipation of the fisc was a more important factor in the dissolution of the Frankish Empire than the local political ambition of the proprietary nobles . . .

The historical fact that the heart of the fisc was situated in central Europe accounts for the partitions of central Europe in the ninth century, and made these regions a battle-ground of kings long before they became a battle-ground of nations. . . .

The dividing frontier between future France and future Germany was drawn in the ninth century because the greatest block of the fisc lay between them.

James Westfall Thompson, *Economic and Social History of the Middle Ages (300–1300)* (New York and London, 1928), pp. 241–2. Cf. by the same author: *The Dissolution of the Carolingian Fisc* (Berkeley, University of California Press, 1935).

3. A. Luchaire, *Les premiers Capétiens* (Paris, 1901), p. 180.

4. C. Petit-Dutaillis, *Las monarchie féodale en France et en Angleterre* (Paris, 1933), p. 8 with following map. For details on the eastern frontier of the western Frankish empire and its movements, cf. Fritz Kern, *Die Anfänge der Französischen Ausdehnungspolitik* (Tübingen, 1910), p. 16.

5. Paul Kirn, *Das Abendland vom Ausgang der Antike bis zum Zerfall des Karolingischen Reiches*, Propyläen-Weltgeschichte, vol. 3 (Berlin, 1932), p. 118.

6. Brunner, *Deutsche Rechtsgeschichte*, quoted by A. Dopsch, *Wirtschaftliche und soziale Grundlagen der europäischen Kulturentwicklung* (Vienna, 1924), pt. 2, pp. 100–1.

7. A. Dopsch, *Wirtschaftliche und soziale Grundlagen der europäischen Kulturentwicklung aus der Zeit von Cäsar bis auf Karl den Grossen* (Vienna, 1918–24), pt. 2, p. 115.

8. Kirn, op. cit., p. 118.

9. A. von Hofmann, *Politische Geschichte der Deutschen* (Stuttgart and Berlin, 1921–8), vol. 1, p. 405.

10. Ernst Dümmler, *Geschichte des ostfränkischen Reiches* (Berlin, 1862–88), vol. 3, p. 306.

11. Paul Kirn, *Politische Geschichte der deutschen Grenzen* (Leipzig, 1934), p. 24.

12. F. Lot, *Les derniers Carolingiens* (Paris, 1891), p. 4; also J. Calmette, *Le monde féodale* (Paris, 1934), p. 119.

13. Beaudoin, quoted by J. Calmette, *La société féodale* (Paris, 1932), p. 27.

14. Luchaire, op. cit., pp. 176–7. A sketch of the distribution of rule at the time of Hugh Capet is given by M. Mignet, "Essai sur la formation territoriale et politique de la France", *Notices et Mémoires historiques* (Paris, 1845), vol. 2, pp. 154f.

15. A. Luchaire, *Histoire des Institutions Monarchiques de la France sous les premiers Capétiens (987–1180)* (Paris, 1883), vol. 2, Notes et Appendices, p. 329.

16. Karl Hampe, *Abendländisches Hochmittelalter*, Propyläen Weltegeschichte, vol. 3 (Berlin, 1932), p. 306.

17. Kirn, *Das Abendland vom Ausgang der Antike bis zum Zerfall des Karolingischen Reiches*, p. 119.

18. A. Dopsch, *Die Wirtschaftsentwicklung der Karolingerzeit, vornehmlich in Deutschland* (Weimar, 1912), vol. 1, p. 162; cf. also the general account of manor and village in Knight, Barnes and Flügel, *Economic History of Europe* (London, 1930), "The Manor", pp. 163ff.

19. Marc Bloch, *Les caractères originaux de l'histoire rurale française* (Oslo, 1931), p. 23.

20. Dopsch, *Wirtschaftliche und soziale Grundlagen der europäischen Kulturentwicklung aus der Zeit von Cäsar bis auf Karl den Grossen*, pt. 2, p. 309: "The greater the real power, the economic and social base, of these officials became, the less the monarchy could contemplate transferring the office outside the incumbent's family on his death."

21. Calmette, *La société féodale*, p. 3.

22. Ibid., pp. 4–5. Cf. on this problem the contrast between European and Japanese feudalism in W. C. Macleod, *The Origin and History of Politics* (New York, 1931), pp. 160ff. Here, admittedly, the explanation of Western feudalization is sought rather in the preceding late-Roman institutions than in contemporary forces of integration: "Many writers appear to believe that Western European feudalism has its institutional origins in pre-Roman Teutonic institutions. Let us explain to the student that the fact is that Germanic invaders merely seized upon those contractual institutions of the late Roman Empire which . . ." (p. 162). The very fact that analogous feudal relationships and institutions are formed in the most different

parts of the world can only be fully understood through a clear insight into the compelling force of the actual relationships, into the dynamics of a specific figuration; and only analysis of them can explain why the feudalization processes and feudal institutions in different societies differ from one another in certain ways.

Another comparison between different feudal societies is to be found in O. Hintze, *Wesen und Verbreitung des Feudalismus*, Sitzungsberichte der Preussischen Akademie der Wissenschaften, phil.-hist. Klasse (Berlin, 1929), pp. 321ff. The author, influenced by the ideas of Max Weber on the methodology of historical and social research, attempts "to describe the *ideal type* underlying the concept of feudalism". But while this study does begin to transform the older historiographical method into one more concerned with actual social structures and so gives rise to useful particular insights, its comparison of different feudal societies is one of the many examples of the difficulties arising when a historian takes over the methodological guiding ideas of Max Weber and tries—in the words of Otto Hintze—to construct "visual abstractions, types". The similarities confronting the observer of different people and societies are not ideal types that have in a sense to be mentally constructed by the observer, but a real, existing kinship between the social structures themselves; if this is lacking the historian's whole concept of types miscarries. If we are to oppose another concept to that of the "ideal type", it could be the "real type". The similarity between different feudal societies is not an artificial product of thought but, to reiterate, the result of the fact that similar forms of social bonding have a strong compelling tendency to develop in a way which in fact, and not only "in the idea", produces related patterns of relationships and institutions at different times and at different locations of global society.

A number of examples for which I am indebted to Ralph Bonwit have shown how remarkably similar the forces of social interweaving that led to feudal relations and institutions in Japan are to the structures and forces which have been established here in relation to Western feudalism. A comparative structural analysis of this kind would prove a more useful way of explaining the peculiarities by which the feudal institutions of Japan and their historical change differ from those of the West.

Similar results have been produced by a preliminary investigation of the Homeric warrior society. To explain the production of large epic cycles—to mention only this feature—in ancient as in Western knightly society and in other societies with a similar structure, we do not need any speculative biologistic hypothesis, the notion of a "youth" of social "organisms". It is quite enough to examine the specific forms of social life that develop at medium and large feudal courts or on military campaigns and travels. Singers and minstrels with their versified reports of the fates and heroic deeds of great warriors that are passed from mouth to mouth, have in the daily life of such feudal warrior societies a specific place and function which differ from those of singers and songs in a tribe living more closely together, for example.

We also gain access to the structural changes in ancient warrior societies from a different angle by examining stylistic changes in the vases and vase paintings of early antiquity. When, for example, in vase paintings originating in particular periods, "baroque" elements appear, affected or—positively expressed—refined gestures and garments, we should think, instead of assuming a biological "ageing" of the society concerned, of processes of differentiation, the emergence of wealthier houses from the mass of warrior society and a greater or lesser transition from warriors to courtiers; or, depending on circumstances, we should look for a colonizing influence from more powerful courts. Insight into the specific tensions and processes within a feudal society which the more abundant documentation from the early European period makes possible can, in a word, in some respects sharpen and focus our observation of material from antiquity. But, of course, suppositions of this kind should in each case be supported by a rigorous examination of material pertaining to the structural history of antiquity itself.

Comparative studies of sociogenesis or structural history of this kind have scarcely begun. Indispensable for their success is an undertaking that has been made especially difficult by the over-sharp distinction between academic disciplines and the lack of collaboration between them which have characterized research hitherto. Essential for an understanding of earlier feudal societies and their structure, for example, is an exact comparative study of living feudal societies before it is too late. A rich knowledge of details and structural connections necessary for an understanding of any society, which the material from the past is too fragmentary to provide, will only become available for interpretation if ethnology bases its research less exclusively on simpler societies, "tribes", and history concerns itself less with past societies and processes, and if both disciplines together turn their attention to those living societies which in their structure are close to the medieval society of the West. Both together should investigate the structure, in the strictest sense of

340

the word, of such societies, the functional dependencies by which people in them are bound together in very specific ways, and the forces of interweaving which under certain circumstan~es bring about a change of these dependencies and relationships in a quite specific direction.

23. On this and the following discussion, cf. A. and E. Kulischer, *Kriegs- und Wanderzüge* (Berlin and Leipzig, 1932), pp. 50f.

24. J. B. Bury, *History of the Eastern Roman Empire* (1912), p. 373, quoted by Kulischer, op. cit., p. 62.

25. Henri Pirenne, *Les villes du moyen âge* (Brussels, 1927).

26. Kirn, *Politische Geschichte der deutschen Grenzen*. For further details on the differences in pace and structure between German and French feudalization, cf. J. W. Thompson, "German Feudalism", *American Historical Review*, vol. 28, 1923, pp. 440ff. "What the ninth century did for France in transforming her into a feudal country was not done in Germany until the civil wars of the reign of Henry IV." Ibid., p. 444.

Here, admittedly (and subsequently in, for example, W. O. Ault, *Europe in the Middle Ages*, 1932) the decline of the western Frankish area is explained primarily in terms of the greater external threat: "Germany being less exposed to attack from outside and possessed of a firmer texture within than France, German feudalism did not become as hard and set a system as was French feudalism. 'Old' France crumbled away in the ninth and tenth centuries; 'old' Germany, anchored to the ancient duchies, which remained intact, retained its integrity" (Thompson, op. cit., p. 443). But another decisive factor in the speed and degree of feudal disintegration in the western Frankish area was precisely the fact that after the Normans had settled invasions by foreign tribes, and therefore the external threat, was less than in the eastern Frankish area. The question whether larger areas, once unified, decay more slowly and whether conversely, once decayed, they re-integrate with greater difficulty than smaller ones, this problem of social dynamics remains to be investigated. But at any rate, hand in hand with the gradual weakening of the Carolingian house brought about at least in part by the unavoidable reduction in its wealth in the course of generations, by the loss of part of its land to pay for services or its division between different family members (this too remains to be examined in more detail), went a phase of disintegration embracing the whole Carolingian dominion. It may be that even in the ninth century this disintegration in the western Frankish area went somewhat further than in the later

German region. But it was certainly more quickly arrested in the latter precisely because of the stronger external threat. Over a long period this threat gave individual tribal leaders the chance to become strong central rulers through military successes over common enemies and so to re-invigorate and extend the Carolingian central organization. And for a time the possibility of colonial expansion, the acquisition of new land on the eastern frontier of the German region, acted in the same direction to strengthen the central authority. In the western Frankish area, by contrast, from the ninth century on both factors were less: the threat of invasion by foreign tribes and the possibility of joint expansion across the frontier. Proportionately smaller was the chance of forming a strong monarchy; the "royal task" was lacking; and so feudal disintegration took place more quickly and completely. (Cf. pp. 15ff. and 36–7 of this volume.)

27. E. Levasseur, *La population française* (Paris, 1889), vol. 1, pp. 154–5.

28. Bloch, op. cit., p. 5.

29. W. Cohn, *Das Zeitalter der Normannen in Sicilien* (Bonn and Leipzig, 1920).

30. H. See, *Französische Wirtschaftsgeschichte* (Jena, 1930), p. 7.

31. Kurt Breysig, *Kulturgeschichte der Neuzeit* (Berlin, 1901), vol. 2, pp. 937ff., partic. p. 948.

If the actions of the three monarchies are compared . . . in seeking the reasons for their varying success, the ultimate cause will not be found in isolated events. The Norman–English monarchy benefited from a circumstance that lay neither in its power nor in that of any mortal being, but was founded in the whole structure of England's external and internal history. By virtue of the fact that in 1066 a new state was established in England from the foundations upwards, it was possible to make use of the experiences gathered by the great monarchies, most of all the closest, the French. The fragmentation of the high nobility and the hereditariness of offices were in a sense only the conclusions drawn by the Norman monarchy from the fate of its nearest example.

32. Pirenne, *Les villes du moyen âge*, p. 53. The opposite view has been taken more recently by D. M. Petruševki, "Strittige Fragen der mittelalterlichen Verfassungs- und Wirtschaftsgeschichte", *Zeitschrift für die gesamte Staatswissenschaft*, vol. 85 (Tübingen, 1928), pp. 468ff. This work is not without interest in that, through its onesidedness in the opposite

direction, it puts into proper perspective certain obscurities in the traditional historical view and certain inadequacies of existing concepts.

So, for example, the idea that the cities of antiquity had completely disappeared by the early Middle Ages is countered by one no less imprecise. Cf. the more balanced account by H. Pirenne, *Economic and Social History of Medieval Europe* (London, 1936), p. 40: "When the Islamic invasion had bottled up the ports of the Tyrrhenian Sea . . . municipal activity rapidly died out. Save in southern Italy and in Venice, where it was maintained thanks to Byzantine trade, it disappeared everywhere. The towns continued in existence, but they lost their population of artisans and merchants and with it all that had survived of the municipal organisation of the Roman Empire."

To the static view whereby the "barter economy" and the "money economy" appear, not as expressions of the *direction* of a gradual historical process, but as two separate, successive and irreconcilable physical states of society (cf. p. 28 and pp. 46–7 above), Petruševski opposed the different conception that no such thing as the "barter economy" ever existed: "We do not wish here to discuss in detail the fact that, as Max Weber has shown, the barter economy is one of those scholarly Utopias which not only do not exist and have never existed in actual reality, but which, unlike others . . . which are likewise Utopian generalizations on account of their logical character, can never have any application to actual reality" (p.488). To this we may compare Pirenne's account (op. cit., p. 8):

> From the economic point of view the most striking and characteristic institution of this civilisation is the great estate. Its origin is, of course, much more ancient and it is easy to establish its affiliation with a very remote past . . . [p. 9]. What was new was the way in which it functioned from the moment of the disappearance of commerce and the towns. So long as the former had been capable of transporting its products and the latter of furnishing it with a market, the great estate had commanded and consequently profited by a regular sale outside . . . but now it ceased to do this, because there were no more merchants and townsmen . . . now that everyone lived off his own land, no-one bothered to buy food from outside. . . . Thus, each estate devoted itself to the kind of economy which has been described rather inexactly as the "closed estate economy", and which was really simply an economy without markets.

Finally Petruševski opposes to the notion whereby "feudalism" and "barter economy" appear as two different spheres of existence or storeys of society, the latter as the infrastructure producing or causing the former as the super-structure, his own view that the two phenomena have nothing to do with each other: ". . . notions wholly at variance with histori-cal fact, such as that of the contingency of feudalism on the bar-ter economy or its incompatibility with a comprehensive state organisation" (p. 488).

It has been attempted to show the real state of affairs in the preceding text. The specific form of barter economy prevailing in the early Middle Ages, the relatively undifferentiated and market-less economies associated with the great courts, and the specific form of political and military organization which we call feudalism, are nothing other than two different aspects of the same forms of human relationships. They can be conceptually *distinguished* as two different aspects of the same human relationships, but even conceptually they cannot be *separated*, like two substances which can exist independently. The political and military functions of the feudal lord and his function as the owner of land and bondsmen are fully interdependent and indis-solubly bound together. And likewise the changes which gradu-ally took place in the situation of these lords and in the whole structure of this society cannot be explained *solely* in terms of an autonomous movement of economic relations and functions, or *solely* in terms of changes of political and military functions, but only in terms of the intertwining human activities comprising both these two inseparably connected areas of functions and forms of relationship.

33. Cf. the Introduction by Louis Halphen in A. Luchaire, *Les communes Françaises à l'époque des Capétiens directs* (Paris, 1911), p. viii.

34. Ibid., p. ix.

35. Ibid., p. 18.

36. Hans von Werveke, "Monnaie, lingots ou marchandises? Les instruments d'échange au XIe et XIIe siècles", *Annales d'histoire économique et sociale* (Sept. 1932), no. 17, p. 468.

37. Ibid. The corresponding process in the opposite direction, the recession of the use of money and the advance of payment in natural produce, sets in at an early stage of late antiquity: "The further the third century proceeds the faster the decline becomes. The only money remaining in circulation is the antonianus. . . ." (F. Lot, *La fin du monde antique* (Paris, 1927), p. 63.) "Wages for the army tend more and more to be paid in produce" (p. 65) . . . "As for the ineluctable conse-

quences of a system which allows services to be rewarded only by payment in kind, the distribution of land, they are readily perceived: they lead to what is called the feudal system or to an analogous régime" (p. 67).

38. M. Rostovtsev, *The Social and Economic History of the Roman Empire* (Oxford, 1926), pp. 66–7, p. 528 and many other places. Cf. Index: Transportation.

39. Lefebvre des Noettes, *L'Attelage. Le cheval de selle à travers les âges. Contribution à l'histoire de l'esclavage* (Paris, 1931).

The investigations of Lefebvre des Noettes, on account both of their results and of their direction of enquiry, have an importance which can scarcely be overestimated. Beside the value of these results, which no doubt need confirmation on particular points, it is no great matter that the author stands the causal connection on its head, seeing the development of haulage technology as the cause of the elimination of slavery.

Indications of the necessary corrections are to be found in a critique of the book by Marc Bloch, "Problèmes d'histoire des techniques", *Annales d'histoire economique et sociale* (Sept. 1932). In particular, two aspects of Lefebvre des Noettes' work are partly accentuated and partly rectified. 1. The influence of China and Byzantium on the inventions of the Middle Ages appears to require closer examination. 2. Slavery had ceased to play an important part in the structure of the early medieval world long before the new harness appeared: "In the absence of any clear temporal succession how can one speak of a cause and effect relationship?" (p. 484). A comprehensive account of the essential results of this work by Lefebvre des Noettes in German is to be found in L. Löwenthal, "Zugtier und Sklaven", *Zeitschrift für Sozialforschung* (Frankfurt/Main, 1933), no. 2.

40. Lefebvre des Noettes, "La 'Nuit' du moyen âge et son inventaire", *Mercure de France* (1932), vol. 235, pp. 572ff.

41. Von Werveke, op. cit., p. 468.

42. A. Zimmern, *Solon and Croesus, and other Greek essays* (Oxford, 1928), pp. 113–14. Cf. also A. Zimmern, *The Greek Commonwealth* (Oxford, 1931).

For some time it has been emphasized—no doubt quite rightly—that in Rome freemen as well as slaves did manual work. Above all the research of M. Rostovtsev (cf. *The Social and Economic History of the Roman Empire*), and then specialized studies like that of R. H. Barrow, *Slavery in the Roman Empire* (London, 1928), e.g. pp. 124ff., have clarified these relationships. But the fact that freemen worked, however highly the share of their work in total production may be estimated, in no way contradicts what was illustrated earlier by the quotation from the work of A. Zimmern—the fact that the social processes and regularities within a society where manual work is done to any considerable extent by slaves differ in a very specific way from those within a society where all urban work at least is done exclusively by freemen. As a social tendency, the urge of freemen to distance themselves from work performed by slaves with the resulting formation of a class of "idle poor" in ancient society, as in modern ones with a large slave-labour sector, is always detectable. It is not difficult to understand that under the pressure of poverty a number of freemen are nevertheless forced to perform the same work as slaves. But it is no less clear that their situation, like that of manual labourers in general in such a society, is decisively influenced by the existence of slave labour. These freemen, or at least a part of them, are forced to accept conditions similar to those of slaves. Depending on the number of slaves available to such a society and on the degree of interdependence of their work with slave labour, the freemen always face a greater or lesser degree of competitive pressure from slave labour. This too is one of the structural regularities of any society of slavemasters. (Cf. also Lot, *La fin du monde antique*, pp. 69ff.)

43. According to A. Zimmern Greek society in its classical period was not a slave society in the typical sense of the word: "Greek society was not a slave-society; but it contained a sediment of slaves to perform its most degrading tasks, while the main body of its so-called slaves consisted of apprentices haled in from outside to assist together and almost on equal terms with their masters in creating the material basis of a civilisation in which they were hereafter to share" (*Solon and Croesus,* pp. 161–2).

44. Pirenne, *Les villes du moyen âge*, pp. 1ff.

45. Ibid., pp. 10ff.

46. Ibid., p. 27. This "recourse to inland areas" and its significance for the development of Western society find confirmation in the fact that the evolution of land transport technology beyond its state in antiquity began, as far as we can see today, about a century earlier than that of nautical technology. The former begins between about 1050 and 1100, the latter clearly not before 1200. Cf. Lefebvre des Noettes, *De la marine antique à la marine moderne. La révolution du gouvernail* (Paris, 1935), pp. 105ff. Cf. also E. H. Byrne *Genoese shipping in the twelfth and thirteenth centuries* (Cambridge, Mass., 1930), pp. 5–7.

47. A. Luchaire, *Louis VII, Philippe Auguste, Louis VIII* (Paris, 1901), p. 80.

48. Calmette, *La société féodale*, p. 71. Cf. by the same author, *Le monde féodale*.

49. Law is, of course, through its fixation by an independent legal apparatus and the existence of bodies of specialists with a vested interest in the preservation of the status quo, relatively impervious to movement and change. Legal security itself, always desired by a considerable part of society, depends partly on the law.'s resistance to change. This immobility is indeed increased by it. The larger the areas and the number of people which are integrated and interdependent, the more necessary becomes a uniform law extending over such areas—as necessary, for example, as a uniform currency; the more strongly, therefore, the law and its apparatus, which like currency becomes itself in turn an organ of integration and a producer of interdependence, opposes any change, and the more serious are the disturbances and shifts of interest that any change brings with it. This too contributes to the fact that the mere threat of force by the "legitimate" organs of power is for long periods enough to make individuals and whole social groups comply with what has once been established as the norm of law and property on the basis of a particular stage of social power relationships. The interests identified with the preservation of existing legal and property relationships are so great, and the weight which law receives through growing integration is so clearly felt, that the constant testing of social power relations in physical struggles to which people in less interdependent societies are always inclined is replaced by a long-enduring readiness to abide by the existing law. Only when upheavals and tensions within society have become extraordinarily great, when interest in the preservation of the existing law has become uncertain in large parts of society, only then, often after intervals lasting centuries, do groups in a society begin to test in physical struggles whether the established law corresponds to the actual social power relationships.

When society had a predominantly barter economy and people were far less interdependent, and when, therefore, the most real though not yet visually representable network of society as a whole did not yet constantly confront the individual with its greater strength, the social power maintaining each legal claim by an individual had to be always fairly directly visible. If it became doubtful, the claim lapsed. Every property owner had to be ready to prove in physical combat that he still had enough military and social power to back his "legal claim". Corresponding to the closer intertwining of human activities at a later stage over large areas with relatively good communications, however, a law has developed that largely disregards local individual differences, a so-called general law, i.e. a law applicable and valid equally over the whole area for all the people within it.

The different kind of social interweaving and dependence existing in feudal society, with its largely barter economy, entrusted small groups and often single individuals with functions that are today exercised by "states". Thus "law", too, was incomparably more individualized and local. It was an obligation and bond entered into by this liege lord and that vassal, this group of tenants and that landlord, this civic corporation and that lord, this abbey and that duke. And a study of these "legal relationships" gives a very vivid idea of what it means when we say that in this phase social integration and interdependence were less and the relation of man to man correspondingly different.

We should take care [says Pirenne for example in *Les villes du moyen âge*, pp. 168–9] not to attribute exaggerated importance to urban charters. Neither in Flanders nor in any other region of Europe do they contain the totality of urban law. They confine themselves to fixing the main outlines, formulating some essential principles and resolving some particularly important conflicts. For most of the time they are products of special circumstances and have taken account only of questions being debated when they were drawn up. . . . If the burghers watched over them for centuries with extraordinary solicitude, it was because they were the paladium of their liberty, because they permitted them to justify revolt in cases of violation, but it was not because they enclosed the whole of their law. They were, as it were, no more than its skeleton. All around their stipulations proliferated a rich vegetation of customs, usages, privileges which were not less indispensable for being unwritten.

This is so true that a good number of charters themselves foresaw and recognized in advance the development of urban law. . . . In 1127 the Count of Flanders granted the burghers of Bruges 'ut de die in diem consuetudinarias leges suas corrigerent', that is, the permission to add from day to day to their municipal customs.

Here again we see how, on that different level of integration, formations of a different order of magnitude, a town and a major feudal lord, stand in the same sort of relationship to each other as today only "states" do; and their legal agreements show the same pattern as those of the latter, following fairly directly shifts of interest and social strength.

50. Calmette, *La société féodale*, pp. 70–1.

51. A. Luchaire, *La société française au temps de Philippe Auguste* (Paris, 1909), p. 265.

52. C. H. Haskins, *The Renaissance of the Twelfth Century* (Cambridge, 1927), p. 55.

53. Ibid., p. 56.

54. Ibid.

55. Eduard Wechssler, *Das Kulturproblem des Minnesangs* (Halle, 1909), p. 173.

56. Ibid., p. 174.

57. Ibid., p. 143.

58. Ibid., p. 113.

59. Hennig Brinkmann, *Entstehungsgeschichte des Minnesangs* (Halle, 1926), p. 86.

60. Wechssler, op. cit., pp. 140–1.

61. Luchaire, *La société française au temps de Philippe Auguste*, p. 374.

62. Ibid., p. 379.

63. Ibid., p. 380.

64. Pierre de Vaissière, *Gentilshommes campagnards de l'ancienne France* (Paris, 1903), p. 145.

65. Brinkmann, op. cit., p. 35.

66. Wechssler, op. cit., p. 71.

67. Ibid., p. 74. Similarly in Marianne Weber, *Ehefrau und Mutter in der Rechtsentwicklung* (Tübingen, 1907), p. 265.

68. De Vaissière, op. cit., p. 145.

69. Wechssler, op. cit., p. 214.

70. Brinkmann, op. cit., pp. 45ff., 61, 86ff. Cf. on this and what follows C. S. Lewis, *The Allegory of Love; a Study in Medieval Tradition* (Oxford, 1936), p. 11.

The new thing itself, I do not pretend to explain. Real changes in human sentiment are very rare, but I believe that they occur and that this is one of them. I am not sure that they have 'causes', if by a cause we mean something which would wholly account for the new state of affairs, and so explain away what seemed its novelty. It is, at any rate, certain that the efforts of scholars have so far failed to find an origin for the content of Provençal love poetry.

71. In England the corresponding term is found in later periods restricted, sometimes even explicitly, to servants. An example of this is the way in which, in an English account of what constitutes a good meal, the "curtese and honestie of servantes" is contrasted to the "kyne frendeshyp and company

of them that sytte at the supper", G. G. Coulton, *Social Life in Britain* (Cambridge, 1919), p. 375.

72. F. Zarncke, *Der deutsche Cato* (Leipzig, 1852), p. 130, v.71 and v.141f. For other aspects of this first main phase in the transition from warriors to courtiers (the education and codes of knightly orders in different countries) cf. E. Prestage, *"Chivalry"; a series of studies to illustrate its historical significance and civilizing influence* (London, 1928); including A. T. Byles, "Medieval courtesy-books and the prose romances of chivalry" (pp. 183ff.).

73. Luchaire, *Les premiers Capétiens*, p. 285; cf. also A. Luchaire, *Louis VI le Gros* (Paris, 1890), Introduction.

74. Luchaire, *Histoire des Institutions Monarchiques de la France sous les premiers Capétiens* (987–1180), vol. 2, p. 258.

75. Cf. pp. 17ff., partic. pp. 31–2.

76. Suger, *Vie de Louis le Gros*, ed. Moliner, ch.8, pp. 18–9.

77. A. Vuitry, *Études sur le régime financier de la France* (Paris, 1878), p. 181.

78. Luchaire, *Louis VI*.

79. "The land from Northumberland to the Channel was easier to unify than from Flanders to the Pyrenees." Petit-Dutaillis, *La monarchie féodale*, p. 37. On the question of size of territory, cf. also R. H. Lowie, *The Origin of the State* (New York, 1927), "The size of the state", pp. 17ff.

MacLeod in *The Origin and History of Politics* points out how astonishing it really was that given the simplicity of their means of transport such large dominions as the Inca or Chinese empires should have proved so stable. Only a detailed structural–historical analysis of the interplay of centrifugal and centralizing tendencies and interests in these empires could, indeed, make the agglomeration of such vast areas and the nature of their cohesion comprehensible to us.

The Chinese form of centralization, compared to that developed in Europe, is certainly very peculiar. Here the warrior class was eradicated relatively early and very radically by a strong central authority. This eradication—however it happened—is connected with two main peculiarities of the Chinese social structure: the passing of control of the land into the hands of the peasants (which we encounter in the early Western period only in a very few places, for example, Sweden) and the manning of the governmental apparatus by a bureaucracy always recruited in part from the peasants themselves and at any rate wholly pacified. Mediated by this hierarchy, courtly forms of civilization penetrate deep into the lower classes of the people: they take root, transformed in many ways, in the code of behaviour of the village. And what has so often been called the "unwarlike" character of the Chinese people is not the expression of some "natural disposition". It results from the fact that the class from which the people drew many of their models through constant contact, was for centuries no longer a warrior class, a nobility, but a peaceful and scholarly officialdom. It is primarily their situation and function which is expressed in the fact that in the traditional Chinese scale of values—unlike the Japanese—military activity and prowess hold no very high place. Different as the Chinese way to centralization was to that in the West in detail, therefore, the foundation of the cohesion of larger dominions in both cases was the elimination of freely competing warriors or landowners.

80. On the importance of the monopoly of physical force in the building of "states", cf. above all Max Weber, *Economy and Society* (New York, 1968).

81. Cf. pp. 99–100 above. It has not been necessary here to follow the present-day custom and offer a mathematical expression for the regularity of the monopoly mechanism. No doubt it would not be impossible to find one. Once it has been found it will be possible to discuss also from this aspect a question which generally speaking is hardly raised today: the question of the *cognitive* value of mathematical formulation. What, for example, is gained in terms of possibilities of knowledge and of clarity by a mathematical formulation of the monopoly mechanism? This question can only be answered on the basis of simple experience.

What is certain, however, is that for many people the formulation of general laws is associated with a value which—at least as far as history and sociology are concerned—has nothing to do with their cognitive value. This untested evaluation often enough leads research astray. Many people regard it as the most essential task of research to explain all changes by something unchangeable. And the regard for mathematical formulation derives not least from this evaluation of the immutable. But this scale of values has its roots not in the cognitive task of research itself but in the researcher's longing for eternity. General regularities like that of the monopoly mechanism and all other general patterns of relationships, whether mathematically formulated or not, do not constitute the final goal or culmination of historical and sociological research. Understanding of such regularities is fruitful as a *means* to a different end, a means of orientating man with regard to himself and his world. Their value lies solely in their function in elucidating historical change.

82. On this see "On the Sociogenesis of Feudalism", especially pp. 57–59. On "social power" see also the "Note on the concept of social power", pp. 62–3, note.

83. Auguste Longnon, *Atlas historique de la France* (Paris, 1885).

84. Luchaire, *Histoire des Institutions Monarchiques* (1891), vol. 1, p. 90.

85. Petit-Dutaillis, *La monarchie féodale en France et en Angleterre*, pp. 109ff.

86. A. Cartellieri, *Philipp II August und der Zusammenbruch des angevinischen Reiches* (Leipzig, 1913), p. 1.

87. Cf. A. Longnon, *La formation de l'unité française* (Paris, 1922), p. 98.

88. Luchaire, *Louis VII, Philipp Augustus, Louis VIII*, p. 204.

89. C. Petit-Dutaillis, *Études sur la vie et le règne de Louis VIII* (Paris, 1899), p. 220.

90. A. Vuitry, *Études sur le régime financier de la France,* nouvelle série, vol. 1 (Paris, 1883), p. 345.

91. Ibid., p. 370.

92. A more exact compilation of these feudal houses is to be found in Longnon, *La formation de l'unité française*, pp. 224f.

93. Vuitry, op. cit., p. 414.

94. Cf. e.g. Karl Mannheim, "Die Bedeutung der Konkurrenz im Gebiete des Geistigen", *Verhandlungen des siebenten deutschen Soziologentages* (Tübingen, 1929), pp. 35ff.

95. G. Dupont-Ferrier, *La formation de l'état français et l'unité française* (Paris, 1934), p. 150.

96. L. Mirot, *Manual de geographie historique de la France* (Paris, 1929), Map 19. This also contains maps relating to the foregoing discussion.

97. P. Imbart de la Tour, *Les origines de la réforme* (Paris, 1909), 1, p. 4.

98. Mirot, op. cit., Map 21.

99. Henri Hauser, review of G. Dupont-Ferrier, "La formation de l'état français", *Revue Historique* (1929), vol. 161, p. 381.

100. L. W. Fowles, Loomis Institute, USA, quoted in *News Review*, No. 35, p. 32.

101. Luchaire, *Les communes françaises à l'epoque des Capétiens directs*, p. 276.

102. Documentation for these and a number of other passages could not be included for reasons of space. The author hopes to append this in a separate volume.

103. P. Lehugeur, *Philipp le Long (1316–1322). Le mécanisme du gouvernement* (Paris, 1931), p. 209.

104. Dupont-Ferrier, op. cit., p. 93.

105. Brantôme, *Oeuvres complètes*, publiées par L. Lalanne, vol. 4, pp. 328ff.

106. J. H. Mariéjol, *Henri IV et Louis XIII* (Paris, 1905), p. 2.

107. Ibid., p. 390.

108. Cf. A. Stölzel, *Die Entwicklung des gelehrten Richtertums in deutschen Territorien* (Stuttgart, 1872), p. 600.

109. Richelieu, *Politisches Testament*, pt. 1, ch. 3, p. 1.

110. E. Lavisse, *Louis XIV* (Paris, 1905), p. 128.

111. Saint-Simon, *Memoiren*, tr. by Lotheisen, vol. 1, p. 167.

112. Cf. Lavisse, op. cit., p. 130.

113. Saint-Simon, op. cit., vol. 1, p. 167.

114. Saint-Simon, *Mémoires* (nouv. éd. par A. de Boislisle) (Paris, 1910), vol. 22, p. 35 (1711).

115. Thomas Aquinas, *De regimine Judaeorum*, Rome edit., vol. 19, p. 622.

116. Vuitry, op. cit., pp. 392ff.

117. Ibid., nouvelle série, vol. 1, p. 145. For another form of the monetarization of feudal seigneurial rights under the pressure of the kings' growing need for money, the liberation, for payment, of bondsmen by the king and his administration, cf. Marc Bloch, *Rois et Serfs* (Paris, 1920).

118. Paul Viollet, *Histoire des institutions politiques et administratives de la France* (Paris, 1898), vol. 2, p. 242.

119. Ibid.

120. Vuitry, op. cit., nouv. sér., vol. 2, p. 48.

121. G. Dupont-Ferrier, "La Chambre ou Cour des Aides de Paris", *Revue historique*, vol. 170 (Paris, 1932), p. 195; cf. on this and what follows the same author, *Études sur les institutions financières de la France*, vol. 2 (Paris, 1932).

122. Léon Mirot, *Les insurrections urbaines au début du règne de Charles VI* (Paris, 1905), p. 7.

123. Ibid., p. 37.

124. Dupont-Ferrier, "La Chambre ou Cour des Aides de Paris", p. 202. Cf. also Petit-Dutaillis, *Charles VII, Louis XI et les premières années de Charles VIII* (Lavisse, *Hist. de France*, IV, 2) (Paris, 1902).

125. Viollet, op. cit., vol. 3 (Paris, 1903), pp. 465–6. Cf. also Thomas Basin, *Histoire des règnes de Charles VII et de Louis XI*, ed. Quicherat (Paris, 1855), vol. 1, pp. 170ff. Details on financial organization are in G. Jacqueton, *Documents relatifs à l'administration financière en France de Charles VII à François Ier (1443–1523)* (Paris, 1897), partic. no. XIX in question-and-answer form, "Le vestige des finances". (A manual for future finance officials of the time?)

126. E. Albèri, *Relazioni degli Ambasciatori Veneti al Senato*,

1st series, vol. 4 (Florence, 1860), pp. 16–18 (Relazione di Francia di Zaccaria Contarini, 1492).

127. L. von Ranke, *Zur venezianischen Geschichte* (Leipzig, 1878), p. 59, and H. Kretschmayr, *Geschichte von Venedig* (Stuttgart, 1934), pp. 159ff.

128. Albèri, op. cit., 1st series, vol. 1 (Florence, 1839), p. pp. 232–5.

It has been frequently pointed out, no doubt with a certain justification, that the first absolutist princes in France had learned much from the princes of the Italian city states. For example, G. Hanotaux, "Le pouvoir royale sous François Ier", in *Études historiques sur le XVIe et le XVIIe siècle en France* (Paris, 1886), pp. 7ff: "The court at Rome and the Venetian Chancellery would have sufficed on their own to spread the new doctrines of diplomacy and politics. But, in reality, in the profusion of petty states which shared the peninsula, there was not one that could not have furnished examples. . . . The monarchies of Europe went to school at the courts of the princes and tyrants of Naples, Florence and Ferrara."

No doubt structurally similar processes took place here, as so often, first in smaller regions then in larger ones, and the leaders of the large regions profited up to a point from their knowledge of the organization of the smaller ones. But in this case as well, only a precise examination in terms of structural history could determine how far the centralization processes and the organization of government in the Italian city states resemble those of early absolutist France, and how far, since differences of size always bring with them qualitative differences of structure, they also diverge from them. At any rate the account given by the Venetian ambassador and its whole tone does not indicate that he regarded the specific power position of the French king and the organization of finances connected to it as something long familiar in Italy.

129. There is today a widespread notion that the forms of social life and particular social institutions are to be explained primarily by the purpose they have for the people who are thus bound together. This idea makes it appear as if people, understanding the usefulness of these institutions, once took a common decision to live together in this way and no other. But this notion is a fiction and if only for that reason not a very good instrument of research.

The consent given by the individual to live with others in a particular form, the justification on grounds of particular purposes for the fact that he lives for example within a state, or is bound to others as a citizen, official, worker, or farmer and not as a knight, priest or bondsman, or as a cattle-rearing nomad—this consent and this justification are something retrospective. In this matter the individual has little choice. He is born into an order with institutions of a particular kind; he is conditioned more or less successfully to conform to it. And even if he should find this order and its institutions neither good nor useful, he could not simply withdraw his assent and jump out of the existing order. He may try to escape it as an adventurer, a tramp, an artist or writer, he may finally flee to a lonely island—even as a refugee from this order he is its product. To disapprove and flee it is no less a sign of conditioning by it than to praise and justify it.

One of the tasks still remaining to be done is to explain convincingly the compulsion whereby certain forms of communal life, for example our own, come into being, are preserved and changed. But access to an understanding of their genesis is blocked if we think of them as having come about in the same way as the works and deeds of individual people: by the setting of particular goals or even by rational thought and planning. The idea that from the early Middle Ages Western men worked in a common exertion and with a clear goal and a rational plan, towards the order of social life and the institutions in which we live today, scarcely answers the facts. How this really happened can be learned only through a study of the historical evolution of these social forms by accurately documented empirical enquiries. Such a study of a particular segment, the aspect of state organization, has been attempted above. But this has also given rise to some insight of broader significance, for example a certain understanding of the nature of socio-historical processes. We can see how little is really achieved by explaining institutions such as the "state" in terms of rational goals.

The goals, plans and actions of individual people constantly intertwine with those of others. But this intertwining of the actions and plans of many people, which, moreover, goes on continuously from generation to generation, is itself not planned. It cannot be understood in terms of the plans and purposeful intentions of individuals, nor in terms which, though not directly purposive, are modelled on teleological modes of thinking. We are here concerned with processes, compulsions and regularities of a relatively autonomous kind. Thus, for example, a situation where many people set themselves the same goal, wanting the same piece of land, the same market or the same social position, gives rise to something that none of them intended or planned, a specifically social datum: a competitive relationship with its peculiar regularities as discussed earlier. Thus it is not from a common plan of many people, but as something unplanned, emerging from the convergence and collision of the plans of many people, that an increasing division of functions comes into being, and the same applies to the integration of larger and larger areas in the form of states, and to many other socio-historical processes.

And only an awareness of the relative autonomy of the intertwining of individual plans and actions, of the way the individual is bound by his social life with others, permits a better understanding of the very fact of individuality itself. The coexistence of people, the intertwining of their intentions and plans, the bonds they place on each other, all these, far from destroying individuality, provide the medium in which it can develop. They set the individual limits, but at the same time give him greater or lesser scope. The social fabric in this sense forms the substratum from which and into which the individual constantly spins and weaves his purposes. But this fabric and the actual course of its historical change as a whole, is intended and planned by no-one.

For further detail on this cf. N. Elias, *What is Sociology?*, trans. Stephen Mennell and Grace Morrissey (London, 1978).

130. For a discussion of the problem of the social process, cf. *Social Problems and Social Processes*, Selected Papers from the Proceedings of the American Sociological Society (1932), ed. E. S. Bogardus (Chicago, 1933).

For a criticism of the earlier biologistic notion of social processes, cf. W. F. Ogburn, *Social Change* (London, 1923), pp. 56f.:

The publication of the *Origin of Species*, setting forth a theory of evolution of species in terms of natural selection, heredity and variation, created a deep impression on the anthropologists and sociologists. The conception of evolution was so profound that the changes in society were seen as a manifestation of evolution and there was an attempt to seek the causes of these social changes in terms of variation and selection. . . . Preliminary to the search for causes, however, attempts were made to establish the development of particular social institutions in successive stages, an evolutionary series, a particular stage necessarily preceding another. The search for laws led to many hypotheses regarding factors such as geographical location, climate, migration, group conflict, racial ability, the evolution of mental ability, and such principles as variation, natural selection, and survival of the fit. A half-century or more of investigations on such theories has yielded some results, but the achievements have not been up to the high hopes entertained shortly after the publication of Darwin's theory of natural selection.

The inevitable series of stages in the development of social institutions has not only not been proven but has been disproven. . . .

For more recent tendencies in the discussion of the problem of historical change cf. A. Goldenweiser, "Social Evolution", in *Encyclopedia of Social Sciences* (New York, 1935), vol. 5, pp. 656ff. (with comprehensive bibliography). The article concludes with the reflection:

Since the World War students of the social sciences without aiming at the logical orderliness of evolutionary schemes have renewed their search for relatively stable tendencies and regularities in history and society. On the other hand, the growing discrepancy between ideals and the workings of history is guiding the sciences of society into more and more pragmatic channels. If there is a social evolution, whatever it may be, it is no longer accepted as a process to be contemplated but as a task to be achieved by deliberate and concerted human effort.

This study of the civilizing process differs from these pragmatic efforts in that, suspending all wishes and demands concerning what ought to be, it tries to establish what was and is, and to explain in which way, and why, it became as it was and is. It seemed more appropriate to make the therapy depend on the diagnosis rather than the diagnosis on the therapy.

Cf. F. J. Teggart, *Theory of History* (New Haven, 1925), p. 148: ". . . the investigation of how things have come to be as they are . . .".

131. Cf. E. C. Parsons, *Fear and Conventionality* (New York, London, 1914). The divergent view, e.g. in W. G. Sumner, *Folkways* (Boston, 1907), p. 419: "It is never correct to regard any one of the taboos as an arbitrary invention or burden laid on society by tradition without necessity . . . they have been sifted for centuries by experience, and those which we have received and accepted are such as experience has proved to be expedient."

132. See the fine account by J. Huizinga, *The Waning of the Middle Ages* (London, 1924), ch. 1.

What was said above also applies, for example, to societies with a related structure in the present-day Orient and, to various degrees depending on the nature and extent of integration, to so-called "primitive" societies.

The extent to which children in our society—however imbued with characteristics of our relatively advanced civilization—still show glimpses of the other standard with its simpler and more straightforward affects and its proneness to sudden changes of mood, is shown, for example, by the following description of what children like in films (*Daily Telegraph*, 12 February, 1937): "Children, especially young children, like aggression. . . . They favour action, action and more action. They are not averse from the shedding of blood, but it must be dark blood. Virtue triumphant is cheered to the echo; villainy is booed with a fine enthusiasm. When scenes of one alternate with scenes of the other, as in sequences of pursuit, the transition from the cheer to the boo is timed to a split second."

Also closely connected to the different force of their emotional utterances, their extreme reaction in both directions, fear and joy, revulsion and affection, is the specific structure of taboos in simpler societies. It was pointed out above (cf. p. 232ff, especially pp. 239–40; cf. also vol. 1, pp. 87ff.) that in the medieval West not only the manifestations of drives and affects in the form of pleasure but also the prohibitions, the tendencies to self-torment and asceticism were stronger, more intense and thereiore more rigorous than at later stages of the civilizing process.

Cf. also R. H. Lowie, "Food Etiquette", in *Are we civilised?* (London, 1929), p. 48: ". . . the savage rules of etiquette are not only strict, but formidable. Nevertheless, to us their table manners are shocking."

133. Cf. C. H. Judd, *The Psychology of Social Institutions* (New York, 1926), pp. 105ff. Also pp. 32ff. and 77ff.

134. Introduction to the French translation of Gratian's "Hand Oracle" written by Amelot de la Houssaie, Paris, 1684. *Oraculo Manuale* published in 1647, went through about twenty different editions during the seventeenth and eighteenth centuries in France alone under the title *L'Homme de Cour*. It is in a sense the first handbook of courtly psychology, as Machiavelli's book on the prince was the first classical handbook of courtly-absolutist politics. Machiavelli, however, seems to speak more from the point of view of the prince than does Gratian. He justifies more or less the "reason of state" of emergent absolutism. Gratian, the Spanish Jesuit, despises reason of state from the bottom of his heart. He elucidates the rules of the great courtly game for himself and others as something with which one has to comply because there is no alternative.

It is not without significance, however, that despite this difference, the conduct recommended by both Machiavelli and

Gratian appears to middle-class people as more or less "immoral", although similar modes of conduct and sentiment are certainly not lacking in the bourgeois world. In this condemnation of courtly psychology and courtly conduct by the non-courtly bourgeoisie is expressed the specific difference of the whole social moulding of the two classes. Social rules are built into the personality of non-courtly bourgeois strata in a different way than in the courtly class. In the former the super-ego is far more rigid and in many respects stricter than in the latter. The belligerent side of everyday life certainly does not disappear in practice from the bourgeois world, but it is banished far more than in the courtly class from what a writer or any person may *express*, and even from consciousness itself.

In courtly-aristocratic circles "thou shalt" is very often no more an expression of expediency, dictated by the practical necessities of social life. Even adults in these circles always remain aware that these are rules that they must obey because they live with other people. In middle-class strata the corresponding rules are often rooted far more deeply in the individual during childhood, not as practical rules for the expedient conduct of life, but as semi-automatic promptings of conscience. For this reason the "thou shalt" and the "thou shalt not" of the super-ego is far more constantly and deeply involved in the observation and understanding of reality. To give at least one example from the innumerable ones that might be quoted here, Gratian says in his precept "Know thoroughly the character of those with whom you deal" (No. 273): "Expect practically nothing good of those who have some natural bodily defect; for they are accustomed to avenge themselves on Nature. . . ." One of the middle-class English books of manners of the seventeenth century, that likewise had wide circulation and had their origin in the well-known rules of George Washington, *Youth's Behaviour* by Francis Hawkins (1646), gives pride of place to "thou shalt not" and so gives behaviour and observation in the same case a different, moral twist (No. 31): "Scorne not any for the infirmityes of nature, which by no art can be amended, nor do thou delight to put them in minde of them, since it very oft procures envye and promotes malice even to revenge."

In a word, we find in Gratian, and after him in La Rochefoucauld and La Bruyère. in the form of general maxims, all the modes of behaviour which we encounter, for example in Saint-Simon, in the practice of court life itself. Again and again we find injunctions on the necessity to hold back the affects (No. 287): "Never act while passion lasts. Otherwise you will spoil everything." Or (No. 273): "The man prejudiced by passion always speaks a langugage different from what things are; passion, not reason, speaks in him." We find the advice to adopt a "psychological attitude", a permanent observation of character (No. 273): "Know thoroughly the character of those with whom you deal." Or the result of such knowledge, the observation (No. 201): "All those who appear mad are mad, and so are half of those who do not appear mad." The necessity of self-observation (No. 225): "Know your dominant fault." The necessity for half-truths (No. 210): "Know how to play with truth." The insight that real truth lies in the truthfulness and substantiality of the whole existence of a person, not in his particular words (No. 175): "The substantial man. It is only Truth that can give a true reputation; and only the substance which can be turned to profit." The necessity for farsightedness (No. 151): "Think today of tomorrow, and of a long time beyond." Moderation in all things (No. 82): "The sage has compressed all wisdom into this precept: Nothing to Excess." The specifically courtly-aristocratic form of perfection, the temperate polishing of a moderated and transformed animalic nature all around, the levity, charm, the new beauty of the animal-made man (No. 127): "Le JE-NE-SAIS-QUOI. Without it all beauty is dead, all grace is graceless . . . the other perfections are ornaments of Nature, the 'Je-ne-sais-quoi' is that of perfection. It is noticeable even in the manner of reasoning. . . ." Or, from a different aspect, the man without affectation (No. 123): "The man without affectation. The more perfections there are the less there is affectation. The most eminent qualities lose their price if we discover affectation in them, because we attribute them rather to an artificial constraint than to a person's true character." War between man and man is inevitable; conduct it decently (No. 165): "Make good war. To conquer villainously is not to conquer but to be conquered. Anything that smells of treason infects one's good name." Over and again in these precepts recurs the argument based on regard for other people, on the necessity to preserve a good reputation, in a word, an argument based on *this-worldly*, social necessities. Religion plays a small part in them. God appears only in the margin and at the end as something outside this human circle. All good things, too, come to a man from other people (No. 111): "Make friends. To have friends is a second being . . . all the good things we have in life depend on others."

It is this justification of rules and precepts not by an eternal moral law but by "external" necessities, consideration of other people, which above all causes these maxims and the whole courtly code of conduct to appear "amoral" or at least "painfully realistic" to the bourgeois observer. Betrayal, for example, the bourgeois world feels, should be forbidden not for practical reasons, concern for one's "good reputation" with other people, but by an inner voice, conscience, in a word, by morality. The same change in the structure of commands and prohibitions that was seen earlier in the study of eating habits, washing and other elementary functions, reappears here. Rules of conduct which in courtly aristocratic circles are observed even by adults largely from consideration and fear of other people, are imprinted on the individual in the bourgeois world rather as a self-constraint. In adults they are no longer reproduced and preserved by direct fear of other people, but by an "inner" voice, a fear automatically reproduced by their own super-ego, in short by a moral commandment that needs no justification.

135. Cf. *The Civilizing Process*, vol. 1, pp. 108ff.

136. C. H. Haskins, "The Spread of Ideas in the Middle Ages", in *Studies in Mediaeval Culture* (Oxford, 1929), pp. 92ff.

137. Cf. p. 66 above. Apart from the *Minnelieder* there is a wealth of material showing this standard, in some cases even more clearly, e.g. the small prose piece by Andreas Capellanus in Marie de Champagne's cycle "De Amore", and the whole literature of the medieval controversy over women.

138. Haskins, op. cit., p. 94.

139. *The Civilizing Process*, vol. 1, pp. 204ff.

140. Cf. pp. 8ff. above.

141. La Bruyère, *Caractères*, 'De la cow' (Paris, Hachette, 1922), *Oeuvres*, vol. 2, p. 237, No. 64; cf. also p. 248, No. 99: "In a hundred years the world will still exist in its entirety. It will be the same theatre with the same decoration, but not the same actors. All those who rejoice at a favour received or are cast into sorrow and despair by a refusal, all will have vanished from the stage. Already other men are moving on to the stage who will play the same parts in the same play. What a background for a comic part!" How strong the sense of immutability still is here, and of the ineluctability of the existing order; how much stronger than in the later phase when the concept of "civilization" begins to displace that of "civilité".

On this development cf. also the passage "Des Jugements": "All foreigners are not Barbarians, nor all our Compatriots civilized."

142. La Bruyère, op. cit., p. 247, No. 94.

143. Ibid., p. 211, No. 2; cf. also p. 211, No. 10: "The court is like an edifice of marble; I mean it is composed of men who are very hard, but very polished." Cf. also n. 134.

144. Saint-Simon, op. cit., p. 63.

145. *The Civilizing Process*, vol. 1, pp. 70ff, partic. 77–8.

146. Ranke, *Französische Geschichte*, bk. 10, ch. 3.

147. Saint-Simon, op. cit., vol. 22, p. 20 and pp. 22f. (1711). What is at stake in these conversations is nothing less than an attempt to win over the heir to the throne to a different form of rule, in which the balance between members of the leading bourgeois and noble groups at court is to be shifted in favour of the latter. The power of the "peers"—this is the goal of Saint-Simon and his friends—is to be restored. In particular the higher offices of state, the ministries, shall be transferred from the bourgeois to the high nobility. An attempt in this direction is actually made directly after Louis XIV's death by the regent with the active involvement of Saint-Simon. It fails. What the English nobility achieve by and large successfully, a stabilization of aristocratic rule whereby various groups and cliques of the nobility contest the occupancy of the decisive positions of political power while observing fairly strict rules, the French nobility fail to achieve. The tensions and conflicts of interest between the leading groups of the nobility and those of the bourgeoisie are incomparably greater in France than in England. Under the cover of absolutism they are constantly discernible. But as in every strong autocracy the struggle being waged around the ruler, in the highest circles, takes place behind locked doors. Saint-Simon is one of the chief exponents of this secret combat.

148. *The Civilizing Process*, vol. 1, pp. 207ff. On the general problem of shame feelings cf. *The Spectator* (1807), vol. 5, no. 373: "If I was put to define Modesty, I would call it, The reflection of an ingenuous Mind, either when a Man has committed an Action for which he censures himself, or fancies that he is exposed to the Censure of others." See also the observation there on the difference of shame feelings between men and women.

149. *The Civilizing Process*, vol. 1, pp. 122ff.

150. Ibid., pp. 204ff.

151. Ibid., pp. 108ff.

152. Attempts have often been made to explain the national character of the English or particular features of it by the geographical situation of their country, from its island character. But if this island character were simply responsible for the national character of its inhabitants as a natural datum, then all other island nations would have to show similar characteristics, and no people should be closer to the English in its character and make-up than, for example, the Japanese.

It is not the island situation as such which sets its stamp on the national character of the population, but the significance of this situation in the total structure of the island society, in the total context of its history. As a result of a particular historical development the lack of land frontiers, for example, has led in England, unlike Japan, to a low evaluation of military prowess and more concretely to the fact that soldiers do not enjoy very high social prestige.

In England the relatively pacified nobility, together with leading bourgeois groups, succeeded very early in sharply restricting the king's control of weapons and the army, and particularly the use of physical violence within the country itself. And this structure of the monopoly of physical force, made possible, to be sure, only by the country's island character, played no small part in the formation of the specifically English national character. How closely certain features of the English super-ego, or, in other words, the English conscience, are bound up with the structure of the monopoly of physical force is shown even today by the social latitude given in England to the "conscientious objector", or the widespread sentiment that general conscription represents a major and dangerous restriction of individual freedom. We would probably not be wrong in assuming that non-conformist movements and organizations have been able to remain as strong and vigorous as they have over the centuries in England only because the official Church of England was not backed by a police and military apparatus to the same extent as were, for example, the national churches in the Protestant states of Germany. At any rate, the fact that in England the pressure of foreign military power on the individual was from an early stage much less heavy than in any other major Continental country, is extremely closely connected to the other fact that the constraint which the individual had to exert on himself, particularly in all matters related to the life of the state, grew stronger and more all-round than in the great Continental nations. In this way, as an element of social history, the island character and the whole nature of the country have indeed, in a great variety of ways, exerted a formative influence on the national character.

153. *The Civilizing Process*, vol. 1, pp. 16ff., pp. 74ff. and p. 292 n. 30. On this question cf. also A. Loewe, *The Price of Liberty* (London, 1937), p. 31: "The educated German of the classical and post-classical period is a dual being. In public life he stands in the place which authority has decreed for him, and fills it in the double capacity of superior and subordinate with complete devotion to duty. In private life he may be a critical intellectual or an emotional romantic. . . . This educational system has come to grief in the attempt to achieve a fusion of the bureaucratic and the humanist ideals. It has in reality created the introverted specialist,

unsurpassed in abstract speculation and in formal organization, but incapable of shaping a real world out of his theoretical ideas. The English educational ideal does not know this cleavage between the world within and the world without. . . ."

154. Cf. pp. 66ff.

155. Cf. pp. 99–100 and pp. 104ff. That the strength of tensions between different hegemonial units is indissolubly bound up with the strength of tensions and the whole social order within them has already been stressed on a number of occasions. It was shown that connections of this kind existed even in the early Western feudal society with its primarily barter economy. The population pressure which led in it to various kinds of expansionist and competitive struggles, the desire for a piece of land in the poorer warriors and the desire for more land at the expense of others in richer ones, counts, dukes and kings, this population pressure is not simply a result of the increase in population but of this in connection with the then existing property relations, the monopolization of the most important means of production by a section of the warriors. From a certain time on land was in fixed possession; access to it by families and individuals who did not already "own" became increasingly difficult; property relationships hardened more and more. In this social constellation a further increase of population in both the peasant and warrior classes and the constant sinking of many people below their previous standard of existence, exerted a pressure which intensified tensions and competition within the whole society from top to bottom, within the individual territories and *between* them, and which kept the competitive mechanism in motion (see pp. 39, 45 and 57ff.). In exactly the same way in industrial society it is not the absolute level of population and still less simply an increase in population which is responsible for pressure within particular states, but the density of population in conjunction with the existing property relations, the relationship of those who control property chances through an unorganized monopoly to those who do not have such chances.

That the social pressure in different Western states varies in degree is obvious. But we do not yet possess any very useful conceptual tools for analysing these pressure relationships, nor any precise framework within which the degree of pressure can be precisely measured, for example, by a comparison of different states. What is clear is that this "internal pressure" is most accessible to observation and analysis from the point of view of the standard of living, if by this we do not mean only the purchasing power of income but also the time and intensity of work needed to obtain this income. Moreover, we cannot gain a proper understanding of the relationships of pressure and tension within a society by comparing the living standards of its different classes statically, i.e. at a particular time, but only by a comparison over extended periods. The degree of tension and the population pressure within a society are very often not explained by the absolute level of the living standard, but rather by the abruptness with which this standard falls in certain classes from one level to another. We must have in view the curve, the historical movement of the standard of living of different classes of a society in order to understand the relationships of pressure and tension within it.

This is the reason why we should not look at one industrial nation on its own if we wish to gain a clear picture of the nature and strength of the relationships of pressure and tension within it. For the level of the living standard, different as it is in different classes of the same society, is always partly determined by the position of this whole society in the global network of different nation states and empires with its further division of functions. In most if not all the industrial nation states of Europe the living standard, which was itself attained in conjunction with industrialization, can be maintained only by constant imports of agrarian products and raw materials. These imports can only be paid for either by income from correspondingly large exports or by income from investments in other countries or from gold reserves. So it happens that it is not only internal pressure, the imminent or actual fall in the living standard of broad classes, which maintains and sometimes intensifies the competitive tension between different industrial nation states, but this inter-state tension in its turn can sometimes contribute to a very considerable extent to an increase in the social pressure within one or other of the competing nation states.

Up to a certain point this no doubt also applies to countries which primarily export agrarian products or raw materials. It applies, indeed, to all countries which have grown into a particular function within the division of labour between different nations, and whose living standard therefore can be maintained only if enough scope for the relevant exports or imports exists. But the sensitivity of different countries to fluctuations in international exchange, to defeats, to slow or rapid decline in the competition of nation states, varies very widely. It is clearly particularly high in nations with a relatively high standard of living in which the balance between their own industrial and agrarian production has tilted sharply to the disadvantage of the latter and which are dependent in both sectors on substantial imports of basic materials, particularly when they are not able to offset such deficits by earnings from foreign investments or from their gold reserves, and when, furthermore, human exports, too, for example in the form of emigration, become impossible. This, however, is a question in its own right which needs more detailed examination than is possible here. Only by such an investigation could we gain better understanding of why, for example, the tensions in the figuration of European states are so much greater than those between, for example, the South and Central American states.

However that may be, one often has the idea that it is only necessary to leave the economic competition between such highly industrialized states to the free play of forces for all the partners to prosper. But this free play of forces is in fact a hard competitive struggle which is subject to the same regularities as such struggles in all other spheres. The balance between the competing states is extremely unstable. It tends towards specific shifts the direction of which, certainly, can only be established through long-term observation. In the course of this economic competition between highly industrialized nations preponderance gradually moves in favour of some and against the others. The export and import capacity of the weakening parties becomes more restricted. To a state in this situation there remain—if, as we have said, it is unable to offset these losses by investments or gold reserves—only two possibilities. It must either force up exports, for example by lowering export prices, or restrict imports. Both actions lead directly or indirectly to a lowering of the living standards of the members of this society. This fall is passed on by those controlling the monopoly of economic opportunities to those who do not control them. The latter thus find themselves surrounded by a double circle of monopoly rulers: those within their own society and those representing foreign societies. The pressure emanating from them contributes to impelling their own representatives and their state as a whole into a competitive struggle with other societies. And thus the tensions within different states and those between them mutually reinforce each other. This spiral movement is, to be sure—it must be emphasized—only one of a large number of different sequential orders of change. But the mention of this sequential order, however fragmentary, may give an impression of the power of the compelling forces which today keep the inter-state competition and monopoly mechanisms in motion.

156. Cf. pp. 159–61 above. A summary of present-day theories on the origins of states is to be found in Macleod, *The Origin and History of Politics*, pp. 139ff.

157. Cf. pp. 104ff. above.

158. Cf. pp. 270ff., esp. pp. 276ff.

159. Cf. pp. 234ff., p. 255, and pp. 258ff.

160. Cf. pp. 254ff., p. 263, pp. 267–68, pp. 292ff; on this question cf. Parsons, *Fear and Conventionality*, p. xiii: "Conventionality rests upon an apprehensive state of mind . . .", and p. 73: "Table manners are, I suppose, one of our most marked class distinctions". Also quoted there W. James, *Principles of Psychology* (New York, 1890), p. 121: "Habit is thus the enormous flywheel of society, its most precious conservative agent. It alone is what keeps us all within the bounds of ordinance, and saves the children of fortune from the envious uprisings of the poor. It alone prevents the hardest and most repulsive walks of life from being deserted by those brought up to tread therein."

The more general question, to the solution of which the present work seeks to make a contribution, has also been posed for a long time by American sociology. For example, Sumner, *Folkways*, p. 418, writes: "When, therefore, the ethnographers apply condemnatory or depreciatory adjectives to the people whom they study, they beg the most important question which we want to investigate; that is, what are standards, codes, and ideas of chastity, decency, propriety, modesty, etc. and whence do they arise? The ethnographical facts contain the answer to this question, but in order to reach it we want a colourless report of the facts." It scarcely needs to be said that this is true not only of the investigation of foreign and simpler societies, but also of our own society and its history.

The problem to which the present work is addressed has more recently been particularly clearly formulated by Judd, *The Psychology of Social Institutions*, even if he attempts a different solution to the problems than is offered here (p. 276): "This chapter will aim to prove that the types of personal emotions which are known to civilised men are products of an evolution in which emotions have taken a new direction. . . . The instruments and means of this adaptation are the institutions, some of which have been described in foregoing chapters. Each institution as it has become established has developed in all individuals to come under its influence a mode of behaviour and emotional attitude which conform to the institution. The new mode of behaviour and the new emotional attitude could not have been perfected until the institution itself was created. . . . The effort of individuals to adapt themselves to institutional demands results in what may be properly described as a wholly new group of pleasures."

Index

Breisig, Kurt, 342
Brinkmann, Hennig, 349
Britain, creation of, 102
British empire, 103
Brittany, 199
~, dukes of, 131, 141, 154, 221
~, house of, 148, 153, 156–7
Bruges, 348
Brunelleschi, 5
Brunner, O., 337
Burdach, Konrad, 78
bureaucracy, 177, 182, 187, 332
burgher class, 131
Burgundy, 23, 27, 37
~, dukes of, 131, 221
~, house of, 148, 153, 156
Bury, J. B. 341
businessmen, 269
Byles, A. T. 350
Byrne, E. H. 346
Byzantium, 30, 345

Calmette, J. 31, 338, 347, 349
Capellanus, Andreas, 361
Capetians, 10, 13–14, 24, 42, 92, 117–18, 120, 123–4, 126–9, 131–5, 138–41, 147–8, 154, 181, 183
capital formation, 231, 291
capitalism, 42
Carolingian empire, 30, 47, 128
~ fisc, 337
~ period, 13, 34, 37, 49–50, 56, 131
Carolingians, 21–3, 42, 341
Cartelieri, A., 352
Catholicism, 295
causation, 26, 32, 48
Cavalli, Marino, 219
central authority, 15, 170–1, 180, 214–15, 350
~ functionaries, 169
~ institutions/apparatus, 27, 163–4, 165, 169, 174, 212–14, 222, 234
~ rulers, 4, 161, 164, 166–7, 171–5, 180–1, 183–5, 187–8, 190, 192, 198, 201–2, 206–7, 223, 225, 259, 302, 304, 342
~ sector, 249
centralization, 25, 65, 112, 114, 135, 154, 162, 165–6, 183, 200, 214, 290, 317, 350–1
centrifugal forces, 15–30, 61–8, 96–7, 101–3, 131–48, 154–5, 162, 183, 199–200, 222, 235, 350
ceremony, 259
chains of action, 236, 248

~ of dependence, 296
chambres des aides, 209, 214
Champagne, 23, 131
chansons de geste, 80
Charlemagne, 15–18, 22, 27, 167, *see also* Carolingian Empire
Charles III, king of France, 19
Charles IV, ~, 128–9
Charles V, ~, 136–40, 142–3, 208–10
Charles V, German–Roman Emperor, 97, 158
Charles VI, king of France, 140, 142–3
Charles VII, ~, 147, 154, 214–15, 217, 220
Charles VIII, ~, 156, 211, 220
Charles of Valois, 139–40
Charles the Bad, king of Navarre, 139
Charles the Bold, duke of Burgundy, 154–15
Charles the Fat, king of the west Franks, 19
childhood, 244–5, 328–30, 358
China, 345, 350, 387
church, 3, 7, 20, 21, 39, 94, 97, 103, 121–2, 181–3, 187, 291
Church of England, 363
civil wars, 180, 188
civilité, 90, 256–7, 267, 309, 361
"civilization", 8, 52, 229, 253, 255–6, 277, 283, 291, 299–300, 311, 313–14, 316, 327, 332, 361
civilized conduct, 167
civilizing movement, 255–6
~ process, 5–7, 32, 71, 113, 166, 229–30, 232, 243–7, 250–1, 253, 270, 281, 286, 293, 295, 312, 319, 333, 358
class, 171–2
clergy/clerics, 20–1, 179, 181, 183, 186, 188, 190, 209, 224
cliques, 271
closure of society, 59, 106, 112, 130, 141, 329, 332, 359, 361, 363
codes of conduct, 239, 254, 360
~ of manners, 314–5
co-existence, 332–3, 356
Cohn, W. 342
colonization, 39, 41, 58, 255, 311, 313–14, 318
commercial functions, 249
commercialization, 67, 69, 130, 175–6
communication, 56
competition, 213, 232, 252, 269, 305, 311, 319–20, 321, *see also*, free competition

373

nations, 15, 56, 253, 256, 365
"nature", 231, 273–4, 297, 319, 327
Navarre, king of, 137
nobility, 3, 11–12, 40, 55, 58, 113, 165, 170, 175–6, 178–80, 187–8, 194–6, 199–200, 206, 208, 209, 222–3, 236, 242, 256, 260–1, 263, 266, 269, 290, 302–3, 316–19, 342, 351, 362–3
noblesse d'épée, 224
noblesse de robe, 176, 224
nomadic tribes, 33–4
non-physical violence, 235
Normandy, 122, 130, 221
Normans, 13, 19, 27, 36, 38, 341
novels, 242

Ogburn, W. F., 356
oligarchy, 111
oppression, 252
Orient, 46, 278, 312, 325, 357
Orléans, 93, 199
Otto I, German–Roman Emperor, 20, 96
outsiders, 250, 251, 311–12, 314
overpopulation, 35–6

pacification, 10, 77, 159, 235–6, 239–40, 297–9, 302–3, 331–2
pain, endurance of, 240
Paris, 5–6, 14, 93, 139, 144–6, 196, 198, 205–6, 212–13, 217, 307
parliaments, 185, 191, 195
Parsons, E. C., 357
patterns of conduct, 253–4, 256, 258, 288, 318
peasants, 262–3, 350
perception, 273
Peru, 262
Petit-Dutaillis, C., 352–3
Petruševski, 343–4
petty-bourgeois, 312
"phenomenon", 83
Philip III, king of France, 127, 134, 139–40
Philip V, duke of Orléans, 143
Philip VI, of Valois, king of France, 134–5
Philip of Evreux, 139
Philip the Bold, duke of Burgundy, 138, 140–3, 210
physical superiority, 292
Pirenne, Henri, 341–3, 346, 348
pleasure balance, 246
~ economy, 326
polarization, 237

Poitiers, battle of, 136, 209
Poitou, 14
"politics", 49–50
power, *see* military power, social power
prestige, 137, 224, 252, 254, 263, 267–8, 301, 305, 313, 329–30
priestly class, 183
"primitive" societies, 325, 357
"primitives", 277, 297
"private economy", 109
~ property, 132, 216, 221
princes des fleurs de lis, 140, 142–4
privileges, 177–8, 224
production, means of, 149–50, 235
professions, 305
proletariat, 165, 170
Protestantism, 295
Proust, Marcel, 275
Prussia, 147
psyche, 284
psychogenesis, 281, 288
psychological change, 231
~ functions, 290–1, 325
psychologization, 275–6, 281–2
psychology, 281
public cause, 216
Puritanism, 295

Quitzows, 92

Ranke, Leopold von, 279, 354, 362
"rational", 230
rational thought, 289, 291
rationality, 278, 282
rationalization, 229, 276, 281–4, 287, 289–92, 326
real type, 339
reduction of contrasts in conduct, 254–5
reflection, 325
Reformation, 196
regularities, 171, 213, 218, 231
regulation of drives, 40, 275
~ of sexual relations, 315
relational dynamics, 160–1
relative autonomy, 231, 356
~ power surplus, 262
religion, 295, 360
religious wars, 188
Renaissance, 5, 52
repugnance, 292, 295
~ frontier, 305
reserve army, 41, 67
restraint of affects, 86, 260